THE COMPLETE GUIDE TO
TREES OF BRITAIN
AND NORTHERN EUROPE

To my sister Christine

David conceived the idea for this book when he first embarked on a full time career as an illustrator back in 1979.

With the information he had learnt by his many studies in the field, he set about creating a design that would best present all the information that the amateur and professional tree spotter needs.

The design David created gave him an intensive 18 month painting challenge to ensure that the book could go to publication. His day had to be very long indeed and it is a credit for someone of the age of 30 years to have met such a demanding deadline with such a high standard of work.

The Publisher

THE COMPLETE GUIDE TO TREES OF BRITAIN AND NORTHERN EUROPE

Alan Mitchell

Illustrated by David More

DRAGON'S
WORLD

Dragon's World Ltd
Limpsfield
Surrey RH8 0DY
Great Britain

ISBN 185028 000 2

Printed in Spain by Cayfosa. Barcelona
Dep. leg. B-6669-1985

Consultant Editor
Kenneth A. Beckett

Editor
Philip Clark

Assistant Editor
Christine McMullen

Designer
Julian Holland

Design Assistant
Martin Smillie

Line drawings by
Nicolas Hall

Contents

Introduction

Britain has an enormous wealth of tree species
from all the temperate parts of the world despite
having few native species. The trees chosen for this
book include all the common and frequently seen
trees and a wide selection of uncommon, rare and
extremely rare kinds. The very rare trees are chosen
from a large number on the basis of the inclusion
of those of particular interest or beauty and those
in which one specimen is prominent or likely to be
easily found in a major tree collection. All the
important cultivars grown long enough to be of
reasonable size are included.

Nearly 500 species are illustrated together with
250 varieties. Trees are shown in typical landscapes
along with much crucial detail of bark, flowers,
fruit and shoots which assist in the identification
of even uncommon variants and rare species.

The text complements David More's detailed
drawings – it does not enlarge on the shapes or
colours shown in the plates, it covers instead in
great detail the origin, history, distribution and
growth. Where a seasonal colour of leaf or fruit is
not shown, it will, if of value for identification, be
mentioned and similarly the dimensions of leaves
and fruit may be given. The main emphasis is on
the introduction and location and size of some of
the best specimens, together with features of
particular interest in botany and growth. Up-to-
date dimensions of many giant and rare specimens
are included.

The biggest cited are either of great age and
unlikely to grow much more or young trees of
immense vigour, which will be much taller and
bigger ten years from now; for instance many of
the Dawn redwoods now 18–20 m tall and 60 cm
in diameter will by then be 25–30 m × 80 cm.

English names are given without a capital initial
when referring to a group like oaks, eucalypts or
maples and with capital initials for the first word
of species, as Sessile oak and Blue gum and for
one-word species like Katsura and Medlar.

Finally, a Practical Reference Section gives
invaluable advice on the choice and cultivation of
trees. It also contains a list of important tree
collections, both public and privately owned, with
the details of trees of special note within the
collections.

Broadleaved Trees
Crack and White Willow

The **Crack willow** (*Salix fragilis*) is the common waterside willow of lowland parts and is native to Britain. It likes to have its roots in streams or rivers with a good flow of water rather than in the still waters of a lake, and some of the best stands are in the swampy margins of fast chalk-fed rivers. Large drainage ditches in flood-plains also grow good trees. Some that are found away from open water, by spring-lines and on clay are no doubt planted but can thrive nevertheless. In former times when willows were pollarded by cutting the stem at 2.5 m, the sprouts that arose were cut every few years for withies and wattle and the stem built up a broad head bearing a score or more shoots. These were so typical of the lowland rural scene and of the haunts of anglers that books on countryside matters were very often adorned by woodcut vignettes showing a background of pollard crack willows – a favourite subject for Thomas Bewick, one of the great engraving artists.

In the present century, the practice of pollarding has almost died out and uncut poles have grown into big branches, crowded on and leaning out from the old head. They may become too heavy for the top of the bole and many have broken out.

The Crack willow is a tree of very rapid growth and a short life. Left uncut, the main stem persists for ten or more metres, even if slightly wavy, and holds an open, upright crown to a height of 25 m. In ten years one specimen grew in bole diameter from 105 to 130 cm, so the rapid growth is maintained and the occasional hulk seen two m in diameter may be only about 100 years old.

The names 'Crack' willow and '*fragilis*' refer to the tree's curious method of vegetative increase. The slender, yellow one-year shoots point forward from their origin, at 45 degrees. When bent gently back towards the right angle they snap off cleanly, and readily, and many are shed during rough weather. Standing near or over running water as the trees so often do, they drop these twigs into the stream and they are borne away, some to come to rest in the slacker waters of muddy bays. Being willow, they send out roots rapidly and so spread the tree downstream. Since the trees, like nearly all willows, are either male or female, a stretch of river colonized by a single upstream pioneer tree will have Crack willows all of the same sex. In order to arrive in the river-system in the first place, and to spread upstream as well, the tree relies on the light, fluff-covered, wind-borne seeds.

A good Crack willow in leaf is identifiable at once by its very large, glossy green foliage, often hanging in lines from long, strong shoots. In winter, and, better, in early spring, the shoots become deeper yellow and pale orange just before the leaves emerge. But all is often not so clear, for there is a wide range of hybrids (*Salix* x *rubens*) between this and the White willow and some are intermediate between the two in leaf size and colour.

The **White willow** (*Salix alba*) is probably a native tree but it comes under some suspicion since it is more southerly in distribution than the Crack willow and occurs only on sites associated with settlements. It is less common and rarely dominates river banks for great distances, but it is more often planted in parks and gardens. It grows even faster than the Crack willow and can exceed 30 m in height. Until its early senility sets in, it maintains an acute-topped crown and with its silvery blue-green leaves it is highly distinctive. Most of the trees collapse soon after they are one m in diameter, which represents barely 60 years growth, but as in the case of Crack willow, some shed branches and survive as hulks to be 1.5 or even two m.

Coralbark willow ('Britzensis' or 'Chermesina') was marketed in Berlin in 1878. It is a male form of much less vigour than the common tree and is widely planted in parks and gardens to give winter colour around lakes. The young shoots are at their best after the New Year and although they give good colour when left alone, they are often cut back annually or every other year to increase the proportion of one-year shoots and to make those strong and long. This process also enables the tree to be grown in a confined space but it can lead to a short, lumpy-topped pollard stem which, with its head of red shoots, resembles an ice-cream cornet on fire. In the summer the shoots show among the leaves distinctively in a very pale orange colour.

Silver willow ('Argentea' or 'Sericea') has a lower, broader, more open crown than the common form and grows more slowly. Seen bathed in sunlight against a dark storm-cloud, it sparkles bright silver, but it is an untidy, formless tree in winter. It is reasonably common in town parks, often around the boundary.

Cricket bat willow ('Coerulea') is the form with the most rapid growth of all. It possesses superior elasticity and resistance to impact on the wood, and hence is the chosen timber for quality bats. It is of unknown origin and first came to notice in East Anglia before 1800.

Silver willow 24m   Cricketbat willow 25m   Pollarded crack willows

Male flower

New leaves

Coral bark willow

White willow

Fruiting catkin

ooting twig

Fruiting catkin

Crack willow

Crack willow 18m

White willow 25m

Golden willow
Cut to ground annually

Weeping Willow

The **Weeping willow** (*Salix* 'Chrysocoma') was for a long time referred to as the 'Babylon willow' and is sometimes still listed as *Salix babylonica*. This compounds several errors. No willow is native to the lower Euphrates River and the weeping tree there that caught the eye of the psalmist is a poplar. The Weeping willow is of Chinese origin, unknown in the wild, a garden form of the Pekin willow and was brought to the Levant very early, along the ancient silk-routes. It was taken from there to Europe before 1730, but remains a tender tree, and no large tree has been known within living memory in Britain although it is the common Weeping willow in the eastern United States from Philadelphia southwards. Reintroduced recently directly from China, it has survived a severe winter at tree-research stations. The shoots are brown and the buds pink.

The Weeping willow in Britain is a hybrid between the Babylon willow and the native White willow (or perhaps a weeping form of the Golden willow variant of the White willow). It is common in parks and gardens throughout England but finds the summers in the north and in Scotland a little cool, and the best growth is in the south.

The Weeping willow is grown from cuttings, and these should be 30–40 cm in the ground and only ten cm with one to two buds above the ground. After the first year it should be cut to the ground to make a single, strong shoot the next year. Cuttings with long tops dangling about make feeble growth and may need tricky internal support from canes to achieve a height from which the tree can 'weep' properly. Good plants can grow up to 15 m tall in as many years and go on to be 23 m × 1.2 m, but are unlikely to live to exceed that. The shoots become brighter yellow after the New Year and are at their best in March when the leaf-buds are unfolding bright green. The flowers extend with the leaves and are occasionally mixed male and female. Entirely female trees are less pendulous and are an older form, *Salix alba* 'Tristis'. In some years many trees are attacked by the fungus 'anthracnose of willows' (*Marssonina*) and lose much of their foliage, although rarely with fatal consequences.

The **Corkscrew willow** (*Salix matsudana* 'Tortuosa') or Dragon's claw willow, is a garden form from North China of the same species, or one very closely allied to it, as the parent of the Weeping willow. It was sent soon after 1920 but has become popular as a small garden tree only since 1950. The contortions are most acute in the new shoots and become gradually smoothed out with the increase in diameter until they are only slight in the bole. It is grown from cuttings and should be over ten m tall in ten years. Apart from the peculiar style of growth it is also of value in the garden as it comes into bright green

leaf very early in the year and retains green leaves very late, often well into December. Since the effect is less in a single-boled tree, the many-stemmed habit often seen will be preferred where there is room for it.

The **Sallow** (*Salix caprea*) is native to all parts of Britain. It grows to its biggest size, 20 m × 50 cm, in the high rainfall of the western Highlands of Scotland in woods of oak and tussock-grass on wet, boulder-strewn soils, but it also springs up on waste ground in dry areas to make a tall bush. The silver-haired, egg-shaped flower-buds enlarge from the first days of the year and in many years a few are open by New Year's Day. However, the majority open over a long period from mid February to mid April. The males have golden anthers and are the familiar 'pussy willow'. The females extend further with green projecting styles and secrete nectar, so the plant is pollinated by insects as well as by wind-borne pollen. The fluffy seeds are like white cotton-wool in mid-June: much remains unshed and the seeds turn brown and untidy.

The **Kilmarnock willow** ('Kilmarnock') is the male, low hummock of very weeping shoots which was found on the banks of the river Ayr. There is a female form, 'Weeping Sally'. The **Grey willow** (*Salix cinerea*) is a native species found in damp woods in Eastern England, and is never more than a bush. The **Eared willow** (*Salix aurita*) is another, even smaller native sallow. The **Osier** (*Salix viminalis*) is seen in willow-beds by lowland rivers, cut annually and making long shoots with 25 cm leaves. The **Almond willow** (*Salix triandra*) is also widely grown as an osier and is native to England. It can be a tree of up to nine m in height. It has furrowed shoots and its leaves are smooth on both sides.

The **Bay willow** (*Salix pentandra*) is native northwards from Derbyshire and is found by streams and in damp woods. It is usually small and shrubby but sometimes, especially when planted in gardens, it can exceed 18 m. Unfortunately, it very rarely is planted and in southern England it can be seen only in an occasional London park, one or two gardens and on a farm or two in a copse. The glossy shoots and leaves are good and the bright yellow male catkins open well after the leaves are out.

The **Violet willow** (*Salix daphnoides*) ranges widely across Europe and was probably introduced long ago although seen remarkably rarely today. A few gardens and town parks grow it beside water and usually cut it back to a stump every two years to obtain the maximum lengths of the brightest-bloomed second-year wood. New shoots will be up to two m long but left uncut they soon slow down.

Corkscrew willow

Goat willow

Kilmarnock willow

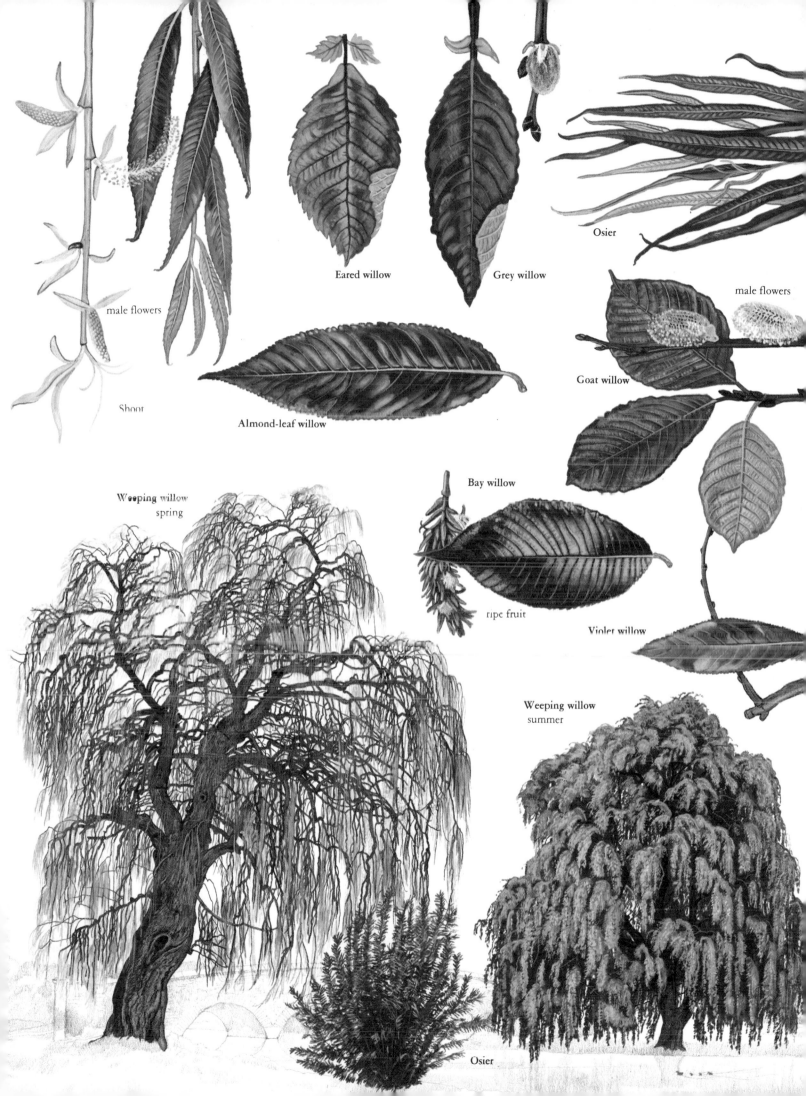

Eared willow

Grey willow

Osier

male flowers

male flowers

Shoot

Almond-leaf willow

Goat willow

Bay willow

Weeping willow
spring

ripe fruit

Violet willow

Weeping willow
summer

Osier

White Poplar

The **Aspen** (*Populus tremula*) is a member of the group of poplars distinguished as White poplars. It differs from the others in not having the shoot and the underside of the leaf thickly covered in white woolly hairs (except when they first emerge) and in the leaves being the same unlobed shape on vigorous young shoots as well as on old wood. White poplars are also distinguished from the Black and the Balsam poplars by having catkin-scales fringed with long hairs and this characteristic is shared by the aspen. This tree is a native of Britain and was among the first trees to return and spread to the far north as the ice retreated some 10,000 years ago. It is common only in the Scottish Highlands where it grows beside streams and rivers.

In southern England the Aspen is local, making thickets here and there at the edges of the woods on damp, low-lying commons and not often found as isolated trees. These thickets usually consist entirely of trees one sex, implying that they are extensions by suckering from a single original tree. Suckers arise in well-spaced dense groups extending ten m or more from quite young trees, beyond and within the thickets. They are very difficult to use for propagation even when lifted with a sector of the root, and seed is the only good method.

Female trees yield copious seed from their early years and the difficulty here is simply one of timing. The seed must be collected just before it is shed, which is usually at least by June. It must be sown at once and, if it is any good at all, it will have germinated by next morning. Self-sown seedlings get into their stride very quickly and within two years will be making annual shoots of 1.3 m or more, but although they can be 15 m tall in as many years, they then lose vigour, rarely exceed 22 m in height or 40 cm in diameter, and so must die early. The male catkins swell and lengthen in January and February and open brown amongst pale grey fluffy hairs by or before March. These are a prominent feature of the rare little **Weeping aspen** ('Pendula').

The **White poplar** (*Populus alba*) is a much less common or robust tree than the Grey poplar and comes from southern Europe, North Africa and western Asia, having been brought to Britain long before such things were recorded. It is sometimes seen growing as an inland defence against blown sand behind dunes where its suckers are not put off by accumulating sand and make thickets which prevent it blowing further. The tree can also tolerate the high lime content and high water-table found in such places. It is also seen as a hedge tree around fields in a few places but otherwise is a far from common park and garden tree. It is short-lived and tends to lean with an asymmetric crown and a sinuous stem. Never an imposing tree and seldom as much as 25 m tall, its best moments nonetheless are spectacular as it stands in sunshine, shimmering silver against a dark cloud. The undersides of the leaves are stark white and also show up well against a blue or a grey sky at any time. They have a particularly pretty effect when they are newly out of the bud. At that time it is only the underside that shows and the whole crown is a cloud of silvery specks.

Pyramidal white poplar ('Pyramidalis', 'Bolleana') is found cultivated in Central Asia and was introduced to Europe in about 1876. It grows rapidly and has a short life so that already the oldest trees have gone and the next oldest are in poor shape, dying at the top. A group of large trees will be admired but a few years later there is nothing left, so there is no point in mentioning the biggest now standing, beyond the fact that they are usually about 27 m × 60 cm when they go, and it is better to note some young ones for future comparisons of size. At Holland Park, London, two were planted in front of the Orangery in 1972. Nine years later they were 19 m × 39 cm.

The form 'Richardii' is not at all common. The gold is not uniform in the crown, there being some areas nearly green, and it seems to be a tree with a short life.

Grey poplar (*Populus canescens*) is intermediate in most features between the Aspen and the White poplar but is very much more vigorous than either. It is thus probably a hybrid between them, showing hybrid vigour. It grows to a great size and must have a life-span well in excess of 200 years. This longevity is helped by its extraordinary resistance to wind, including salt-laden sea-winds and its tolerance of soil conditions. In fact a large tree, 28 m × 130 cm, grows at Dunrobin Castle in Sutherland on the beach outside the wall, and must even have to contend with a salty soil. The Grey poplar grows best in broad valleys in chalk or limestone areas, and the finest is beside the River Brosna in central Ireland at Birr Castle, County Offaly. It is about 38 m × 172 cm and another nearby is 38 m × 145 cm.

The chalk valleys in Hampshire and Dorset hold many good specimens, some of them in lines along roadsides. This tree is not popular with farmers as a field boundary as it has an extensive superficial root-system and suckers freely. If it were less invasive it could be planted more widely as a replacement for the elm which has much the same needs and stature. The Grey poplar is often mistaken for the White poplar, but it is very different in its big sturdy trunk and strong heavy branches rising to make multiple-dome crowns, and the foliage is considerably less white. The haircover is less strikingly white and when a leaf from each is put side by side seems grey. The late-season leaves have a thin cover and before autumn all the leaves are nearly free of this woolly hair. It is hard to find a female tree and only a few are known at present. The male has been planted in preference because it does not spread cotton-wool at fruit-shedding time in July.

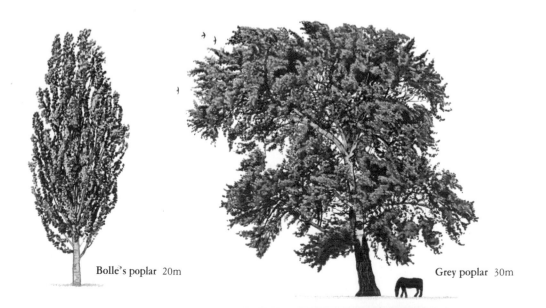

Bolle's poplar 20m

Grey poplar 30m

Weeping aspen

Female catkins

Male catkins

Fruiting catkins

Underside

Aspen

Sucker

Leaf

Richardii

Sucker leaf, underside

Aspen bark

Bark

Bark

Bark

Grey poplar 35m

Aspen 15m

White poplar 18m

Black Poplar

The native **Black poplar** (*Populus nigra* var. *betulifolia*) is a fine tree that has become scarce in the countryside. This odd position arises from the replacement of the big trees in lowland valleys by the hybrid Black Italian poplar which grows even more rapidly, and, being necessarily a male tree, does not strew the area with cotton-wool in summer, whereas some of the wild trees are female and shed the woolly fruit. But the native tree was found to be remarkably resistant to the smoky air once normal in cities, and a male form was widely planted under the name 'Manchester poplar': it is still common in industrial cities and suburbs. Big old trees, like that in the town car park in Newtown, Powys and by the A39 at Cannington, Somerset (27 m × 1.85 m) appear only at first glance to be like the more frequent Black Italian. Second and subsequent views reveal the big burrs breaking the run of some of the ridges in the brown, rugged bark. In addition, the largest branches arch out to hold dense brushes of shoots, and, if viewed at the relevant time, show the early leafing out, briefly pale brown and then bright green.

As a decreasing native species, this tree has been sought and mapped intensively. Only one or two female trees have been found growing with adjacent males. Seed collected from one of these near Tewkesbury was distributed by Edgar Milne-Redhead. It germinated profusely and two-year plants were over two metres tall. Poplar seed must be sown within a few days of collection and if it does not germinate and sprout overnight it will not do so at all. Two-year plants are cut back to base before planting out, to cause a new stem to grow. The two-year root-system means that this is a sturdy shoot, far superior to the slender one it replaces, which would not have been able to add very much after replanting. The new one makes a good foundation for a strong, shapely tree. One specimen only 23 years old at Cambridge Botanic Garden was 23 m × 52 cm. Cuttings from stout shoots are similarly cut back to base after the first year, when they are planted out.

Lombardy poplar (*Populus nigra* 'Italica') is an upright, narrow form of the southern European Black poplar. It arose in Northern Italy and was brought to Britain by Lord Rochford in 1758. He planted it at St Osyth Priory, Essex, where suckers of the original tree now grow. This true form is a male tree and in early spring it bears numerous dark-red catkins on the upper shoots. The tapering spire crown leads the eye upwards and seems to be taller than it actually is. Only one in Britain is currently known to be 39 m tall but numerous trees, often many of a line or group are 35–36 m. One in Tacoma, Washington, is 40 m tall, and the tree is common in almost every state of the USA and in southern Canada, although afflicted by diseases and pests in some parts of the eastern Rocky Mountains. In California and New Mexico articularly, the hot, sunny autumns turn the trees into towers of bright gold, as the occasional hot season can in England. The first 30 m can be grown in 40 years but increase in height thereafter is at risk from damage by lightning and storm, from disease and perhaps from over-use as a perch by carrion crows.

In towns, the authorities too often yield to pressure to lop Lombardies to some 12 m, on spurious grounds of safety. In fact, trees left alone resist windthrow very well until they die, but trees cut back regrow to over 30 m within 15 years. However, they now have six tops instead of one. These arise from zones prone to rot from the old cuts and so are likely to be blown out as well as to destabilize the whole tree. No trees seem to be known with planting dates before 1900, although many lines and trees are obviously older than that. However, the scarcity of diameters larger than one metre (which can be grown in less than 100 years) suggests a life-span little above 150 years. A form scarcely half the width of the usual one and verging on the ridiculous is quite frequent and often 31 m tall. It may be 'Elegans'.

Gigantea is a female tree of unknown origin, quite often seen in plantings of Lombardies and locally in large groups of its own, as in Elgin, Grampian, and by the river at Guildford, Surrey. Just before the leaves emerge it is densely hung with long, slightly curved, pale green catkins. This often confirms an identification made at other times of the year on the grounds of several diverging trunks. As the bigger branches and crown suggest, it grows faster in diameter of bole than the narrow males but is seldom above 25 m tall.

Plantierensis is probably common among the Lombardies, but is seldom distinguished. It has down on the young leaves and shoots, and tends to be a more leafy, vigorous tree, with a broader apex. It is a cross between the Lombardy and the Black poplars, arising in the Plantiere Nurseries near Metz before 1884, and on sale after that year.

Berlin poplar (*Populus* x 'Berolinensis') is a cross between the Lombardy poplar and an Asiatic balsam poplar, which occurred in Berlin before 1865. It is a female and inherits from the balsam poplar the wedge-shaped base to the leaf and the whitish underside. Once much planted, it is now scarce in Britain but less so in Europe.

Lombardy poplar

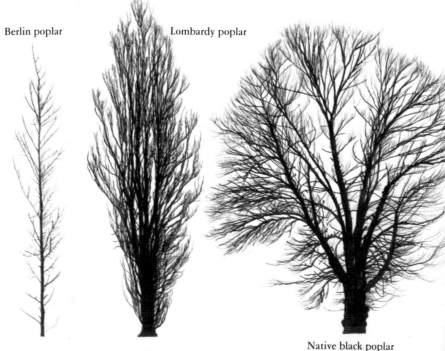

Berlin poplar

Lombardy poplar

Native black poplar

Male catkins

Lombardy poplar

Native black poplar

Shoot

Female catkin with fruit

Berlin poplar

'Elegans'   'Gigantea'   'Plantierensis'   Native black poplar

Balsam Poplar

A group of poplars that spreads across North America and Central Asia to the Far East, the Balsams are distinguished by large, very resinous buds, stout shoots and large leaves with whitish undersides. The Asiatic species are not very well suited to the British climate, preferring one much less equable and so they are scarce and usually small trees. Two of the more northerly species from North America are, however, more at home in Britain and one of them, the Western balsam, is common and widespread and often grows rapidly to a size that causes embarrassment and a need for its removal. The first to be grown in Europe and Britain was the Eastern balsam poplar, (*Populus balsamifera*), sent some 300 years ago, but now scarce. It does not grow well or achieve any great size in Britain and was soon confused with an obscure hybrid, also from north-eastern North America but not known in the wild, the Balm of Gilead (*Populus* x *candicans*). Both of these suffer badly from Poplar canker and tend to die young.

The Balsam poplar grows a thicket of slender suckers, often to a considerable distance from the stem and has rounded shoots without the ridges or wings that are found on the Western balsam. In Canada, the change from Balsam poplar in Alberta at Lake Louise to Western Balsam a few miles through Kicking Horse Pass into British Columbia is at once obvious from the appearance of heavier leaves and leafier crowns.

The **Balm of Gilead** is a more spreading tree with downy leaf-stalks and young shoots. It is now often planted in the form 'Aurora' which arose in Devon. It is at its striking best in midsummer when the earlier foliage of mainly dark green is the background to the midseason leaves unfolding white, cream and pink. Poplar canker usually strikes before this tree has exceeded 18 m but when cut back hard it makes new shoots which for some years at least make it peculiarly attractive.

The **Western balsam poplar** (*Populus trichocarpa*) is the biggest broadleaf tree of the Rocky Mountains and western slopes, being known to reach 60 m in height. It was not introduced until 1892 but it is the common Balsam throughout Britain. It is the tree planted to scent the spring air with the sweet balsam aroma from its expanding buds and new foliage, although both the Eastern balsam and the Balm of Gilead will do so also, but will not thrive so well. Easily grown from cuttings, this is the tree so often planted in small gardens and so rapidly regretted. Within five years it will be as tall as the house and its suckers will have taken over the garden. Western balsams spring up in suburban gardens and are cut down with great regularity. In plantations they have grown to 30 m in 15 years and in parks and large gardens many are 36–38 m tall. The columnar crown is made untidy by the sprouts and dead twigs on the bole. It is distinctive for the white undersides of the leaves and for their very varied size. Short shoots bear relatively broad leaves 10 cm long, and strong shoots growing fast add bigger and bigger leaves as the season advances so that those towards the tips may be long-tapered triangles over 30 cm long. In autumn they can be glorious towers of bright gold.

Unlike the Black poplars, the Western balsam particularly has no need of rich, basic soils and hot summers. It thrives on somewhat acid soils and in cool, damp regions so it is much planted in northern Scotland and in the west of Britain generally. A number of specimens suffer from canker but there are others that are resistant. Many selections of these have been made but they are used only in forestry and in a few gardens where attention is paid to this sort of detail. The male trees bear big thick catkins eight cm long which become dull dark red before the leaves unfold and usually seem to be shed or blown off before the pollen is shed. Female trees have green catkins which ripen into fluff-covered fruit which are shed in May.

Two hybrids between the Western and Eastern balsams are now quite widely grown. Called 'TT Hybrid' poplars because when they were raised the name current for the eastern one was *P. tacamahaca* and this was crossed with *P. trichocarpa*, they are exceedingly vigorous, narrowly columnar trees. One, 'TT 32', is much the more slender, with more steeply ascending branches in whorls two to 2.5 m apart (because that is the annual rate of growth) and this is the commoner of the two. One in Green Park, London, is over 30 m tall. Many little patches of damp land planted with this may be seen from motorways. The other, 'TT 37', is noticeably broader with less steeply-angled branches, and grows as fast in height and somewhat faster in diameter of stem. The leading shoot of both these hybrids, unbranched and 2.5 m long, has its biggest leaves at the top in autumn and tapers regularly in outline to its base where the smallest leaves are.

The **Chinese necklace poplar** (*Populus lasiocarpa*) is the only one of the world's poplars that has flowers of both sexes on the same tree. It is also the only plant in the whole Willow-Poplar family to do this, with the exception of one or two hybrid weeping willows. Furthermore, it is absolutely the only member of this family to have both sexes on the same catkin, and still further it is the only tree with catkins of mixed sex to bear the females at the outer end. Normally, as in the sycamore, the males are on the outer end which can thus be discarded after flowering. This peculiar flowering may, however, be an odd individual quirk rare in the wild, for the trees that show it are all derived from one of the six plants that were raised from the cuttings sent in 1900 from China by Ernest Wilson.

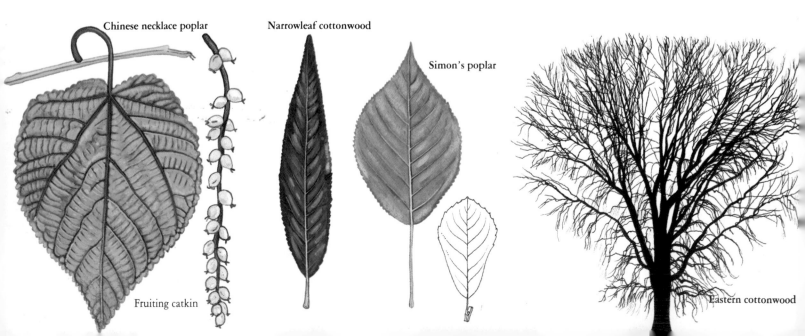

Chinese necklace poplar

Narrowleaf cottonwood

Simon's poplar

Fruiting catkin

Eastern cottonwood

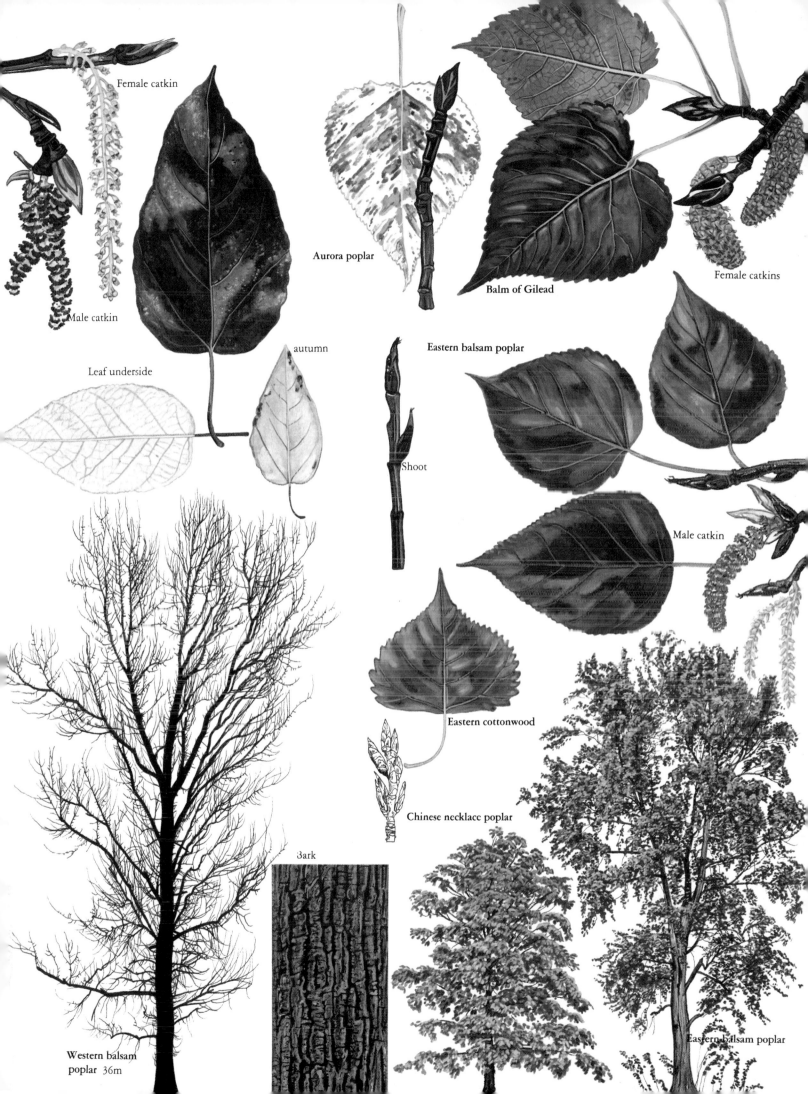

Female catkin

Male catkin

Leaf underside

autumn

Aurora poplar

Balm of Gilead

Female catkins

Eastern balsam poplar

Shoot

Male catkin

Eastern cottonwood

Chinese necklace poplar

Bark

Western balsam
poplar 36m

Eastern balsam poplar

Hybrid Black Poplars

The **Black Italian poplar** (*Populus* x *'Serotina'*) was the first of a number of hybrids to arise in European nurseries between the European Black poplar (*Populus nigra*) and the American Eastern cottonwood, (*Populus deltoides*). For 200 years it was also the most widely planted. Only since about 1950 has it been replaced to a considerable extent by another, 'Robusta'. The Black Italian was favoured at the expense of the native Black poplar because of its more rapid growth, its often straight and long trunk clear of burrs, and because, being a male raised from cuttings, it could never litter the area with woolly fruits. It is the common big poplar in the wide vales and chalkland valleys of south-eastern England, and is also often planted to screen water-towers and in city parks. It has become a liability in public places, however, and is now little planted in parks because it matures rapidly as a huge tree with heavy branches and it is not long before senility sets in and these are shed.

The Black Italian poplar needs warm summers and fertile, basic soils for good growth, a combination which limits its range as a useful tree to lowland England. It withstands considerable exposure and many of the biggest trees stand alone in riverside meadows, but it is in belts of mixed trees that the best, clean boles are grown and these may be without a branch for over 15 m.

This is the last countryside tree to come into leaf, in late May, but at least six weeks before that, and along with most other poplars, it opens its flowers – dark red male catkins. When the leaves unfold they are dark orange-brown, paling in a week or two to become the distinctive greyish-green that they will remain during the summer. Until maturity the crown is shaped like a huge goblet but the branches open out with age and in public places the biggest trees have usually had to be cut back severely and have grown dense masses of sprouts giving a very different outline, now equally characteristic. Young trees grow fairly broadly conical crowns, open, with unswept branches, the stronger ones in whorls. When 20 years old they can be 25 m × 55 cm, and may still be seen in small roadside plantations and by motorways, planted largely for the matchbox market which no longer requires them, and soon to be replaced by newer hybrids, once they have been felled to make pallets and boxes.

The **Golden poplar** ('Serotina Aurea') arose soon after 1870 as a branch-sport in a Belgian nursery. It is normally very much slower in growth than the parent, green form and does not develop the same goblet-shaped crown. In its earlier years it is a more rounded, more densely crowned tree and then develops a tall, open, rather irregular domed crown which can be over 32 m tall. A few such trees have some high branches which have reverted to green foliage. Young trees are a good butter-yellow throughout the summer. Old, tall trees are paler yellow but they also shine out splendidly, particularly in the sunshine between showers when in front of a dark cloud. This is a tree of English city and town parks, not very often seen in gardens.

Railway poplar ('Regenerata') is another European black and Eastern cottonwood hybrid which arose in France, this time in 1818. Some time around or after 1900 it was much planted in the Royal Parks and on the properties of the railway companies. The Regent's Park area in London and the sidings, coalyards and embankments of railways around London and to the south still have numbers of this tree and so do the hop-garden areas of Surrey and some market-garden areas where it was planted as shelter.

Railway poplar leafs out quite early and bright green, and before the leaves unfold fully the female catkins hang in lines beneath them like bright green caterpillars. The arching branches and hanging, slender shoots, together with the burred and sprouted bole distinguish the tree at a distance from the Black Italian poplar.

Another member of this hybrid group, the **Maryland poplar** ('Marilandica') probably a cross between the European black and the Black Italian poplars, arose in about 1800. A female, it has a dense, rather rounded crown until mature when it has big, spreading branches bearing clumps of foliage, leaving daylight between the branches. The leaves are markedly triangular with slender tips drawn out from a broad base. A few very big trees can be found in some town parks.

Eugene's poplar ('Eugenei') owes its slender, small-branched crown in youth to having the Lombardy poplar as one parent. It was once planted on spare farmland (also the matchbox market) but is now rare. The big trees are those planted in 1888 in the main botanic gardens and, as at Kew, now the biggest trees in these gardens, but they tend to deteriorate when around 36 m × 1.1 m.

'Robusta' poplar arose in a French nursery in 1890 and is the closest of the hybrids to the Eastern cottonwood parent, with much of its luxuriance of foliage. In summer, this abundance of big, firm leaves identifies 'Robusta', while in spring the profusion of big red catkins is an equally sure guide, as is the bright orange of the unfolding leaves – far more spectacular as well as six weeks or so earlier than those of the Black Italian poplar. Young trees have grown 30 m in 15 years and an occasional tree is now 40 m tall. This is common in small plantations, screens and shelterbelts, and is also sometimes on traffic roundabouts and roadside verges in semi-urban areas and parks.

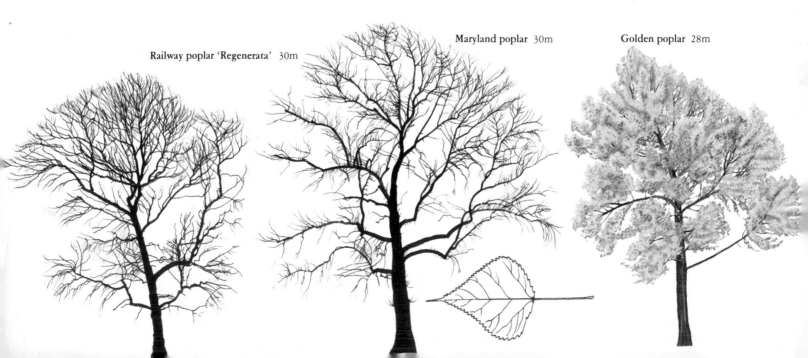

Railway poplar 'Regenerata' 30m

Maryland poplar 30m

Golden poplar 28m

Male flowers

Black Italian poplar

Base of leaf showing glands

Fruiting catkin

Female flower

Railway poplar

Robusta poplar

Male flowers

Black Italian poplar

Black Italian poplar 42m   Robusta poplar Coming into leaf   Eugene's poplar 36m

Common Walnut

The name 'walnut' comes from the Anglo-Saxon for 'foreign nut' and so was in use before the Norman Conquest and probably dates from Roman times. It may refer to the fruit rather than the tree but the **Common walnut** (*Juglans regia*) has been grown in Britain for a very long time. The Romans associated their god Jupiter (Jove) with this tree, hence the Latin name *juglans*, 'Jove's acorn (*glans*) or nut'. To Americans it is the 'English' or 'Persian' walnut as opposed to their several native species. The latter name puts it within its natural range, which is from China and Central Asia through Iran and Asia Minor to the Balkan Mountains, but north and east from there it is present only from early, unrecorded plantings. It is common in Britain only in southern and central England north to eastern Yorkshire, where there are many beside roads in farmland, but it is present as quite large trees in parks and gardens northwards to Skye (Armadale Castle) in the west and to Easter Ross.

For good growth the walnut needs deep, fertile soils, well drained but moist. The brick-earths of the hop-garden areas of the Weald in Kent and Surrey grow good trees as do clay loams and gravels. Sandy soil can also be suitable, if it is shallowly underlain by clay. Warm summers are also a factor in the better growth in the south-east. Although the unfolding leaves are frost-tender, they expand late enough to avoid damage from frost except when the rare June frost strikes. Then the leaves are killed although they are soon replaced.

There is a group of walnut orchards in Essex, and many garden trees may have been planted for the nut-crop, but it usually takes a long, hot summer to ripen the nuts for dessert, and only green nuts for pickling will be yielded, squirrels permitting. The tree, however, still merits planting for its handsome foliage alone, as well as its pale whitish-grey bark and picturesque winter aspect. So young trees are frequent in parks and gardens on clay and gravel soils and, becoming established after a few years, they grow fast. When 20 years old they should be about ten m tall and 30 cm through the bole. Growth in height almost ceases quite early and few trees exceed 23 m in height, but the bole expands rapidly for about 100 years, after which time it is one m in diameter.

This is a short-lived tree and few boles are more than 1.3 m in diameter but the position is unclear because the timber is so valuable that trees with good boles have rarely been left to become senile. A few old hulks were two m in diameter and fell to pieces while other old trees have low branches and are difficult to assess for age. The limit seems to be around 200 years. One remarkable specimen, standing at the time of writing, is quite without equal. By the drive to Gayhurst on the Northamptonshire–Buckinghamshire border, it is like a prime oak, with a bole 1.94 m in diameter and 2.5 m clear of branches. Even in 1907 it was among the finest recorded at 1.65 m. Its growth in the last 80-odd years indicates an age of about 270 years. The foliage of walnut readily gives a scent like some kinds of shoe-polish and a sprig in a jar by an open window is said to deter flies from entering.

The **Cutleaf walnut** ('Laciniata') is a rare tree striking for its lacy purple-tinged leaves and very open crown. **Black walnut** (*Juglans nigra*) is so-called because in its native woods in the Appalachian region its dark, blackish bark distinguishes it at a distance from the silvery-grey barked Butternut or White walnut. It is a magnificent tree in England, in stature and in foliage, but is almost confined to the south-east of a line from Lincoln to Exeter, although there is one fine example in Easter Ross. It likes warm summers and deep, fertile soils and thrives around London where one in Battersea Park is 33 m.

The bark is dark, very scaly and ridged even when the stem is only a few years old. Seed imported from the United States, fresh in damp peat, can give first year plants 50 cm tall. These should be planted out the following spring and, preferably stumped back (that is, cut to the base) for sturdy growth the next year. On the better sites early growth is rapid and well maintained but on less good sites it is moderate or slow. The fruit, which are freely borne, fall still green in late autumn. Scratching the skin gives a juice with a strong, sweet aroma and which yields a highly persistent brown dye. The wood is like that of the Common walnut and both are unsurpassed for use as gunstocks because once seasoned, neither moves at all after having been worked, and they withstand shock particularly well. They are also valued similarly in furniture for their good colour and figure and ability to take a high polish.

Butternut (*Juglans cinerea*) also comes from the Appalachian region of north-eastern America, extending further north than the Black walnut across Maine and into Quebec. It was introduced to Britain before 1650. But it remains scarce, almost confined to botanic collections although by far the finest is in the garden at Cliveden, Buckinghamshire, 25 m × 60 cm. The leaf can be 60 cm long and its stalk is covered in dense short hairs.

Japanese walnut (*Juglans ailantifolia*) grows as a broad low dome, well covered in summer with very large dull greyish-green leaves. Their stalks are thickly covered in sticky hairs. Japanese walnut is at its most decorative when the female flowers show their red styles on the long spikes. Sometimes a leaf may be one m long.

The **Manchurian walnut** (*Juglans mandschurica*), from the mainland of north-eastern Asia, differs only in the more abruptly pointed apex on the leaf. Both trees are scarce except in botanical collections.

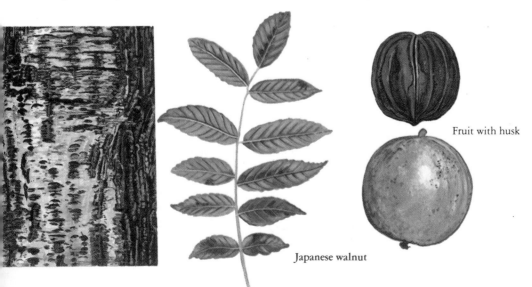

Fruit with husk

Japanese walnut

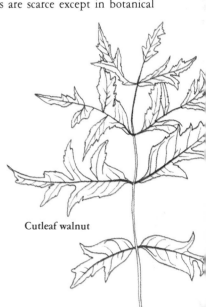

Cutleaf walnut

Female flower

Common walnut

Male catkins

Sliced twig to show chambered pith

Fruit with husk

Manchurian walnut

Butternut   Nut

Black walnut leaf

Black walnut bark

Common walnut 23m   Black walnut 30m

Caucasian Wingnut

The wingnuts are a small group of splendid trees of the walnut family and (unlike the hickories which are also members) share with the walnuts the odd feature of the pith being closely divided into chambers by numerous crosswalls, visible when a shoot is cut across on the slant. Unlike either walnut or hickory, most wingnuts have no budscales, preferring to spend the winter with two downy, un-expanded leaves pressed together over the tip of the shoot. Another strange feature is that the axillary buds – those arising between a leaf and the shoot – are one cm or more above the origin of the leaf and on a two–four cm stalk.

Wingnuts grow in China and Japan, except for one species from the Caucasus Mountains. This was introduced to France in 1780 and to Britain soon after, the magnificent tree at Melbury in Dorset which dates from about 1800 being probably the first. This tree is about 35 m tall, has a bole 1.8 m in diameter, and is unusual in this being its only stem and without a branch for eight feet.

Liking a rich, moist soil, the wingnut is often planted on the bank of a lake. This at least confines it in one direction but it soon occupies an inordinate length of the bank. It is less exuberant in the cool north and is not often seen north of the English midlands.

Hybrid wingnut (*Pterocarya* x *rehderana*) arose first when seed was sent from France to the USA in 1879. It came from a tree of the Chinese wingnut standing near a Caucasian one and yielded hybrid plants. This has occurred also in Borde Hill Gardens in Sussex. The hybrid has its leaf-axis deeply grooved and slightly flanged, inter-mediate between the elaborate, broad, toothed flange on the Chinese tree and the smoothly-rounded stalk of the Caucasian. It also lies somewhere between the two in its propensity for throwing up root-suckers, which the Chinese species does with far less abandon and vigour than the Caucasian. It is, however, not intermediate at all in speed of growth, being possessed of an astonishing vigour. A rooted cutting in its second full year in a Surrey garden grew a shoot 2.3 m long. A tree by the Main Gate at Kew, planted in 1953, was 22 m × 77 cm by 1981. Suckers taken with some fibrous root and cut to the ground make good trees and soft shoots rooted in June as cuttings do even better.

The **Chinese wingnut** (*Pterocarya stenoptera*) is, like the Hybrid, much less often seen than the Caucasian. In some cases this is because it was grafted on to the Caucasian, which has taken command and swamped it. It is quite rapid in growth if regarded as a normal tree, but among the wingnuts it is a laggard. At Dyffryn near Cardiff, one planted in 1902 was 24 m × 85 cm in 1979. A good one at Wakehurst Place in Sussex is 24 m × 90 cm.

The **Hickories** consist of a dozen species in eastern North America and one in Indo-China. The **Bitternut** (*Carya cordiformis*) is the most elegant and the most frequently seen among the six grown in Britain. The slender yellow but and the leaf with more than seven leaflets are features shared only by the very rare Pecan, and the terminal leaflet tapering to a stalkless base is its own. There are two fine pairs in the Pagoda Vista at Kew, 24–28 m tall, and two 26 m tall towards the Hermitage at Bicton Garden, Devon. The biggest, however, is by the duckpond at Leeds Castle, Kent and is 33 m × 88 cm. The airy, open crown of slender, upraised and outward-arching branches is most unlike that of the Shagbark but similar to the Shellbark. The Bitter-nut is the only hickory to have a brown bark with a network of ridges.

The **Shagbark** (*Carya ovata*) lives up to its name early in life as the loosely-held, long curving plates on the young stem soon begin to lift away at the top and the bottom. Its crown is distinctively heavily branched, the lower branches are horizontal, and the five-leafletted leaves are either thick and leathery or hard like parchment. They turn bright gold in the autumn.

The **Pignut** (*Carya glabra*) is the odd one out in terms of the small size of the leaf, often with only three leaflets when on weaker shoots; and in the shiny smooth purplish bark on old trees. It colours superbly in autumn, but it is very scarce and is grown in some collections and a few large gardens. The best is a fine tree near the Cumberland Gate at Kew which is 21 m × 49 cm. There is also a good one (17 m × 50 cm) in the Glasnevin Botanic Garden near Dublin. A tall one in Cannizaro Park, Wimbledon, has two stems and reaches to 22 m, while in the Serps, Wakehurst Place, Sussex there is one of 24 m.

The **Shellbark** (*Carya laciniosa*) combines the elegant crown of the Bitternut with the bark of the Shagbark, but has seven leaflets, and is somewhat less frequently encountered than either of those. One at Bicton is 22 m × 40 cm, and among the six at Wakehurst Place that in the flower-bed is 17 m × 40 cm. An even bigger one is by the church at Tortworth, Gloucestershire, and that is 17 m × 51 cm.

The **Mockernut** (*Carya tomentosa*) has very big leaves which when crushed give a pleasant paint-like aroma, and the down on the leaf-stalk is hard and dense. One at Kew was 23 m × 52 cm when 106 years old in 1978. The **Pecan** (*Carya illinoiensis*) which makes a monu-mental tree of up to 50 m tall with flaky, very pale grey bark in the south-eastern states of the USA is not happy in England and only five have been seen: two 9 m trees at Bedgebury, Kent; one 16 m tree at Wisley in Surrey; and two at Cambridge Botanic Garden, the older being 21 m × 38 cm. The numerous long-tapered bright green leaflets are unlike any others grown in Britain.

Bitternut

Shagbark hickory

Shellbark hickory

Mockernut hickory

Pecan

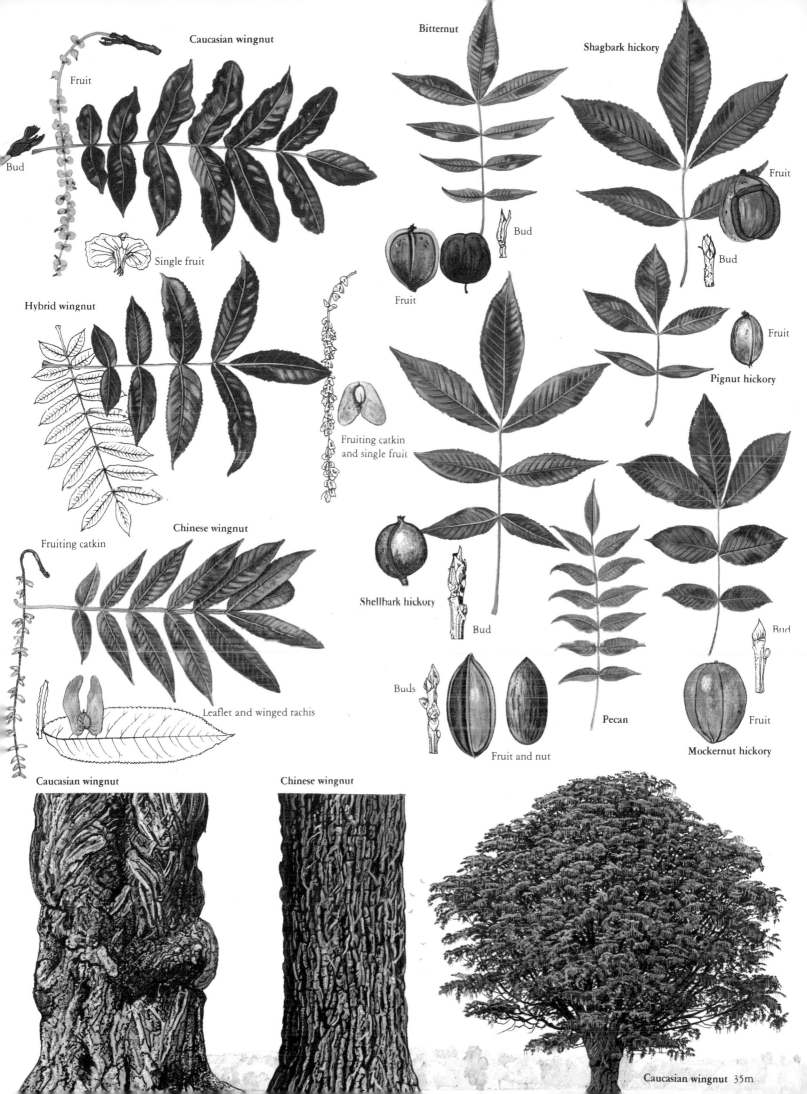

Caucasian wingnut

Fruit

Bud

Single fruit

Hybrid wingnut

Fruiting catkin
and single fruit

Fruiting catkin

Chinese wingnut

Leaflet and winged rachis

Bitternut

Bud

Fruit

Shagbark hickory

Fruit

Bud

Bud

Pignut hickory

Shellbark hickory

Bud

Buds

Fruit and nut

Pecan

Bud

Fruit

Mockernut hickory

Caucasian wingnut

Chinese wingnut

Caucasian wingnut 35m

Silver Birch

There are two different species of birch, both of them widespread and native to Britain, which are commonly called 'silver birch', and to most people that is the end of the matter, but in fact the two are quite distinct when looked at closely. Even from a distance, the weeping outer crown and the black diamond shapes on the bark proclaim the true species.

The true **Silver birch** (*Betula pendula*) is the one common on the dry parts of heaths, in open woods on sands and gravels and on the quick-draining slopes of mountain glens. It is a pioneer species, and the first tree to appear on cleared, burned or disturbed land on open soils. Its light seeds are blown far from woodlands. Dense drifts of birch on many southern heaths mark the passage of past fires. As with other pioneers, completely open sky is required for early growth, which is very rapid to enable the tree to grow clear of herbage and shrubs. In two years it will be 1.5 to two m tall and in 25 years 20 m, but from then on growth in height may be slow and few trees attain 25 m. The stem also expands rapidly and will be 30 cm through in 25 years.

In the wild in England, these trees begin to show signs of old age when about 50 cm through and 60 years old, but in gardens many survive to be 70–80 cm through and may live to be 100 years old. In Scottish glens growth is slower and some trees only 60–70 cm through are 200 years old and more.

This tree is always shedding something. In spring it is the bud-scales coming down like chaff, then the male catkins, and after them all the summer it deposits systems of dead twigs, as it may too in winter. There is then a long period during which seeds float down by the million, helped by the redpolls, siskins and tits for which this is a main source of autumn food. Then the remains of the fruit come down. On loamy soils, this birch makes an ideal lightly shading screen from the midday sun for many rhododendrons, and in spring it gives enough light to suit most bulbs. But on poor sandy soils, its roots are too invasive and competitive for any but tough plants.

Swedish birch 'Dalecarlica' is the name used in Europe for this gracefully pendulous tree with deeply-cut leaves. In America, however, where it is almost the dominant tree in streets through all the central states, it is often named 'Gracilis' and some may be of different origin. The true Swedish form was found in the wild in 1767 and grafts were taken well before it was blown down in 1887. The tallest birch of any sort in Britain is an early one of these, and now stands 33 m tall beside Loch Tay near Kenmore. There are groups of good trees up to over 20 m in Windsor Great Park and in Sheffield Park, Sussex, and young trees are now appearing in many parks and gardens.

'Fastigiata' is occasionally seen as a street tree and when young its shape is very suitable for this purpose, but it will open out somewhat with age. The biggest is in Alexandra Park, Hastings, Sussex and was 29 m tall when 100 years old. **'Tristis'** is a slender tree with short, level branches holding dense, hanging masses of shoots which are tinged deep purple in winter. **'Youngii'** arose in Milford, Surrey and is grafted, usually at 1.5–two m on a stem of Silver birch. It usually mushrooms down from a little above that point but a few trees grow up to 12 m and hold many layers of foliage. The leaf is small and dark green. **'Purpurea'** is rarely seen and is even more rarely thriving but a young tree can be a small feature. **Dwarf birch** (*Betula nana*) is a subshrub growing to scarcely one m found wild on mountain tops in Northumberland, the Borders Region in Scotland, and the Grampians.

Downy birch (*Betula pubescens*) is the other tree commonly known as 'silver birch'. It replaces it in damp hollows on heaths, by streams and pools in open woodland and by the ditches and streams along the bottoms of highland glens, where its fuzzy outline contrasts with that of the weeping Silver birch above it. It occurs frequently in town and city parks on clay soils and is similar to the Silver birch in the sizes and ages achieved.

Paper birch (*Betula papyrifera*), also known as Canoe birch, ranges from Labrador to Alaska near the northern limit of tree growth, south to Oregon and North Carolina. With such a vast extension of populations it is almost inevitable that there should be regional varieties and six are recognized. Only one, the typical form, is generally seen in British parks and gardens. It is recognized more by the large leaf having few veins than by the bark, for that can vary quite widely. Few are clear white all over; most are tinged with or have patches of pink, orange or dark purple. For a tree introduced as long ago as 1750 and so hardy, at least in parts, it is remarkably uncommon, but there is a scatter of good trees northwards as far as the Grampians.

Sichuan birch (*Betula platyphylla* var. *szechuanica*) is the south-western Chinese form of the East Asian equivalent of the Silver birch, and is the form least scarce in British gardens. The chalk-white bark rubs off on the hand as white dust, more freely than occurs in other birches. The species has new shoots even more roughened by little warts than the Silver birch and jaggedly toothed, long-tailed leaves: the Sichuan variety has more rounded leaves and these are firm and thick in texture.

Sichuan birch   Paper birch   Paper birch 16m   'Tristis'   'Fastigiata' 20m   Young's weeping birch 3m

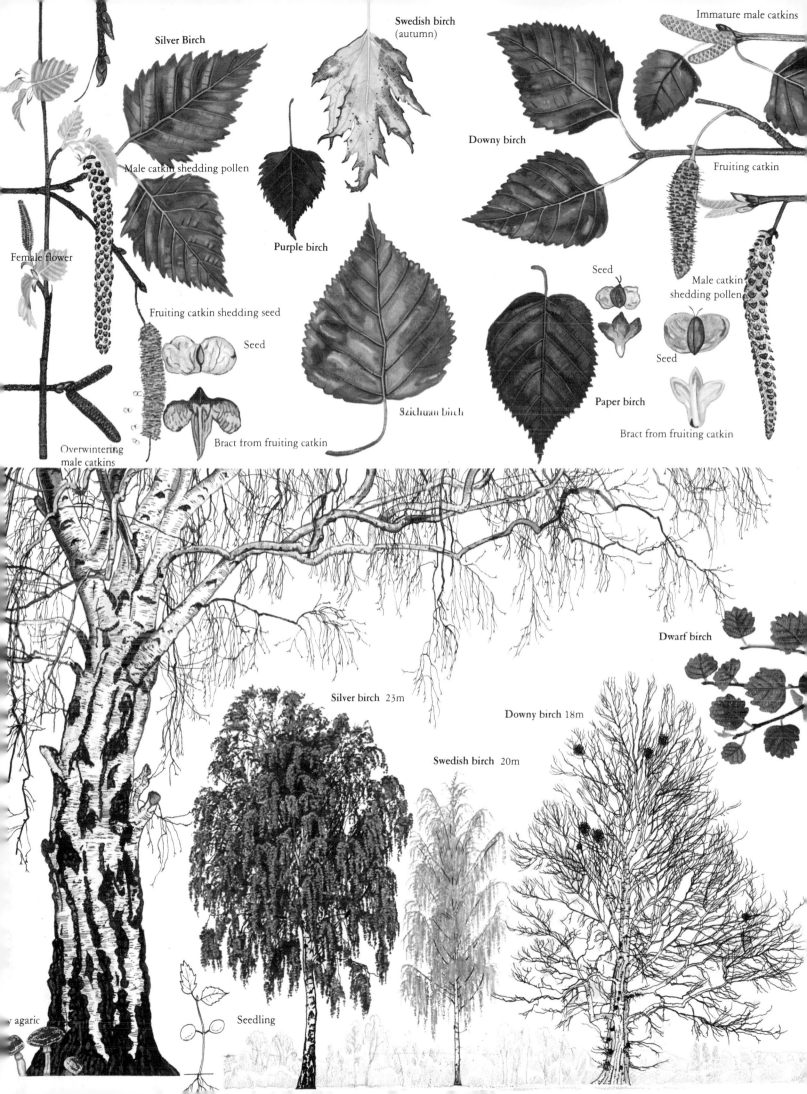

Silver Birch

Swedish birch (autumn)

Immature male catkins

Male catkin shedding pollen

Downy birch

Fruiting catkin

Female flower

Purple birch

Male catkin shedding pollen

Seed

Fruiting catkin shedding seed

Seed

Seed

Overwintering male catkins

Bract from fruiting catkin

Szichuan birch

Paper birch

Bract from fruiting catkin

Dwarf birch

Silver birch 23m

Downy birch 18m

Swedish birch 20m

y agaric

Seedling

Other Birches

Kashmir birch (*Betula jacquemontiana*) is the western form of the Himalayan birch planted now in many gardens mainly for the benefit of its strikingly white, smooth, shiny bark. In fact, this kind of bark also occurs elsewhere in the Himalayan birch, and many trees planted as Kashmir birch are botanically Himalayan. The division is not precise, but the true Kashmir birch should have no more than nine pairs of veins on each leaf. The beautiful bark is cast at times and for a short while the new bark is orange-brown.

Himalayan birch (*Betula utilis*) is a variable tree. Many specimens now planted are selected for their clear white bark and differ from the Kashmir birch only in the leaf having ten to 12 pairs of veins. Others may have similar bark, or one that is largely orange, or orange, grey and white, but their leaves are broader, darker and firmer, with stout, grooved, hairy stalks and more down beneath. They have strong ascending branches making a broad-conic crown. The very white-barked form is notable in the Royal Botanic Garden, Edinburgh and at Trinity College, Dublin, from which seed was sent to Kew in 1934. One at Hidcote, Gloucestershire, is 12 m × 21 cm; another at Kew is 14 m × 38 cm.

River birch (*Betula nigra*), or Black birch, extends its natural range further south than any other birch in America, reaching Georgia and Florida. The decidedly few specimens in Britain show a strong southerly grouping, with few outside Berkshire, London and Surrey. There are even two growing in a street in Horsell near Woking. A northern outlier is one at Thorp Perrow, Yorkshire, 14 m × 30 cm. The silvery underside of young leaves is a mark of the species, and young trees are somewhat erect with an orange-pink or pale brown bark which has blackish flaking ridges before it becomes dark purplish red. The numerous cylindrical fruit stand erect.

Transcaucasian birch (*Betula medwediewii*) from the southern shores of the Caspian Sea and on the surrounding Elburz Mountains, remains an upright bush on a single bole seldom more than 30 cm long. It is only exceptionally ten m tall. The bark is flaky and brown with some silvery grey and is very like that of the hazel. Leafy spurs persist on the interior parts of the branches which, on older plants, radiates from the base before turning upright. The foliage is handsome, if dark green in summer, but the glory of the tree is the rich golden colours in autumn. There are half a dozen or more trees in the Autumn Glade at Thorpe Perrow, and several at Westonbirt.

Erman's birch (*Betula ermanii*) is widespread in Eastern Asia and was received from Japan in 1890. It is most attractive as a young tree when it has a slender crown of strongly raised branches with pure white bark for most of their length. With age, the crown spreads more widely and the bark becomes pink and hung with fraying strips. The leaf is prettily marked by about ten pairs of close, straight, parallel veins, and is usually wedge-shaped at the base. The four cm diameter fruit are abundant and persist into the winter, enough often to identify the tree from a distance.

Yellow birch (*Betula lutea* or *alleghaniensis*) from eastern North America merits planting much more widely than has been the case so far. The bright gold autumn colour may be brief, but the large leaves and shapely crown make it an excellent foliage-tree. Skinning a twig with a fingernail gives rise to a strong scent of oil of wintergreen but unfortunately this test cannot be used for distinguishing Yellow birch from the very similar Cherry birch (*Betula lenta*) as that behaves in the same way. However, the Yellow birch has dark-grey bark with brown areas and a yellow cast rather than a dark red one, and usually has broader, flatter leaves, with 12–15 pairs of veins rather than 9–12 pairs. Both are equally infrequent and seen mainly in the big gardens with tree collections. A big tree, for this species, is in Tilgate Park, Crawley, Sussex (20 m × 67 cm at one m) and another is at Innes House, Grampian (11 m × 51 at 0.5 m) showing a fine disregard of latitude for the species. The biggest Cherry birch is at Hollycombe, Sussex, 23 m × 62 cm.

The **Monarch birch** (*Betula maximowicziana*) is a splendid tree from Japan, bearing most unbirchlike leaves to 15 cm × 12 cm, more like a lime, and with a bigger tooth between the others where each vein reaches the margin. Its big branches are less upright than in most birches and have much pink in the bark. Young trees have orange down over the new leaves but in older trees the leaves are smooth and glossy. In autumn they turn bright yellow. The male catkins become 12 cm long when shedding pollen and yellow and are grouped in threes and fives. A tree at Killerton, Devon, is 18 m × 55 cm and two at Westonbirt, near the main road, are as tall. In Holland Park, London, one 30 years old is 18 m × 25 cm.

The **Chinese redbark birch** (*Betula albosinensis*) has been introduced in two forms, differing chiefly in the size and hairiness of the leaf, but both are grown for the exceptional beauty of their bloomed bark. The northern form has sparsely-set leaves which may be 17 cm long and have tufts of hair in the angles of the veins and midrib on the underside. The best features of the bark seem to be shown particularly well in Scotland, where at Branklyn, Tayside and Innes House, Grampian, trees 16 m tall are outstandingly good for colour and bloom.

Chinese redbark birch

Monarch birch

var *septentrionalis*

Cherry birch

Old bark

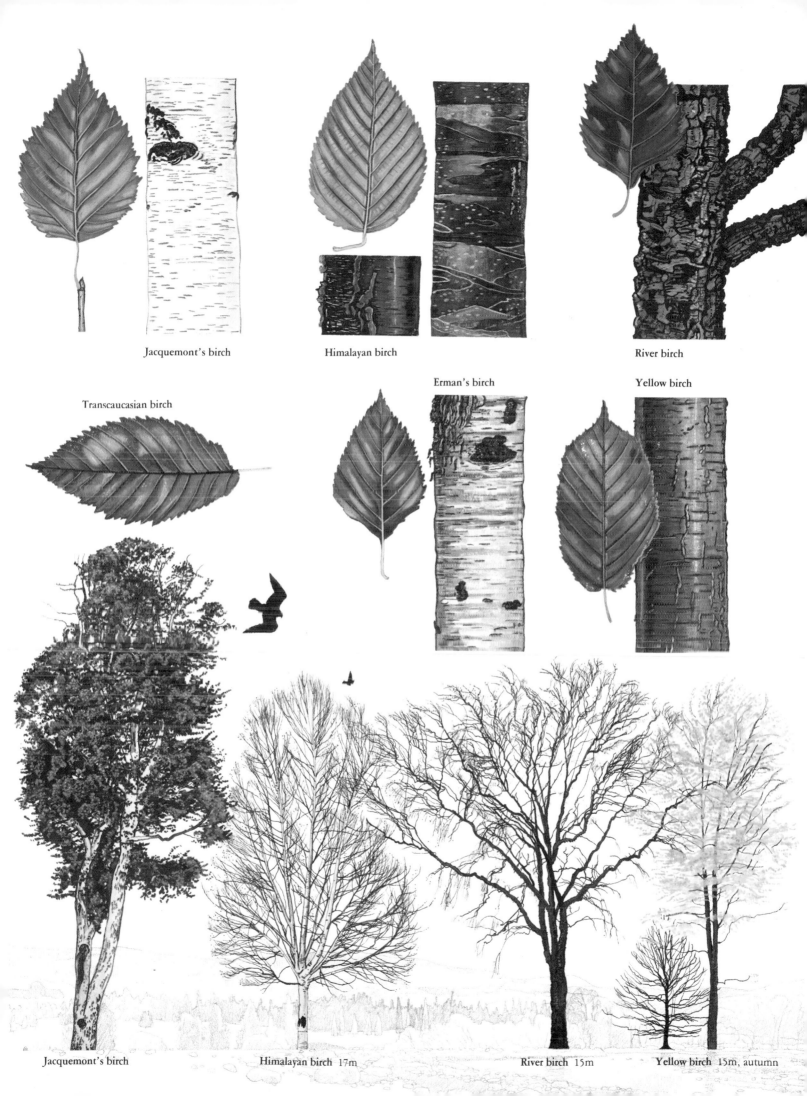

Jacquemont's birch

Himalayan birch

River birch

Transcaucasian birch

Erman's birch

Yellow birch

Jacquemont's birch

Himalayan birch 17m

River birch 15m

Yellow birch 15m, autumn

Alder

Common alder (*Alnus glutinosa*), a native of Britain found mainly by still or running water, was among the first trees to recolonize the country after the Ice Ages. It is able to grow on wet and often flooded sites and in soils lacking the nitrates essential for growth because its roots have nodules which harbour a bacterium which extracts them, in effect, from the air. It is thus a valuable pioneer, improving new soils for other trees. All the alders have this facility.

The alder was formerly valued for its timber, used where continual wetting and drying soon rot most woods, for example in mill-clogs and some canal-lock works, as well as for high quality charcoal. For this last and other smallwood produce, the strong coppicing ability of alder is a great asset. Sprouts from an older root-system can grow 1.3 m or more in a season. The dark-red roots that this tree grows in adjacent fresh water in dense bunches were appreciated as defence of mud-banks against erosion from floodwater and the wash from passing craft before rivers came to be treated only as agricultural drains.

The flowering of the male catkins is a protracted event in a group of trees as some will lengthen, colour and shed pollen towards the end of a mild January and others will still be doing so in April. In autumn the only diversity is in the time of leaf-fall – there is never a chance of a golden leaf, they all fall dark green. In summer the foliage is a dull dark green too, so as an ornamental tree the alder has distinctly limited appeal, and its use in gardens rarely goes beyond a lakeside fringe whose seeds may attract feeding siskins, redpolls and goldfinches.

Cutleaf alder ('Laciniata') is the same in every way except in the narrowly-lobed leaf and is seen only in few gardens and slightly more town parks. It is able to grow to much the same sort of size as the Common alder.

Imperial alder ('Imperialis') is a very different kind of tree. In leaf it has a pale filigree elegance foreign to other alders. For most of the season, large persistent stipules at the base of each leaf add a yellow-green variation equally out of character. A slender tree at any time, a young Imperial alder will often have such lax, thin shoots that the top of the crown leans out, and the plant looks feeble, although a few have become relatively sturdy with age. The usual places to plant this tree are by the streams that often traverse city parks and big gardens, or in a damp hollow nearby.

Golden alder ('Aurea') is a regrettably rare, slow-growing, rounded little tree with foliage of a fine soft golden colour. **Grey alder** (*Alnus incana*) is a tough and hardy tree from northern Europe which, far from needing a wet site, grows best in well-drained soil and even

thrives in the often dry and difficult soils of spoil-tips. It also grows well in broken, rocky soil in high rainfall areas, and is to be seen in car parks and public areas in the western Highlands of Scotland in recently laid out recreation sites. There are remarkably few old or big trees in gardens or even in collections but this is a fast-growing tree and in a few plantations in western Scotland many trees were 25 m tall before being felled when still quite young. Maturing trees are notable for their smooth, pale grey-green bark. In autumn the leaves stay on the tree until late November, turning black as they are shed.

'Aurea' is a small tree, also decorative in winter because the shoots are orange and the catkins in bud are bright orange. It is, however, upstaged and now usually replaced by **'Ramulis Coccineis'**, in which the shoots are bright red and the catkin-buds sealing-wax scarlet. In leaf the latter is distinguished by the underside of the leaf being almost smooth instead of downy.

Italian alder (*Alnus cordata*) is the aristrocrat of the commonly seen alders, the finest in foliage and the champion in growth, stature and size of fruit. Its southern origins – in Corsica and southern Italy – affect it not a whit and one of the tallest is in eastern Scotland. The tallest, currently 30 m, is in Marble Hill Park, London and is a metre or so taller than one in Westonbirt, Gloucestershire. A fine group on the Fen, Cambridge City, must be about 50 years old but it is only in the last 15 years or so that park, town and roadside plantings have become common. In good rich soil a tree can grow a shoot 1.5 m long and even on a drier site over chalk it may add one m in a year and quickly build a sturdy stem. The male catkins become bright yellow and open with the first of those of the Common alder, or sometimes even a week or two earlier: they are much longer and more impressive. The season is, however, shorter as they all flower within a few weeks of each other. The main veins on the underside of the leaf have at their base attractive groups of pale brown hairs lying at right angles to the vein and straight. The crown maintains a good conical shape with a spire until the tree is 20 m or more tall, which adds to the other features of robust growth and pretty foliage that make this such a good tree for precincts and roadsides.

Green alder (*Alnus viridis*) is the alder of the Alpine streamsides and the only one likely to be seen that has buds lacking stalks. It is not, however, often encountered. When it is, it usually appears in the form of an upright bush, except for the occasional moderately large tree like the one in the Royal Botanic Garden, Edinburgh. The substantial, bright yellow catkins ripen late for an alder, usually not being fully out until early May.

Cutleaf alder   'Imperialis'   Weeping grey alder   Golden grey alder

Female flowers

Lengthening male catkin

Immature fruit
in summer

Common alder

Green alder

Male catkin

Italian alder

Male catkin

Female
flower

Female flowers

Opened fruit in winter

Male catkins ripening

Grey alder

Immature flowers in winter

Opened fruit in winter

'Ramulis-coccineis'

Grey alder 20m

Italian alder 27m

Common alder 25m

Common alder

Hornbeams and Hazels

Common hornbeam (*Carpinus betulus*) is a native tree which arrived late in Britain and did not spread far. The few woods of pure hornbeam are in Essex, notably in Epping, Hainault and Hatfield Forests, as well as in Hertfordshire and East Anglia. It also occurs in a more scattered form among other trees in Kent, Sussex and Surrey and beyond these areas is probably a planted tree, uncommon in Scotland. The name 'hornbeam' means 'hard wood'. It is one of the hardest and strongest of all timbers and is a good fuel-wood, also making high quality charcoal. It was grown for smallwood uses, and for charcoal, often where deer would prevent young trees from growing and so was 'lopped' or pollarded. The stem was cut as high as an axe could reach, about 2.5 m, and the sprouts were cut when of suitable size. Each cutting produced more new sprouts than the previous one until a broad-topped pollard resulted, like those in Essex.

Hornbeam wood is still used today for piano hammers, and larger pieces form the centres of chopping-blocks. Before the invention of cast iron, hornbeam was the one wood strong and hard enough to take the strain of a watermill wheel and the wear of its cog-teeth. It was also used for the hub of a cartwheel, which, being bored to take the axle and the spokes, requires extreme strength.

Hornbeam grows better than all but a few trees on heavy clays, a useful feature for a tree whose main population is on the London clay of Essex and Hertfordshire. It grows well on lighter soils but not on poor, acid sands and it needs some shelter in order to thrive and even some high shade when it is young. Early growth consists of a slender, straight leading shoot up to some 70 cm long, with rather few, level, less straight side-branches snaking out for some distance. Upward growth slows gradually and few trees reach above 25 m although here and there, in well sheltered conditions, 30 m is achieved. The male catkins, which are inside buds in the winter (unlike those of Hop-hornbeam) are very prolific every year and expand before the leaves over several weeks in March and April.

'Incisa' or Oakleaf hornbeam is seen in some parks as a bushy tree which may be 15 m tall and at least as broad. Not only does the depth of lobing vary from twig to twig but most of the older plants have some shoots bearing normal leaves. This gives rise to local myths that the tree is a beech grafted on to an oak. Otherwise it is a dull, rather dark, untidy plant.

'Fastigiata', the **Pyramidal hornbeam**, however, is a very attractive and useful tree. It grows well on heavy clays or with paving over its roots; as well as in towns where its formal shape is valued for keeping clear of street furniture while giving a leafy crown in summer; for its fine autumn colours and for its extremely fine winter tracery of close, straight slender shoots.

Japanese hornbeam (*Carpinus japonica*) is a rare, small but handsome tree. The bark has pink stripes on smooth grey green, and the extra-long tooth at the end of each of the 22 pairs of veins curls upwards. **Eastern hornbeam** (*Carpinus orientalis*) is also rare. It comes from Asia Minor and the Balkan Mountains and has purplish-grey bark well streaked in buff. The little leaves, no more than five cm long, are folded concertina-wise in the bud and remain slightly folded at each vein.

European hop-hornbeam (*Ostrya carpinifolia*) is a sturdy, scaly-barked tree, sometimes with several stems and quite vigorous, although none is very big in Britain. It is infrequent and is most easily found in the summer when the fruit hang white among dark, rather flaccid leaves. The male catkins are exposed from autumn to spring, in small bunches like those of alders and hazels, and lengthen to shed pollen in March or April. This tree is wild and quite common across southern Europe from eastern France to the Black Sea and in Asia Minor.

Hazel (*Corylus avellana*) was an early immigrant after the Ice Ages and extends everywhere in the British Isles except in the Shetlands. It is not, however, officially a tree, as it fails to achieve six m on a single stem, although some bushes may be taller than that. Growing as it does it can yield wood only for turnery and tool-handles but its supple shoots were once in demand for being woven into hurdles. It also yielded bean-poles and faggots for ovens. Its strong sprouting growth when cut makes it ideal for coppiced growth under clean-boled oaks. This 'coppice with standards' was a widespread system in the woods of southern England until this century. The periodic clearing of each area encouraged a rich growth of bluebells and also favoured nightingales, so some woods are being managed as coppice today by conservation-minded bodies. A few catkins can be found in some years just before New Year's Day, but in most seasons they start in late January and may still be found on some bushes in April.

Turkish hazel (*Corylus colurna*) from the Balkan Mountains, Asia Minor and western Asia has been in Britain for 400 years but has only recently been appreciated as the splendid, adaptable and vigorous tree it is, ideal for city planting, with a shapely conic and leafy crown. There are some old trees, now most un-hazel-like in their fine boles up to one metre through, and in being 25 m tall, as at Syon Park, London or the Abbey Gardens at Bury St Edmunds. The catkins open in January and the softly spiny fruit are bright green in summer.

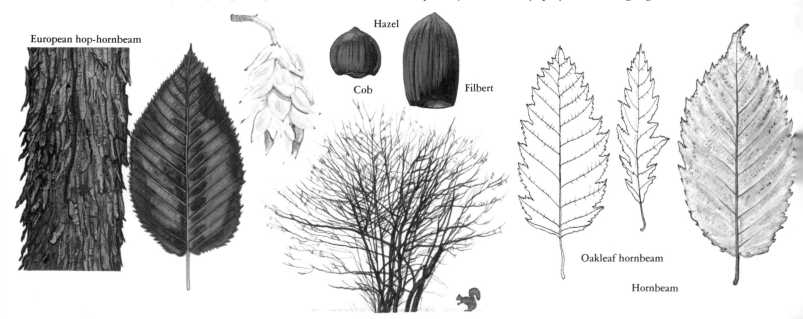

European hop-hornbeam

Hazel

Cob

Filbert

Oakleaf hornbeam

Hornbeam

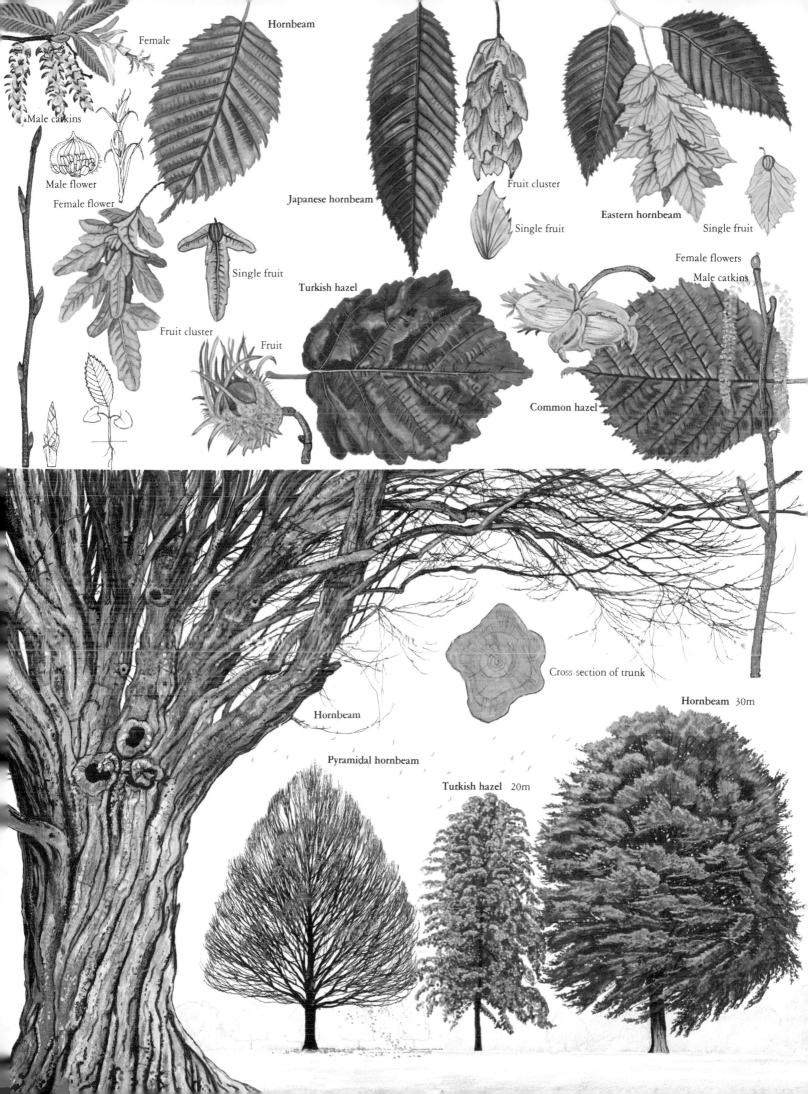

Female

Male catkins

Male flower

Female flower

Hornbeam

Japanese hornbeam

Fruit cluster

Single fruit

Turkish hazel

Fruit cluster

Fruit

Eastern hornbeam

Single fruit

Female flowers

Male catkins

Common hazel

Single fruit

Cross-section of trunk

Hornbeam

Pyramidal hornbeam

Hornbeam 30m

Turkish hazel 20m

Beech

No tree can grow up under the shade of its own kind but the **Beech** (*Fagus sylvatica*) can do so under any native tree except yew. Hence, in time, all suitable soils left undisturbed would become beechwoods. Beech, however, will not grow on heavy clay or other wet soils but must have open, well-drained soils, so the clay vales and river-bottoms would become oakwoods. Beech dominates on chalk and limestone uplands and on mildly acid sands. Its roots penetrate far through open soils and chalk rock to find the moist layers it needs with its high demands for water, but its roots will not go into these and in shallow sands over clay old beech are often blown over, raising root-plates of great extent but no depth.

Adapted to growing in existing woodland, beech cannot start life on its own on exposed open ground among grass. It has to be planted with, or after, species like sycamore, larch or Lawson cypress which nurse it through the early years with shelter and by suppression of the grass mat. The 'nurses' are cut out when saleable, so leaving a pure beechwood and giving early returns to defray costs. Once established, beech resists exposure very well and is an invaluable shelter-tree in upland areas. Chanctonbury Ring in Sussex on the crest of chalk downs at 230 m was planted in 1770 with Scots pine, ash and sycamore for nurses. Some of these remain today.

A curious feature of the beech is the 'juvenile cone', a zone about two metres broad at the base, tapering to an end 2.5 m high, within which the foliage looks the same as the adult but remains in winter rich red-brown on the tree. Beech hedges are cut to remain within this zone and where clipping is neglected and shoots project beyond it, the part beyond sheds its leaves. Similarly, sprouts on the boles of old trees retain their leaves where they are within this zone.

New shoots are expanded during three weeks in May, well after the older wood is in leaf, and extend some 15 cm a week, drooping, soft grey and with long hairs. Young trees make a second similar addition in July bringing the increment for the year to about one metre for a few years. After 30 years they should be some 15 m tall. In the open they grow eventually to 25 or 30 m but in deep wooded combes many exceed 40 m. One rather less sheltered at Beaufront Castle, Northumberland, is about 44 m. In the fine old stand at Slindon, Sussex, many trees are 40 m and reputedly over 240 years old. They have been thinned well from an earlier fairly dense stand and so have clean boles for up to 20 m and small branches. Trees grown more openly, with heavy branches rarely survive so long but die suddenly and break up rapidly. Very few boles exceed 1.8 m in diameter, which represents about 200 years' growth in the open.

The **Golden beech** 'Zlatia' arose in Yugoslavia before 1890. It grows at least as fast as any other beech, and its fresh, pale, golden foliage is a splendid addition in spring. However, by August, it is little different from an ordinary beech.

The **Copper beech** 'Purpurea' was first known in Switzerland by 1680, and also arose twice later in Germany. The name is a general, if seldom apt one applied now to an array of seedling forms as well as to two superior forms, 'Swat Magret' and 'Rivers' Purple' which are both a good deep red colour. Growth of purple beeches is as rapid as that of the green, and several old ones are two metres in diameter.

Fernleaf beech 'Aspenifolia' can be identified in winter by its finer shoots, more densely twigged, and numerous sprouts on bole and branch as well as from the sign of a graft near the base. The crown in summer is a delicate shade of green with a finer texture, easily identified from a great distance. The biggest are now over 25 m tall with boles up to 1.2 m in diameter.

Roundleaf beech, 'Rotundifolia' arose near Woking, Surrey before 1870. It remains fairly rare. Of those planted recently, many are the form 'Cockleshell' with even smaller leaves.

Crested beech, 'Cristata' is curious not only in its jagged-toothed, crumpled leaves but in its crown of long, wandering branches sparingly arising from the bole. It is rare, but a big one grows in Bath Botanic Garden and another near the lawn at Wakehurst Place, Sussex.

Weeping beech 'Pendula' can be a narrow tree to 30 m or, like the Knaphill Nursery original five (planted in 1826) form huge, broad grooves in rings of layered branches around the main bole, in which case, it will rarely be more than 24 m tall.

Dawyck beech was found in a plantation made at Dawyck estate near Peebles and was moved, in about 1860, down to a gate to the garden where it stands today 27 m tall and 0.8 m diameter at one metre. It was available in the trade only after 1938 when the first planting was by part of the Basingstoke by-pass, but a few were grafted before this and given by the Balfours of Dawyck to friends. One of these, at Wakehurst Place, at 29 m is now taller than the Dawyck tree. **Dawyck purple** is a seedling raised by Mr van Hoey Smith at Trompenburg Arboretum, Rotterdam and was launched in Britain in 1980.

Oriental beech (*Fagus orientalis*), the species found in the Balkan Mountains, the Crimea and from Asia Minor to Iran, is found in a few gardens. Its bigger leaves are more widely spaced and some of the bristles on the husk are flattened and green.

Copper beech   Fernleaf beech   Roundleaf beech   Crested beech   Weeping beech

female flowers

male flowers

Ripe fruit

Summer foliage

Oriental beech

'Luteo Variegata'

'Zlatia'

Shoot

Bole

Common beech

'Dawyck Purple'

Dawyck beech

Southern Beeches

Only a single, small branch of the large and important Oak-Beech-Chestnut family, *Fagaceae*, is native in the southern hemisphere. The pattern of its occurrence there has great geological significance, showing the breaking up of the earlier great southern continent – Gondwanaland – and the dispersal of the major pieces. Southern beeches grow in the southern parts of South America, in Tasmania, New Zealand, Australia, New Caledonia and New Guinea. Of the 17 temperate region species, seven are deciduous, six of which occur in Argentina and Chile and one in Tasmania. Three of the South American species are evergreen, as are two more in Tasmania, all five in New Zealand, the one in Australia as well as the remaining twenty or so from the Tropical Region.

The name 'Southern beech' translates into botanical Latin/Greek as *Notofagus* and this was probably the word intended by the first author to distinguish the group, but he wrote *Nothofagus* and so this form must be retained. (It actually means 'False beech'.)

The **Rauli** (*Nothofagus procera*) comes from a small area of Chile, a little north of Chiloe Island, and spreads just across the Argentine border. The first trees in Britain were raised from seed sent in 1910 and were planted in 1913 and 1914.

Leading shoots of two m may sometimes be grown and in Devon a tree nine years from sowing the seed was 16 m tall. The large, one cm bright chestnut brown buds begin to open early, sometimes in about mid-March, and the unfolding leaves are then nearly always held back by late frosts, although growth resumes in May as if nothing had happened. Trees one or two years old can be killed down to the ground during a severe winter but usually sprouts will grow from the stump in June and be one–1.5 m long by September. The strongest should be selected and the others cut out by midsummer. In autumn the handsome leaves, which may have up to 22 pairs of veins, turn pale orange, often with much crimson before falling.

The **Roble** (*Nothofagus obliqua*) was called the 'oak' (*roble* in Spanish) by the early Spanish settlers in Chile. It comes from the same area as the Rauli but extends a little further north into hotter, drier parts around Santiago. It was introduced in 1902 and several trees of this origin are known, the biggest being in the Sunningdale Nursery in Surrey (23 m × 105 cm in 1975) and one by the drive at Grayswood Hill, Surrey (24 m × 89 cm in 1982). The shoots are slender and the buds, half the size of those of Rauli, open later and are seldom damaged by frost, although a severe winter can cut young trees back to base in the same way as in that species. The leaves are variable in the presence and depth of lobing, even on the same tree and late

season leaves may have eight to ten quite well divided lobes. The slender, arching branches high in the crown are rather fragile and prone to getting broken in strong winds, so a sheltered position is best, but tolerance of different soils is quite high and some of the best growth is on poor and rather dry sands and on clay. On light soils it may seed itself abundantly from two or more trees together.

Antarctic beech (*Nothofagus antarctica*) extends in range from the region of Rauli and Roble right down to Cape Horn and should therefore be very hardy, but it is not happy in exposed places and is seen only in some sheltered gardens. Growth can at first be rapid, with slender leading shoots up to one metre long, but it soon becomes slower and has rarely made a tree 12 m tall. It is often more of a bush or a low tree with spreading low branches. It comes into leaf bright shiny green and is then dark green until very late in autumn when it turns a fine old gold colour.

Silver beech (*Nothofagus menziesii*) comes from New Zealand and is seen in a few of the most westerly gardens. It will scarcely grow east of Cornwall except that by far the biggest, 21 m × 70 cm, is in that strange outlier in the hills of central Sussex where many tender trees thrive, this one being at Nymans. The bark in Britain is not the pale silvery grey that gives the tree its common New Zealand name but shiny deep red-purple banded with corky strips of lenticels. The underside of the leaf has minute hair-filled pockets at the base of the main veins.

Red beech (*Nothofagus fusca*) from New Zealand is evergreen but shows autumn colour most of the year as some of the thin leaves turn orange and red before being shed. It is hardy enough to grow well in Edinburgh but most of the specimens are in the west and in Ireland, although the biggest is, again, at Nymans in Sussex (26 m × 90 cm).

Mountain beech (*Nothofagus solandri* var. *cliffortioides*) although so different in aspect from the Red beech, has the same distribution in Britain, including good growth at Edinburgh and the biggest at Nymans, where it is 24 m × 66 cm. Also from New Zealand, it has the smallest leaf of any broadleaf tree grown in Britain. The bark is smooth and black on a deeply-ridged bole.

Coigue (*Nothofagus dombeyi*) from Chile is the hardiest evergreen Southern beech and grows well at Kew. In Ireland it grows even faster and two at Mount Usher, County Wicklow, were 27 m × 104 cm when only 47 years old. Purplish bark scales off with age leaving red patches. *Nothofagus betuloides* is similar but less vigorous and ranges south to Cape Horn. New foliage is slightly sticky and the bright red male flowers are like small Fuchsia flowers.

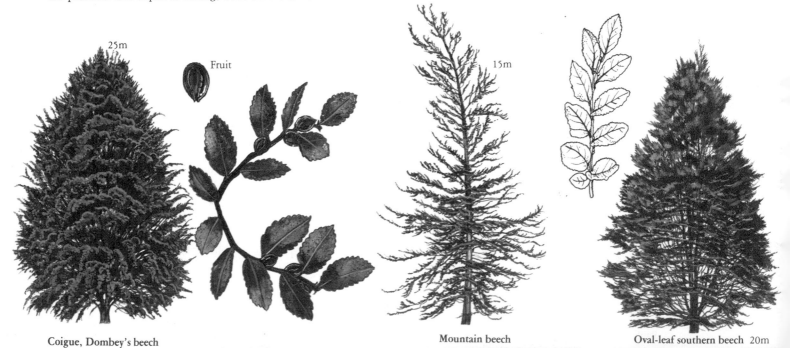

25m   Fruit

15m

Coigue, Dombey's beech

Mountain beech

Oval-leaf southern beech 20m

Rauli

Shoot

Rauli fruit (enlarged)

Silver beech

Black beech

Antarctic beech

Red beech

Roble beech

Fruit

Rauli 25m

Roble beech 30m

Antarctic beech 12m

Sweet Chestnut

The **Sweet chestnut** (*Castanea sativa*) is a tree from southern Europe that may have been introduced by the Romans, who certainly brought the nuts to eat, but it may not have been grown in Britain until much later. It has in any case been established in Britain since very early times and behaves as if it were native. It grows happily far northwards in Scotland and the oldest tree of any kind with a known planting date is a Sweet chestnut at Castle Leod, Strathpeffer, Easter Ross. Two were planted at the seat of the Earls of Cromartie in 1550. One was blown down in 1979 and the other was 2.46 m through in 1980. Growth is much faster in the south of England, with warmer summers and many trees are bigger than that when about half the age. In County Wicklow too, Sweet chestnuts grow very fast and one at Rossanagh, not shown in an engraving of the house made in 1798, had a diameter of 3.25 m in 1966.

The most famous Sweet chestnut is at Tortworth Church in Gloucestershire where a plaque states that it was said to have been '600 years old on January 1st, 1800'. It is, however also reputed to have been a boundary marker in the reign of King Stephen, implying a sizeable tree before 1150, and to have been planted in the reign of King Egbert (d. 839). In 1820 it was said to be 16 m round the bole. Magnificent in decline, it has long had two huge limbs which have taken part of the bole with them to lie on the ground and continue growth.

Groves of Sweet chestnut at Croft Castle, Herefordshire, are said to have been planted in the pattern of the Spanish Armada fleets and raised from the seeds washed ashore from the wrecks therefrom (and hence believed to date from 1590). There is, however, some evidence that they were planted in about 1760 and the trees, although many are over 2.5 m in diameter, support this rather than the earlier date.

There are some young trees of known date to show the rapidity of the early growth. One in Kent 43 years old was 14 m × 79 cm and one at Killerton, Devon is 19 m × 58 cm when 29 years old. The prominently spiralled bark is a feature of age and, unlike snails or bindweed, the Sweet chestnut does not have strong views on which way to twist. Until they are about 50 years old or 60 cm through, the boles have few fissures and these tend to be straight. From then on fissures divide more and more shallow ridges and lean into a spiral. When about one m through the bole, the tree has the ridges in a marked spiral only a little out of true vertical but by the time it is two m through, the spiral is at about 45 degrees and it flattens further with greater age.

The arrangement of the sexes of the flowers is odd. The first to open are the male catkins, always profuse, from buds behind the shoot-tip. They are joined by the females – brilliant green little rosettes with white styles – from buds at the tip and sometimes on little branches of their own but usually at the base of some short catkins which are not open. Weeks later these may open as male flowers and stand up as spikes of flower with a completely different aspect from the earlier males. In good years the nuts will enlarge and ripen to be comparable with imported nuts for dessert, but in most years the cool summer makes them of little use for that purpose.

The timber of Sweet chestnut has most of the good features of that of oak but lacks the figure in the grain. The trees also have a nasty habit of yielding 'shaken' timber, either from the felling impact or from 'shakes' already there. These are cracks which render the wood worthless for any but the smallest uses. Smallwood chestnut is still grown for the palings made by splitting, for it cleaves easily and is durable in the ground. It was formerly grown for hop-poles and both uses exploited the excellent growth in coppice, when sprouts from old 'stools' are cut every fifteen years or so. The periodic removal of shade in these woods made them ideal for strong growth of bluebells and some coppice is worked mainly for the flowers and insects today. In some years the leaves fall when pale yellow or turning dull brown but in others most of them become deep yellow turning orange and orange-brown.

'Laciniata' is a rare form with narrow lobes extended into long filaments. It seems to be curiously unstable for in one year a high proportion of leaves can be like the normal form and the tree will be dismissed as having reverted to type, but the next year it can be nearly all as it should be. One at Westonbirt, Gloucestershire is 16 m tall but most trees are usually rather low and small.

'Albomarginata' is a little less scarce and a few big trees are seen in gardens. They will have some leaves in the interior of the crown that are entirely white, but young trees have all the leaves prominently varigated although an occasional reverted shoot of all green leaves will sprout and must be cut out.

The **Golden chinkapin** (*Chrysolepis chrysophylla*) is one of a small group intermediate between the oaks and the Sweet chestnuts and grows in the Coast Range of Oregon and California. Introduced in 1844 it is occasionally seen as a tree to 17 m or, more as a bush, as in the Royal Botanic Garden, Edinburgh. The male catkins flower after midsummer and the leaves are hard and rigid.

Golden chinkapin 15m

Seed

Fruit

Female flowers

Male flowers

Fruit

Seed

Seedling

'Laciniata'

'Albomarginata'

Shoot enlarged

Male flower enlarged

Female flower enlarged

35m

Sweet chestnut

English Oak

The **English oak** (*Quercus robur*) ranges across the plains of northern Europe to the eastern lowlands of Britain, leaving the west and the mountains largely to the Sessile oak. It has been planted quite widely in southern Canada and the northern USA but is common only in Rhode Island, much less so in Vancouver, and in Ohio and Pennsylvania, while elsewhere there are only single trees in some city and Capitol parks. It grows best on damp, heavy clays but will grow on sandy soils, rooting deeply and never the worse for drought. It is a singularly robust tree and remains in full health while its leaves, flowers, fruit and roots nourish a vast array of insects, including many gall-wasps. These festoon the trees in often colourful galls like cherries, currants and apples and one like the hop fruit, while a recent addition causes hideous distortions to acorns. The bark may carry ferns, mosses and lichens, while dead branches, pensioned off when not needed, support many fungi and larvae of beetles and moths. The open pattern of woodland of this oak allows many other trees and shrubs to grow, so it is the form of woodland that is richest of all in wildlife. It is also the best for bluebells and nightingales, so the preservation of the remaining remnants is of the greatest importance.

Being resistant or indifferent to so many pests and diseases, the oak has a long life. When the trunk eventually becomes hollow, the strong wood of the outside holds the tree together for some two hundred years or more, to become among our oldest trees. Not old enough, however, to make believable many of the associations claimed for surviving individuals, with remote historic characters or events. The trouble is that this oak grows much faster than is generally known and few of these trees are anything like the size they would have to be were the stories true. A fully crowned oak a hundred years old is already 87–97 cm in diameter if it is going to reach a ripe old age. When 300 years old it can hardly be less than two m in diameter. Any oak that was known to William the Conqueror would have to be much bigger than that. The second biggest now, 'Majesty' in Kent, is 3.76 m in diameter and growing so fast that comparison with its size in the past shows that it is about 420 years old.

The biggest, at Bowthorpe Farm, near Bourne, Lincolnshire, cannot be dated in that way but is perhaps 600 years old, while the Major Oak in Sherwood Forest can be so dated. It is about 410 years

old. Robin Hood might have known its grandparents.

Oaks in the open countryside are usually about 23–25 m tall but in sheltered glens in Perthshire and Angus many are 35 m. Height decreases with age beyond about 200 years and the biggest, oldest trees are often mere hulks with all the main branches much died back or lost. In former times, oaks were often cut back when quite young, at about 2.5 m. Trees 'pollarded' like this sprouted new branches at that height, where they could grow out of reach of the browsing deer and could be cut again at intervals to produce smallwood. Left uncut for the last 150 years or more, pollards have made hugely spreading crowns and can replace the main branches when they die, by new sprouts.

The **Cypress oak** 'Fastigiata' is a narrowly erect form found in south Germany and multiplied by grafting. It is now often planted near buildings and grows about 60 cm a year, remaining shapely even when 27 m tall. Its leaves are larger than the wild oak's usually are.

The **Sessile oak** (*Quercus petraea*) arrived before the English oak, and is the common oak of the Western mountains with outliers in Enfield Chase, and in the Weald. It grows faster into a cleaner, more shapely tree than the English oak and holds its firmer, larger, stalked leaves more evenly. It also grows in a more uniform woodland and shades out shrubs, making flycatching space for Pied flycatchers and redstarts. It likes a freely draining soil but a fairly high rainfall. Its branches tend to be straight and it seldom has sprouty burrs on the bole.

The **Hungarian oak** (*Quercus frainetto*) is the most handsome of all the oaks and grows very fast. Native to southern Italy and the Balkans, it was introduced to Britain in 1837 and was usually, as now, grafted on to English oak. In 80 years it can be 30 m tall and one metre in diameter, with a hugely domed crown on straight radiating branches, and pale grey finely fissured bark.

Mirbeck's oak (*Quercus canariensis*) is wild in Algeria and southern Spain and was probably sent to Britain in 1835. It is exceedingly attractive and vigorous and is semi-evergreen. In autumn about half the leaves turn yellow and fall and the rest remain green until the New Year. It has a rugged, nearly black bark and a neat egg-shaped crown which can exceed 30 m in height. It is extremely hardy.

Mirbeck's oak

Pollard oak

Hungarian oak

Female flowers

Male flowers

Hop galls

Cherry galls

Acorn

English oak

English oak

English oak

Sessile oak

English oak

Mature oak

English oak

Cypress oak

Sessile Oak

The earlier of the two native British oaks to recolonize after the Ice Ages, the **Sessile oak** (*Quercus petraea*) puts the later arrival, the Common oak, firmly in the shade, for leaves, crown, growth and health. Each leaf on its 2.5 cm yellow stalk is firm and solid, free of galls, symmetrically lobed and tapering to an acute tip. On the tree the foliage is spread evenly, not clustered. On the ground the shed leaves persist, being substantial, and the undersides show a pale, coffee-brown with the strong venation being dark chocolate-brown.

The bole tends to be straight and to be clear of branches until at 5–10 m it bears a head of radiating straight branches. The trees can therefore grow more closely set than the wide-branching Common oak. The evenly-spread foliage also casts more shade and few other trees or tall shrubs are able to grow in Sessile oak woods so with the crowns held high, there is much flycatching-room. Hence the breeding areas of the Pied flycatcher which are restricted to the hills of Wales, the eastern Pennines, Cumbria and parts of Tayside; these are all the home of the Sessile oak and also attract redstarts and wood-warblers.

The Sessile oak is dominant in high rainfall areas with light soils while the Common oak predominates in drier areas on heavy soils and in the broader glens in Scotland. There are, however, two well-known exceptions in which this scheme is reversed. The highest oakwoods on Dartmoor are Common oak, above much Sessile in woods below, and the clays and gravels in Enfield Chase on the west bank of the River Lee north of London support Sessile oak.

Intermediates between the Sessile and the Common oak are common, with their acorns on stout, variably short stalks and their leaves lacking the clean wedge-shaped base to a long stalk, but it is remarkable how often a tree noticed among Common oaks for its superior height and shape will prove to be an intermediate, but much closer to the Sessile.

There are very fine isolated true Sessile oaks at Kenwood House and on Hampstead Heath, London. Two near the polo ground at Midhurst, Sussex are 35 m × 2.5 m.

'**Mespilifolia**' has variably waved or faintly lobed strap-shaped leaves to 22 cm long with thickened margins and is sometimes seen 25 m tall.

The **Chestnut-leafed oak** (*Quercus castaneifolia*) from the Caucasus and Elburz Mountains by the Caspian Sea not only has unusual and very handsome leaves 20 cm long, but grows exceptionally rapidly into a magnificent specimen. The original tree in Kew Gardens, planted in 1846 is 34 m × 2.05 m and one raised from it in 1953 was already 18 m × 68 cm by 1981. The bark of the young tree is very like black polished leather. On the old tree it is dark purple-brown and much ridged. A good tree in Alexandra Park, Hastings, dating from 1880 was 23 m × 111 cm in 1983 but there are very few old trees generally and not nearly enough young ones as this species is hard to obtain.

Chestnut oak (*Quercus prinus*) from the Allegheny Mountains in the eastern United States has firm broad leaves 18 cm long on stout stalks one to two cm long. The bark is dark brown, broken into short thick ridges. It is seen in a few collections like Kew Gardens where there are several examples. By the Round Pond area of Kensington Gardens, London, there is a splendid tree of the Chinkapin oak (*Quercus muehlenbergii*) from the same region, and often confused with Chestnut oak, but having more elegant leaves, acute and on a three cm yellow stalk. That specimen is 20 m × 92 cm.

Caucasian oak (*Quercus macranthera*) is a vigorous and handsome tree with leaves very like those of Mirbeck oak but downy, and on downy stalks and shoots. It also differs in being fully deciduous and in the bark being broken by dark fissures into short, pale-grey, scaly ridges. The two oldest trees of this species in Britain were planted in 1876 at Westonbirt Arboretum and one is 28 m tall.

Pyrenean oak (*Quercus pyrenaica*) is nearly always seen as the very pendulous form, 'Pendula' grafted at two metres on Turkey oak. It is the last oak in leaf and also in flower when it has spectacular long bunches of golden catkins. In leaf it is hoary grey from the dense short down.

Armenian oak (*Quercus pontica*) makes up for its low-branched, broad bushy growth by its exceptionally fine foliage and good bright yellow and brown autumn colours. The shoot is very stout, ribbed but smooth and the pale brown buds are tall and conic. The leaf can be 18 × 10 cm and is lightly silvered beneath. It is a rare tree but is found in collections in several countries.

The **Lebanon oak** (*Quercus libani*) is mostly confined to oak-collections, but the National Pinetum at Bedgebury, in Kent, has two 20 m specimens. In leaf it is an attractive tree, narrowly conic with an airy open crown of slender 12 cm leaves. In winter, the sparse branching and dark, slightly corky, orange-fissured bark give it a gaunt aspect. The bud at the end of each shoot is surrounded by dark grey whiskers. The acorns, on short, very stout stalks, take two years to ripen and in hot countries grow big, but in Britain they attain about two cm and hardly protrude from the big, deep cup.

Macedonian oak (*Quercus trojana*) resembles the Lebanon oak but has a knobbly bark and smaller leaves which stay brown on the tree in late autumn and into the winter. It has downy new shoots and stalk-less acorns. A fine tree at Batsford Park, Gloucestershire, is 24 m × 85 cm.

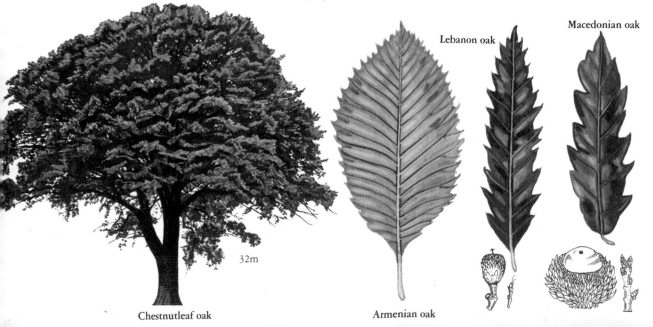

32m

Chestnutleaf oak

Lebanon oak

Macedonian oak

Armenian oak

Sessile oak

Fruit

Male flower enlarged

Female flower enlarged

'Mespilifolia'

Fruit

Common oak

Common oak

Chestnut oak

Caucasian oak

Chestnutleaf oak

Sessile oak

Pyrenean oak

Red and Other Oaks

The **Red oak** (*Quercus rubra*) is typical of a group of North American oaks characterized by small acorns that take two years to mature and by leaves with large lobes bearing a few big whisker-tipped teeth. They nearly all have smooth bark and are good for autumn colours. There are no Red oaks native to Europe, where the English and the Sessile oaks are White oaks, another group also strongly represented in North America.

The Red oak grows much faster than the Common oak and has a shorter life-span. The first-year shoot from the acorn can be one m long and by the third year the leading shoot may be 1.5 m long growing at 20 cm a week in two short bursts, one towards the end of May and the other in July. The shoots droop as they extend and bear pale yellow unfolding leaves. The entire foliage is bright yellow for two or three weeks in a normal season but if a cold spell sets in before they leaves are green it can hold them back; still yellow until warmer weather or, if the cold is long and severe, the foliage is killed and the tree has to start again. The female flowers are borne on very short, thick stalks along the middle section of the new shoot and become minute acorns for a full year before expanding the next summer.

When a young tree is cut down, the stump sends up a few strong shoots which, like the sprouts at the base of some of the old trees, bear extra large leaves, almost unlobed. Trees two metres in diameter have been known but were very senile and have collapsed so this size is about the limit and indicates an age of little over 200 years. Few trees grow to this size in the vast native range that extends from Nova Scotia to Texas.

'Aurea' is scarce and slow growing, but a fresh, bright gold in late spring, gradually greening. **Scarlet oak** (*Quercus coccinea*) is greatly superior to the Red oak in autumn colouring but is not its equal in growth. At any age it turns brilliant scarlet to deep red, often by way of a striking orange-red with a brown tinge, and rarely fails to be spectacular. It is short-lived and trees over one m in diameter are rare. It has a sinuous bole bearing a few large, widely-angled branches making a thin, highly irregular, domed crown. With the more attractive designation and better reputation for colour, the Scarlet oak's name is, regrettably, sometimes used to sell Red oaks, but the true species can be identified by the gloss on both the upper and lower surfaces of the usually smaller, more deeply lobed leaf. The form 'Splendens' has larger, less glossy leaves and grows very fast, but it differs from Red oak in having small tufts of hairs in the angles of the veins beneath the leaf.

The **Pin oak** (*Quercus palustris*) is also a tree for southern, warm parts only. Here it rapidly makes a splendidly domed crown on a smooth, straight bole. The underside of the leaf has prominent tufts of pale brown hairs in the vein axils and the bark is a shiny deep purplish-brown. The lower branches fan out, downwards and straight in a dense skirt round the clean two-metre bole.

The **Black oak** (*Quercus velutina*) extends from Maine to Texas, almost the full range of the Red oak, but it is oddly scarce in Britain. A big tree stands below the car park at Killerton Garden, Devon and a bigger one is in the Knaphill Nurseries, Surrey but there are few others in such public places. The leaf is big and parchment-like, softly downy beneath and on the long stalk. A strange, definitive feature is the midrib, which forks in perhaps a quarter of all the leaves so that there are two unequal and clumsily divided tips.

The **Louisiana oak** (*Quercus* x *ludoviciana*) is a natural hybrid found in that State in 1913. It unfolds shiny orange-red leaves which turn deep green and remain so well through the autumn until in November they turn orange-brown. It is a choice tree in collections.

Swamp white oak (*Quercus bicolor*) has big, wedge-based leaves variably white beneath and turning rich brown in autumn. The bark is craggy with pale grey ridges.

Bur oak (*Quercus macrocarpa*) grows from around Winnipeg to southern Texas where the acorns are four cm × 3.5 cm. The few in Britain are in the south.

The **Daimyo oak** (*Quercus dentata*) from Japan, is grown in a number of gardens for its remarkable leaf. Growing on a stout, hairy shoot, it can be 40 × 20 cm and is thick and heavy. The tree is broad and usually low. One on the lawn at Osterley Park, Middlesex is 12 m × 51 cm. It grows slowly and some trees have their new shoots killed back in hard winters and so bear only small shoots in bunches on the stout branches.

Bartram's oak (*Quercus* x *heterophylla*) is a natural hybrid between the Willow oak and the Red oak. The leaf varies in the number and size of the small, whisker-tipped teeth. In autumn the leaves turn pink, red and brown. In summer, the underside of the leaf is glossy and has tufts of hairs in the angles at the base of the veins. It grows fast into a shapely tree but is seen only in collections.

Lea's hybrid oak (*Quercus* x *leana*) was found by a Mr Lea in Ohio in 1830. It is a hybrid between the Black and Shingle oaks, occasionally seen in gardens and collections, and can be a fine tree. One at Hollycombe Steam Fair near Liphook, Hampshire is 23 m × 70 cm.

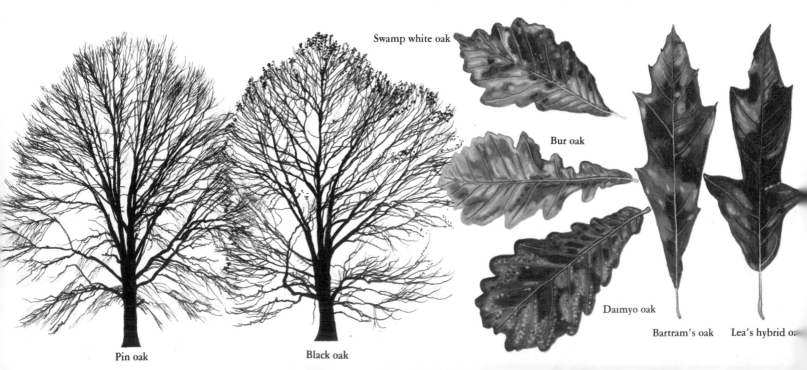

Swamp white oak

Bur oak

Daimyo oak

Bartram's oak   Lea's hybrid oak

Pin oak

Black oak

Pin oak

Scarlet oak

Female flowers

Male catkins

Red oak

Black oak

1st year acorn

Louisiana oak

2nd year acorn

Red Oak

Red oak

'Aurea'

Scarlet oak

Turkey Oak

The **Turkey oak** (*Quercus cerris*) is a tree of Southern Europe from France to Romania which owes its name to the old extension of Turkish rule into the Balkans rather than to the modern Turkey of Asia Minor. It seems to have been introduced into Britain by Lucombe and Pince, nurserymen of Exeter, as late as 1735, but behaves as if it has always been there and it may indeed have been sent before that time. Like the Sweet chestnut from the same region, it seeds itself freely in the south of England on light soils, and grows extremely well far into the north-east of Scotland, although growth is less rapid there than in the south.It is able to thrive in city parks and quite large specimens are frequently seen in small urban parks, while there is a long avenue in Central Park, New York. The biggest, however, tend to be in Devon, perhaps because that is where Lucombe and Pince sold and planted many trees which survive today.

Outside Devon there are many fine trees in Sussex especially, but the outstanding specimen is at Bulstrode Park, Buckinghamshire, and that was 41 m × 2.11 m in 1983. Growth is very rapid and because the central bud is dominant and maintains the axis of the tree in a straight line, the Turkey oak makes a quality bole from its early years; while the Common oak, in which a side-bud often makes the main shoot, may take a long time before it has thickened sufficiently to smooth out its bends. The timberman is, however, unimpressed by the fine boles of Turkey oak because they are usually flawed by 'shakes' – serious internal cracking. Although this tree colours well in autumn, when it may be a rich orange-brown, it is dark foliaged and dull all the summer. It is good therefore to see a little recent planting of the boldly white-splashed **'Variegata'** although it will not grow so fast.

The **Downy oak** (*Quercus pubescens*) has short, quite dense down all over its shoots, leaves and leaf stalks. It is the common oak on dry hillsides from Spain eastwards across southern Europe but, unlike the Holm oak from the same areas, it has completely failed to interest any but the dedicated oak-collector, although it is fully hardy and grows at least as fast as the Common oak. From a short distance it looks just like a Common oak with darker, dull foliage and this may explain its rarity. The finest is 27 m × 1.01 m on the northern fringe of the valley at Melbury in Dorset, and there are about ten in Kew Gardens.

Lucombe oak (*Quercus* x *hispanica* 'Lucombeana') arose in the Exeter nursery of Lucombe and Pince in 1763 when acorns from their first Turkey oak were sown. Two of the plants made remarkable growth in the first season and remained evergreen in the winter. Mr Lucombe reasoned that those acorns had been pollinated by his nearby Cork oak and that this hybrid would be a good tree so he planted one each side of the entrance to the nursery. He then made many grafts from them on Common oak rootstock, and sold them to many gardens in the area in 1770.

In 1792 the two original trees bore acorns and several distinct forms were planted in the nursery and later sent out as grafts. One of these is the common Lucombe oak of most parks and gardens and is fully evergreen except in the hardest winters and has dark, only slightly corky bark. Another has pale, very corky bark and one of these grows by the Chapel at Killerton.

In about 1830 Mr Lucombe cut down one of the original pair to make boards for his coffin, which he stacked under his bed. They perished before he did, so he cut the other one and was buried in it when he was 102. The numbers of Lucombe oaks thin out northwards but there is a very splendid specimen at Innes House, Grampian, and quite a large one even further north at Coul House Hotel in Easter Ross. The original forms inherit from the Turkey oak the swelling out of the bole where the branches spring, in exaggerated form, but the later, smaller-leafed, more evergreen forms hardly show this characteristic. The original forms hold on to an outer fringe of leaves after shedding the rest in autumn and then shed those during the winter, when they are dark olive-green.

Cork oak (*Quercus suber*) is all too often an inordinately dull, bushy plant with a tendency to rest big low branches on the ground. Only a few in Cornwall are respectable specimen trees and notable among these are one in a field at Mount Edgcumbe (26 m × 1.63 m) and another at Antony House (20 m × 1.46 m). This tree comes from the Mediterranean region but is hardy in the north of Scotland. The very thick, deeply-fissured, often pale cream bark is sometimes fixed to the walls and pillars of orchid-houses and used for growing the epiphytic species, but in Portugal and Spain it is not allowed to become so mature and is stripped away every few years for its cork.

Chinese cork oak (*Quercus variabilis*) is an altogether superior tree. With the same deeply-fissured bark but tinged with pink, it has elegant leaves silvered beneath, large and handsomely veined with a little whisker-tooth at the tip of each. Unfortunately it is also rare.

Vallonia oak (*Quercus macrolepis*) is also very rare and covers a group of closely-related oaks from Turkey grown as *Quercus aegilops* and *Q. pyrami*, one form of which bears acorns in cups five cm across (although not in Britain).

Lucombe oak types in winter

Cork oak

Male catkins

Downy oak

'Variegata'

Lucombe oak types

Cork oak

Acorn cup

Chinese cork oak

Turkey oak

Vallonia oak

Turkey oak

Turkey oak

Downy oak

Holm Oak

The **Holm oak** (*Quercus ilex*) derives its English name from an old word 'holm' meaning 'holly', but in the botanical names, things are the other way about. This oak is the classical Latin 'Ilex' and the holly has been given this name for its genus and is *Ilex aquifolium*. These references to holly arise from the hard, spine-toothed leaves borne by the Holm oak while it is young and while its foliage is at hazard from grazing. Like the holly itself, but more uniformly and positively, its adult leaves are untoothed, unspined and unlobed. The undersides are then more thickly covered in short white down, like the shoots, and newly unfolded adult leaves are white all over. These features should somewhat lessen the dark, uninspiring aspect of the tree, but in large numbers and in the avenues commonly seen in some coastal areas, the general effect is of unchanging gloom throughout the year. For all that, in the south of France this is *la chêne verte* and is very nearly black.

This tree comes from the western Mediterranean area and has grown in Britain since about 1500. Although the massed plantings are in coastal parts, it is common throughout the land, and as one of the few large evergreens able to survive, if not grow well, in the old smoky city air, it is frequent in city parks and – for which its gloom is no great drawback – in cemeteries.

In Devon, Sussex, Norfolk and Lothian especially many estates and farmlands shelter from sea-winds in the lee of extensive plantings of Holm oak. For this purpose it has few rivals as it is efficient in absorbing salt spray carried by the wind and is unharmed by it. Further, it can grow on shallow soils over chalk in severe exposure and for these qualities it has been the tree that gives the shelter so vital to the success of Abbotsbury Tropical Gardens in Dorset: the occasional gap from a gale blowing out some old trees is replanted assiduously.

In shelterbelts, the marked tendency for this tree to grow as a big bush with many spreading stems is an advantage but after some 150 years, trees of this shape are vulnerable to having a stem or two torn off by a gale. Single-boled trees branching low are common, but long clear stems are not often seen outside Devon, where some trees are 30 m tall.

Trees like this survive much longer than those with many stems and some may be over 300 years old. One at Chilham Castle, however, which may date from 1619 divides very low, on a sheltered site and is 2.39 m in diameter (at 0.3 m). The timber is hard and exceedingly heavy. It has so many medullary rays that on a crosscut surface they nearly obscure the annual rings. It must have a figure better than the prized one of Common oak when 'quarter-sawn' to expose a radius, but it is difficult to work, seasons badly and is very little used.

Turner's oak (*Quercus x turneri*) is a hybrid between the Holm oak and the Common oak which arose before 1780 in Turner's nursery in Essex. It is usually broad of crown and of low stature but is always a handsome tree. It is nearly evergreen, shedding its leaves while still dark green only a month or so before the new ones unfold.

White oak (*Quercus alba*) is one of those trees of eastern North America that has been tried on and off in Britain for over 350 years with negligible results. Small trees grow, but without great enthusiasm, in a few oak-collections from Kew to Edinburgh: one in Windsor Great Park excels them all at 18 m × 60 cm. At their best the leaves have elegantly curved cuts between the lobes and turn rich reds and purples in autumn.

California live oak (*Quercus agrifolia*) is only found in a few oak-collections and has dark, hard evergreen leaves, shiny beneath, with tufts of hair at the bases of the veins. The best of six at Kew, 17 m × 63 cm, shows well the black, smooth, almost leathery bark.

Sawtooth oak (*Quercus acutissima*) from China and Japan is a little gaunt in winter with dark grey rough bark but it has big, bright green leaves and merits the planting in towns that it receives in the USA. In Britain it is still confined to the biggest gardens.

Blackjack oak (*Quercus marilandica*) has leaves of great substance, leathery and shiny bright green to 12 m × 11 cm, but except for one in Station Road, Desford, Leicestershire, it is grown in Britain only in a few collections. One in Osterley Park, Middlesex is 20 m × 40 cm and the bigger of two at Wakehurst Place, Sussex is 18 m × 50 cm. It grows slowly, however, and is normally a small, upright-branched tree.

Willow oak (*Quercus phellos*) is much more of a southern tree in North America than is the White oak, and yet it is the Willow oak that thrives in Britain, if nearly confined to the south of England. One at Powis Castle in Wales is 20 m × 80 cm and in the Knaphill Nursery in Surrey a grand tree is 20 m × 125 cm. The leaves unfold yellow before becoming green.

Shingle oak (*Quercus imbricaria*) also unfolds yellow leaves, bright gold for weeks. They are twice the size of those of the Willow oak and well-stalked. This tree comes from the same southern parts of the eastern side of the USA, but is more scarce in Britain where one of the biggest is 20 m × 76 cm in Alexandra Park, Hastings, Sussex. The tallest is by Flora in Syon Park, Middlesex (27 m × 56 cm).

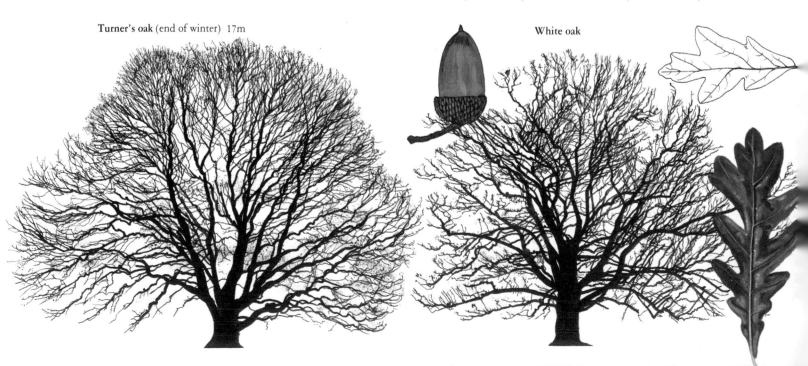

Turner's oak (end of winter) 17m

White oak

Male flower enlarged

Female flower enlarged

Female catkin

Male catkins

Leaf of young tree

Two forms

Turner's oak

California live oak

Holm oak

'Foordii' Exeter oak

Sawtooth oak

Blackjack oak

Willow oak

Shingle oak 25m

Holm oak 28m

Sawtooth oak

Willow oak 25m

Shingle oak

Wych Elm

The **Wych Elm** (*Ulmus glabra*) is an undisputed native of the British Isles, whatever view may be held about the English Elm. The Wych, or Mountain Elm is common in hillside woods in the Highlands of Scotland wherever it is shady and damp. It spreads into higher open land, growing among boulders by streamsides in Scotland, Cumbria and on the Pennine Hills. The tallest and finest trees are in the sheltered glens in the Highlands on deep, moist soils and this was so even before Dutch Elm Disease killed nearly all the big trees in southern England. It resists the disease when that first arrives and there are other, more susceptible elms around, but when the Elm-bark beetles, which carry the fungus causing the disease, are driven to feed on Wych elm through lack of an alternative, this elm succumbs fairly rapidly.

The Wych elm was much less common in the south, being rather local in damp woods and much less a hedgerow tree than the English elm, but there were many specimens in parklands with widely-spreading crowns on boles two m in diameter.

The botanical name 'glabra', or 'smooth', seems out of place in a tree with exceptionally harshly hairy leaves which feel rather like sandpaper, and with densely hairy shoots and leafstalks, but in fact it refers to the bark of young trees. At an age and size when other elms have bark prominently fissured into blocks or ridges, that of the Wych elm is smooth and pale grey. After the tree is some 80 years old, the bole is shallowly ridged, but the branches maintain a smooth grey bark. In parkland trees there is a tendency for the lowest branches to extend a great distance and to droop to rest an elbow on the ground. In such trees the spread is much in excess of the height. Confined by other trees in woodland, the crown is a dome high on a clear but often somewhat sinuous bole. This elm is not supposed to grow sprouts from its base so the few that have been found so disfigured are taken to have at least a small amount of Smoothleaf elm in their make-up, for these two elms do hybridize.

The shoots of Wych elm are stouter than those of other elms and sprays of shoots are sparse, with short side-shoots perpendicular to the main shoot, with prominent ovoid buds. The flowers open, pressed close to the shoot, in February or March, and the fruit are fully developed and prominent in apple-green bunches well before the leaves unfold. In June they turn pale brown and they fall in July when they lie thick on the ground in many Scottish woods. The leaves emerge bright green, pleated at the veins and in the autumn most of them turn pale yellow before they are shed.

Wych Elm is one of the most resistant of all trees to smoky city air.

In London and the south generally this was unimportant, as the English elm was the city tree and only the Camperdown form of the Wych elm was much seen, but in the north and in Edinburgh particularly, the Wych elm is the important tree. Without it, the Prince's Street Gardens, Atholl and other squares in the New Town and the Meadows would be almost treeless wastes. Glasgow and Dundee would be as bad and the further spread of Dutch Elm Disease in Scotland is a depressing possibility.

The **Camperdown elm** (*Ulmus glabra* 'Camperdown') was found in 1850 as a seedling at Camperdown Castle near Dundee, growing as a mat of twisted shoots on the ground. Grafted at two m on a stem of ordinary Wych Elm, it goes through multiple contortions before sending sinuous shoots down to the ground, forming a bower. The leaves are larger and more harshly hairy than those of the ordinary tree, up to 20 cm long, and the shoot is slightly bloomed. This tree was popular in city churchyards and parks and survived the first onslaughts well, but most in the south have now died. Many still grow in Scottish cities but this species was less commonly planted in the north than in England.

'Pendula' is very much less a weeping Wych Elm than Camperdown, so it would be misleading to give it that English name. It was first described as 'Horizontalis' so that is now the accepted name. It was always less common than the Camperdown form and grew quite tall, often to 15 m, but few are now seen. Fine shoots spray out in herring-bone patterns at only a slight downward angle, bearing normal-sized leaves.

The **Exeter elm** (*Ulmus glabra* 'Exoniensis') arose in a nursery in that city before 1826 and was planted more in that area than in other parts. There were, however, some in London parks: one (16 m × 65 cm) survives in Battersea Park and another (15 m × 70 cm) in Finsbury Park. It is used as a street tree in a few places, a site for which the upright branching makes it suitable, since the crown is narrow until a fair age and size are reached. The leaves themselves are upright, and do not expand fully but remain as bunches strung along the numerous shoots from tip to base.

'Lutescens', the Golden Wych Elm, differs from the golden-leafed forms of other elms in its smooth pale grey bark and much bigger leaf. It is also a broader, level-branched tree when grown in the open, although one in a wood in Dumfries and Galloway was 27 m tall and slender in the crown. Normally it is very short boled and quite bushy. The disease killed many good plantings in south Devon and only small young trees are now to be seen.

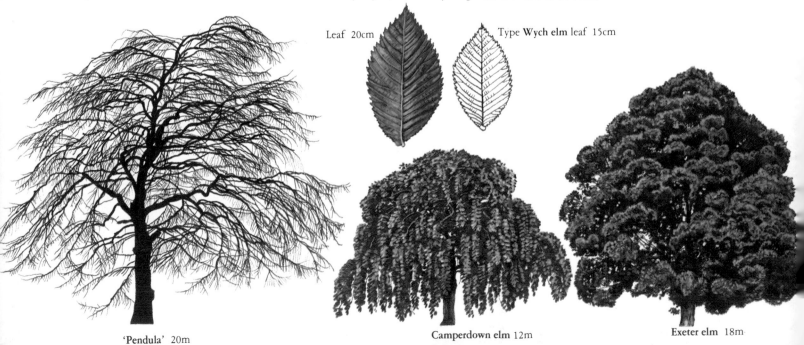

Leaf 20cm

Type **Wych elm** leaf 15cm

'Pendula' 20m

Camperdown elm 12m

Exeter elm 18m

Male flower
enlarged

Immature fruits, April

Variation in leaf-shape

'Lutescens'

Wych elm 38m

English Elm

There is grave doubt as to whether the **English elm** (*Ulmus procera*) is in fact English at all, in the sense of being a native tree. No matching population has been found along the Channel coasts of the Continent, where the Field elm or Smoothleaf elm (*U. carpinifolia*) takes its place; nor is it likely that a population should have spread, as the Ice Age waned, into a new area and left no trace behind. Also, the pattern of distribution in England has been linked with the spread of certain tribes before the Iron Age, and the inference is that they brought it with them. It almost never sets good seed, instead being spread by root-suckers, and it was used both for forage for cattle and for marking boundaries.

The English elm is thought by some to have been introduced, probably as a selected local form of Field elm from the south of France, to the Vale of Berkeley. It is not found to the east of Canterbury and all eastern Kent is, or was, Smoothleaf elm country. It fades out north of York and it enters Wales only in the Usk Valley and the far south. In Devon it did not cross the A386 Okehampton to Barnstaple road, to the west of which is Cornish elm country and it was similarly replaced south of Dartmoor from Kingsbridge westwards except for a few patches to Plymouth.

Within its main range, however, the English elm dominated great tracts of the land, creating a unique rural landscape. This was notably developed on the eastward slopes of the Cotswold Hills, in the Vale of Aylesbury and along the south coast seaboard from Dorset to east Sussex. Today, only the eastern part of the Sussex coast strip, from Worthing to west of Beachy Head, retains this character, being defended along the south by the sea, and from the north and east by elm-free chalklands, with a narrow strip open to the disease-afflicted area of Chichester needing vigilance to halt the slow advance.

There are two species of Elm Bark beetle which carry the fungal Dutch elm disease in England and one of them extends into Scotland. The disease is not Dutch in origin but probably Central Asiatic and the Dutch are associated with it only in that they worked hard in studying it and in raising elms with resistance to it. Unfortunately, although the hybrids selected successfully resisted the form of the disease then prevalent, they failed in the face of the virulent strain that was imported from Canada in about 1965. The new strain can grow through the new wood of the summer growth of the elm shoot, unlike the old strain which was restricted by it, and can move down the stem and into the root-systems which often interconnect along much of a hedgerow, and so pass from tree to tree without help from the beetle. Before 1970 there were many old English elms 30 m × 2.0 m and a few with boles 2.5 m through.

'**Argenteovariegata**', the Silver elm, is an old variety which was planted in some parks and gardens and was sometimes over 25 m tall. Where one was growing in a Surrey hedge, the hedgerow was similarly variegated for some 40 m. '**Viminalis**' is, or was, a slender tree with a light, narrow crown which could be 30 m tall. '**Louis van Houtte**' kept its good colour through the season and a small, neat tree.

The **Wheatley** or **Jersey elm** (*Ulmus carpinifolia* 'Sarniensis') is apparently a selected form of the elm common in the Channel Islands and Brittany, introduced in 1816, for it is of more regular shape than is usual there. It was extensively planted along bypasses, in avenues and city parks, partly because its very numerous branches remain small enough not to be a danger, and in fact almost never break out. It is much more resistant to the disease than is English elm, and many of these trees survive in the English Midlands and in Scottish cities, but most have eventually been infected where they were in severely diseased areas. One near Winchester was very much bigger than any other and was 32 m × 186 cm before it died. This species differs strongly in its bark from the Cornish and other Smoothleaf elms which have deeply divided parallel ridges, for it has no marked ridges but is divided into rectangular plates like the bark of the English elm. In late autumn the leaves turn well before shedding and make the tree a tower of gold which later turns pale orange.

Cornish elm 'Cornubiensis' is either native or of pre-Roman introduction to all of Cornwall and the part of Devon west of Dartmoor, replacing English elm, and mixed with it round the south Devon coast; it was also introduced to much of Counties Waterford and Cork in Ireland. There were highly localized areas of planting in southern England which have been mostly killed by Dutch elm disease. Walsingham Abbey in Norfolk was such an area, as were the Regent's Park area of London, the neighbourhood of Devizes, and the famous Waterloo Elms planted in 1815 around the Cathedral Close in Salisbury, where two were 36 m tall. These trees are somewhat resistant to the disease and remained in places like Halliford Park, Sunbury, Middlesex after the English elms around had gone: however, they were then the only choice between feeding and starving for the beetle, and they in turn died. Their very late leafing out is some protection, but only when there are other elms nearby. In Cornwall, where seawinds also may inhibit the beetle, there are currently many healthy trees.

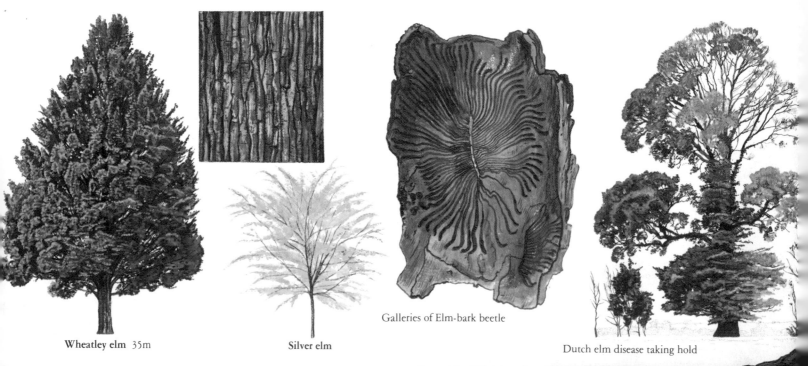

Wheatley elm 35m

Silver elm

Galleries of Elm-bark beetle

Dutch elm disease taking hold

Wheatley elm

Cornish elm

English elm

Adult beetle maturation
-feeding damage

Fruit

Flowering shoot

Cross-section of diseased branch
showing blockage of vessels

Elm bark beetle
(*Scolytus multistriatus*)

'Louis Van Houtte'

'Viminalis'

'Variegata'

Flower enlarged

Young tree

English elm 36m

Cornish elm 37m

Other Elms

The **Smoothleaf elm** (*Ulmus carpinifolia*) is the common Field elm of Europe, but its status in Britain is a matter of some dispute. One faction maintains that it is an undoubted native. The other points to peculiarities in the numerous distinct forms and their distribution to support the view that it was introduced by pre-Iron Age tribes, each bringing its own form and marking out its local territory with it. For example, east of Canterbury, the English elm is replaced by a Smoothleaf with typical small leaves and hanging slender shoots. Essex and Suffolk have a complex pattern of forms with large but not pendulous leaves, and the typical form was in Hertfordshire: towards Essex and Cambridge there was a very mixed pattern again.

Outside these areas, the tree is very local and of more recent planting. Since 1980 there are few surviving the elm disease in the south. There are currently, two in Green Park, London, near Piccadilly and one in Finsbury Park. In Cambridge city there is one on The Fen and a superb, narrow tree 36 m × 137 cm on Jesus Green. Further afield, one at Cathays Park, Cardiff is 26 m × 108 cm and the best of all is 40 m × 106 cm on the North Inch in Perth. Before the disease struck, hugely domed trees over two metres in diameter were found as far west as Gloucestershire. This elm is very late to unfold its leaves and is bare for six weeks or more after the English elm is in full leaf, but its red flowers open at much the same time in late February or early March. It is much beset by basal sprouts and by fine shoots from bosses on the bole.

'**Wredei**' is a tree that grows up to 18 m, with a narrow form and small bright golden leaves. It is sometimes seen in town and other gardens, surviving where disease has removed other elms, although these are lucky escapes rather than resistant trees. It is regarded by some as a form of Dutch elm.

Dutch elm (*Ulmus* x *hollandica* 'Hollandica') is one of a group of hybrids between the Wych and the Smoothleaf elms that have arisen in many places. It was once thought to have been brought to Britain from the Netherlands towards the end of the seventeenth century but its origin is doubtful. Although valued for its easily worked timber and of very rapid growth from suckers, it was of peculiarly restricted distribution, largely in the region now nearly devoid of elms. It was frequent as a roadside tree only in North Hampshire and adjacent parts of Wiltshire and Berkshire.

The bark is unlike other elms in being finely flaky and red-brown, and the crown is equally distinctive. The sinuous bole bears a large, ascending branch at the outside of each of its two or three big curves

and these rise to hold a sparse, flat-domed umbrella. The leaf is dark and coarse, leathery and almost completely smooth on top.

Huntingdon elm (*Ulmus* x *hollandica* 'Vegeta') arose in 1760 when seed was collected from a fine Smoothleaf elm standing near a Wych elm in Hinchingbrook Park, by the Huntingdon nurserymen, Ingram and Wood. It is very distinct in its crown, a high dome held on strong, radiating and very straight branches. The leaves are leathery, smooth and 12 cm long on a two cm pink and yellow stalk. It is very vigorous and its shapely crown makes it a good avenue tree that is also much planted in city squares and in parks. The fruit are also big, 6 cm × 6 cm in bunches, very prominent pale green before the leaves unfold at the end of April. The seed is sterile.

The **White elm** (*Ulmus laevis*) from Europe has fruit with a fringe of white hairs like the American elm, which it also resembles in foliage and in the vase-shaped crown of arching branches. It was grown in several collections before the disease struck and one 17 m tall survives in Kew Gardens.

The **Plot elm** (*Ulmus plotii*) is better named the 'Lock elm' since this is not the tree originally described by Plot. It is a form of the Smoothleaf elm found in the northern part of the English Midlands. Lines of the curious, slender, straggling swept-topped crowns used to be seen on roadsides, notably at Towcester and Thrapston in Northamptonshire, at Stone in Staffordshire and from the main line railway around Grantham in Lincolnshire. The crossgrained timber would lock the saw, hence the alternative name.

The **Chinese elm** (*Ulmus parvifolia*) is an exceptionally attractive small tree with a broad crown densely clad in pretty little three cm leaves which remain green on the tree until the end of the year. It flowers in October. Although highly resistant to elm disease, two of the best trees have died from other causes and it now is rare. One in Benenden, Kent is 16 m × 71 cm and there are somewhat smaller specimens at Dyffryn Gardens near Cardiff and at Glasnevin Botanic Garden, Dublin. It is a street-tree in parts of the USA, and in the heat of California the red-brown bark flakes away, revealing a pale grey-blue colour.

The **Siberian elm** (*Ulmus pumila*) also resists the disease but has remained very rare. There is one in Battersea Park, London, that is 16 m tall and one in Alexandra Park, Hastings, 17 m tall; while Wakehurst Place, Sussex, and Colesbourne, Gloucestershire, each have two around 20 m × 60 cm. This tree flowers in spring and has a thin, open crown.

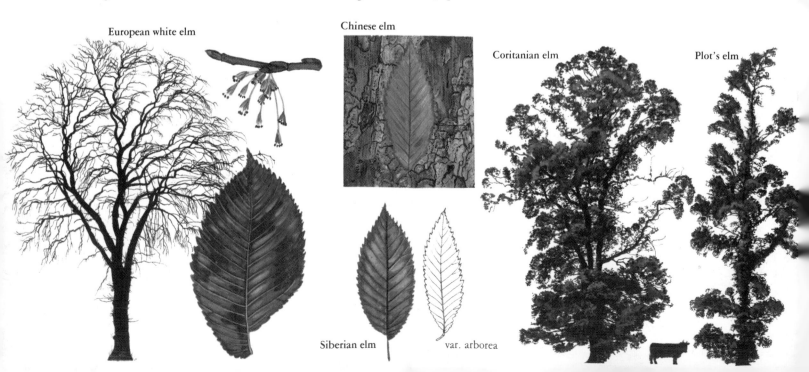

European white elm

Chinese elm

Coritanian elm

Plot's elm

Siberian elm

var. arborea

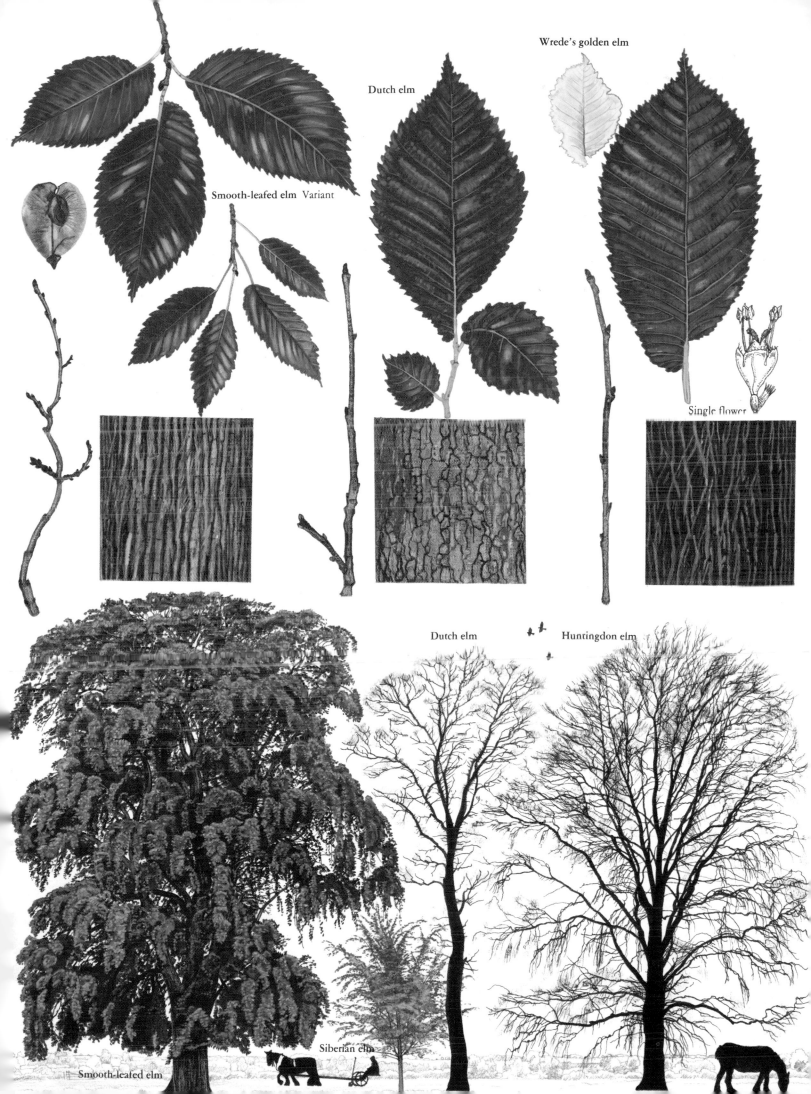

Smooth-leafed elm Variant

Dutch elm

Wrede's golden elm

Single flower

Dutch elm

Huntingdon elm

Smooth-leafed elm

Siberian elm

Zelkova and Nettletree

The **Caucasus zelkova** (*Zelkova carpinifolia*) is often called the Caucasian elm, but since other true elms are native there too, and the Zelkovas, although closely related to elms, are a distinct group, it is better to use the name given here. This tree grows wild in the Elburz and Caucasus Mountains and the strange thing is that there, by all accounts, it is a normal tree. In Britain it is sometimes, but usually it grows into what can best be described as a giant erect bush on a stout short leg. It is hard to see how this form can be a selected cultivar, for the original five trees, believed to be from seed probably via France in 1760, are of this form and so are the biggest and oldest of the other specimens in Britain and Ireland.

The deeply fluted bole, usually one–two m long but sometimes scarcely that, holds aloft a tall egg-shaped crown of over 100 almost vertical branches, many of about equal small size. And yet there are several specimens of normal tree shape, having long, if slightly sinuous boles clear of branches for perhaps 12 m and then bearing moderately ascending branches in normal numbers. These can be mixed with the bushy kind, as in Hyde Park, London, where one of three close to Hyde Park Corner is long-boled, and, until 1983, in the University Parks, Oxford where they were nearly side by side until the slender one died.

The most extreme 'normal' tree is at Langley Park near Slough (30 m × 64 cm), is grafted on to Smoothleaf elm at 1.5 m, and has a long clean bole. A remarkable group at Wardour House in Wiltshire is so closely planted that the trees had no choice but to be slender-crowned and six in the circle are 30–35 m tall. Another old planting has three trees widely spaced along a slope near Chudleigh, Devon with more in a hedge beside the old A38. Some 300 m of the hedge consists of Zelkova suckers with the trees to 28 m × 165 cm, and these and the bigger ones above, to 30 m × 190 cm, are of very bushy form on clear two m boles. Another very big bushy one is at Worlingham, Suffolk, where a plot in Park Drive was left unbuilt on because of the tree. It is 28 m × 216 cm but can be measured only at one m as it scarcely has a stem.

At Kenwood House, London a very bushy one is 22 m × 200 cm but is not in good health. One at Bicton House, Devon is 31 m × 200 cm and another in the Gardens is 33 m × 153 cm. Young trees are slender and slow for some years before they start to grow rapidly and the bole thickens. The autumn colours are old gold and pale brown. In most years the little nuts are borne in plenty. On many of the old bushy trees some of the interior vertical branches are dead, and, unable to fall away, rot slowly where they are.

Cutleaf zelkova (*Zelkova verschaffeltii*) is of unknown origin but seems to be a variant of the Caucasus tree. It has the same bark, flaking to leave crumbling orange patches. At its best it is a bushy plant with slender spreading branches, but slow to grow. Two of the best trees are almost as far south and north as they could be in Britain, at Wakehurst Place in Sussex and Crathes Castle on Deeside; while a third is in the Midlands, in the Jephson Gardens, Leamington Spa, 12 m × 40 cm.

Chinese zelkova (*Zelkova sinica*) is also a rare tree, spread widely but thinly from Tayside to Sussex where a tall but poorly-shaped tree is in Alexandra Park, Hastings (15 m tall). It can be recognized by the untoothed wedge-shaped base of the leaf.

The **Keaki** (*Zelkova serrata*) from Japan has more elegant foliage than the Caucasus tree, with smooth, well-stalked, long-tapered leaves hanging each side of slightly drooping shoots. The crown is a light, open hemisphere (sometimes flatter and more spreading). It also gives subtle yellow, amber and pink shades in the autumn. Found in eastern American cities, it thrives in heat with paving over its roots. It is now being planted more frequently in Britain, having long been grown in parks and squares in West London. Introduced in 1862, a tree grown from the original seed is at Lower Coombe Royal in Devon and is 18 m × 90 cm, while one of the same size beside a road from Horsted Keynes to Handcross in Sussex dates from 1890. This tree is quite easily raised from seed but makes a feeble stem for some years and may need help in sorting out a strong upward shoot from numerous lax, spreading ones.

Southern nettletree (*Celtis australis*) comes from southern Europe, where it makes a big tree: its impressive smooth grey bole is familiar in cities like Nîmes and Auch in France. It feels the lack of warmth in Britain and is confined to the south where, even then, few are more tree than bush. The biggest is most oddly placed in a town road – Grove Road off the busy main street of Shirley, Southampton. It has a bole 83 cm in diameter at one m, above which it divides. A more shapely tree is in the orchard at Lacock Abbey, Wiltshire (14 m × 66 cm). The long-tapered leaf is rough to the touch above and sharply toothed all round.

The leaf of the **Hackberry** (*Celtis occidentalis*) from eastern North America is more abruptly pointed and lacks teeth on varying lengths from the base, sometimes on all of one side. One of the best is in Cannizaro Park, Wimbledon, and there are three – one unlikely to last long – in Battersea Park, London. The bark is curiously adorned with knobs and winged ridges.

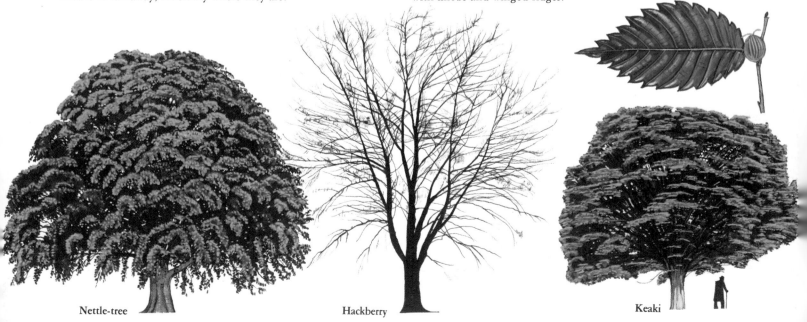

Nettle-tree   Hackberry   Keaki

Caucasian zelkova

Chinese zelkova

Cutleaf zelkova

Hackberry

Nettle-tree

Caucasian zelkova

Mulberry

The common mulberry in Britain is the **Black mulberry** (*Morus nigra*) a tree so long in cultivation and planted so widely that its natural range is unknown beyond the fact that it is Oriental. It must also be of a relatively southern origin because it is common in southern England, rare north of the Midlands as far north as Cumbria and not grown in Scotland, despite its being much prized as an ornamental tree in gardens. It has been planted for its fruit and also for raising silkworms on its foliage. These caterpillars probably prefer and make better silk from the White mulberry, which is scarcely suited at all to northern climates, but they will mature and spin cocoons on the Black in Britain although there has been no success in doing so on a large scale. The famous attempt by King James I in 1609 was probably mostly based on this tree, as the White mulberry had been introduced only 13 years previously, and seeds and trees imported from the south of France were unlikely to have flourished sufficiently.

The Black mulberry grows very slowly for many years from seed and does better as summerwood cuttings. However, the traditional method of propagation was by 'truncheons'. These are 1.5–two m lengths of branch from an old collapsing tree, and with one m or so in the ground they sprout great numbers of shoots around the cut top and from burrs below it. They soon make broad, bushy trees and bear fruit within 20 years in warm sites. By then they look old, almost venerable, and with decay almost inevitably setting in at the cut, where the main branches spring, they in turn become collapsing old trees. Some were then mounded up to support the branches, which soon root into the new soil. The old bole, one-time branch, is hidden.

The reputation of the mulberry as a very slow, very long-lived tree is largely derived from these circumstances. In fact, it is, as its luxuriant leafage clearly indicates, a tree of quite rapid growth and short life. Trees that were not truncheons, and which therefore started with no ready-made bole, grow at the rate expected of a moderately vigorous tree.

Truncheon trees, known by their low break into numerous branches, start with some 30 cm diameter and can be measured only at or below one m. If this were a long-lived tree the pattern of sizes found would be very different from the present position where the biggest trees are nearly everywhere around 50 cm in diameter – very few exceed 70 cm and none are as much as one m. From the rates of growth given, this shows that most of them date from after 1910 and that very few are much older. One which is considerably older is at Weathersdane Hall in Kent. It is 94 cm in diameter at one m, possibly a truncheon, but with a good lower bole and has long, spreading branches supported on props. Another is at Hatfield House in Hertfordshire and is more probably a truncheon with a shorter bole, only measurable at 0.3 m where it is 96 cm in diameter. One at Broadlands in Hampshire is claimed to have been planted in 1605. A small part of its bole has fallen away and the diameter of the remainder is 72 cm. Some other trees with reputed early connections, like that under which Milton wrote *Lycidas* in Cambridge, have been mounded leaving nothing significant to measure and so giving little away.

A splendid courtyard tree, the mulberry should not be planted where it overhangs pavings for, unless the fruit is picked, it will fall when over-ripe and black and be spread by blackbirds, making a slippery walk. The leaves on strong shoots are often deeply and irregularly cut into broad lobes. All leaves have the unusual combination of a glossy surface yet a harsh texture from being covered in short, hard hairs. The autumn colour is a pleasing pale yellowish brown. A remarkable aspect of the tree is that in all its thousands of years of widespread cultivation it has yet to produce a single distinct variant.

White mulberry (*Morus alba*) is native to China and is the tree upon which the silk industry is founded. It was brought to Britain in or about 1596, but has found no part of this country to its liking and is a bushy, fragile plant much given to dying back in the few places where it has been planted. There is one as far north as Crathes Castle on Deeside and one each at Thorp Perrow and Owston in Yorkshire, but very few are outside southern England. The bark of branches and bole, and the green of the leaf are paler than in the Black mulberry and the leaf has a smooth, hairless upper side. The fruit are white for a brief period before turning pink and finally red.

The **Weeping mulberry** ('Pendula') is among the most dramatically weeping of all trees and makes a splendid bower, but it is rare in Britain although one of the most widely planted garden trees from Virginia to Arizona (where they even have a non-fruiting form 'Acerifolia' with larger, darker glossier leaves).

The **Osage orange** (*Maclura pomifera*) is native to the eastern parts of Texas and is accustomed to more heat than it can have in Britain. It is easily raised from imported seed and makes a spiny little bush which usually perishes in its first hard winter. It must, however, toughen greatly with age when it does survive because the tree at Kew is a fine specimen, being 19 m × 69 cm; while one of two in the Botanic Garden at Cambridge is 12 m × 38 cm. The tennis-ball-sized fruit are borne on the female trees and are full of a woody, stringy white substance. Before laminated woods were used, the timber was regarded as the best for longbows, even better than yew.

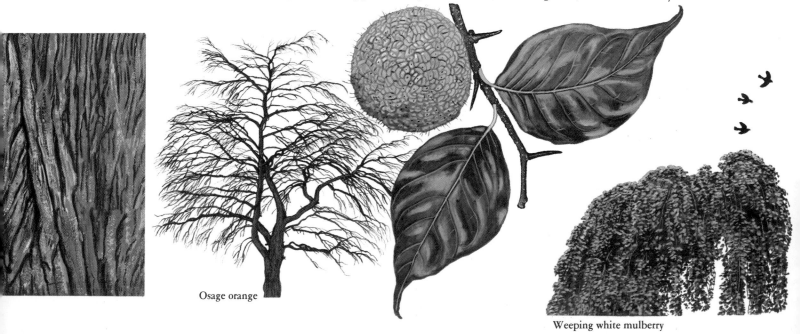

Osage orange

Weeping white mulberry

White mulberry

Male catkins

Black mulberry

Female flowerhead

Female flowerhead

Silkworm caterpillar

Osage orange

Black mulberry

Fig, Katsura and Paper Mulberry

The **Fig** (*Ficus carica*) has given its name to a huge genus of some 800 members of the mulberry family, all evergreen and mostly tropical. This group includes plants of strange habits like the strangler-figs and banyans, as well as climbers such as the neat little *Ficus pumila* often grown on conservatory walls. They are typified by their strange flowers which are almost entirely enclosed in a cup. Insects are lured into this through the small aperture and before they can escape collect an amount of pollen, which is then taken to another flowerhead and fertilizes the flowers within. Then the whole succulent head becomes the fruit.

The Common fig is, however, an ancient selection of a female plant which bears fruit without the need for fertilization. This is just as well since the necessary fig-wasps are specialized insects which do not live in Britain. The fig may have been introduced by the Romans or even before their time. It is native to western Asia and is only marginally hardy in Britain except in the south. In London and other warm parts it can manage well without a wall, as can be seen from the relatively tall specimens in St James's Park, but it is rarely expected to do so, and if edible fruit is the aim, a wall will be a great help, especially in cool summers. The front of the National Gallery in Trafalgar Square, London, has the most notable planting of this kind. North of the Thames Valley there are few free-standing figs and in the Midlands a wall is advisable while to the north of that figs are mostly under glass.

The **Paper mulberry** (*Broussonetia papyrifera*) comes from Japan and China. It has been widely cultivated in the East for the paper made from its bark and for its fibre which makes good quality white linen. It is often planted as a street tree from New York to Texas and there are some remarkable old hulks in the streets of Colonial Williamsburg in Virginia. The leaves can be 18 cm each way and deeply lobed in a most irregular fashion. They have soft hairs all over them, standing out from the margins. Thicker, harder, dark-brown hairs cover the zigzag shoots. Male trees bear bright yellow, rather curled, 6–8 cm catkins on stalks. Female flowers are little one cm globules, brown, shaggy with styles, on one cm stalks: they ripen into red fruits. Botanic gardens from Bath to Cambridge and some south-eastern gardens grow this tree, whose bark is not as papery looking as might be thought. It can be brown or grey-purple, ribbed and pitted, but not usually coming away in sheets.

The **Katsura tree** (*Cercidiphyllum japonicum*) is, rather unexpectedly for such an elegant, almost delicate-looking tree, easily the largest deciduous tree in both China and Japan. It is also a botanical curiosity, the position of which in the scheme of Orders is uncertain, partly because it is undoubtedly extremely primitive and of early origin, the only survivor of a single group of Families and so is now isolated from known relatives. Although quite evidently an Angiosperm, or 'flowering plant', it has a wood structure like that of a conifers, but even more primitive – its timber would be classed as a softwood. The timbers of normal Angiosperm trees like oak, beech and ash are hardwoods. In this, more advanced structure, the sap is carried by wide vessels butting directly on to each other and giving little restriction to the flow. The vessels can still be thin-walled because the rigidity and hardness of the stem is taken care of by specialized fibre-cells. This was a later development from the Gymnosperm confier wood in which the cells had to combine both functions. They are tracheids and must be thick-walled and have long overlaps where they join in order to remain strong, yet leave the sap as clear a passage as possible.

The Katsura was introduced from Japan in 1881 and was found in China only in 1910. Although among the most decorative of trees, it was little appreciated until recently, and old trees are not common.

With the big increase in planting since 1950 and the rapid growth of the tree, there are now handsome specimens in many more gardens. It is hardy and grows well as far north as Inverness although very slowly beyond that. It suffers from drought in hot summers so it needs a good, moist soil and grows well beside water, but frost-hollows should be avoided. A late spring frost can scorch the beautiful coral-red unfolding leaves and although it leafs out again, this process not only slows its growth but spoils one of its set-pieces which is very attractive. While the leaves are still red, although now dark red, the flowers come out. There are both male and female trees and both flower copiously and prettily if not making a great spectacle. The male flowers are tight bunches of stamens tipped with golden anthers. The females are like dark red claws and ripen bloomed blue-grey. Any pair of nearby trees will yield good seed (from the female) and the seedlings grow rapidly into shapely plants. All too many trees have numerous stems but those with single boles show how desirable it is to keep them that way when young so that they mature into columnar trees with domed tops and level branches drooped at the tips. Autumn colours vary from tree to tree and year to year but most young trees turn a bright, deep red while many of the big trees turn shades of gold, amber, pink and sometimes orange. With leafing spurs spreading along the big branches right back to the stem, a 20 m tree is a stirring sight.

Paper mulberry

Katsura-tree

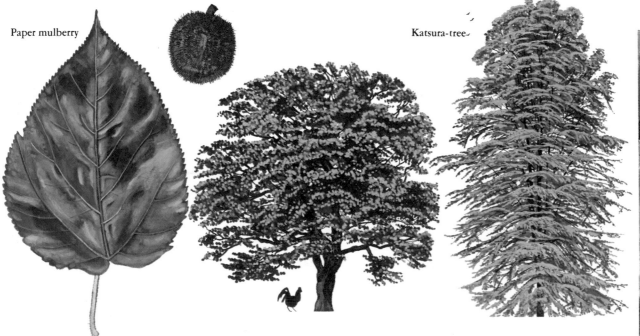

Female flowers

Male flowers

Unripe fruit

Ripe fruit

Katsura-tree

Fig

Ripe fruit

Leaf variant

Cross-section of fruit

Katsura-tree

Fig

Tulip-Tree, Sweetgum and Sassafras

The **Tulip-tree** (*Liriodendron tulipifera*) belongs to the magnolia family and has magnolia-like flowers but very different buds and leaves. It is very common in the USA from New England to Louisiana where it is known as the Tulip-poplar or Yellow poplar. It grows with an open, narrow crown until 40 m tall.

Big trees are frequent across England south of the Midlands and in South Wales but thin out rapidly to the north to be of moderate size at best in northern England and in the south of Scotland. There is one 24 m tall at Reelig near Inverness and two small ones in wall-gardens further north. Flowers will be few in such places, and in the south it is 25 years from planting before they can be expected, but they are largely hidden in the July foliage anyway, and it is as a foliage tree that this species excels. In any case, flowers only leave unsightly brown seed heads throughout the winter. In autumn the leaves turn splendidly gold and pale orange. The wood of tulip-tree is the soft, even-grained whitewood with which intending joiners learn their skills.

'Aureomarginatum' has a more open crown and grows less rapidly. 'Fastigiatum' is becoming almost frequent now and is highly effective as a young tree. The few older specimens 18 m or so tall have broadened only a little but have become very open in the lower crown.

The **Chinese tulip-tree** (*Liriodendron chinense*) has the whole crown of leaves deeply lobed like those on sprouts of the common tree, and they unfold orange-brown. The leafstalk is stained dark red and the leaf is usually bigger, to 22 cm × 25 cm and variably silvered beneath. The bark is smoother and pale grey. It has the same fine autumn colours as the American tree and may grow even faster. It is more frequent in the big gardens in Ireland than in England where several – none of which were planted before 1907 – are 24 m tall.

Sweetgum (*Liquidambar styraciflua*) is a superb foliage-tree in summer and autumn in southern regions. It can be grown as far north as Grampian but is low and slow and hence seldom planted in Scotland or anywhere north of North Wales. The best trees and autumn colours are seen in southern England. The finest is at Stratfield Saye in Hampshire and is 29 m × 96 cm with about nine m of clear straight stem, thus outclassing the tree (30 m × 90 cm) at Syon Park, Middlesex and one at Kew of 28 m × 70 cm. The native range is from Long Island, New York to eastern Texas and from eastern Mexico to Honduras, where it is largely evergreen. The aptitude of the American name – sweetgum – is seen when a leaf is crushed and the sticky remains emit a strong sweet, balsam-like scent.

The leaf is somewhat like that of some species of maple, but is alternate with, not opposite to, the adjacent leaf and sweetgum is a member of the Witch-hazel family. It is notably variable in the time and hues of its autumn display. Many trees turn early, first going bright scarlet and then deep red. Others turn in the middle of the colour season, often beautifully mottled with mixed rich red, orange and yellow leaves, while some remain green into November when some of the leaves turn pale yellow, lilac or deep red, although some fall green.

Oriental sweetgum (*Liquidambar orientalis*) was brought from Asia Minor in 1750. It makes a bush that is sometimes four m high, with smaller, quite hairless leaves and may be seen in Battersea Park and at Kew Gardens but is otherwise rare. **Chinese sweetgum** (*Liquidambar formosana*) is a splendid tree which, when it is not trying to be evergreen, becomes a tower of rich orange, purple and scarlet in late autumn. The leaf is very hard with rigid fine teeth, and it unfolds shining red-brown. The bark is pale grey, smooth until cracking finely into square plates.

Sassafras (*Sassafras albidum*) is a member of the laurel family and shares its aromatic foliage, although with less pungence than the Bay, the scent being sweet vanilla spiced with orange. It occurs over almost the whole of the eastern USA and, suckering widely as it does, forms big hedges in some parts, differing from an English hedgerow in the densely leafed umbrella-crowns which become a spectacular mixture of orange and scarlet in the autumn. In Britain it lacks the sun for this display and is a muted yellow and orange. It is also quite rare. There is one 12 m tall in the ravine at Bodnant, Gwynydd, but the species is otherwise almost entirely confined to the south of England. The Sassafras centre there is Cannizaro Park, Wimbledon, where despite the threatening demise of the biggest, 21 m × 68 cm, there will still be two more unequalled elsewhere, the larger measuring 20 m × 57 cm. Old trees tend to grow out of the odd, irregularly-lobed, often mitten-shaped leaves and settle down to plain ellipses.

Persian ironwood (*Parrotia persica*) is from the same family as the Sweetgum – the Witch-hazel family – and unlike the Sweetgum it shares their habit of flowering in the winter as well as giving good autumn colours. The flowers are usually out in the second half of January. In its native mountains beside the Caspian Sea, this is a tall, slender tree but a bole of two m before determined bushing out is unusual. The plants are sometimes 12 m tall but even these are broader than they are tall. The long, low-arched upper branches usually change colour in the autumn before the lower crown and are bare by the time that turns. This is a plant of southern gardens, but there is one at Lingholm in Cumbria, and one in Edinburgh.

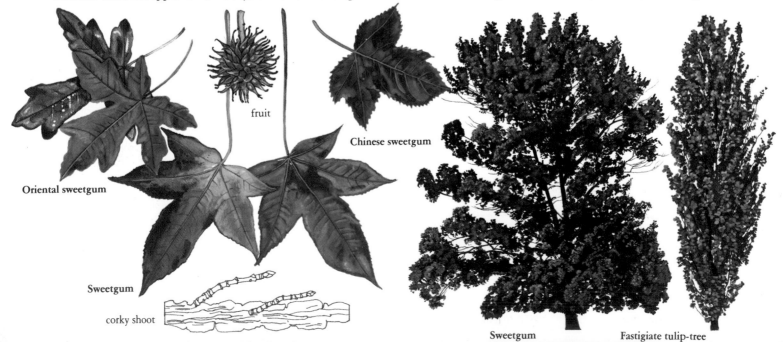

fruit

Chinese sweetgum

Oriental sweetgum

Sweetgum

corky shoot

Sweetgum

Fastigiate tulip-tree

Tulip-tree

flower

Chinese tulip-tree

flower

'Aurcomarginatum'

fruit

Tulip-tree

fruit

Chinese tulip-tree

Sassafras
fruit

fruit

flowers

Sassafras

shoot

Persian ironwood

variation in leaf

bark

Tulip-tree

Tulip-tree

Persian ironwood

Sassafras

Magnolia

The Magnolias have the most primitive flower of all the non-conifers: the segments are not divided into distinguishable sepals and petals but are graded from smaller in outer rows to bigger in the inner whorls, and are all classed as 'tepals', a handy anagram. Those prominent in the spring with flowers on bare wood are Asiatic whereas all the American species flower when in full leaf.

Southern magnolia or Evergreen magnolia (*Magnolia grandiflora*) native from North Carolina to Texas, is a favourite plant for the south-facing wall of an English mansion and is seen free-standing, up to 12 m × 40 cm, only south and west of the Thames. The sweetly fragrant flower may open to 25 cm across from midsummer.

The **Chinese evergreen magnolia** (*Magnolia delavayi*) is also a wall-plant, occurring as far north as North Wales, and a free-standing tree from London westwards when given the chance, for it often outgrows a wall and flourishes above it. The bark is yellowish-white, thick and corky. Its bold foliage with silvery highlights makes up for its sparse flowering.

Wilson's magnolia (*Magnolia wilsonii*) was discovered by Ernest Wilson in West China in 1904. Its hanging, fragrant red-stamened flowers open when the leaves are fully out. A small, open, bushy plant, it is best placed to hang its flowers from a bank or wall.

The **Japanese bigleaf magnolia** (*Magnolia hypoleuca*) can be a sturdy tree to 15 m × 50 cm but it is shortlived and sometimes consists of a ring of big sprouts from a stump. It will grow and flower as far north as Innes House near Elgin, Grampian, but is scarce north of North Wales. The sweet scent of the flower can be detected 30 m from the tree and the fruit is 20 cm long.

Saucer magnolia (*Magnolia x soulangiana*) is the popular front-garden magnolia, broad and bushy and full of flower. It is a hybrid between the Chinese Yulan (*M. denudata*) and a Japanese species. It has given numerous variants, a few with pure white flowers but mostly with some purple or deep red. Among the best is **'Lennei'** with bigger, darker leaves and a white interior to each rosy-purple tepal. This also bears a few flowers throughout the summer.

The **Cucumber tree** (*Magnolia acuminata*) is wild from Lake Ontario to Texas. Young trees grow quite rapidly and have a shapely conical crown, but with age the increase in bole size becomes very slow. The bark is warm brown, and has narrow ridges which shed little rectangular plates to leave bright red-brown patches.

Bigleaf magnolia (*Magnolia macrophylla*) from the southern Allegheny Mountains, bears the biggest simple leaves of any tree we grow, 60 cm long and lightly silvered beneath. They occur in short whorls at the tips of the branches. New shoots are bloomed blue-grey, and the few flowers are faintly creamy white, and egg-shaped until they open to 30 cm across, showing purple stamens.

Veitch's hybrid magnolia (*Magnolia x veitchii*) was raised by the Exeter firm of that name in 1907 in order to obtain a plant with flowers like Campbell's magnolia but hardier and able to flower in less than 25 years, by crossing it with the Yulan Lily (*M. denudata*). The result is a vigorous tree, occasionally 24 m tall, floriferous from its tenth year, and four of the five raised had white flowers.

The **Willow magnolia** (*Magnolia salicifolia*) from Japan holds clouds of small, pure white flowers aloft on a high-domed delicate crown in late April. The flowers have six tepals, three large and three small. It is almost entirely confined to southern and western gardens and is often 15 m tall. The bark of a skinned shoot or a torn leaf emits a sweet heliotrope or aniseed scent. There is variation among specimens in the narrowness of the leaves and the bronzy tinge retained in summer.

The **Northern Japanese magnolia** (*Magnolia kobus*) is usually seen in the tall tree form (var. *borealis*) as a very sturdy plant with smooth dull grey bark. It has been known to take over 30 years before starting to flower and once flowering it can either be very profuse or rather sparse. The flowers have six tepals and are among the smallest of the magnolias, opening to ten cm. The abrupt point on the leaf and its shiny green underside are distinctive.

Campbell's magnolia (*Magnolia campbellii*) is regarded by some as the queen of the genus and in the Himalayas when 45 m tall and covered in huge rosy-pink flowers it must be spectacular. In southern and western gardens, when a broad tree to over 18 m tall, it also makes its mark. In normal years, the flowers open between mid-February to late Match. Once the big, hairy bud-scales have parted, the flower is likely to be killed by frost, so a few weeks without any frost must follow any early warm spell for there to be any display. It also takes about 25 years from seed before there are any flowers. In mid-flower, the outer eight–12 tepals droop leaving the inner four erect. The white flowered form 'Alba' grows more strongly.

The **Fraser magnolia** (*Magnolia fraseri*) comes from the southern Allegheny Mountains and is grown in a few English gardens from Sussex to Devon. It is like the Bigleaf Magnolia but with a leaf half as long, and lacks the silver underside.

Sweetbay (*Magnolia virginiana*) is scarce but very attractive with its brilliant silver-blue beneath the pale green leaf, and little pointed white flowers. Often a bush, as at Kew, it can also be a tree of 12 m.

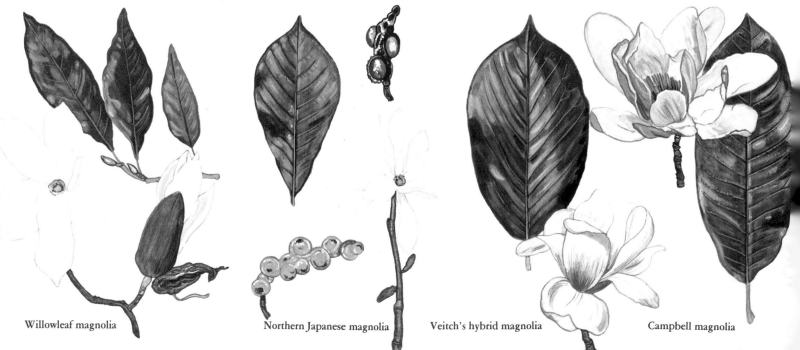

Willowleaf magnolia   Northern Japanese magnolia   Veitch's hybrid magnolia   Campbell magnolia

Wilson's magnolia

Southern magnolia

Chinese evergreen magnolia

Japanese bigleaf magnolia

Saucer magnolia

'Lennei'

'Lennei'

Cucumber-tree

Bigleaf magnolia

Saucer magnolia

Sweet bay

Fraser magnolia

Plane

The **London Plane** (*Platanus* x *acerifolia*) was a source of puzzlement and confusion for 250 years until in 1919 it was shown to be a hybrid between the Oriental plane and the American plane. Until then it had been variously called the American plane or a variety of the Oriental. It seems certain that the many early references to the American plane in Britain referred to London plane, but the American species has always failed at Kew and only one specimen more than ten years old is known.

As well as being intermediate between the parents in depth of lobing on the leaf and in the number of fruit on each stalk, the tree shows hybrid vigour to a large degree. This is really the secret of its success in cities, which has been ascribed to its large-scale shedding of the outer bark and is probably also enhanced by the short season in leaf, like the Catalpas, and by the hard shiny leaf surface washing clear of soot. But the ability to grow in poor rubble-filled soils beneath paving and in the conditions often inflicted upon this tree, must depend upon the most robust root-system and foliage. It often grows too large to be suitable in such places and then has to suffer amputation of its branches. It is, in fact, singularly odd to plant the largest growing British tree in confined squares and courts, where complaints about blocking the light are bound to arise. It is also apt to lift pavings and its leaves block drains and make skid-pans. Further, the fine hairs its leaves shed in summer, as well as those from its seeds, break into minute fragments which are carried by the wind and cause irritation to the eyes of some people.

The London plane is one of the many trees that needs all the warmth it can find and its stature falls away sharply towards the north. This factor is quite handy in making it a small, untroublesome tree for the streets in Glasgow and Edinburgh but northwards from there the only two trees of any size are, surprisingly, in Easter Ross. It is in the south of England on good soils with plenty of space that this tree shows its paces. The finest by far is in a private park in Gloucestershire, 37–39 m × 268 cm, with a cylindrical bole for five m. The famous tree at the Bishop's Palace in Ely is 35 m × 281 cm (1983) but a vast limb leaves the bole at 1.5 m and when the measuring tape is taut, about ten people could stand between it and the tree in a concavity. This tree is reputed to date from around 1680 and to be one of the first planted, but it may well have been planted after 1730.

A superb tree by Festival Walk, Carshalton, Surrey is 39 m × 214 cm and a similar one at Witley Rectory in Surrey by the main road is 38 m × 207 cm. A bigger bole is at Pusey House, Oxfordshire, 32 m × 240 cm and a rather absurd squat tree in the middle of Chilton

Foliat is 250 cm in diameter. The tallest, and easily the tallest of any broadleafed trees in Britain, are three in a line of four planted in 1740 near the river at Bryanston School in Dorset. All are over 47 m tall and one may be nearer 50 m × 183 cm. In Magdalen College, Oxford, a London plane planted in 1801 was 37 m × 205 cm in 1978. Hybrid vigour may also confer robust good health, and until recent and local outbreaks of plane-tree anthracnose which kills new shoots and flowers in some seasons but does no serious harm, this tree was free of disease. Since dead planes or planes dropping branches are almost, if not quite, unknown and the oldest are still growing fast, this will increasingly be the biggest British broadleaf tree.

'**Pyramidalis**' is the form common in London and other cities, with a brown, burry bark, small, three-lobed, bright shiny green leaves, and only one or two big fruit-balls. None of the big trees is of this form, which has been known since 1850. '**Augustine Henry**' is a very superior form, occasionally seen in London parks, in Kew and a few gardens. It has bark exposing much white on a clean, straight bole and few ascending straight branches. The leaves are large and dark and held sparsely, slightly hooded and pointing downwards.

'**Suttneri**' has leaves boldly variegated white, with some inner ones white all over, and so cannot be expected to grow fast. Young ones must be more widespread but only three sizeable trees have been found. The best is by the Jolly Farmer at Puttenham in Surrey and is 21 m × 80 cm. One in Holland Park, London, is 19 m × 58 cm and one in Glasvevin Botanic Garden near Dublin was 19 m × 37 cm in 1974.

The **Oriental plane** (*Platanus orientalis*) has a tendency to grow huge low branches and to rest them on the ground ten m or more away, so it is even less suitable for street planting than the London plane. It seems to be rather less sensitive to cool summers than that tree, and there are sizable trees in Cumbria and Tayside, but it is much less widely planted everywhere. It was introduced before 1600 but there is no old tree whose date is precisely known. The oldest must be the immense tree at Rycote House near Thame, Oxon, which is 21 m × 273 cm (1983); the tree at Woodstock Park, Kent, 28 m × 260 cm measured round its considerably swollen belly at 1.5 m; and the well-known one at Weston Park, Shifnal in Shropshire, 24 m × 232 cm. One planted at Jesus College Cambridge in 1802, the earliest fixed date, was 28 m × 165 cm in 1972, an interesting comparison with the 1801 London plane cited, in Oxford. Var. *insularis* from Cyprus and Crete is a minor variant but '**Digitata**' with its deep, slender lobes is very attractive although scarce.

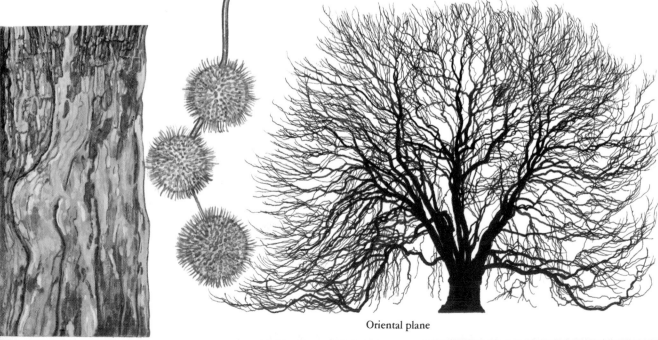

Oriental plane

London plane

'Pyramidalis' with fruit

'Digitata'

Female flowers

Suttner's plane

Oriental plane

London plane

Thorn

The **Hawthorn** (*Crataegus monogyna*) is a native species seen at its best as a tall, broad bush clothed to the ground on chalk downlands or sandy commons. In this state it covers itself all over with flowers and scents the air during mid-May. It provides birds with great quantities of dark red berries in October and after. It is mostly birds of the thrush family that feed on hawthorns, especially the redwing and fieldfare which arrive about that time. When berries are left in December or January they may attract waxwings. In the very earliest seasons an occasional bush will open some heads of flower by the first of May, but this was the normal time of full flowering before the Gregorian Calendar was introduced to Britain in 1752 and May 1st became May 13th.

Hawthorns are also seen as genuine trees, in parks and gardens more than in the countryside, because the tall plants in uncut hedges seldom count as trees, but are tall shrubs with many stems. In town and city parks, where the hawthorn is highly valued for its all-round toughness, growing in poor soils, dry places and polluted air and with branches resistant to all but the most determined vandal, there are commonly hawthorns ten or 12 m × 40 cm. These have single boles clean for two m and easily qualify as proper trees, and sometimes they are over 15 m tall. By far the greater number of hawthorn plants, however, are in hedges bounding fields, and most of these are clipped and so lose most of their flowering wood. Easily raised by the million from cuttings, robust when transplanted without great care, clipping into low, thorny, cattle-proof barriers, this was the obvious plant for the big hedge-planting of the Enclosures after 1820. The timber is very hard and an excellent fuel, burning slowly and hot with a lilac flame.

'**Fastigiata**' is too severely upright to be used anywhere but in a very formal planting or confined space. It moves well even when five m tall and will grow to 12 m. As tough as the normal May, it is even more resistant to vandalism and so recommends itself for planting in precincts.

The **Midland thorn** (*Crataegus oxyacantha* or *laevigata*) prefers the shade of woods on heavy soils and so has a habitat distinct from that of the common May, but hybrids between them commonly blur the distinctions in both habitat and tree. In the wild, pink-flowered variants are common, and a selection from these is very common in suburban gardens and parks, although a somewhat dull tree. However, a truly red-flowered branch grew on one, and in 1858 this was propagated as '**Paul's Scarlet**' and is now more common and a far better tree.

The true **Cockspur thorn** (*Crataegus crus-galli*) is very rarely seen, nearly all the trees so regarded being hybrids that lack the close rows of long, curved ferocious thorns. They also all have downy flower-stalks instead of smooth ones.

The **Plumleaf thorn** (*Crataegus* x *prunifolia*) or Broadleafed hybrid cockspur, is the tree most commonly taken for the true cockspur although the much fewer, purple thorns and broad, dark glossy leaf are so unlike it. This splendid plant, rugged, free-flowering and fruiting, and uniquely coloured in autumn in gold, burnished copper, orange and scarlet, is common in town parks and by roadsides near villages as well as in gardens. Unless planted after training to a single stem, it grows into a low, broad, bushy tree. The fruit fall with the leaves. This tree is not known wild and is a cockspur hybrid with another American thorn although it is uncertain which one.

Carriere's thorn (*Crataegus* x *lavallei*) is another hybrid cockspur, the other parent being the Mexican thorn whose large yellow fruit are common in markets in Mexico. It arose twice, the first time in Paris, the second in Segrez. It is more common as a street tree than the Plumleaf thorn because it is less bushy and less well armed. It is often planted in rows by arterial roads, especially in West London, but is also frequent in large gardens including, although less frequently, those in the north of Scotland. In winter it is unmistakeable with its grey vertically-plated bark and level branches clothed along their upper sides only with short bunches of twigs. The leaves remain shiny dark green until about November and briefly turn dark crimson before falling, leaving the orange-red fruit on the tree for a few months.

Oriental thorn (*Crataegus laciniata*, formerly *orientalis*) is tough, hardy and attractive but although occasional in roadside suburban gardens, it is quite rare. It has hardly any thorns and the leaves are soft with thick down. The fruit, large for a thorn, being over two cm across, are also downy and may be red, orange or nearly yellow.

The **Azarole** (*Crataegus azarolus*) from southern Europe and North Africa is similar to the Oriental thorn but has thicker leaves and bigger fruit, up to nearly three cm. At Thorp Perrow, Bedale, Yorkshire, it is eight m × 26 cm. It is comparatively rare. The **Tansyleaf thorn** (*Crataegus tanacetifolia*) is another in this group. It has deeply-cut downy leaves and big fruit, and is almost thornless. It is distinguished in fruit by the deeply-cut bracts at the base.

Washington thorn (*Crataegus phaenopyrum*) is a pretty little tree in foliage and in fruit. The small one cm flowers ripen into clusters of brilliant scarlet fruit which last through to the spring. It is scarce and seen only in the south of England.

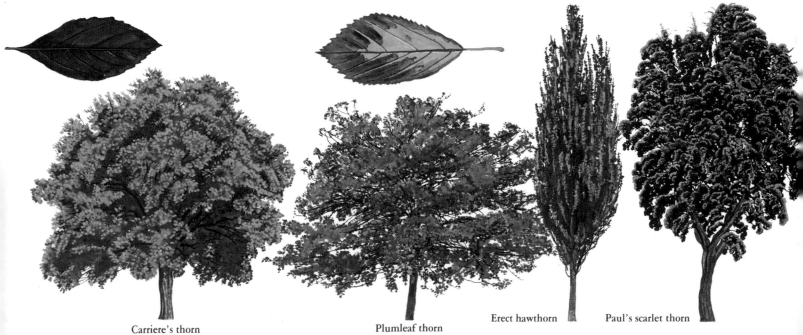

Carriere's thorn   Plumleaf thorn   Erect hawthorn   Paul's scarlet thorn

Carriere's thorn

Plumleaf thorn

Hawthorn

Fruit with single stone

Fruit with two stones

Cockspur thorn

Washington thorn

Midland hawthorn

Oriental thorn

Azarole

Tansleyleaf thorn

Hawthorn

Cockspur thorn

Hawthorn

Rowan and Service Tree

The **Wild service tree** (*Sorbus torminalis*) is a native British tree on or near chalk and limestone and clay from Kent to near Carnforth, Cumbria in the west and near Sheffield in the east. It is of particular interest to botanists and ecologists since it will sow itself only in primary woodland, that is, only on land that has never been cultivated. Its occurrence has been closely studied and mapped and it is found that in some woods there is a long history of the tree replacing itself through suckers.

The Wild service tree is in a group of its own but it has hybridized with the Whitebeam many times in the wild. By contrast, the **True service tree** (*Sorbus domestica*) is, despite its rowan-like leaves, in a quite isolated group of its own, crossing with no other. Even without fruit it can be told from any rowan by its ovoid shiny green buds and its rich, dark-brown, finely ridged bark. The fruit are big, up to three cm, green and brown tinged with red, and either globular (var. *pomifera*) or pear-shaped (var. *pyrifera*).

The **Rowan** (*Sorbus aucuparia*) is native throughout Great Britain and Ireland and grows at a higher altitude – over 1000 m in Scotland – than any other tree. In the remote north it is the brightest of the autumn foliages, being coloured fine orange and scarlet, but where day-length is shorter, as in England where the tree is extensively planted in town streets and gardens as well as growing wild in open woods, it is at best a mottled orange and dark red and usually the leaves blacken and fall early. The berries turn from green to yellow within a few days in July and then suddenly, within a day or two, they are red and being eaten by blackbirds, thrushes and starlings.

Young rowans are narrowly erect, but '**Fastigiata**' is more so and is of unknown origin: it may be a hybrid with an American rowan for it differs in bigger fruit and many details of foliage. '**Fructo Luteo**', the Yellow-fruited rowan, is grafted on to common rowan rootstock and unless rescued it can be overwhelmed by its sucker shoots. It is more speading in the crown but equally or more floriferous with slightly domed flowerheads.

'**Beissneri**' was until recently growing only in a few unexpected places like a street in Edgbaston, Birmingham, the reserve at Begbroke, Oxford and in Kensington Gardens. Now its great merits have won it more of the popularity it deserves. The bark has a thin film of bluish wax and this becomes translucent when wet so that in sunshine after a storm the stems shine out like jewels. The prettily shaped leaves turn pale gold and amber in the autumn.

The **Scarlet rowan** (*Sorbus* 'Embley') achieves a flaming scarlet in autumn unequalled by any other rowan and by few trees of any sort.

Strangely this comes after the outer leaves have turned deep purple. This tree has been widely planted (as '*Sorbus discolor*') by public authorities for many years, in parks and streets and around hospitals and schools but only recently has it become common in gardens. A few older ones like four at Sheffield Park in Sussex are around 17 m × 45 cm. In summer the fern-like foliage on slender, slightly arched branches can soon be recognized from afar without the need to look for the scarlet buds like dunces' hats.

Sargent rowan (*Sorbus sargentiana*) also turns scarlet but a slightly darker colour than 'Embley', and often with a greater admixture of yellow. It also has long red buds but these exude clear resin and are larger on very stout shoots. It makes a broad little tree of slow growth.

The **Hupeh rowan** (*Sorbus hupehensis*) also comes from western China, but was sent to Britain in 1910. It is becoming frequent in public plantings, for which its ability to survive planting when four m tall is a great asset, as well as in private gardens. Its foliage has a grey cast and is pale grey-green beneath, which together with its red stained central leafstalk make it distinctive in leaf. In fruit it is even more so, laden with open, red-stalked fruitheads of dull white or sometimes rosy pink fruit.

The **Kashmir rowan** (*Sorbus cashmiriana*) has much bigger and whiter berries than the Hupeh rowan, big enough to incommode the blackbirds who then turn to picking or knocking them off and attacking them on the ground. The pink flowers are fragrant. The leaves fall early, a pale straw-yellow.

The **Vilmorin rowan** (*Sorbus vilmoriniana*) makes a low, spreading tree most at home in high rainfall areas and seeding itself in some western gardens. The berries are a deep bright red in summer and fade through dark pink in autumn to pale rose and then white. It comes from western China.

'**Joseph rock**' arose from a single rogue seed in a batch of another species which was sent by the American collector Joseph Rock to Edinburgh from China. The seedlot was split and the portion containing this seed went to Wisley Gardens in Surrey. It was raised, recognized as something different, and planted on Battleston Hill where it is now 16 m × 31 cm. All true 'Joseph Rock' plants are grafts from this tree, but seedlings are almost the same. Even before it assumes its fine autumn colours, the foliage is beautiful with a leaflet here and there prematurely scarlet, touches of red on the stalks and bright yellowish green and deep green mixed together. Its slender crown and small leaflets fit it well for street planting even without regard to its foliage, fruit and autumn colours.

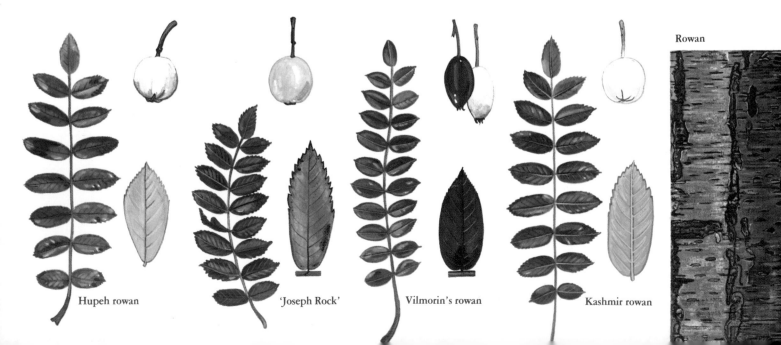

Hupeh rowan   'Joseph Rock'   Vilmorin's rowan   Kashmir rowan   Rowan

True service tree

Rowan

Japanese rowan

var. *pomifera*

var. *pyrifera*

Scarlet rowan

Beissner's rowan

Sargent rowan

Fastigiate rowan

Rowan

Alderleaf whitebeam

True service tree

Wild service tree

Whitebeam and Medlar

The **Whitebeam** (*Sorbus aria*) is native to chalk and limestone hills from Kent to the Wye Valley, and in County Galway in Ireland, and is commonly planted all over England in gardens, streets and town parks, particularly around London. It is, however, uncommon in Scotland. It is a feature of the woods on the Chiltern Hills, showing up strongly against dark yews, hollies and other backgrounds, when it leafs out brightly silvered and again in autumn when it turns a subtle biscuit-brown, still showing white undersides to the leaves. The berries have usually been eaten by birds before this and are at their best when they have just ripened in late summer, against the dark green and silver foliage.

Although this tree is most at home on chalk, seedlings grow up from seeds which have passed through birds and been voided in roosts in wood and scrub on sandy, acid soils or clays nearby, in small numbers. In woods and hedgerows the trees are low-crowned with short stems but in parks and gardens, where a clean stem of two m is desirable, they are kept to a single bole which turns with age from smooth silvery grey to scaly-ridged dark purple-grey. Trees like this are sometimes 20 m tall and 60 cm in diameter.

'Lutescens' is usually preferred for planting in streets and small gardens, partly because it has a neater and more shapely crown. It is more dense and for many years it is upswept and egg-shaped. Its other good point is that it has dark purple shoots against which the unfolding silvery leaf-buds show to advantage.

'Majestica' or 'Decaisneana' is of unknown French origin, but had been brought to Britain by 1858. It is seen more often along streets, especially in the western approaches to London, than in gardens, and there are groups in Regent's Park and Primrose Hill in London.

The **Himalayan whitebeam** (*Sorbus cuspidata*) has been grown in Britain since 1820, but no tree without doubts about its true identity is known to be more than about 40 years old, and these are confined to a few major gardens. Westonbirt has about eight specimens, an undue proportion of the national total, and they are all currently very healthy, shapely and bearing splendid foliage; elsewhere, however, this has been a short-lived species. Good specimens are narrowly conical with an acute apex at 18 m or more. The flowers have a strong scent like hawthorn.

'Wilfrid Fox' is probably a hybrid between the Himalayan and the Common whitebeams. It is a good tree for restricted spaces or where a spreading crown is unsuitable, and is seen in town precincts and car parks. It is also well suited to northern parts, two gardens north of Aberdeen growing two of the biggest specimens. Young trees are very

narrow and upright and can be planted when oversize with good chances of success.

'John Mitchell' has even bigger, rounder and thicker leaves and is becoming better known. It is a form of *Sorbus thibetica* which was raised by W. J. Mitchell at Westonbirt, and planted in 1938.

The **Chinese whitebeam** (*Sorbus folgneri*) is a rare tree notable for the metallic silvering under the leaves of the best trees and the rich, very late autumn colours. The **Swedish whitebeam** (*Sorbus* x *intermedia*) is one of a series of hybrids which occur in the wild among several species of *Sorbus*, in this case apparently between the whitebeam and the rowan. It is very hardy and tough and is commonly planted in city streets and parks. It can cover itself in flowers almost like a hawthorn and makes a very sturdy tree with a trunk more than 70 cm in diameter.

Another complex of these Whitebeam x Rowan hybrids includes the **Finnish whitebeam** or Bastard service tree (*Sorbus* x *thuringiaca*) among several with leaves having a pair or two of free leaflets. This has a bigger and longer leaf than the other similar hybrids, up to 15 cm long. It is naturally very upright and compact in crown, but a more strict form is also grown, 'Fastigiata'. They both have dense crowns and are planted in car parks and cities. Some older trees in gardens have shown a tendency to lie down with age.

Alderleaf whitebeam (*Sorbus alnifolia*) has pleasant foliage but stands out most in the autumn when its abundant long-lasting fruit stay on orange-red. **Fontainebleu service tree** (*Sorbus latifolia*) is a hybrid between the Whitebeam and the Wild service tree and is found wild only around that town, but a complex of hybrids of the same parentage occurs in many forms in isolated patches in Britain, in Devon, in Avon in the Avon Gorge and similar forms occur in Brecon and Somerset. The Fontainebleau form is seen in some old gardens and in city parks.

The **Medlar** (*Mespilus germanica*) is separable from the closely related thorns, apples and pears by its big solitary flower and fruit. It was introduced from Europe in very early times and was grown in orchards. The fruit were left on the tree until very ripe in October and then stored to ripen further until they began to decay, at which point they were, apparently, ready to eat. Although reported as running wild in some Sussex and Kent woodlands, this plant is not at all common in gardens. It is most likely to be seen in old gardens associated with cathedrals and abbeys or other ancient foundations. It is either a bush or has a short stem and in either case it is broader than it is tall. In autumn the big leaves turn a pleasant yellow-brown.

Medlar

flower

bark

fruit

Himalayan whitebeam

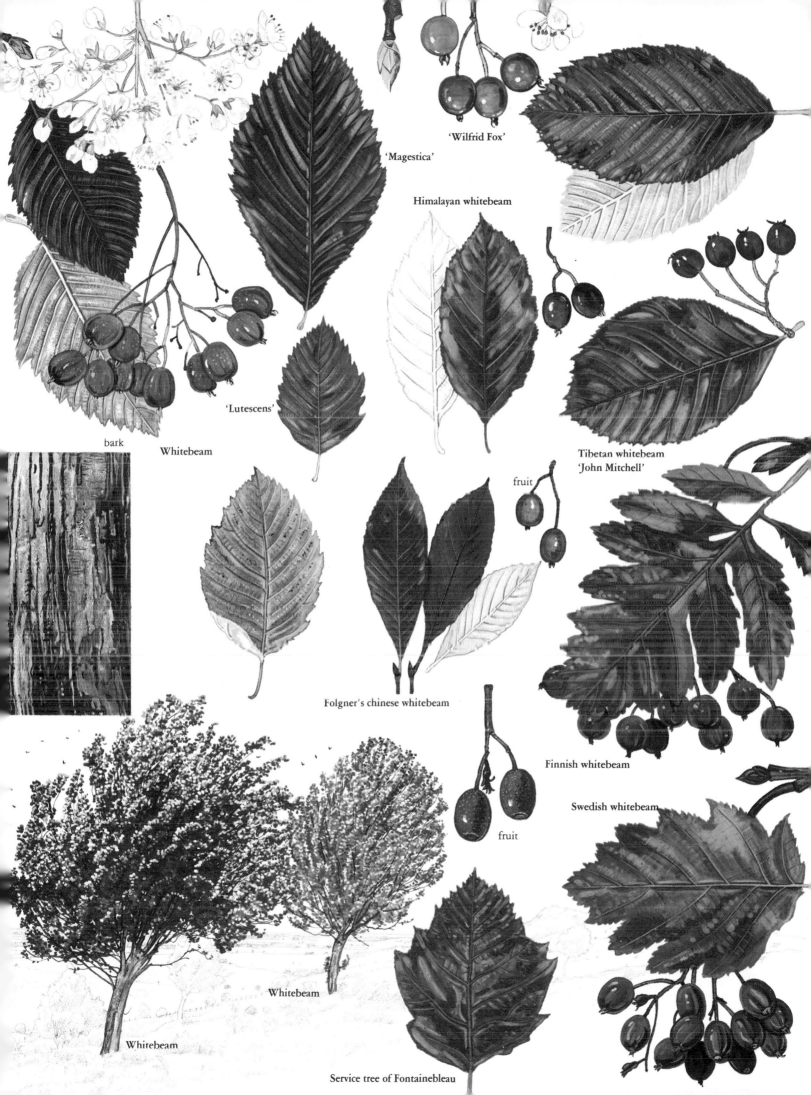

'Wilfrid Fox'

'Magestica'

Himalayan whitebeam

'Lutescens'

bark

Whitebeam

Tibetan whitebeam
'John Mitchell'

fruit

Folgner's chinese whitebeam

Finnish whitebeam

fruit

Swedish whitebeam

Whitebeam

Whitebeam

Service tree of Fontainebleau

Crab Apple

The term **Crab apple** has been extended in horticultural use from just the small-fruited woodland and hedgerow tree to embrace all the small-fruited non-orchard apples. This means that it now includes all the apple trees grown for their flowers or autumn colour – all the exotic species and cultivars grown in gardens. The one garden apple often prized for its fruit and for making into jelly or jam, 'John Downie' is also highly decorative in fruit; the fruit are small so this is also a Crab apple.

The **Wild crab** (*Malus sylvestris*) is a native British tree found scattered in all parts in oakwoods and hedgerows. In one common form it can be told from the 'wild' seedlings arising from discarded cores of orchard apples, which are quite frequent near picnic-places and along roads, by bearing some thorns and having white flowers. Other forms lack spines and have flowers flushed pink: they can be distinguished by their smooth shoots and underside of the leaf. The Wild crab is only one of at least four species that went to make the orchard apple.

'**Golden hornet**' is a hybrid from a Japanese species, raised at Bagshot, Surrey, and much planted since 1950. '**John Downie'** was raised near Lichfield, Staffordshire, and has been available since 1885. It is splendid in flower, with masses of pink buds opening white, as well as in fruit. These can be picked after two or more weeks of decorating the tree, to be made into a jelly of superb flavour and colour.

Chinese crab (*Malus spectabilis*) is known only as a cultivated tree from China, unknown in the wild. It makes a relatively big tree, to 12 m × 55 cm with big double flowers up to 5.5 cm across on a broad crown of twisting branches and rather pendulous shoots.

Siberian crab (*Malus baccata*) is a smaller-growing and small-flowered version of the Hupeh crab, with similar leaves and fruit. More frequently seen is one of the **Hybrid Siberian crabs** (*Malus x robusta*) a form in which the much larger fruit hang as dark red, globular apples in large numbers through the winter. The **Manchurian crab** (var. *mandschurica*) makes a larger tree than the ordinary Siberian and differs from it also in the hairy flower-stalks. It is sometimes seen 15 m × 60 cm.

The **Hupeh crab** (*Malus hupehensis*) is an outstandingly good garden tree, found in West China in 1900. It grows fast – seedlings planted out two years previously should make shoots over one m long and in 40 years it can be 12 m × 70 cm. It will not cross with other crabs, however closely related, so it comes true from seed and is very fertile. The opening flowers, of which a few sprays are borne in the fourth year from seed, are of unsurpassed elegance when in masses on a tree 15 years or so of age. The big buds are globular and pale pink.

They open pure white up to six cm across with a golden centre. At the height of flowering, the whole tree is a cloud of clear white flowers hiding all the foliage. Within a few weeks the innumerable little fruit, in long-stalked sprays, are yellow and orange, and for most of the summer they are bright, shining dark red.

The **Magdeburg apple** ('Magdeburgensis') may have an orchard-apple in its parentage. It is frequent in village gardens and on trading-estates and is among the first apples to flower. It is also the most fully double in the flower, having 12 petals. The newly-unfolded leaves are soft grey-green when the flowers open among them on a low, drooping crown.

The **Japanese crab** (*Malus floribunda*) is a hybrid that arose long ago in Japan and was sent to Britain in 1862. It is the commonest crab in most suburban gardens and parks, along with some of the Purple crabs, and although its crown is twiggy and untidy it is a vast improvement on theirs. It comes into leaf remarkably early, before the end of March, and every year it seems that the abundant foliage must obscure the flowers. Without fail, however, by early May the tree is foaming with red buds and pink and white flowers and hardly a leaf remains unhidden. Every few years there are myriads of tiny yellow fruit.

Hall's crab (*Malus halliana*) was brought to America by Dr Hall in 1862 from Japan, where it is known only as a garden tree. The flowers are often semi-double and are always very pretty but rarely profuse.

The **Purple crab** (*Malus x purpurea*) is almost acceptable when first into flower. Then the flowers fade badly and the thin foliage, looking blighted and stained an ugly purple, is borne on branches which grow at awkward angles. Several forms are common. '**Lemoinei**' grows bigger, bears many lobed leaves, and has deep rosy purple flowers. 'Aldenhamensis' is a better, richer red and partly semi-double, but '**Profusion**' is the best in flower. It has sprays of dark red flowers wreathed along the shoots among very deep purple leaves and persistent, flattened, dark red fruit.

The **Pillar apple** (*Malus tschonoskii*) is a rare native of Japan, sent to Kew in 1897 from America and now, thanks to extensive planting since about 1950, a common tree. It could hardly be ignored any longer by those planting in public places, for it is tailor-made for streets, precincts and difficult, confined spaces. As an apple, it is almost indifferent as to the poverty or poor aeration of the soil and positively welcomes lime in it. It also moves with relative ease and high chances of success when far too big for good garden-planting practice, four or five m tall.

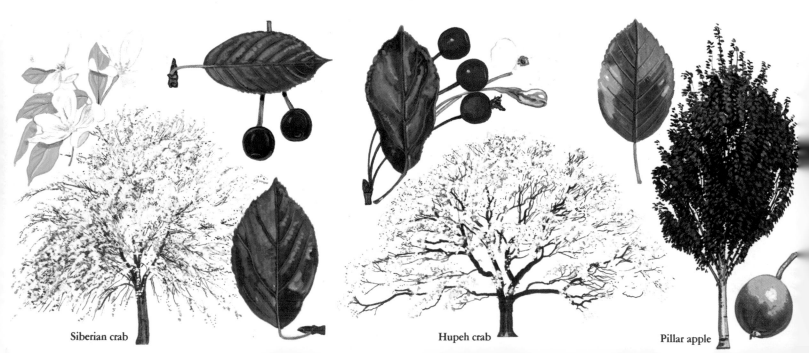

Siberian crab   Hupeh crab   Pillar apple

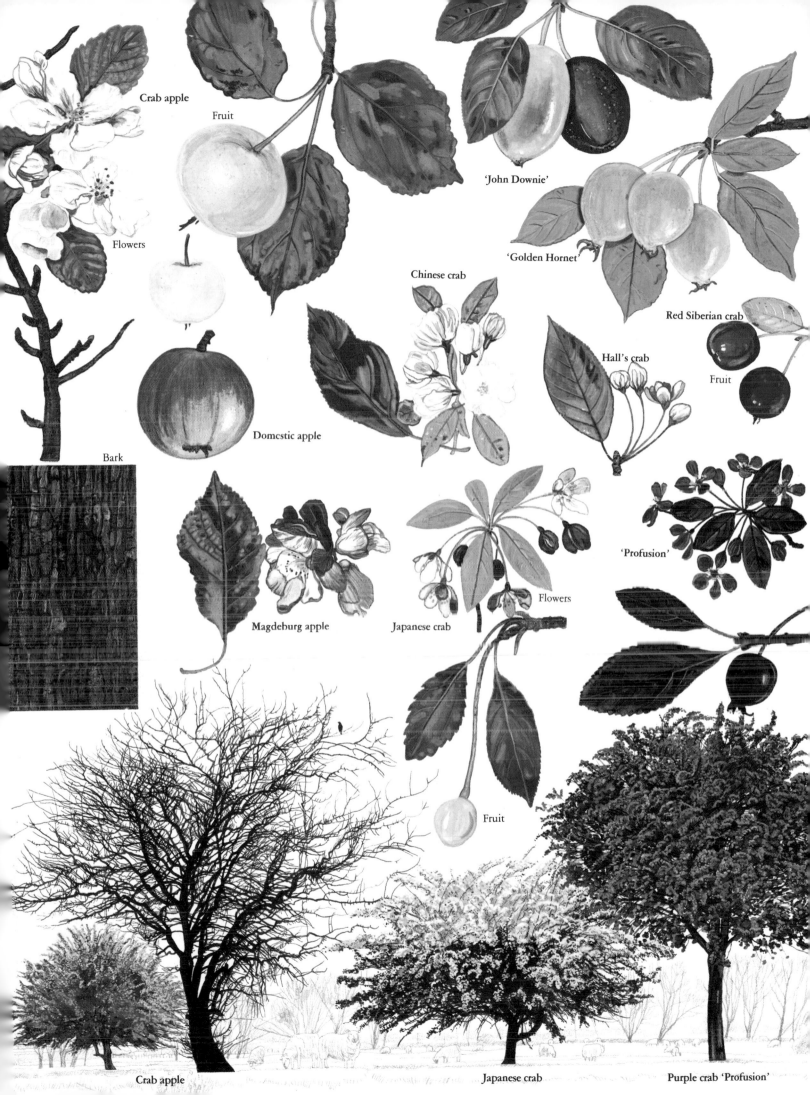

Crab apple

Fruit

Flowers

'John Downie'

'Golden Hornet'

Chinese crab

Red Siberian crab

Hall's crab

Fruit

Domestic apple

Bark

Magdeburg apple

Japanese crab

Flowers

'Profusion'

Fruit

Crab apple

Japanese crab

Purple crab 'Profusion'

Pear and Snowy Mespil

The pears are a small group of Old World trees with white flowers that open before the leaves unfold, and fruit with abundant grit-cells. Their wood is dense, very hard and strong and takes a good polish. It is used in turnery and any that can be spared for burning makes a first-class fuel, burning hot and slowly with a pleasant scent.

The **Common pear** (*Pyrus communis*) is probably not a native of Britain, at least in the form commonly found. These trees are descendants of orchard pears which have long been naturalized and which derived originally from hybrids between the wild pear and other species from southern Europe. The truly wild form, found in south-western England, is *Pyrus cordata*, which has little three cm leaves deeply heart-shaped at the base and globular brown fruit speckled white. A specimen in Kew Gardens was 16 m × 56 cm in 1976. The Common pear as a wilding is occasional in hedgerows and at the edges of woods and may be thorny. As a garden tree it is frequent in city parks and usually has a good bole many metres long and branches that originate ascending quite steeply before arching out bearing clusters of short spurs. The bark is very dark brown or black cracked into small, shallow, square plates.

Willowleaf pear (*Pyrus salicifolia*) grows in the Caucasus regions of Russia, Turkey and Iran and was introduced to Britain in 1780. It is naturally pendulous in the outer crown, and 'Pendula', the low-crowned plant with steeply-arched branches that is seen most frequently, is actually 'weeping', although some trees are indeterminate. Some of the tallest may be the wild type, like the 14 m trees in Holland Park, London and Kelvingrove Park, Glasgow. The most weeping trees achieve about half that height. This plant is at its best when the flower-buds are nearly ready to open, for each bud is tipped bright red, but when the flowers open white they are lost among the silvery opening leaves. In its leafless state 'Pendula' is unattractive, and in late summer its leaves lose their brightness so this tree, now very popular in small gardens, is difficult to place. It looks best overhanging a small pool or as a spring feature shining out against dark yew hedges.

The **Snow pear** (*Pyrus nivalis*) is a more strikingly white tree in spring than the Willowleaf, but is dark green in summer. It is thornless and not weeping and has leaves nearly as broad as they are long. It comes from south-eastern Europe and is rare.

The **Ussuri pear** (*Pyrus ussuriensis*) from China, Korea and Mongolia, is less scarce and a much bigger tree. It grows easily from seed and is soon making shoots over one m long, with erect branches, dark purple shoots speckled white and long, slender spurshoots often spined at the tip. The leaves are dark yellowish-green, glossy with a dark red tinge and turn pale orange very late in autumn. One tree at Winkworth Arboretum in Surrey at the foot of a steep bank is 15 m × 50 cm and is very handsome in flower.

Almondleaf pear (*Pyrus amygdaliformis*) from southern Europe is often written off as a bush of no merit, but at Benenden Grange in Kent it is the showpiece when in flower. It was planted in 1920 and in 1981 it was 15 m × 70 cm. In early spring it is a tower of white flowers.

The **Chanticleer pear** (*Pyrus calleryana* 'Chanticleer') is the best of all pears, with so many great merits that its growing popularity can only accelerate as quickly as supplies permit. The Chinese species from which this was selected by Ed Scanlon of Cleveland, Ohio, had already given the splendid, densely ovoid-crowned, glossy leafed 'Bradford' which adorns so many downtown precincts in the USA.

'Chanticleer' is narrowly erect, very like the Pillar apple, and like it also is exceedingly tough, robust and vigorous. It is early into flower with silvery foliage unfolding before the flowers fade. The leaves are soft grey-green and become shiny, and through the summer some of them turn yellow and red. In the autumn, most of the rest turn yellow, orange, red and crimson and meanwhile at least some trees put out more flowers. Then the coloured leaves fall but some remain evergreen for a month or two.

Stranvaesia (*Stranvaesia davidiana*) is a tall shrub or small tree from China related to the thorns. It is more or less evergreen but among its dark leaves there are always some which are orange or red, and some plants colour all over in autumn. It bears masses of fruit even when growing in some shade and they last well, not being of much interest to birds. It can be 13 m tall and, like many of its relatives – the pears, whitebeams and others – it can be attacked by the fungal disease fireblight, killing the flowers.

The **Snowy mespil** (*Amelanchier lamarckii*) may be a garden hybrid or an obscure American species and has run wild on sandy commons in the south of England, spread by birds eating the berries. It is bushy as a garden-escape but in old gardens it may grow into a nine m tree with a dark-barked, sinuous, clear bole. In mainly sandy areas like south-western Surrey it is abundant as a suckering shrub, often self-sown, but it is scarce in northern England.

The flowering is about the best of any tree for marking the earliness or otherwise of the seasons, because it is easily seen when the flowers open. They all open within a few days on any one plant and all the plants flower together. It takes a very early season to bring them out before March is over and a late one holds them back until early May.

Willowleaf pear   Snow pear   'Chanticleer' pear

'Bradford' pear

Snowy mespil

Ussuri pear

Willowleaf pear

Fruit

Heartleaf pear

Common pear

Fruit

Almondleaf pear

Spring

Winter

Bole

Almond, Cherry and Blackthorn

The **Almond** (*Prunus dulcis*) is the first big-flowered tree of the cherry group to open its flowers, which it does several weeks after the opening of the massed little pale flowers of Myrobalan plum forms. In areas noted for early flowering, like London, Exeter and Torquay, there will be almonds out in late January in very early seasons but more usually it is late February: in late areas like rural Surrey and much further north it is often late March. The usual form in parks and gardens is not the one grown for fruit, which is usually white-flowered, but an old selection or the hybrid with the peach, with earlier and larger flowers, *Prunus × amygdalo-persica* '**Pollardii**'.

Almonds suffer much from the fungus that causes peach-leaf curl, turning leaves bright red and puckered then brown and black. The fruit hang black and unsightly into the winter. The tree is often short-lived and the best displays of flowers are likely to be in relatively recently built-up areas. Fading flowers have white petals and red stamens and appear at a casual glance to be another species.

The **Apricot** (*Prunus armeniaca*) came long ago from China despite its supposed origin in Armenia. To yield good fruit it needs to be grown against a wall. The **Peach** (*Prunus persica*) is also, contrary to its botanical name, of ancient Chinese origin, having been brought along the old trade-routes to western Asia and later to Europe. The form grown against a wall for fruit has pale pink single flowers but 'Klara Mayer' makes a fine little tree well covered in rich pink, double flowers in close clusters along slender shoots.

Bird cherry (*Prunus padus*) is native to Scotland, Ireland, Wales, northern England and parts of the Midlands. It is most common by streams high in the limestone mountains of the Pennines and Cumbria and in Scottish glens. Bird cherry is very attractive in flower in June and in its soft yellow and amber autumn colours. It is planted in some gardens in the south and sometimes in streets where it needs to have been trained in the nursery, for it tends to be bushy with more than one stem.

Much more commonly planted is the coarse growing form '**Watereri**' which can be 18 m tall. Its bigger leaves are scattered along whip-like shoots, but it can be a fine sight in flower in good years. The flower-spikes are 15–20 cm long and curved. 'Colorata' is a gem when in flower but dull in summer and not strong in growth. The **Saint Lucie cherry** (*Prunus mahaleb*) from Europe is not often seen, but can be a tree of 12 m and splendid in flower, when the fragrance can be appreciated over a wide area.

The **Black cherry** (*Prunus serotina*) grows in one form or another from Nova Scotia to Arizona and in Guatemala, Ecuador and Peru. In Michigan and in the Great Smoky Mountains of Tennessee it is often 35 m tall. It was introduced in 1629 but is not often seen as a big single tree, when it can be 20 m × 60 cm. More frequently, it seeds itself around in thickets on the edges of estates or on commons. This is because it was at one time planted as cover for pheasants and to provide them with a supply of the berry-like cherries. Many other birds eat them too and the seeds are spread widely, but the seedlings seem to thrive only in good but light soils. They grow very fast with shoots sometimes two m long, but they do not often go on to make good trees in these conditions, and in gardens they have to be cut back or removed as too invasive. *Serotina* means 'late', but it is not notably late in leaf in Britain, although the flowers do not open until late May; this is later than the related species it grows with in America. The midrib on the underside of the leaf is ornamented with pale orange or white hairs both straight and at right angles to it in little groups.

The **Manchurian cherry** (*Prunus maackii*) was introduced in 1910. It belongs to the Bird cherry group, which has small white flowers gathered on spikes and includes the familiar, coarse but cheerfully foliaged Cherry laurel and the more elegant, dark-leafed Portugal laurel. The spikes of the Manchurian cherry are short, about four cm long when the flowers first open, and the crowded one cm flowers make it nearly globular or beehive-shaped. The flowers have a strong sweet scent, and open early in May when the tree is newly into full leaf. Young trees are narrow and upright and if they are grown closely among other trees they remain quite narrow with small branches. If grown in the open, however, they have a few big, spreading branches and are as broad as they are high, with the branch ends bending low.

The Manchurian cherry grows rather too fast for its own good, for its attraction is the beauty of the bark of the young tree, smooth and silky honey-brown. But within 30 years it is on a stem 50 cm through and part of the expansion comes from broadening grey fissures. The coloured parts between them become dark orange and much of the attraction is lost.

Blackthorn (*Prunus spinosa*) is a spiny suckering shrub wild all over the British Isles, but it can be trained into a small tree and is sometimes seen in gardens in this form. The red-leafed form 'Purpurea' is more inclined to be a tree and can be eight m tall. The wild bush is valued by those who like sloes, which are the fruit, and by those who like longtailed tits, as it makes a low, relatively dog-proof nesting place they greatly favour. It is a great ornament to countryside hedges when it is in flower.

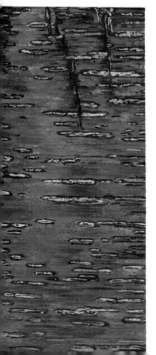

Manchurian cherry

Black cherry 22m

Almond Fruit

Apricot

Waterer's bird cherry

Saint Lucie cherry

'Klara Meyer'

Peach

Purple blackthorn

Almond Bark

Bird cherry Bark

Blackthorn Sloe

Pollard's

Bird cherry 'Colorata'

Cherries and Cherryplums

The **Wild cherry** (*Prunus avium*) has an older, less academic name, Gean (with a hard 'G') in more general use in Scotland. It is a native tree of great value in decorative plantings and of some value to wildlife and for its timber. It grows very fast, preferring a fairly rich soil or one with some lime in it, but it grows acceptably on almost any soil. It has, while still making height, a form highly unusual in a broadleaf tree and frequent in the conifers, having rising branches in well-spaced whorls on the trunk with bare lengths between them. The shoots are wreathed in sprays of large single white flowers as the leaves unfold, and the little berry-like cherries are eaten by birds as they turn red in August. The leaves give a long autumnal display of yellow, orange and dark red.

The timber is very strong with a beautiful figure and takes a high polish, but is not durable out of doors. Growing trees for the furniture trade is a specialized side of forestry on a few estates in the Chiltern Hills. The Gean has a powerful, spreading but superficial root-system very ready to send up suckers. Its vigour suits it for use as the rootstock for grafts of the Japanese 'Sato' cherries and others, and it is universally so used but the suckering is a drawback. It can grow to over 30 m in 60 years but is short-lived.

The **Double gean** Plena', is a magnificent spectacle in flower, with long-stalked sprays of large, markedly double flowers below bright green opening leaves. The flowers open two weeks or more after those of the wild form, alongside 'Kanzan', diluting that strident pink most usefully, and they last for weeks. Although not quite as opulent as the double white Sato cherries, it can be 20 m tall whereas they spread out below six m.

The **Myrobalan plum** (*Prunus cerasifera*) is not known wild but has long been grown from Central Asia to the Balkans. In England it is common in semi-wild hedges and suburban gardens, a twiggy, bushy tree and the first to flower, covered in little white flowers among opening green leaves, in early February or in March in late seasons. It is commonly mistaken for the blackthorn, which should not open for a month or more after that time. It bears little red edible plums in some years.

Pissard's plum 'Pissardii' was found by Monsieur Pissard in Iran in 1880 and now pervades suburbia like privet. The very early starry white flowers from pink buds are pretty until the yellowish-brown leaves unfold among them, and spoil their effect. The leaves go on to make their gloomy, mud-purple splashes which disfigure every street and park for the rest of the summer. A much improved form, **'Nigra'** opens its rich pink flowers a week later and they last longer and escape

bullfinch damage. The leaves are even passable, being glossy and a true dark red.

Double cherryplum (*Prunus* x *blireana*) is a low, twiggy tree with leaves no better than Pissard's plum but it is redeemed by almost equally early flowers, fully double and coloured a rich rosy pink.

Sargent cherry (*Prunus sargentii*) from Japan is very common in towns, with a spreading head of stout red-brown branches much banded by lenticels and bearing short spurs, arching flatly from the Gean rootstock stem at two m. When Almonds have faded, Sargent cherries blossom forth as fine pink clouds of three to four cm single flowers in short-stemmed bunches of ten. The dark, sharply toothed and abruptly pointed leaves hang rather lifelessly in summer but are the first leaves to turn colour in the autumn, reliably displaying scarlet and then deep red. 'Spire' is a hybrid from the Sargent cherry, narrowly upright with small, pink, single, early flowers fading almost to white, a neat and·attractive small tree.

'Accolade' is a hybrid raised in Surrey from seed of Sargent cherry received from America in 1925, and has been much planted since 1950. Its soft pink, semi-double flowers begin to open on low, inner shoots by early February but the full flowering, more profuse every year is in March, two weeks before the Sargent cherry. It has slender, sparse dark leaves and whippy shoots.

The **Yoshino cherry** (*Prunus yedoensis*) from Japan wreathes its bare shoots in masses of large single flowers, at first pale pink then pure white and becomes loud with bees in early spring. Bullfinches make it almost a non-flowering tree in country gardens but it is spectacular in busy streets. Out of flower it is no ornament, poorly shaped and coarsely foliaged.

Winter cherry (*Prunus subhirtella* 'Autumnalis') opens its first flowers among the yellowing leaves of autumn, nearly white, and throughout the winter it opens more, pinker and semi-double, renewing them in periods between sharp frosts which kill them, until a final burst in April among the new leaves. It is an untidy sprawl of twiggy branches grafted on a stem of Gean. **'Pendula rubra'** opens all its dark pink flowers together in April on sharply down-curved weeping branches in an asymmetrical crown.

The **Tibetan cherry** (*Prunus serrula*) is grown for its bark, which is kept free of dark scales and in prime condition when it is stroked and admired, so planting by a busy path is best. 'Sheraton' cherries use this stem to carry heads of one or other of the opulent-flowered Sato cherries. The Tibetan cherry itself has small white flowers hanging among fully opened leaves.

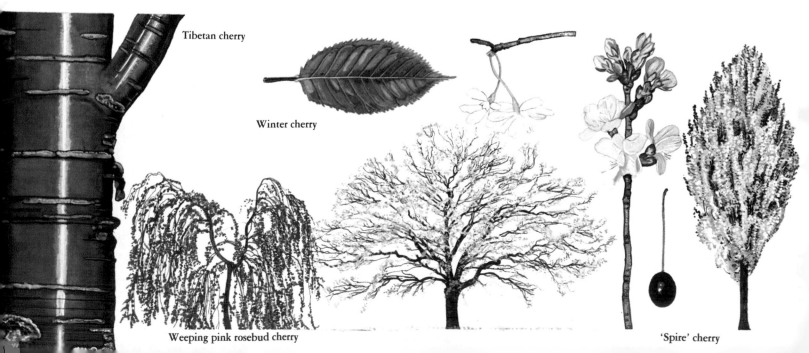

Tibetan cherry

Winter cherry

Weeping pink rosebud cherry

'Spire' cherry

Wild cherry

Sargent cherry

Myrobalan plum

'Accolade' cherry

Pissard's plum

Double cherryplum

Pink Pissard's plum

Tibetan cherry

Pink Pissard's plum

Yoshino cherry

Sargent cherry

Wild cherry

Japanese Cherries

The very floriferous, late-flowering, mostly double, Japanese cherries are selections from hybrids raised long ago in Japan and there known as 'Sato' cherries, or ornamental as opposed to eating-cherries. The precise origins are unknown so it is now the practice to give them only the cultivar name without ascribing them to any species. Formerly they were named as varieties of the Hill cherry (*Prunus serrulata*). They all have big leaves tapering to a fine point, and sharp, whisker-ended teeth. They begin to flower at the beginning of April in early years: the date varies by many weeks, but the sequence in which they come into flower is almost unchanging

The first is '**Shirotae**', a flat, widely-spreading, low tree with big, five–six cm pure white flowers in long-stemmed bunches below unfolding bright green leaves. They are single on young trees, becoming increasingly semi-double with age, and show a red eye before they fade. This tree is known even in the summer by the gloss on the bright green leaves.

Cheal's weeping cherry has a spidery crown of sinuous arching and hanging shoots, and fully double flowers with more petals than any other cherry except '**Asano**', which is the same thing upside-down, with sinuous, steeply-rising branches.

Next comes '**Taihaku**' with the biggest flowers of any cherry, often seven cm across, single, opening from a pink globular bud to pure white beneath dark red unfolding leaves. It had been lost for 200 years in Japan, but a dying tree was found in a Sussex garden in 1923. A few healthy shoots were taken for grafting by Collingwood Ingram, and every tree known in the world now derives from these. In summer it can be identified from its very oblong, dark, 20 cm leaf and strong growth of raised, spreading branches.

'**Ukon**' opens its flowers primrose yellow beneath khaki brown leaves at about the same time. They fade to white as the leaves go green, and then resemble those of 'Taihaku'. Similarly, they show a red eye are are nearly as big (six cm) but they are semi-double, with more than five petals.

'**Hokusai**' follows, with beautiful, large bunches of rose-pink, semi-double, short-stemmed flowers fading to blush-pink and opening to show a dark centre. In the autumn its leaves turn scarlet.

'**Kanzan**' has for a long time now been the universal, off-the-shelf Japanese cherry planted by the million. It achieved this popularity by its early strong growth and abundance of flower, weighing down the branches. The dark pink buds among dark brown unfolding leaves, however, are not pretty and they unfold the same colour.

These faults were rectified by a bumble-bee in the Bagshot nurseries in 1935. It crossed 'Kanzan' with 'Shimidsu' and made the only Sato cherry which has not come from Japan. It is '**Pink Perfection**' and its big globular red buds hang well below bronze yellow-green unfolding leaves in generous bunches. As the leaves turn green, the buds open to bright rose-pink and fade gradually to blush pink.

'**Shimidsu**', the other parent of 'Pink Perfection', begins to open its flowers with pink buds among unfolding leaves covered in violet hairs. The big bunches extend on long stalks as the leaves green and the flowers open snow-white, fully double with frilly petals. It is entrancingly beautiful but a poor grower.

'**Amanogawa**' is the tightly erect cherry, opening rather untidily with age and at its best when a few years old and encrusted with large bunches of wide open, semi-double, pink and white fragrant flowers.

'**Ichiyo**' is scarce but is a choice tree with a long season and hanging rows of big, pale pink flowers, each a flat circular disc with a green eye and semi-double. It grows very strongly into a tall, widely-spreading tree.

'**Shirofugen**' is the last to flower, and a fitting climax. Soft pink globular buds hang beneath rich dark-red leaves, and open to very big, double, frilled flowers, pink at first, then dazzling white. The leaves then turn green, and soon the flowers turn pink again. This tree grows very strongly with a flat crown of long, level branches drooping at their tips.

'**Pandora**' is not a Sato, but an early, single-flowered hybrid between the Yoshino and Rosebud cherries, of recent origin and with a neat, upright crown. It flowers a little after Pissard's plum and its flowers are much superior, paling from red buds to pale pink, soon becoming white, a little larger and more densely borne. It has dark green slender leaves which turn bright orange in the autumn.

'**Okame**' grows stout, twisting branches from its rootstock union at two m and crowds them with little bunches of tiny flowers right down to their bases. Having dark purple stems and calyces and very small, narrow, notched, deep pink petals, the effect is of a tree of dusky purplish-pink flowers. These open very early, often alongside those of the later Pissard's plum. It is a recent hybrid of the same origin, raised by Collingwood Ingram, as is '**Kursar**', which flowers about a week later. This has a more upright, open crown and the flowers have broad petals, making a bowl-shape of rich rosy pink. Although it has the same purple calyx and stem as 'Okame', the effect is of a bright pink tree of great charm.

(Numbers show normal sequence of flowering, early April to early May)

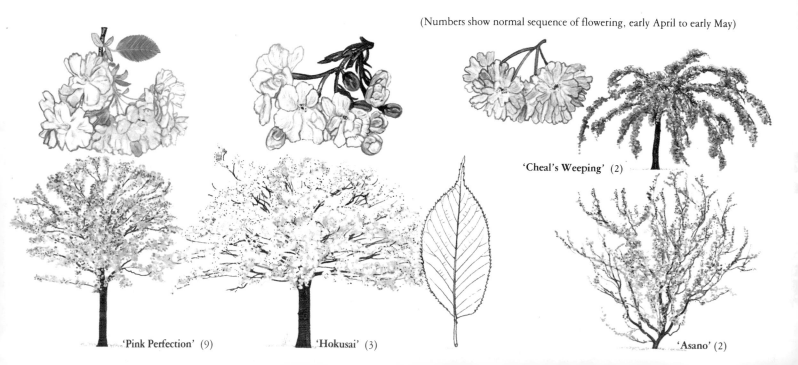

'Cheal's Weeping' (2)

'Pink Perfection' (9)   'Hokusai' (3)   'Asano' (2)

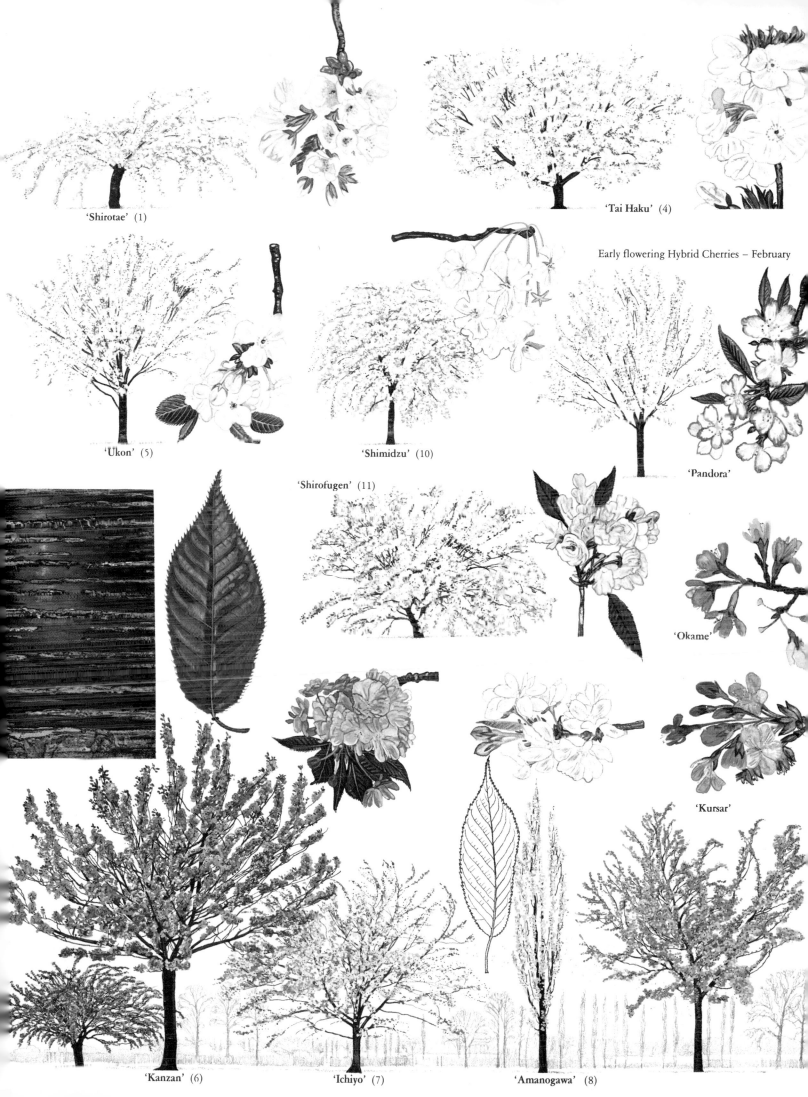

'Shirotae' (1)

'Tai Haku' (4)

Early flowering Hybrid Cherries – February

'Ukon' (5)

'Shimidzu' (10)

'Pandora'

'Shirofugen' (11)

'Okame'

'Kursar'

'Kanzan' (6)

'Ichiyo' (7)

'Amanogawa' (8)

Cherry Laurel and Laburnum

The **Cherry laurel** (*Prunus laurocerasus*) is often referred to as just 'the laurel' but it is a Bird cherry and the true laurel – Poets' Laurel – is the Bay with its own, quite different Family. The leaf of the Bay is the one to put in stews; the cherry laurel leaf is better in a killing-bottle for insects. With its sweet almond scent when crushed, it yields a little hydrocyanic acid gas, enough for the insects in the bottle but harmless to people in the open. This plant from south of the Caspian and Black Seas has been in Britain for over 300 years and has largely taken over big tracts of the country, using every conceivable method of spreading: seeds, suckers and layers. Nothing else can grow in the shade of its evergreen crown or come up through the heavy, slow-rotting leaf-litter; trees on woods and hillsides on many estates, especially on good soils in warm, damp areas, have perished from its invasion.

Only *Rhododendron ponticum* is more pervasive, at least on sandy soils. The flowerheads are prominent in the winter and in mild spells appear about to open in February, but never quite succeed until April, when their heady, sweet scent travels far. Left to itself, this laurel will, in humid places, reach tree-size, up to 16 m × 70 cm. Most commonly in gardens and parks, however, it is a clipped bush. That makes the branching much more dense and in this state it is much favoured as a nesting site by song-thrushes and blackbirds.

'**Magnoliifolia**' with leaves to 30 cm long is sometimes seen as a tall bush in old gardens. '**Otto Luyken**' is a popular little shrub with small, dark, glossy leaves and prolific flowers in April sometimes followed by more in September. The **Portugal laurel** (*Prunus lusitanica*) is common as a hedge or as a small tree. In western parts it is sometimes a moderately large small tree, with a smooth or slightly scaling black bark. The very sweetly scented flowers open in mid-June and are very numerous on old trees.

Common laburnum (*Laburnum anagyroides*) was brought to Britain from its native southern Europe at least 400 years ago. Being thoroughly poisonous in all parts it had to wait until plants were valued purely as ornaments or it would probably have arrived sooner. It spreads itself by seeds and grows fast for a few years. It is usually very short-lived, a fact much appreciated by those who await an irre-futable excuse for felling it for its wood. The canary yellow sapwood and the well-figured brown heartwood polish well and make its wood sought after for turnery and carving. Few trees in fact live long enough to have a bole more than 50 cm across.

The **Scotch laburnum** (*Laburnum alpinum*) seems to be irrevocably burdened with that spurious adjective, but even were the more civil-ized 'Scottish' adopted, it would be only slightly appropriate. The tree comes originally from the southern Alps, but it does thrive par-ticularly well in Scotland, where big ones still survive from long avenues along main roads, especially in Angus on the Aberdeen to Perth road. It is a stronger growing, bigger leafed tree than the Com-mon laburnum and its flowers, opening two or three weeks later, are on longer heads up to 35 cm long, and more densely set although smaller.

The hybrid between these two laburnums, which is **Voss's labur-num** (*Laburnum* x *watereri* 'Vossii') has the best of both worlds. It has long tassels, even longer than in the Scotch, densely set, as also in the Scotch, but with the big flowers of the Common. These tassels can be 60 cm long and neither these nor the leaves deteriorate noticeably with age.

Adam's laburnum (*Laburnocytisus adami*) is for 50 weeks of the year about the ugliest, most untidy tree of all, but for the other two it is a bizarre and fascinating sight and a good conversation-piece. Monsieur Adam, at Vitry in France, grafted in 1823 a shoot of the dwarf purple broom, *Cytisus purpurea*, on to a leg of laburnum to make a mophead. Its early shoot was accidentally broken and it threw out shoots bearing mainly laburnum flowers of a new and unheard-of purplish pink. Later the plants from this, grafts in their turn, began adding some ordinary yellow laburnum flowers and some bunches of Purple broom shoots, leaves and flowers.

The **Judas tree** (*Cercis siliquastrum*) is one of the seven species and among the few in the entire vast family of Legumes to have simple leaves. The flowers grow on last year's shoot, the length of the branch bearing it and even on the bole. To be abundant they really need one hot June for them to be laid down in the bud followed by another hot spell in the middle of the next May to bring them out. So they are rarely at their best in Britain and then only in the south-east of England. In some years the leaves come out with the flowers, spoiling their effect. It becomes slow in growth but is long-lived, although old trees tend to lie down.

Mimosa or **Silver wattle** (*Acacia dealbata*) although very common on the Isle of Wight, in south Devon, Cornwall, the Isle of Man and in Ireland, is cut to the ground by hard winters in England. This makes little difference, however, for it seeds itself and also sprouts from the stump and grows back again at two–three m a year.

Mount Etna broom (*Genista aetnensis*) is a tree of ten m by Kew Green in London, but is normally only a tall shrub. The green stems do the work of leaves so the flowers stand out on the bare shoots in July.

Judas-tree

Cherry laurel

Portugal laurel

Common laburnum

Mimosa

Scotch laburnum

Voss's laburnum

Mount Etna broom

Cherry laurel

Adam's laburnum

Mimosa

Voss's laburnum

Locust and Pagoda Trees

The **Locust tree** is generally referred to as the 'acacia', a name which properly refers to the mimosas. The Americans, whose tree this is, call it 'Locust', 'Yellow locust' or, more generally, 'Black locust', while botanists and gardeners in Britain and worldwide call it the 'Robinia' after the French herbalist, Jean Robin. It is native to the Allegheny Mountains and middle Mississippi Valley, but is now found commonly in every state of the Union. It was brought to England by John Tradescant in 1638 and was, 200 years later, an enthusiasm of William Cobbett's. He raised these trees by the million and wanted everyone with an estate on soil too light for growing good oak to plant them, as they grow even more durable timber than oak on the poorest sandy soils.

This tree can be a nuisance in a garden because its vigorous growth is not confined to the main stem but shows also in root-suckers, which put up two m of spined growth in a year, far from the original tree. It comes in useful, however, when this vigour is channelled into growing a tree in sites too inhospitable for other trees. It tolerates great heat and drought and can flourish with its roots in dry soil under pavings and its top in a windy corner, hot in summer and cold in winter.

As a legume, its roots have nodules of nitrogen-fixing bacteria, so it can grow on sterile, and even hot, mine spoil-heaps. It does need warm summers and is not a good tree north of the English Midlands. It is good in cities and in industrial areas partly because it has a short season in leaf in England, where it is not hot enough to bring the leaves out before June. By the end of September it has begun to discard them before they have had too great exposure to soot or dust.

Unless there is a good warm period in June, the Locust tree cannot bear many flowers the next year and it needs another warm period in that year to open them properly. When this does happen, the tree is well covered in masses of highly fragrant flowers, but if there is cold weather instead, the leaves remain half folded and yellow and the flowers scarcely open. After a prolific season the tree is festooned all winter in ugly dark brown pods.

In the south, young trees achieve about ten m × 25 cm in ten years but very few old ones are 100 cm through so they either soon relapse into very slow growth or they die quite young. One does, however, survive from a 1762 planting at Kew, brought from the Hounslow estate of the Duke of Argyll to help start the botanic garden, when the Duke died.

The **Pink locust tree** (*Robinia* x *ambigua* 'Decaisneana') can be distinguished only when in flower or from its sticky young shoots. It grows reasonably frequently to much the same sizes, and also needs hot weather to develop its flowers well. It is a hybrid with a pink-flowered species from (necessarily in Locust trees) North America, that was raised in France in about 1860.

Mophead acacia (*Robinia pseudoacacia* 'Umbraculifera') is a spineless, globular-crowned little tree frequent only in the older suburban areas of London where it used to be the drill to cut it back annually to the top of the stump.

Golden acacia ('Frisia') is a feature somewhere in almost every recent planting scheme in southern England. The oldest British trees date from about 1950 and are now 14 m tall. Unexpectedly, the foliage greened considerably in the very hot summers of 1976 and 1983, while in normal cool summers it remains butter-yellow until turning orange for autumn.

'Fastigiata' or **'Pyramidalis'** is too severely upright and slender to be attractive, especially during the long season without leaves. It is often over 15 m tall but is not long-lived and is rarely seen to flower. **Single-leaflet acacia** ('Unifoliola') is an oddity seen in some parks and occasionally in suburban gardens. The large terminal leaflet makes the tree appear to bear only simple leaves but there are usually two little leaflets below it.

Rose acacia (*Robinia hispida*) is a low, widely suckering shrub on hillsides in the Allegheny Mountains, not normally producing seed. In gardens it is grafted on to Black locust and is grown either as a mophead or a broad shrub against a wall. The shoots and leafstalks are covered in purple spiny bristles as are also the calyx of the flower.

The **Pagoda tree** (*Sophora japonica*) is also called the 'Scholar's tree' because a schoolmaster in old China ranked sufficiently highly to be allowed this species planted on his grave. It comes only from China despite the botanical adjective 'japonica', and was first grown in Britain in 1753. The tree resembles a Black locust but differs in its warm brown bark and bright bluish green shoots without spines and in the leaflets which taper to a point. The widely branched flower-heads appear in Britain only on trees after about their fortieth year, but in warmer places like Washington DC where the tree had a big vogue in street planting, much younger trees flower well.

Weeping pagoda tree ('Pendula') was being sold 150 years ago by a Hammersmith nursery, but it is not known where they obtained it. The branches make the most complicated contortions before they bear the long, weeping shoots. It is found occasionally in most parts, but is probably nowhere bigger than one of two in the Knaphill Nurseries in Surrey, which is ten m × 63 cm.

Pagoda-tree 23m   Weeping pagoda-tree   'Rozynskyana' locust   Mophead locust

Rose acacia

Single-leaf locust

Pink locust, 'Decaisneana'

Pagoda-tree

'Frisia' golden locust

Fastigiate locust

Locust-tree 30m

Tree of Heaven and Honeylocust

The **Tree of heaven** (*Ailanthus altissima*) is not really deserving of its name since it attains no great height. *Ailanthus* means 'reaching to the heavens' and *altissima* means 'very tall', but the first Latin word was transferred from a taller species growing in Molucca and the last, like the English name, was presumably given to keep in line. This tree was introduced in 1751 from northern China and thrives remarkably well in the southern cities of England. It would thrive far too well were these much warmer for, in the hot cities from Washington DC to Atlanta and beyond, it is out of control. Spreading by seed and even more by long-distance suckering it has invaded gardens, vacant lots, road reserves and even sidewalks to a point well beyond what is reasonable.

In London squares and parks it rapidly makes a fine, clean pewter-grey bole marked by silvery or buff streaks, but soon afterwards it is 80–90 cm in diameter and is removed as it is liable to shed branches. A tree in Devon did achieve 100 feet (30.5 m) but it then blew down.

The leaves unfold very late in the season, deep red, and are scarcely fully out before the end of June. They fall early without colouring and the central leafstalks remain beneath the tree when the leaflets have rotted. Each leaflet has one or more large, broad teeth or small lobes at the base, with a raised gland on it. This is helpful because of the number of trees unrelated to Trees of heaven with similar big compound leaves – these teeth are unique to the Ailanthus species. The leaves on young trees and on sprouts from cut-back stumps can be 90 cm long with 43 leaflets, but the normal leaf is about 50 cm with 15 leaflets.

The trees are either male or female, and in most years the females bear multitudes of bunches of fruit, highly attractive when scarlet but very different when dismal brown and hanging on into the winter. The steps up to the top of the Mound Stand at Lord's Cricket Ground pass in effect through the crown of a female tree; and very pretty they look during the finals of competition cricket.

The **Downy tree of heaven** (*Ailanthus vilmoriniana*) was sent from west China to France in 1897, and one plant from that importation planted a year later at Kew is 17 m × 53 cm. The down that gives the tree its English name is on the underside of the leaflet and on the bright red leafstalk. Plants cut back hard may grow leaves one m long on shoots that have numerous soft green spines towards the tip.

The **Honeylocust** (*Gleditsia triacanthos*) has a natural range covering broadly the area of the Mississippi Basin, and is planted in almost every city in the United States as, together with the Ginkgo, it is the only tree to flourish in all the impossible places of downtown areas. In Britain it feels the need of hot summers and thrives mainly in Cam-

bridge, London and Chichester. The biggest, however, is in Victoria Park, Bath, 25 m × 130 cm (at 0.5 m).

The fruit are not often borne in Britain and keep to about 25 cm long, but in hotter regions they are 40 cm and prolific, causing some inconvenience on the paths in, for example, Central Park, New York. Non-fruiting forms like 'Moraine' are now favoured there. The autumn colour should be a good gold but it is fleeting in Britain and the merits of the tree are its tolerance of hot dry places and its pretty leaves, although the ferocious, bunched spines have their advantages.

'Inermis' lacks those spines on the bole and so is the one usually planted in streets. Instead, it has curious raised flanges of bark. It grows to the same size as the Honeylocust and flourishes best in the same areas and sites. A specimen at Emmanuel College, Cambridge, is 24 m × 74 cm and one at Avenue House, Barnet, is 22 m × 69 cm. 'Sunburst' was raised in the Middle West of the United States in about 1950. Although the leaves green as they age, it is a very bright green and new leaves unfold through most of the summer. It is becoming popular for small gardens in southern England.

The **Kentucky coffee tree** (*Gymnocladus dioicus*) ranges from Lake Ontario to Arkansas and, like the Honeylocust, is a legume without the customary pea-flower. It tends to be found more in long-established city parks than in gardens. There are ten in Battersea Park and one or more in Finsbury, Victoria and Regent's Park, London. One in Brompton Cemetery, London, is 12 m × 43 cm. These trees occur west through South Wales, and there is even one in County Cork, but none north of the Jephson Gardens, Leamington Spa, Warwickshire.

The leaves unfold pink and may be 115 cm long. In autumn the leaflets turn yellow and fall away to leave the common stalk on the tree. Male and female flowers are on different trees, small white stars streaked with green, but are seldom seen in Britain so neither are the pods. The shoots are remarkably beautiful, being blue-green bloomed with violet, pink and purple, although they are stout and knobbly with buds.

The **Yellowwood** (*Cladrastis lutea*) comes from hill-country from North Carolina to Arkansas, but even there in its home woods and in nearby states it is usually a battered plant with a broken main stem. In Britain it probably does not live long enough to achieve that and is only occasionally above 12 m tall but it is grown as far north as Crathes Castle, in shelter on Deeside, and in Edinburgh. The markedly alternate placing of the leaflets is its most distinctive feature but it does flower in the south, late in the summer, and turns bright yellow in autumn.

Kentucky coffee-tree 17m

Yellowwood

Tree of heaven

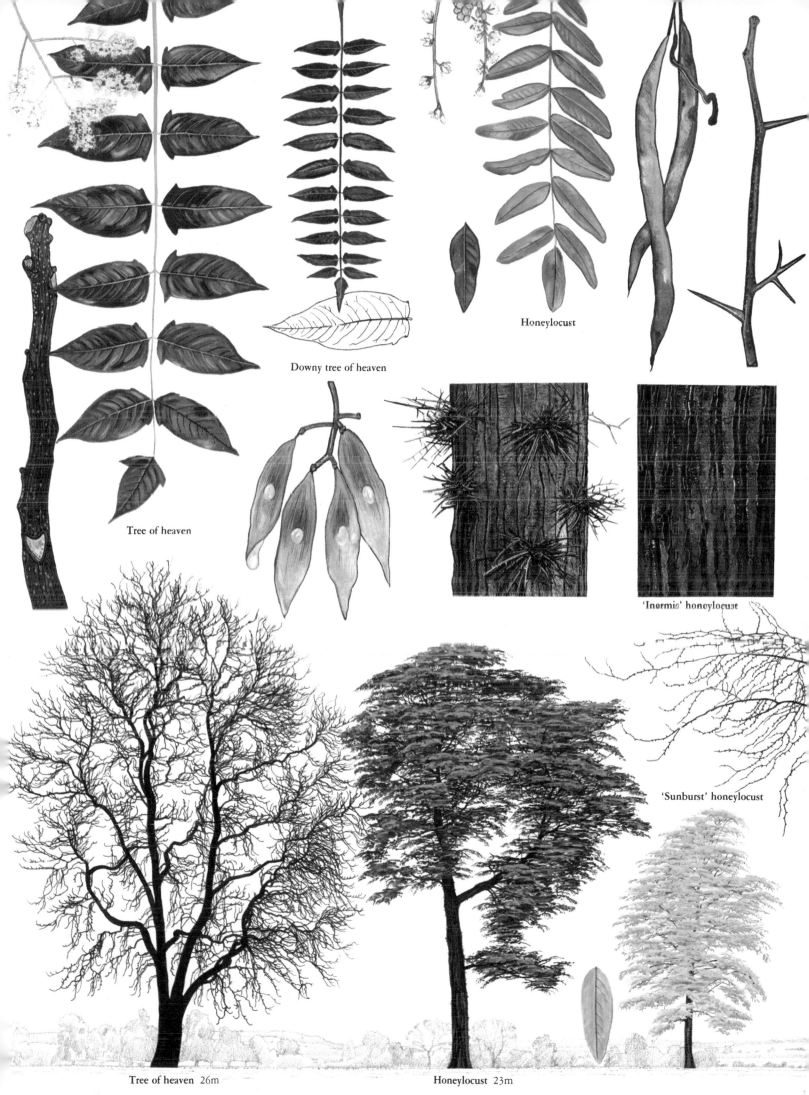

Downy tree of heaven

Honeylocust

Tree of heaven

'Inermis' honeylocust

'Sunburst' honeylocust

Tree of heaven 26m

Honeylocust 23m

Holly and Box

The **Common holly** (*Ilex aquifolium*) is a native tree growing on almost any soil, from what little there is among mountain streamside boulders to deep woodland soil and chalk. It will grow in the shade in oak and beech woods but has there a thin, open, straggling crown and can scarcely flower, while in the open hedgerow the trees are densely leafed, prolific in flower and, until old, conical with a spire top. The familiar strongly crinkled and spined leaf is usually replaced on old wood above the lower crown by elliptical leaves without teeth.

Every autumn a few trees are stripped early of their berries by birds, yet others nearby are, like the great majority, left alone. The berries are still there in May unless a long and very severe spell threatens birds with starvation. The buckled leaf distinguishes this holly and some of its forms from the hybrid group, the Highclere hollies mentioned below.

Laurel-leaf holly ('Laurifolia') grows the elliptical, flat, untoothed leaves from the start and makes a narrow crown of up to 20 m high. **Hedgehog holly** ('Ferox') has buckled and spined leaves with many rows of short spines on the upper surface. It is quite frequent, as is the variegated form 'Ferox Argentea' which has white margins and surface spines. **'Handsworth New Silver'** has small, very strongly toothed leaves, although they are nearly flat and have white margins. With its purple shoots it is very attractive.

'Pyramidalis' has smooth-edged leaves; big, thick and brighter green than most. As a female which flowers well it is splendid in autumn, its shapely conic crown laden with bright berries. **'Pendula'** has strongly-buckled leaves hung in regular alternation down the arbour-forming weeping shoots. It is a female, as is **'Perry's weeping'** which makes a delightful fountain of white-margined, cream-mottled foliage. **'Madame Briot'** has purple shoots and is female which saves us more of the inevitable banter about Silver Queen and Golden King which have their sexes reversed. **'Golden milkmaid'** is a name now loosely applied to several good forms with leaves well splashed centrally with gold but variously toothed. **'Bacciflava'** has normal and very dark foliage which sets off the lemon-yellow fruit and makes this a fine tree.

The **Highclere hollies** (*Ilex* x *altaclerensis*) arose at Highclere (which Latinizes as 'Altaclera') in Hampshire in 1838 but also arose at many other mansions at various times. The reason is that in these houses the generally tender Madeira holly (*Ilex perado*) was grown in the conservatory for its winter display of berries. In the summer their places were needed for more decorative hothouse plants so the tubs were hauled out and put on the terrace or in the kitchen-garden. This was also good for the Madeira holly and helped it to flower better. Then some gardeners, wanting to raise more of this holly for the winter, sowed the berries. But, being outside, the flowers had often been pollinated by bees coming straight from the Common holly around and so the plants raised were hybrid.

None is more robust than **'Hodginsii'** which can grow in industrial cities or exposed to the salt winds of sea-fronts as few trees can, and today shelters more promenade gardens and putting-greens than any other tree. In a little less exposure it is often a tree of 17 m × 50 cm. The leaves near the base have many straight teeth but a little above that they are down to an asymmetrical one or three, and all have a metallic greyish sheen from a distance. It is a male form with the flowerbuds prominent in purple bunches on the stem.

The equivalent female tree, **'Hendersonii'** has big berries although not in great numbers nor very bright red and its foliage is very dull green. Unfortunately this tree was the origin of the decorative **'Lawsoniana'**, which reverts to it all too often and thus needs watching, with the secateurs to hand. It also gave rise to **'Golden king'** which is therefore female but is seldom seen to revert. It differs from the gold-margined forms of Common holly in its solid, almost untoothed leaf, and is among the richest coloured of those with this pattern of gold.

'Wilsonii' has the most handsome, polished, boldly-toothed leaves of all, although some high in the crown are nearly entire. The new growth is purplish-brown and the shoots are green. **'Camelliifolia'** makes a narrow, conical tree to 15 m, with whorls of level branches. With its large, polished leaves and plenty of berries, it is a fine specimen tree. **Perny's holly** (*Ilex pernyi*) can be seen in a few big gardens in all parts as a slender tree to nine m with very few branches: its shoots are rather pendulous. New growth is pale brown and the flowers are yellow. **Himalayan holly** (*Ilex dipyrena*) is a sturdy tree, often with a stem forking low and a broad crown to 15 m tall.

The **Box** (*Buxus sempervirens*) was presumably the last tree to colonize Britain after the Ice Ages before the Channel opened up, and hence to qualify as a native. There are a few groves on the North Downs, the Chiltern Hills and in the Cotswolds. The best of these have shapely, narrowly conic-topped trees to six m with dense, hanging foliage and a clean bole. In gardens it is much more often a broad, not very densely branched bush.

The flowers open in mid-March and are unusual in their arrangement, there being five–six males around a central female. The wood is not only the heaviest of native timbers but the only one which does not float in water.

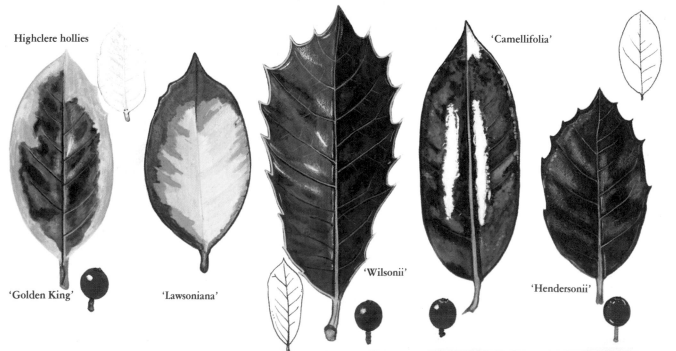

Highclere hollies

'Golden King'

'Lawsoniana'

'Wilsonii'

'Camellifolia'

'Hendersonii'

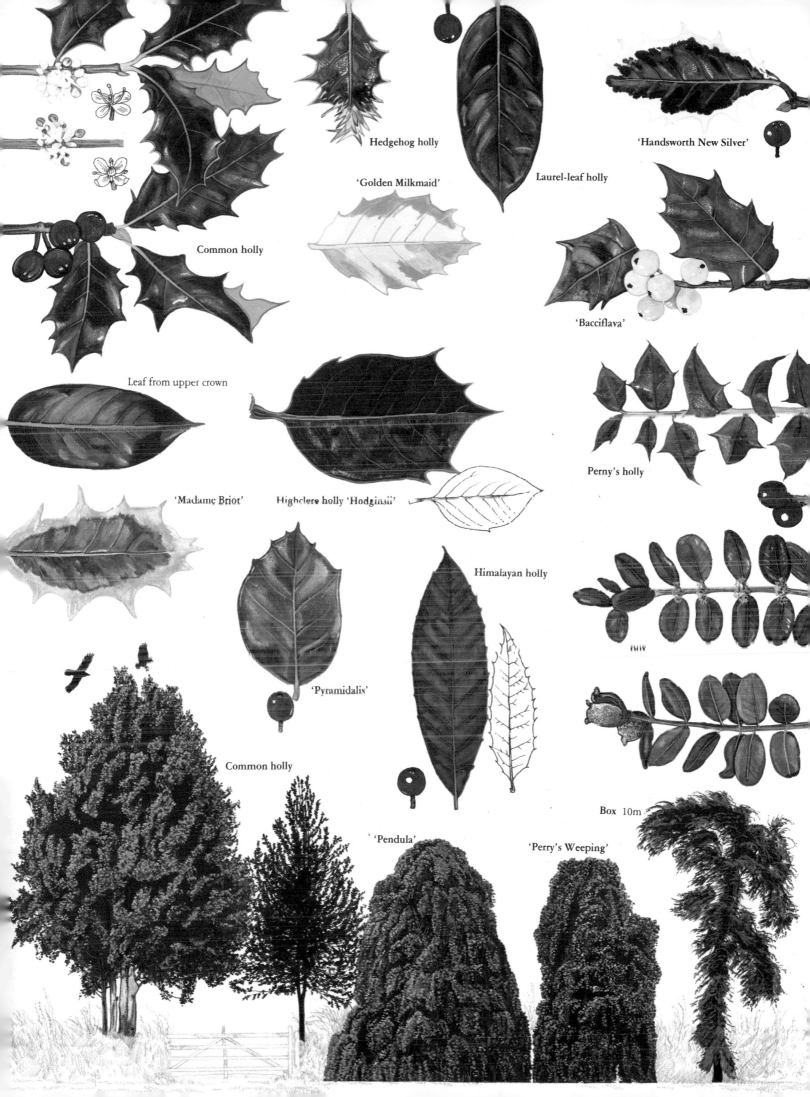

Hedgehog holly

'Golden Milkmaid'

Laurel-leaf holly

'Handsworth New Silver'

Common holly

'Bacciflava'

Leaf from upper crown

Perny's holly

'Madame Briot'

Highclere holly 'Hodginsii'

Himalayan holly

'Pyramidalis'

Common holly

'Pendula'

'Perry's Weeping'

Box 10m

Norway Maple

The **Norway maple** (*Acer platanoides*) was about the first tree to miss the land-connection between Continental Europe and Britain and so fail to reach there by its own efforts, when the ice had receded. It is not known when it was brought across the water but the date must have been after 1600 because it is a thriving and conspicuous tree, setting good seed quickly and yet the first note of it was not until 1683.

This species ranges widely across Europe from the Caucasus Mountains and occupies only a small area in the southern corner of Norway, so the reason why we use the name is obscure. For many reasons this is a tree of great importance in amenity planting. It grows with great vigour and health in every part of the British Isles, is easily raised and transplants well.

The Norway maple starts its displays very early, since the flowers, with big petals for a maple (some of which lack them) shine out, a brilliant acid-yellow, before most other trees have any leaves in late March or the first half of April. Its crown is very leafy but neither oppressive nor dull, and the colours in autumn are reliable and various. A few trees that are early to colour turn from orange to red; most turn butter yellow over a long period and some hold on to their leaves to turn a late orange.

Young trees should grow annual shoots one m long and sometimes two m. Soon after this they diffuse into a domed crown, and mature with a short bole bearing heavy low branches. The flowering is in every possible arrangement of the sexes, a few trees being either male or female. A branch may be of a single sex, a flowerhead may contain only one sex or both – one usually open before the other – and some flowers are perfect, with both together. In the winter small bunches of fruit-stalks remain at the tips of many branches.

Drummond's maple ('Drummondii') arose in a Stirling nursery in 1903 and is frequent in the better suburban areas. It should be watched closely with secateurs at hand because it usually throws a green-leafed shoot which, being stronger, and with more chlorophyll, will grow at the expense of, and eventually largely replace, the variegated crown. This form has a low, rounded crown and holds its leaves in dense layers.

'Cucullatum' makes a strongly upright growing tree of slightly curious, shrivelled aspect when in leaf. Towards the north-west corner of Kensington Gardens in London there is a group of five trees, all between 21 and 22 m tall.

'Dissectum' is a low, broad, dark-leafed little tree, usually planted in small groups. **Schwedler's maple** ('Schwedleri') is popular as a roadside and village green tree and in parks and gardens is sometimes 25 m tall. The winter-buds are dark red, as are the unfolding leaves, the flower-stalk and calyx and this colour suffuses the leaf in summer, turning to crimson and orange early in autumn.

'Crimson King' arose in Orleans in 1946 and has rich ruby-red leaves when the sun shines through them, as they have dark red undersides. The name is now also used for the inferior **'Goldsworth Purple'** and the true Crimson King is seldom found. 'Goldsworth Purple' is a seedling of Schwedler's maple and has bigger leaves, 15 cm × 20 cm, a dull green beneath with dark red veins. Their so-called purple upper sides make unsightly blotches in new plantings everywhere.

Lobel's maple (*Acer lobelii*) from Italy is, remarkably, a strictly fastigiate wild species and for its first 20 years or so it has very few, long, near-vertical branches with spurs but hardly a side-shoot and reaches 15 m in height. It opens out to some extent as it grows on to 25 m. It is distinguished by blue-white shoots and leaves held level with tapering twisted lobe-tips, and is often surrounded by suckers.

The **Sugar maple** (*Acer saccharum*) makes the most intensely flame-coloured orange-scarlet of all trees in the fall colouring in eastern America but has only a brief and uncertain display in Britain. It is not quite as rare as is sometimes thought, and some good trees in gardens have been passed over as Norway maples.

The Sugar maple is distinguished most easily by its dark-grey bark, which has two or three broad fissures and a tendency to become shaggy. The leaf is more deeply lobed and there is usually a band of dark purple around the shoot at each pair of leaves. The sap from a broken leaf-stalk is clear, where in Norway maple it is milky.

Heldreich's maple (*Acer heldreichii*) from the Balkans looks like a superior sycamore with deeply cut leaves, but its sharply-pointed, dark brown bud and its erect umbels of flowers show it to be from a different section of the maples.

The **Cappadocian maple** (*Acer cappadocicum*) is frequent in large gardens everywhere and occasionally found in streets. In woods it throws so many suckers which grow so tall that the parent tree can be hidden. One sucker at Westonbirt is 26 m tall. The well-domed crown is reliably covered in mid-October with a mass of butter-yellow leaves.

The **Golden Cappadocian maple** ('Aureum') is a bright and dainty young tree with bright gold new leaves among bright green early leaves, and is becoming popular. Old trees spend the summer a pale, dull, but pleasing yellow all over.

Lobel's maple 26m   Sugar maple 27m   Heldreich's maple 22m   Norway maple

Sugar maple

Heldreich's maple

Norway maple

Drummond's maple

'Aureum'

Lobel's maple

'Dissectum'

'Cucullatum'

Cappadocian maple

'Crimson King'

Schwedler's maple

'Goldsworth Purple'

Norway maple 27m

Golden cappadocian maple

'Goldsworth Purple'

Sycamore and Other Maples

The **Sycamore** (*Acer pseudoplatanus*) has been called the Great maple. This is a good name for it, since it is easily the biggest of the European maples, and the name 'sycamore' does not really belong to it. It means 'fig-mulberry' and has been transferred from a fig in the Middle East. In North America the name is used for the plane trees, while in Scotland the planes are called the 'sycamore'.

The sycamore ranges widely across the middle of Europe and was brought to Britain at an unknown time at least 400 years ago. It spreads itself rapidly by seed on good woodland soil and in gardens, even inside cities, where it is as impervious to pollution in the air as it is to salt-laden winds by the coast. It is liable to take over woodlands to the detriment of wildlife in general, for its leathery leaves make a mat which suppresses the flowers and grasses, and although heavily infested by greenfly in spring and autumn it is unattractive to birds.

The sycamore is a very long-lived tree and there are many huge specimens, but the best are curiously confined to Kent, Yorkshire, Lincolnshire, Dumfries and Galloway and the Highland glens. One of the two 'Birnam Oaks' near Dunkeld is a magnificent sycamore, 32 m × 237 cm. The wood is ideal for kitchenware as it is white, hard, can be scrubbed without the grain picking up, takes no stain from nor gives any taint to food. It also polishes well and can be cut to give the pretty grain used in string instruments.

'**Variegatum**' is an old, slow-growing variety frequent in old parks and gardens. '**Erectum**' is rather gaunt and of recent planting only. '**Purpureum**' is seen as a big parkland tree, passable when the wind flutters the leaves to show the greyish undersides tinged with purple. The form with the best colour is 'Atropurpureum' but one is enough in any garden.

The **Corstorphine sycamore** ('Corstorphinense') arose in that Edinburgh suburb in, it is said, 1600, and the original survives there. It is also seen in old gardens and parks. '**Worleei**' is an improved form which keeps its colour through the season and has red leafstalks. It has replaced the Corstorphine tree in recent plantings. '**Leopoldii**' originated in Belgium and is frequently planted. '**Brilliantissimum**' is often a mophead grafted at 1.5 m on a stem of ordinary sycamore, but at other times it is grafted lower and makes a big, broad bush to 12 m × 40 cm. The leaves begin to unfold bright red: they then go through a remarkable performance lasting two months, turning coral-red, shrimp-pink, pink-orange, pale orange, a good yellow, and then white before relapsing into very dull green.

'**Prinz Handjery**' differs only in somewhat less dense growth and in having a purple underside to the leaf in summer.

The **Horned maple** (*Acer diabolicum*), so-named from two styles persisting between the wings of the fruit, is Japanese and confined to collections. The parachute flowering is a feature and the purple-red, big-petalled female flowers of '**Purpurascens**' are notable. **Van Volxem's maple** (*Acer velutinum* var. *vanvolxemii*) from the Caucasus Mountains looks at first like a smooth-barked sycamore with outsize leaves. These can be 15 cm × 18 cm on a stout stalk 27 cm long. But its sharp, dark brown buds and erect panicles of flowers show it to be in another section of the maples.

The **Balkan maple** (*Acer hyrcanum*) is rare, but there are two in Silk Wood, Westonbirt, one of them 23 m × 60 cm; and one in Oxford University Park, 13 m × 38 cm. The long, slender leaf-stalk and the parallel-sided inner parts of the lobes help to identify it. **Trautvetter's maple** (*Acer trautvetteri*) looks like a pink cherry in full flower from a distance, when it bears many fruit in summer. It comes from the Caucasus region and its flowerheads and buds show that despite the similar leaf, it is not a sycamore.

Amur maple (*Acer ginnala*) is very resistant to cold and is common in Winnipeg, which proves it. In Britain it is as frequent in small gardens around country towns as in more formal gardens. It is among the first trees to change colour in autumn and the deep red leaves are shed early. It is either an open bush or a small tree on a twisting stem.

The **Tartar maple** (*Acer tataricum*) from south-eastern Europe is closely related to the Amur maple and has similar but more prominent flowers. It is a bush or low tree and, particularly when in flower, suggests a kind of thorn rather than a maple. The **Hornbeam maple** (*Acer carpinifolium*) from Japan makes a broad, open, bushy tree of great merit for its foliage, which is bright green in summer and gold in the autumn; and for its appearance when strung with slender catkins of bright green starry flowers.

The **Montpelier maple** (*Acer monspessulanum*) with its hard dark leaves looks evergreen but is not. It is slow-growing and scarce. One at the north end of the Serpentine in Hyde Park is 14 m × 57 cm and there is one at Inveraray Castle, Argyll. The biggest is in a field near St Briavels Common in the Forest of Dean (13 m × 70 cm). The **Cretan maple** (*Acer sempervirens*) looks evergreen and is. Its leaves show a variety of shapes.

The **Trident maple** (*Acer buergeranum*) from China has flaky, pale orange bark. The prominently three-veined leaves unfold covered in pale orange silky hairs, and are variably blue-grey beneath. Some trees bear a few leaves with one lobe or with none at all. The flowers are yellow on umbels.

Amur maple

Montpelier maple

Tartar maple

Hornbeam maple

Trident maple

Cretan maple

Fastigiate sycamore

Horned maple

var. *purpurascens*

Van Volxem's maple

Sycamore

Leopold's sycamore

Balkan maple

Trautvetter's maple

Golden sycamore 'Worleei'

Purple sycamore

Variegated sycamore 24m

Sycamore 35m

'Brilliantissimum'

Field Maple

The **Field maple** (*Acer campestre*) is the only maple native to Britain, although probably only strictly so in England northwards as far as Cumbria and to Wales, having been introduced early to Scotland and Ireland. It is a tree of chalk and limestone soils and is most common on and near the chalklands of southern England. It is often in a clipped hedge and that makes it grow a much higher proportion of its shoots with corky wings than is seen in uncut trees. When it grows into a hedgerow tree with plenty of room it has a large, domed crown of curved branches and straight shoots, to 15 m or more tall, and a stout bole to 80 cm diameter often much encumbered by burrs and sprouts. Uncut hedges grow to some nine m as bushes and these can show the best autumn colours, turning dark red and purple whereas the clipped hedge and the big tree turn gold to old gold and russet.

Although regarded as a small tree (the name 'Hedge maple' may suggest a bushy plant although it should only imply a tree that is found in hedgerows) this maple can be quite a big tree, over 25 m tall and with a trunk 1.2 m in diameter. New foliage unfolds pale pink in May and a second flush on sprouts and hedges in July unfolds bright red. A tough tree, able to grow in a city it is only in city parks that it is sometimes planted on its own. In a garden it is a little dark and dull in summer so is more likely to be placed as a background for late autumn colour. **'Postelense'** has new leaves in spring and summer bright gold turning dark green and is rare.

The **Oregon maple** (*Acer macrophyllum*) in fact extends far each side of that State, growing from well north in British Columbia south to the Mexican border. It was one of David Douglas's early introductions, in 1827, and a fine, handsome tree tolerant of most soils and all regions but had not been much planted until recently. This treee is also called the Bigleaf maple and no other can match a leaf 28 cm × 30 cm on a 30 cm stalk. The flower catkin is also somewhat outsize, 30 cm long and thick enough to bring to mind the fluffy grips on a church-bell rope. The nutlets in the fruit are covered by stiff, white bristles. The fruit are borne freely in large bunches. Autumn colour in Europe does not aspire to the rich orange shades seen in the riverside woods in Oregon, and is brief and fairly early, a biscuit colour, or darker brown. The bark on young trees is smooth and brownish purple, but soon grows orange fissures and divides into grey ridges, at first in a network but later making square grey blocks.

The **Italian maple** (*Acer opalus*) may look like a sycamore with its coarsely scaling orange-brown bark in the winter and in the summer, with its leaves differing only in their shallow, bluntly rounded lobes, but in the spring and the autumn it is patently another species. No sycamore has those large-petalled, soft yellow, hanging flowers, nor is there one with the same rich orange, yellow and brown autumn colour. The Italian maple comes from the south of Europe generally but it grows as well in Scotland as it does in England. It is, however, not very often encountered except for the small number in nearly all London parks. Two quite big specimens grow north of the lake in St James's Park. They flower in April, before most other trees except catkin-bearers and early cherries.

The **Rough-barked maple** (*Acer triflorum*) was so named to mark its prime distinction from the otherwise similar Nikko maple. The leaf is also smaller and each leaflet usually has a short, broad tooth but it has the same blue-white hairs beneath and the yellow flowers in threes. Sent from Korea in 1923, it has a reputation for brilliant red autumn colours but is seen only in maple collections.

The **Ashleaf maple** (*Acer negundo*) puzzles the general public continually and its American name 'Box-elder' is no help at all. Being very commonly planted in town gardens it is frequently seen and it is, with the Lucombe oak, the leaf most often sent for identification. It has a most remarkable natural range, being not only one of the very few trees to cross the Rocky Mountains in North America, but also extending coast-to-coast, although patchy in the west, and down to southern Mexico. It changes a little on the way, having little three-leaflet leaves in Arizona and softly hairy shoots in California that become almost furry in Mexico. It was sent to Bishop Compton in 1688 but is short-lived and no old tree is known. With age it sprouts from the bole and tends to lie down but young trees grow very fast. In Britain it is a dull-foliaged tree, although shining rich green in New England, so it is seldom planted deliberately.

The form usually planted is **'Variegatum'** a female clone with the most boldly white-variegated leaves available. Even the wings of the fruit are largely white, stained pale purple or pink. **'Auratum'** comes into leaf a rich gold and fades almost to green by the autumn but is a first class addition to many colour-plantings and town parks and gardens.

Miyabe's maple (*Acer miyabe*) was sent from Japan in 1895 and grows in some of the larger British gardens. The base of the leafstalk is so swollen that the pair meet round the shoot. It has yellow flowers hanging in slender racemes and the leaves, which can be 20 cm × 28 cm, turn clear yellow in autumn when their stalks turn red.

The **Vineleaf maple** (*Acer cissifolium*) is a rare Japanese three-leaflet maple growing a broad, low, tabletop crown on a 1.5 m stem with pale grey bark acquiring white patches with age.

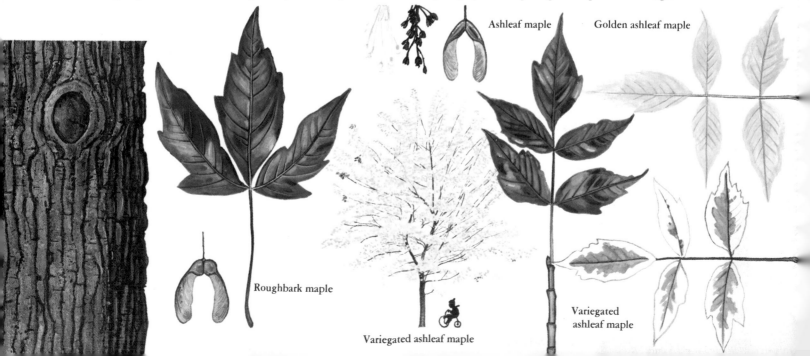

Ashleaf maple   Golden ashleaf maple

Roughbark maple

Variegated ashleaf maple

Variegated ashleaf maple

Miyabe's maple

Oregon maple

Field maple

Vineleaf maple

Italian maple

Cork-winged bark

Cross-section of
cork-barked twig

Field maple 25m

Golden field maple

Italian maple in flower 20m

Silver and Japanese Maples

The **Silver maple** (*Acer saccharinum*) occurs in nearly all the eastern United States as well as southern Quebec and Ontario. It is quite common in the south of England but gets progressively less frequent northwards until it is rare in Scotland. The leaves unfold a glossy red-brown two months after the flowers have faded. Seed, if borne at all in Britain, is shed by June.

Cutleaf silver maple (*laciniatum* 'Weiri') is a selection from a range of similar trees in the wild populations. More elegant and pendulous, with shiny brown shoots, it is used in town precincts, and there are large trees in some city parks.

Smooth Japanese maple (*Acer palmatum*) was brought out of Japan in 1820, when it was still a closed country, by Philip von Siebold, a privileged eye-surgeon whose services were highly valued. Often seen as a front-garden shrub, it grows in woodland gardens to over 15 m tall. There is variety in the size and detailed shape of the leaves and in the colours to which they turn in autumn: yellow, orange, scarlet or dark red. The bark is smooth and dark brown with a pattern of buff stripes. It is often grown in the form **'Atropurpureum'** or as similarly coloured forms. **'Osakazuki'** is greatly superior, with large, nine cm × 12 cm seven-lobed leaves, green in summer when the bunches of scarlet fruit hang beneath them, and flame-scarlet in October. Unlike other trees turning red in autumn in Britain, this needs no fully sunlit position to do so and not only is this quality valuable in a shady site but it means that all the foliage, shaded and unshaded, on the plant becomes equally scarlet.

The **Coralbark maple** ('Senkaki' – now usually 'Sangokaku') has prettily-cut little leaves which turn amber, pink and orange in the autumn but it is best known and most grown for the colour of the winter shoots. It is liable to be killed back somewhat by late frosts but pruned hard it makes longer shoots for the winter colour.

The **Downy Japanese maple** (*Acer japonicum*) grows into a small tree with many sinuous, upright, smooth grey stems, and 1.5 cm purple flowers in nodding bunches before the leaves unfold fully. **'Vitifolium'** is a bigger tree, to 14 m, with bigger leaves (up to 15 cm each way, or occasionally over 20 cm) and dazzling autumn colours. Wherever the sun strikes, the leaves are bright royal-red, those beneath are gold and some are green but turn violet or orange.

Golden full moon maple ('Aureum') is very slow to grow and only in the oldest gardens is it more than a low, rounded shrub. In the south it tends to scorch in full sun. It is expensive and not easy to establish but is worth the trouble for the way it ornaments rock-garden or small

border. The **Korean maple** (*Acer palmatum coreanum*) is a form of the Smooth Japanese maple, with low, shrubby growth noted for the long-lasting bright and deep red of its autumn colours.

The **Zoeschen maple** (*Acer* x *zoeschense*) is named from the German nursery in which it arose. It is a hybrid between the Field maple and the Cappadocian maple and inherits the suckering abilities of the latter. It seems to have been in commercial use from about 1870 and has been planted in several gardens that specialize in maples, although it has not become a tree of general use. It grows quite fast. At Talbot Manor in Norfolk a 17-year-old tree was 13 m × 30 cm and the bigger of two at Westonbirt was 16 m × 64 cm (at 0.5 m) when 53 years old. A good tree at Winkworth Arboretum in Surrey is 14 m × 50 cm when about 45 years old. The petal-less flowers are yellowish-green in erect rounded heads and the fruit are five cm across the pink-flushed, level wings.

The **Nikko maple** (*Acer nikoense*) has the largest leaves of the trifoliate maples – those with three-parted leaves – each leaflet being about 10 cm × 4 cm. They have dense blue-white hairy under-surfaces and the stalk is densely hairy pink-brown. The bark is smooth and dull grey. This is a sturdy tree but slow-growing and of 15 specimens around 50 years old at Westonbirt, the biggest is 15 m × 40 cm. One at Sheffield Park, Sussex, near the gate is 15 m × 42 cm. It is mainly in such major gardens as these that the tree is seen and it is planted largely for the bright red late autumn colours. In Japan its native woods are on limestone so it is usefully tolerant of chalk where other Japanese maples may not do so well. The flowers are cup-shaped with broad yellow petals and hang in threes in early May.

The **Paperbark maple** (*Acer griseum*) was sent from China in 1901 and was little planted for the next 30 years only because little seed could be imported and seed on the trees in Britain was seldom fertile. Imports from Italy and elsewhere have allowed the tree to be more widely available but it is slow to start and there are shortages in the trade in some years. The striking bark of well-placed, fine trees in many famous gardens such as Stourhead, Bodnant and Leonardslee, as well as in Preston Park, Brighton and Howick, Northumberland, brings the tree into public prominence. It may make a shoot of 40 cm a few years after planting but it soon returns to slow growth and a tree 12 m tall is a rarity. So also is one with a proper bole to show the bark off well and it is extraordinary how so many who have planted a tree have not bothered to give it a respectable bole, but have left it to fork low into two or three or to grow big low branches.

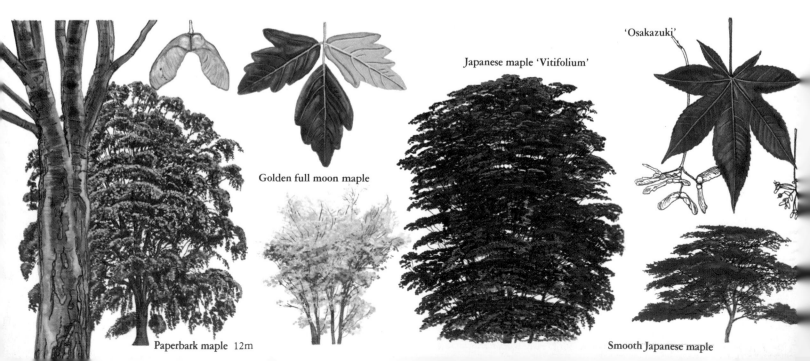

'Osakazuki'

Japanese maple 'Vitifolium'

Golden full moon maple

Paperbark maple 12m

Smooth Japanese maple

Smooth Japanese maple

Leaf variant

'Atropurpureum'

Korean maple

Silver maple

Coralbark maple

'Osakazuki'

Japanese maple 'Vitifolium'

Zoeschen maple

Cutleaf silver maple

Nikko maple

Silver maple 30m

'Atropurpureum'

Red and Snakebark Maple

The **Red maple** (*Acer rubrum*) was among the earliest trees to be brought to Europe from eastern North America, where it grows almost everywhere from Newfoundland to mid-Texas. It was introduced in 1656 by John Tradescant the younger and in all that time has never become a common tree although it is moderately frequent in all parts, and is hardy, adaptable and highly desirable. Although flowering abundantly and regularly, it sheds what little seed it bears by July and even if that is collected, it is rarely of good quality. The name 'Red maple' was not given it for its autumn colours but for its flowers. They open from mid-March for a month or so, from well before until the start of the unfolding of the leaves. The tree may appear to change its sex once or twice during that time as succeeding waves of flower alternate between male and female on some trees or branches.

The Red maple's autumn colour in America is highly variable. Hillsides as far as the eye can reach are often solid scarlet, yet in a roadside group adjacent trees can be brilliant gold, bright red and the deepest rich purple. In Britain, young trees tend to colour best, through bright red to deep red and older trees turn gold before some or all of the foliage turns red: in some the gold is pale and the red fleeting. The crowns of old trees are at best untidy, with slender, whippy shoots curving at odd angles and they are liable to become mis-shapen through damage. In places they carry mistletoe.

One way to be confident of a less straggling crown is to plant **'Scanlon'**. When in charge of tree-planting in Cleveland, Ohio, Ed Scanlon formulated strict criteria for good street trees and spent the rest of his life finding and selecting them. Typical of these, this maple has a neat crown and good, bright autumn colours.

Père David's maple (*Acer davidii*) is typical of the Snakebark maples, a fascinating group of small trees all but one of which come from China and Japan. (The exception is the Moosewood from eastern America.) Père David's maple comes in at least four very different forms, all of which grow very rapidly when young with shoots one m long. They fan out to make a cascade of long shoots and attain no great height. The two most often seen both have the dark red shoots striped chalky white, but their leaves differ greatly. One has slender, lanceolate leaves 15 cm × 8 cm long turning orange in the autumn, and the other, known as 'George Forrest' has broad ovate leaves with a few small lobes, blackish green in summer and with no marked autumn colour.

The **Red snakebark maple** (*Acer capillipes*) has red shoots and scarlet leafstalks. Its leaves differ from those of other snakebarks in having a longer central lobe, prominent and numerous parallel veins and glossy green upper surface with, like Père David's maple but unlike the others, little red pegs in the angles of the basal veins beneath. It also has one of the brightest of the barks and rich orange and scarlet colours in autumn. It has been planted in many gardens but tends to suffer from rot at the base and succumb after about 50 years of life.

The **Moosewood** (*Acer pensylvanicum*) grows from Nova Scotia to Georgia and has been in Britain since 1755. It has never become common, perhaps because it has so often been short-lived, but although less elegant than the Asiatic snakebarks, it makes the most impressive tree. It can be known from afar by its apparently blue-white trunk and stems holding large, luxuriant, rich green foliage. In autumn its leaves turn early to a pale, bright yellow and fall early. Like the other snakebarks it bears large numbers of paired catkins early in life, strung with little fruit in the summer.

Hers's maple (*Acer hersii*) has the greenest bark in this group with the clustered fine blue-white lines making prominent stripes. It also has green buds and almost everything about the tree is olive-green. The fruit are bigger with broader wings than in any other, and just as copiously borne. In autumn, however its leaves turn bright orange and crimson. It is probably the snakebark seen most frequently in new plantings.

The **Grey-budded snakebark maple** (*Acer rufinerve*) differs from the others in that its buds on the spur-shoots are blue-white, its leaves are broader than long, with faint rusty hairs or stains in the vein angles beneath, and in its largely grey bark with pink fissures in some trees. The arched top branches show autumn dark reds before the rest of the crown and shed their leaves first.

Hawthorn maple (*Acer crataegifolium*) is a slender-stemmed little tree from Japan with thin branches holding crowded little spur-shoots on their upper sides and a red stain or tinge about all its foliage and red veins. The stem does not grow big enough to show a full snakebark and is dark red and grey with some narrow white stripes.

Forrest's maple (*Acer forrestii*) is a rare Chinese tree with polished rich green and white snakebark, and scarlet stalks on its long-pointed dark leaves. The foliage hangs on long, weeping, scarcely branched shoots making a splendid cascade, but it is not usually a good grower.

The **Birchleaf maple** (*Acer tetramerum*) spreads from China into Burma and Tibet. Its foliage and sometimes its bark suggest a snakebark but it is in a different section of the genus. A strange tree, it sends up five or six vigorous willowy stems and seems healthy enough yet seems never to exceed 15 m except for one in Wisley Gardens on Battleston Hill which is 19 m.

The **Limeleaf maple** (*Acer distylum*) from Japan holds its flower-spikes vertical and has hard, substantial leaves. It is grown in only a few collections.

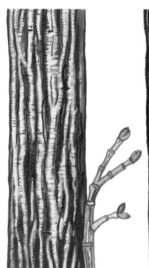

Pere David's maple   Red snakebark maple   Moosewood   Hers's maple   Grey-budded snakebark maple

Snakebark maples

'Ernest Wilson'

Moosewood

Red snakebark maple

'George Forrest'

Small-leaf form

Pere David's maple

Birchleaf maple

Grey-budded snakebark maple

Red maple

Lime-leaf maple

Forrest's maple

Hawthorn maple

Hers's maple

Red maple

Red maple 23m

Fastigiate red maple

Pere David's maple 15m

Horse Chestnut

The **Horse chestnut** (*Aesculus hippocastanum*) masquerades very successfully as a native British tree without which no village green nor rectory lawn is complete. It was even featured as one of four 'British Trees' on a postage stamp set, although it was unknown even to botanists until 1596. It was introduced between 1605 and 1617 and is native to a few mountains in Greece and Albania. It does not really look like a native of Britain when laden with thousands of big panicles of showy flowers. A point about the flowers which has only recently been made is that the blotches are yellow on a newly open flower and become crimson once it has been pollinated, usually on the same day or the next.

The wood is among the best for both toys and artificial limbs because it is light, works easily and does not splinter or have a sharp and dangerous fracture. On the other hand its weakness gives rise to one dangerous feature of the tree. A sudden shower of rain adds to the weight of the foliage, and this is often sufficient to break out a heavy limb without warning just when there may be people sheltering within the danger zone. After a July thunderstorm a big tree may often be seen with a large branch lying beneath it.

There is great variation in the time in spring when the leaves and flowerheads expand. Many districts have one tree that is almost in leaf and flower before March is out but the others are still in bud until the end of April with flowers that open by mid-May.

Although this is often a tree with a short life – and trees about 150 years old and one m in diameter may decay and collapse, especially where the crown has been cut back over many years as in some street trees – there are some true veterans. A line of four at Busbridge Lakes, near Godalming, Surrey, said to date from 1664, was in good order in 1963 with the best trees 30 m × 170 cm and 38 m × 129 cm. A tree at Castle Ashby, Northamptonshire, planted in 1762, was 31 m × 171 cm in 1983.

Horse chestnuts in public places can be a source of danger in conker-time from the fall-out of assorted missiles. A few chemicals have been tried that might prevent the fruit from forming, but so far without practical success. The alternative now frequently adopted is to plant the double-flowered **'Baumannii'** which is sterile, although some consider this if not unsporting at least missing an important autumn feature of the tree. The flowers of 'Baumanii' are frilly and pretty but not, from a distance, any more showy than those of the single form. Out of flower this tree can be known only by the evident sign of grafting on an otherwise ordinary horse chestnut or by its local reputation as being useless for conkers. A remarkably big one (32 m × 122 cm) is on the edge of a group by the picnic area at Westonbirt. In a fine line of seven in Henrietta Park, Bath, the biggest by a small margin is 26 m × 117 cm.

The **Red horse chestnut** (*Aesculus* x *carnea*) probably arose in Germany as a hybrid between the Common horse chestnut and the American red buckeye (*Aesculus pavia*) and was being marketed in 1820. By a quirk in its genetics it is not only fertile but breeds true despite its hybrid origin, although that only ensures that each new plant is as dull as its parents. Most of the trees seen are grafted, anyway, at 1.3–two m on a stem of the common horse chestnut. Sometimes a shoot from the stock enlivens the crown with white flowers. In autumn some trees turn a dingy brown. By the time the tree is about 17 m × 60 cm it is disfigured by big craters of canker, is crumbling inside and is doomed to die before very long.

Only the form **'Briotii'** has good red flowers and reasonable foliage fit for an occasional group or line, but it is less common and village greens and city parks are mostly planted with the unimproved form. **'Plantierensis'** is a great improvement. A backcross between the Red and the Common horse chestnuts, it has more of the stature and health of the latter, the influence of the Red being largely limited to making the flowers a soft pink.

The **Japanese horse chestnut** (*Aesculus turbinata*) was a favourite tree of Sir George Holford who had the original on his lawn at Westonbirt House, where it still stands. He planted others later around the Arboretum. The oldest of these, by Circular Drive, is now 20 m × 80 cm and the tallest, off Main Drive, is 25 m × 63 cm: none is bigger in other gardens, but this tree is almost entirely confined to the biggest gardens and collections. The leaves on young trees are outsize, to 40 cm × 65 cm on a 40 cm stalk, and differ also from those of the Common horse chestnut in tapering gradually to the tip. They are colourful in autumn when they are rich orange-brown, while the main veins remain white. The bark is a smooth, pinkish grey. Young trees have chalky white streaking, and corky, flaking, pale grey bark. The conkers are dull and small but the flowerheads are 30 cm long and it is always worth growing for the size of the leaf.

The **Sunrise horse chestnut** (*Aesculus neglecta* 'Erythroblastos') was also pioneered by Sir George Holford at Westonbirt, who had the first in Britain in 1931. It had been raised in Germany from a rather obscure American species not known in the wild. After the brilliant leafing out, the tree turns briefly yellow and then white. It forms a broad, low-domed crown. There are trees of up to eight m in a few collections and more recently planted gardens.

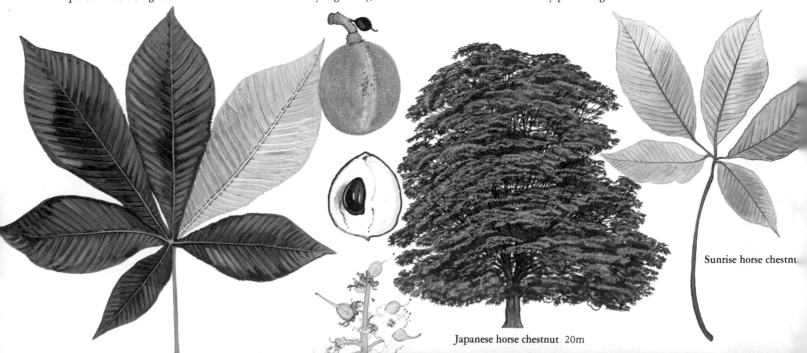

Sunrise horse chestnut

Japanese horse chestnut 20m

Red horse chestnut

'Briotii'

'Plantierensis' hybrid

Horse chestnut

Horse chestnut 35m

Red horse chestnut 22m

Indian Horse Chestnut

The Horse chestnuts are a very distinct little family spread rather thinly right across the Northern Hemisphere. There is one species in California, and another in Baja California, Mexico. Eastern North America has six or nine depending on the views of the botanist, with at least nine natural hybrids between them. In Europe, there is one in Greece. In Asia there are two species in the Himalayas, two in China and one in Japan. The common European and the Japanese species differ from the others in having resinous buds and stalkless leaflets. The leaflets of all the rest, with the sole exception of the Ohio buckeye, in which the stalks are very short, have very positive stalks which together with slender blades give them a far more elegant foliage than the European and Japanese varieties.

The **Indian horse chestnut** (*Aesculus indica*) has leaflets with long, stout stalks, which in most trees are pink or red, as is the leafstalk. The leaves tend to droop from the shoots and this makes the colour more prominent and distinctive. The leaflets can be up to 32 cm long, and are dark and often crinkled, which adds to the individuality of this species. In late spring it is also quite different from others, as the leaves unfold bright orange, fading to khaki before turning green. The flowers are not open until early July, which adds to the value of the tree in extending the season to a time when parks and gardens are more frequented than in May, when the other species are in flower.

From a moderate distance, the flowers of many specimens appear rose-pink all over. The conkers are either very dark mahogany or coal-black. They fall later than the common ones and persist on the ground in good repair until January. Left to itself, this tree all too often grows big low branches or several stems at the expense of a good central bole and should always be pruned up to a clear stem for two m at least. The finest specimen has been cared for in this way and has well repaid the effort. It is at Hidcote in Gloucestershire, 18.5 m × 85 cm.

'Sydney Pearce' was selected from seedlings raised from the Kew trees by the late Curator there whose name it bears, and was planted in 1935 near the Main Gates. It has big leaves on green stalks, without silvering on the underside. It has 30 cm panicles of flowers that are dark pink in bud and very freely borne. In 1981 the original tree was 13 m × 56 cm. Grafts from it grow in some gardens.

The **Yellow buckeye** (*Aesculus flava*, formerly *octandra*) is one of the most outstandingly beautiful and adaptable trees that can be grown in Britain, and it is nothing short of a scenic and horticultural disaster that it has not been planted more widely in the place of the Red horse chestnut. The Americans are no better. It is their tree, and in the Great Smoky Mountains of Tennessee it grows to 44 m tall, yet in the streets of every town in the northern States there are European horse chestnuts and no Yellow buckeye can be seen planted.

In Britain it is difficult to raise from seed as home-collected crops seldom germinate and it takes a special effort to bring American seed here sufficiently fresh to yield plants. But the tree has been grown in Britain since 1764. It grafts easily on to European horse chestnut, and nearly all the British specimens are evident grafts. The change in the bark at the union, often at one m but preferably lower, is marked, the scaling pink-brown rootstock abruptly changing to the red-brown, smooth bark ringed by bands of lenticels.

The tree does need hotter summers than those of northern Europe to grow fast and to bear fertile fruit, but it flowers well and although slow-growing it makes a good tree in time even in the far north, adorning many Scottish gardens. The leaves have a singular elegance and beauty from their slender leaflets, long-stalked, finely and evenly toothed, and bright glossy green colour. The way the leaflets are held, combined with a rounded, concave curving or cupping, makes the highlights from the glossy surface much more interesting than they would be from a plane leaflet. In autumn, even in the less sunny parts of Scotland, the riot of orange, scarlet and crimson is a standing reproach to the poor, brownish Red horse chestnut.

London parks, as usual the best places for the uncommon trees from eastern North America, grow some of the biggest Yellow buckeyes. The biggest of all, 23 m × 96 cm, is at Twickenham in a residents' private garden, but Victoria Park, Hackney has them to 22 m × 62 cm; Holland Park has one 20 m × 68 cm and the best in Hyde Park, near the Serpentine, is 22 m × 58 cm.

Hybrid buckeye (*Aesculus* x *hybrida*) includes the wild and the garden crosses between the Yellow and the Red buckeyes. The form sometimes seen in gardens is a coarse-foliaged, red-flowered Yellow buckeye and displays the same autumn colours. However, there are some with similar foliage to that tree.

The **Red buckeye** (*Aesculus pavia*) from the Southern States is occasionally seen as a small tree with twisting short branches and pendulous shoots. It ought to be seen more often, for the flowers are a really fine bright red. **Bottlebrush buckeye** (*Aesculus parviflora*) is a suckering shrub quite often seen in large gardens but of no account until its flowers open in August. Its leaves turn various shades of red in late autumn.

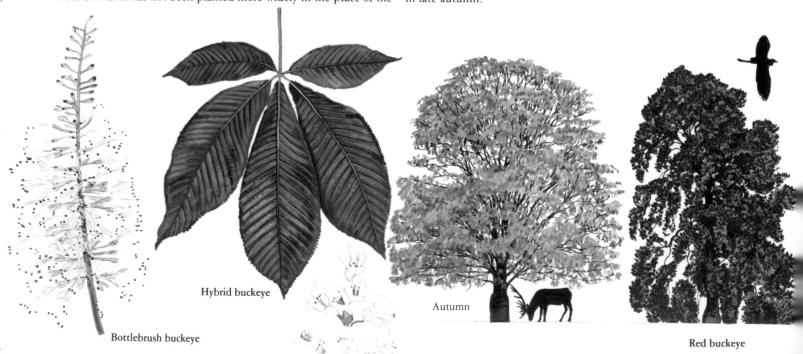

Bottlebrush buckeye

Hybrid buckeye

Autumn

Red buckeye

Red buckeye

Indian horse chestnut

Fruit

Yellow buckeye

'Sydney Pearce'

Seed

Bud

Fruit

Seed

Indian horse chestnut

Yellow buckeye

Indian horse chestnut

Common Lime

Although the **Common lime** (*Tilia* x *europaea*) is one of the most abundant, widespread and largest trees, its early history is unknown. That it is a hybrid between the two native limes, Small-leaf and Broadleaf, is suggested by its flowers being halfway between theirs in number, size and date of opening and by features of the foliage. However, when and where this hybrid arose is not known at all. Since Common lime seeds are rarely fertile, at least in Britain, the lack of any population in undisturbed woodlands and away from settlements is only to be expected if the cross has not occurred here but was brought from other parts of Europe where both species grow.

The earliest reported plantings date from soon after 1600, but these may not have been the first. References to 'lime-trees' in early times do not distinguish among the three. The early plantings are, like so many since, in the form of avenues along drives. Despite the ability to grow to the required imposing stature and survive to a great age, this lime is among the least suitable trees for lining a drive. The choice is often regretted two hundred years later, a new drive made and the limes are abandoned to the parkland cattle. They sprout so vigorously from the base that an annual cutting back is necessary or the drive becomes unusable; sprouts from burrs on the bole soon hide the trunk and make untidy, shapeless trees. The tops may be loaded with mistletoe.

As a tree for town streets the Common lime has no rivals for bottom place. In addition to the defects mentioned, it has roots good at lifting paving; it casts a dense shade; it fails to colour in autumn, and worst of all, is hugely infested with greenfly which rain sticky honeydew on its leaves and anything within its shade. Naturally, then, it was until very recently the tree most frequently planted in town streets. Another feature inconvenient in streets is the great heights to which it can grow. Many trees are 42–43 m tall and one is 46 m, a height exceeded among broadleaf trees only by one Black Italian poplar and three London planes.

Growth in diameter of bole slows down greatly after some 50 years of quite rapid progress, and boles larger than 1.5 m increase very slowly. Many boles about two metres across are far too sprouty to allow any useful measurement, but a few are clean and one such at Charlton Park, Northants is 2.2 m across. This seems likely to have needed more than 400 years to grow and is in good shape for surviving a long time yet. Some people like to chew newly emerging lime leaves, and cattle soon clean a tree up to the browsing-line. There remains some bare branchwood too stout and woody to eat, below the lowest leaves.

This makes ideal perches for Spotted flycatchers which are attracted by the dungflies on the droppings and find the dense sprouts on the bole a good place to nest. Colonies of jackdaws often nest in the higher sprouty parts, and so will a pair of kestrels.

'**Wratislaviensis**' is now sometimes seen, planted for the fresh yellow of the opening leaves which turn fairly green by midsummer. It arose about a hundred years ago in Breslau.

Caucasian lime (*Tilia* x *euchlora*) or **Crimean lime**, introduced in 1860, has been much planted in the last 40 years in streets and parks. It was welcomed as a smaller growing and neater tree than the Common lime, with luxuriant, glossy foliage, and rich yellow flowers a month later. Some of the earlier trees were grafted at the base on Broadleaf or Common lime and may be encircled by their sprouts, but the majority have good, smooth, gun-metal grey boles, clean for two metres, and shapely domed crowns. Unfortunately they do not stay like this but grow into mushrooms of awkwardly downward bent branches. However, the leaves are nearly always clear of greenfly.

Silver lime (*Tilia tomentosa*) from the Balkans and Asia Minor is a remarkably robust tree even in city parks. The rather hard, parchment-like leaves are held out level and are free from greenfly probably because their undersurface, like the shoots, is densely covered in white down. For about the first 50 years and more the crown is an exceptionally regular dome, as attractive in winter as it is in leaf. Trunks often increase in diameter by two cm a year and some trees are 30 m tall. The abundant, fragrant flowers are among the last of the limes to open, at about the end of July.

Silver pendent lime 'Petiolaris' is unknown as a wild tree and is thought to be a selected variant of the Silver lime in the Caucasus region. There being no seed import, the trees are all grafts – probably of the same individual. Hence, good seed will not be grown and all must still be grafts. They are put on a two metre stem of Broadleaf lime and from then onwards two or three sinuous trunks grow strongly upright. Grown here only after 1840, many are very big trees now, notably one in Bath Botanic Garden (37 m × 1.3 m) and the biggest, on the golf course at Beauport Park, Sussex (open to the public) 38 m × 1.6 m.

Mongolian lime (*Tilia mongolica*) is now much in demand for its elegant, unusual foliage, but until the recent plantings it was known only from the four fine trees planted in the lime collection at Kew in 1908; one even better at Thorp Perrow, Yorkshire and two (in Coates' Wood) at Wakehurst Place, Sussex.

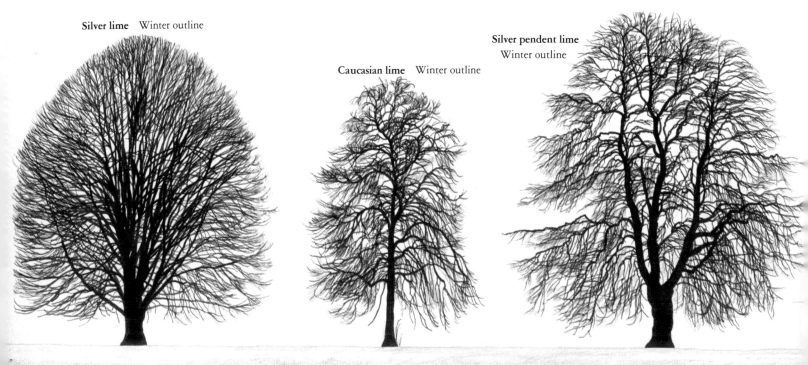

Silver lime Winter outline

Caucasian lime Winter outline

Silver pendent lime
Winter outline

Silver lime

Mongolian lime

Flowers

Underside

'Wratislaviensis'

Silver pendent lime

Common lime

Common lime

Bole

Broadleaf Lime

The **Broadleaf lime** (*Tilia platyphyllos*) is native to some woods on old limestone from the Wye Gorge above Chepstow to Swaledale in the Pennine Hills, but is very local and scarce in the wild. It is widely but not abundantly planted in parks and a few big gardens and replaces the ubiquitous Common lime in a town street here and there. It has also been planted instead of Common lime to make some greatly superior avenues, but all too seldom. In the long lime avenue into Clumber Park in Nottinghamshire the single Broadleaf somewhere about the middle stands out as the one tree of class as well as the biggest, 33 m × 120 cm.

The bowl-shaped crown of immaturity later becomes less regular but still remains finely domed and free of excrescences, in stark contrast to Common lime as usually seen. Neither the stem nor the base sprout suckers, except in a few cases, and that has recommended the use of this species as a general rootstock upon which to place nearly all the cultivars of limes that need to be grafted. Then, to be perverse, it usually grows strong basal sucker-shoots. The flowers are the first of all the limes to open and are fragrant like those of the Common lime. The fruit remain on many of the lower branches after the leaves have been shed, a useful way to identify this tree in early winter. The softly hairy shoots and leafstalks distinguish it in the early summer and the way the leaf is slightly raised in the centre and round the margin is a spot characteristic that can be memorized.

Red-twigged lime ('Rubra') has been much planted recently but big trees are scarce. In the summer the shoots are green but the leaves are brighter, more yellowish-green.

Cutleaf lime ('Laciniata') is a remarkable sight in flower with the foliage almost hidden by the crowded lines of big bracts and big yellow flowers which attract every bee in the district. From a distance it seems to be a yellow-variegated tree. An exceptionally big one at Beaufront Castle in Northumberland is 21 m × 60 cm and trees of 15 m × 40 cm are present in many parks and gardens in all parts. A form with variegated leaves and upright crown is, on the other hand, almost confined to a few gardens in Ireland.

The **Small-leaf lime** (*Tilia cordata*) is the other native British lime, and a highly decorative and desirable tree too. In the wild it is locally an important part of some woods from Avon to Cumbria, notably in the Forest of Wyre in Worcestershire and in parts of Lincolnshire. Before Saxon times it was more dominant than the oak is now, but its seedlings are readily grazed and the tree was so useful that it was extinguished very early in most forests. It is very long-lived as a tree and much longer as an individual spreading by suckers: one such

group of regenerated trees in a circle in Westonbirt is judged to be about 1000 years old. It is widely planted, not in streets but often by roadsides and in gardens and is most easily recognized when its flowers shine out as bunched, yellow stars, at all angles – including erect – so different from the other limes with their flowers hanging below big bracts.

The noticeably dainty foliage shows well in summer but the winter feature of more intricate tracery of fine shoots can be uncertain. As an avenue tree it is better than Common lime for 100 years or so but eventually becomes even more congested with sprouts, burrs, mistletoe and heavy branches.

Oliver's lime (*Tilia oliveri*) is a very superior species sent from China in 1900. The big, very flat leaf is silvered beneath and is held out level from a drooping stalk. The smooth pale grey bark is rather prone to the sap-sucking activities of woodpeckers. An outstanding tree by Specimen Drive in Westonbirt is 25 m × 55 cm and another near Acer Glade dating from 1943 is 18 m × 40 cm (even that has few competitors as there are all too few collections or gardens that grow this tree).

The **American lime** (*Tilia americana*) known there as Basswood or Linden has had mixed fortune in Britain. There are not very many specimens and some of them grow huge leaves, 20 cm × 18 cm or, on a sprout on the tree at Killerton in Devon, 30 cm × 25 cm, but make little real progress. There are, however, other trees with leaves like those normal in America, 15 cm, rich dark green with prominent, pale, parallel veins, and these are good trees to 23 m × 80 cm. A small one by the Totem Pole in Windsor Park is densely ringed from root to upper branch by woodpeckers sap-sucking, as is one at Winkworth Arboretum in Surrey where another is 19 m × 40 cm. There may be more trees about than is generally noticed because there are some at the Middle School in Farnham, Surrey and a pair by a farm entrance at Kingsley eight miles away, which until recently no-one had recognized.

Von Moltke's lime (*Tilia* x 'Moltkei') is a hybrid between the American lime and Silver pendent lime raised in Germany. It can be very vigorous as a young tree with a shoot two m long and leaves 25 cm × 15 cm with soft, fine, white hairs beneath. Older trees, rare in Britain but less so in Irish gardens, have smaller leaves.

Amur lime (*Tilia maximowicziana* or *amurensis*) is taken from a single tree at Westonbirt of uncertain species. It is so powerfully and sweetly fragrant when in flower in July that it draws people from 100 metres away or more to see what can be the origin of the scent. It is near the north end of Morley Ride and was planted in 1941.

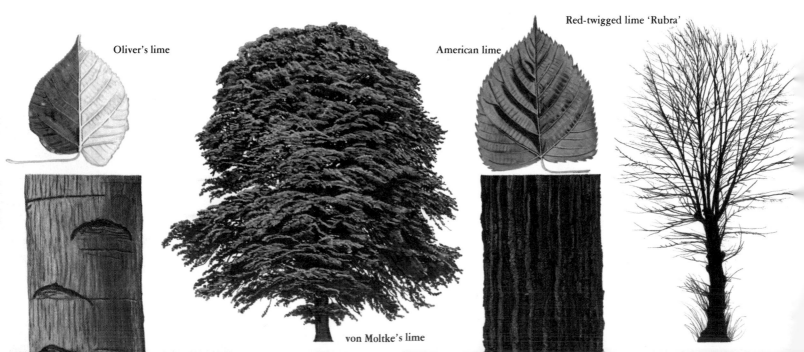

Oliver's lime

American lime

Red-twigged lime 'Rubra'

von Moltke's lime

Broadleaf lime

Small-leaf lime

Amur lime

Underside

Fruit

'Laciniata'

Seedling

Small-leaf lime

Young tree

Broadleaf lime

Tupelo and Dove Tree

The **Tupelo** (*Nyssa sylvatica*) has an extensive range from Maine to Texas, scattered among the hillside woods and showing bright autumn reds in their shade. In Britain the colours stop at mottled cream and pink in any sort of shade and for the scarlet and deep red to appear the tree must be well in the open. Even so, it is peculiarly attractive at all stages of colouring.

The single large planting in Britain is at Sheffield Park in Sussex where 400 were raised and many of them planted throughout the garden in 1909. The biggest of 20 measured recently is 22 m × 50 cm.

The **Dove tree** (*Davidia involucrata*) was discovered by Père David in Sichuan Province in 1869. The main motive in training Ernest Wilson at Kew in 1899 and sending him to China was to collect this tree. He had to visit Augustine Henry in Yunnan for the details and was given a postcard with a few features and an 'X' for the tree. The card covered the entire province, an area three times that of England and Wales, but Wilson found the tree. It consisted of a stump, having just been felled to make the roof of a house. He went on to find more and in 1901 Kew received enough seed from 11 trees to raise thousands after two years germinating. These turned out to be var. *vilmoriniana*, and Wilson sent the true species as described by David in 1903. Many of these were grafted on to the variety, as is the big one at Wakehurst Place, Sussex, 17 m tall with two stems. This form is much less common than the Vilmorin variety and grows less rapidly. The leaf has soft white down all over the underside and turns orange and crimson in autumn. The fruit is bigger, four × three cm on a much longer stalk 14 cm.

Vilmorin's dove tree (var. *vilmoriniana*) was sent, unknown to Wilson, by Père Farges to France in 1897. It is the one most often seen, with a shiny green underside to the leaf, a more purple bark, stronger growth and shorter flower-stalks. A few in sheltered woodland gardens are 22 m tall. Strong suckers may grow from the base and there is a tendency to double or multiple stems and big low branches, so early pruning is required for a shapely tree to result.

Nymans hybrid eucryphia (*Eucryphia* x *nymansensis* 'Nymansay') is a hybrid between two Chilean species of Eucryphia, one a deciduous hardy shrub, *E. glutinosa*, and the other a rather tender tree, *E. cordifolia*, nearly confined to western and Irish gardens where some have fine smooth trunks and are 20 m tall. The hybrid now in many gardens arose in 1914 at Nymans in Sussex and two seedlings were selected, 'A' and 'B'. It was 'A' that was shown and won the Award of Merit as 'Nymansay'. It flowers from August sometimes until December. The coarsely toothed and irregularly divided leaves are hairy and evergreen. The stems are among the most favoured of all for sap-sucking by great spotted woodpeckers and are often closely ringed by lines of pits.

The **Rostrevor hybrid eucryphia** (*Eucryphia* x *intermedia* 'Rostrevor') is a cross between *E. glutinosa* and a Tasmanian species, *E. lucida*, which arose in Rostrevor garden, County Down. It has far more elegant, smaller, nearly smooth leaves, many of them simple and elliptical, and a dense crown of slender twigs. The flowers usually form a perfect circle and have the same season as 'Nymansay'.

The **Deciduous camellia** (*Stuartia pseudocamellia*) is, like the familiar camellias, in the family of the tea plant. Sent from Japan in about 1880 it is grown for its fine bark and its late summer flowers, but it can also be a tower of bright red and crimson in the autumn. It grows slowly and remains uncommon. None is known bigger or of better form than the specimen prominent above the House at Killerton in Devon, which is 17 m × 44 cm and shows well the smoothly-fluted bole.

The **Chinese stuartia** (*Stuartia sinensis*) is grown largely for the bark, but its five cm flowers are scented. It is hardy in Innes garden in Grampian, but is little encountered outside the major southern gardens. One in Tilgate Park, Crawley, Sussex is 15 m × 34 cm.

The **Idesia** (*Idesia polycarpa*) from Japan and China could be taken for a small-leafed Catalpa until the smooth bark and scarlet leafstalks are seen. If female trees are grown fairly near males they bear big crops of berries.

Pittosporum (*Pittosporum tenuifolium*) is the hardiest of this large group of trees and shrubs of which many more are grown in Cornish and Irish gardens. It grows to 15 m in the south and west but is also grown as a tall shelter hedge. In town gardens it is an upright bush surviving the worst winters unharmed across the south of England where its pale crinkled foliage is unlike any other.

Pride of India (*Koelreuteria paniculata*) is a Chinese tree, more aptly called 'Golden Raintree' in America. It likes warm summers and grows best, although slowly, in southern cities like Chichester, London and Cambridge although there are a few specimens as far north as Crathes Castle on Deeside. The leaf is about 45 cm long and unfolds dark red at the end of May. It then turns pale yellow before becoming dark green. In autumn it is rather briefly yellow, brownish and dark red. The flowers open in mid-August and quickly mature into the coloured fruit.

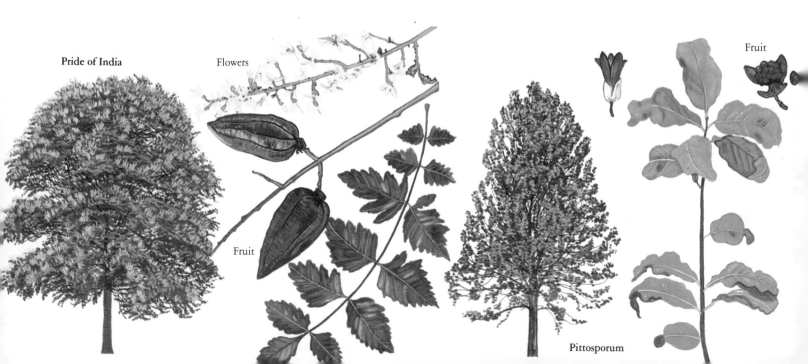

Pride of India | Flowers | Fruit | Fruit | Pittosporum

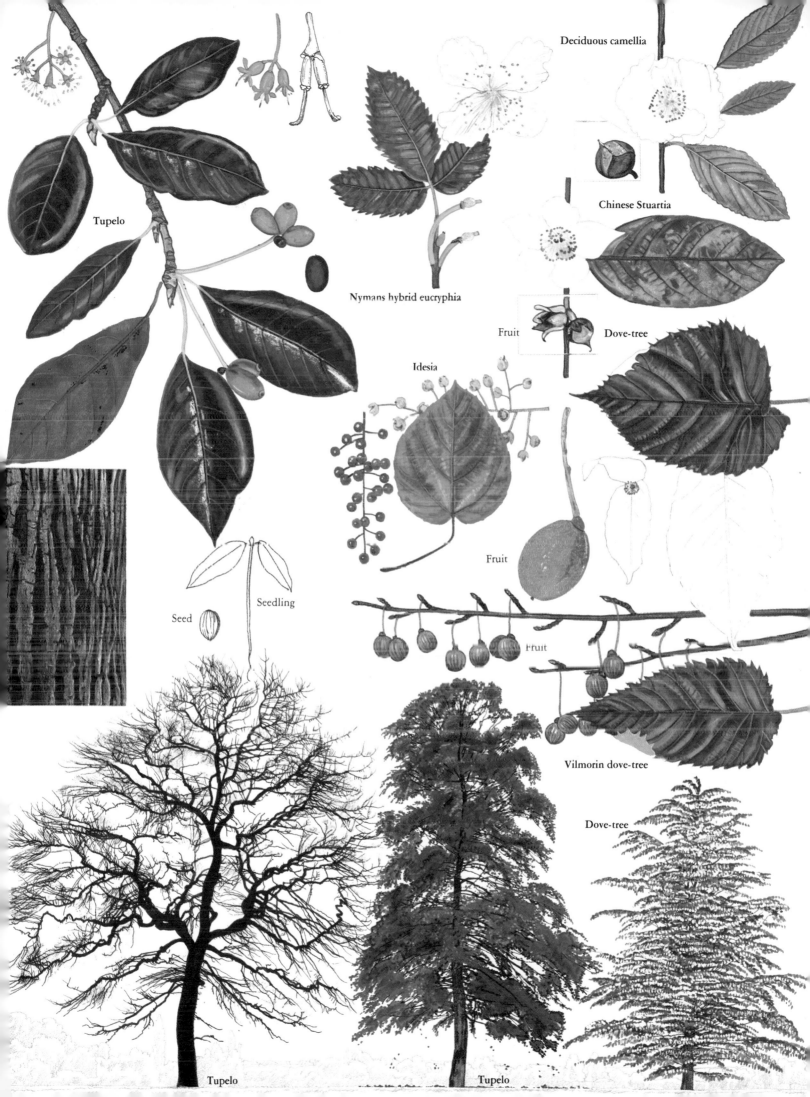

Tupelo

Nymans hybrid eucryphia

Deciduous camellia

Chinese Stuartia

Idesia

Fruit

Dove-tree

Fruit

Seed   Seedling

Fruit

Vilmorin dove-tree

Dove-tree

Tupelo

Tupelo

Eucalyptus and Myrtle

The Myrtle Family is a huge one, consisting of evergreen, aromatic plants bearing flowers with prominent bunches of stamens. They are found throughout the warmer regions. The Eucalypts or Gums are in several respects among the most remarkable trees in the world. First, no other genus anywhere in the world even approaches the total dominance of the Eucalypts in the forests across the continental landmass of Australia and Tasmania, although they did not reach New Zealand. Secondly, they include the tallest known broadleafed trees not only in the native woods but already, after less than 100 years planted there, in most other countries in warm regions. Thirdly they hold all the records for rapid growth both in the first few years and to 30 and 60 m in height. Fourthly, they set no winter bud at all but merely pause in growth until any cold period passes. In many places some species flower, fruit and seed continually as well as growing. And lastly, in juvenile growth, they have opposite leaves, rounded, clasping the stem or combined into a circle round the stem, and most of them soon turn to bearing alternate, long, slender leaves.

The **Blue gum** (*Eucalyptus globulus*) is not the tallest species in Australia, where it is largely confined to Tasmania, but is the one that has rapidly overtaken all other broadleafed trees almost everywhere it has been planted. In the British Isles this is true of Ireland and the Isle of Man and nearly so for Northern Ireland, but in mainland Britain it has never survived long enough to make any impact at all. Between the severe winters it makes enormous progress, if not quite the 15 m in five years it has grown in County Kerry. One in Ventnor Park on the Isle of Wight was 19.5 m × 48 cm when nine years from seed in 1978.

In 1980, one at Glencormac in County Wicklow was 44 m tall but the one at Eccles Hotel in Glengarriff, County Cork, was 42 m × 190 cm in 1968. There is a tree at Bangor Castle near Belfast, 36 m × 110 cm, and on the Isle of Man at Laxey Glen trees about 60 years old are 36 m × 120 cm. However, the oldest and biggest of all is a little further north even than those. Situated at St Macnissi School near Garron Point, County Antrim, it dates from 1856, and in 1982 it measured 31 m × 241 cm. The effect of even a small stretch of sea in making east winds tolerable to Blue gum is evident there, but is more so in Killiney or Bray on the coast south of Dublin, where Blue gums 35 m tall stand in every other garden; yet in Wales, which is visible on a clear day, they cannot survive many winters.

The **Broadleaf gum** (*Eucalyptus dalrympleana*) is the gum most like the Blue gum in foliage, with adult leaves up to 20 cm long. It is almost fully hardy, at least in the south and the west. It can be distinguished from the Blue gum by its flowers, which are borne early in life, as they are in most gums. They are in little umbels of three and are very small while those of the Blue gum are solitary and three cm long in bud. The big blue-white capsules of this tree always lie thickly beneath it. The hardiness of Broadleaf gums is unpredictable, since in 1981 one of several sometimes died completely and the others were unharmed. The beautiful tree at Wisley Gardens in Surrey was planted in 1960 and had grown to 20 m × 55 cm by 1983. One at Mount Usher in County Wicklow was 24 m × 61 cm when 30 years old and in St Leonards, Sussex a tree ten years planted was 14 m × 35 cm.

Cider gum (*Eucalyptus gunnii*) is the standard garden eucalypt and has run wild in Brightlingsea on the Essex coast. Normally completely hardy, this species was killed here and there in 1979 and 1981, but survives to be common in gardens everywhere. It is a Tasmanian tree which was introduced in 1845, but the oldest so far found, and also the biggest, dates from 1885 at Sidbury Manor, Devon and was 22 m × 148 cm in 1977. The larger of a pair planted in 1912 at Sheffield Park, Sussex is 32 m × 112 cm and one in an old avenue at Castle Kennedy, Dumfries, is 31 m × 121 cm. Even as far north as Dunrobin Castle in Sutherland, one planted only seven years was 12 m × 15 cm. This is among the fastest in growth for young trees which are variable in this feature, although in the Tavistock Woods in Devon a 12-year-old tree was 18 m × 21 cm. The flowers are prolifically borne after about ten years and open from June until the autumn.

The **Snow gum** (*Eucalyptus niphophila*) is of quite recent introduction from the slopes of Mt Kosciusko, Australia, and was found to survive the worst winters until one or two in Britain failed in 1981. New foliage unfolds bright orange-brown on some trees and the shoots are red or bright orange until they become blue-white. The flowers are very big and white in bunches, and the speed of growth is variable and often slow for a gum.

The **Mount Wellington peppermint** (*Eucalyptus coccifera*) was introduced from Tasmania in 1840 and an original tree from this seed in Devon was killed by the winter of 1963 when it was 26 m × 200 cm. The little curved spine on the tip of the leaf and the bright white bloomed club-shaped buds identify this tree, together with a twisted bole. A few grow in gardens by the east coast, but this is much more a tree of mild western gardens.

The **Orangebark myrtle** (*Myrtus luma*) runs wild in gardens in Ireland, both North and South, and in Cornwall. It can be a 12 m tree in Dumfries and Galloway and reach ten m in the Highland Region, but it will hardly grow at all east of Dorset. The foliage has a rich, fruity, spicy aroma when crushed and the masses of flowers open in August. It is a native of Chile and Argentina and was introduced in 1844.

Urn-gum

Cider-gum

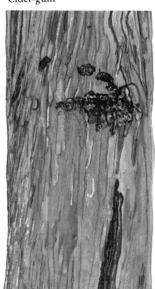

Broadleaf gum

Snow-gum

Blue gum

Broadleaf gum

Adult leaf

Juvenile shoot

Adult leaves

Urn-gum

Snow-gum

Fruit

Juvenile leaves

Blue gum

Mount Wellington peppermint

Adult leaves

Juvenile leaves

Juvenile leaves

Fruit

Adult leaves

Flowers

Adult leaves

Cider-gum

Fruit

Cider-gum

Fruit

Blue gum

Orange-bark myrtle

Snow-gum

Cider-gum Young tree

Dogwood and Styrax

The Dogwoods all have small flowers of white or yellow, but in one group these are in globose heads which are surrounded by big white, yellow or pink bracts, like large petals. The biggest 'flowers' of this sort, sometimes 15 cm across but more usually 10 cm, are borne by the **Pacific dogwood** (*Cornus nuttallii*). This is a tree of the damp woods from southern British Columbia, near the coast, southwards to the far end of California. It was brought to Britain in 1835 but there are no old or big trees there.

For some unexplained reason it flourishes for a few decades and then dies. The biggest and oldest is, or was in 1980, at Killerton in Devon. It was planted in 1930 and was 10.5 m × 42 cm.

The flowerheads are visible all the winter at the tips of the shoots with the bracts green, short and broad, and the true flowers purple in tight bud. There are usually six bracts but there may be eight. The flowers open and the bracts colour in May. In some cases more open in October amongst the red and dark red of the autumn leaves. The bole is broadly fluted, with smooth dark purple bark.

The **Table dogwood** (*Cornus controversa*) is one of the only two Dogwoods with leaves held alternately. A much rarer tree very like the Table dogwood has opposite leaves and is the Bigleaf dogwood (*Cornus macrophylla*). Table dogwood comes from Eastern Asia and is uncommon but not confined to any region, growing well from Cornwall to Cumbria and Grampian but although so attractive it has been very little planted. The bark is in smooth grey folds until it ages to broad flat ridges. The shoots shine out in winter, ruby-red at the ends of the curious, flat branch-systems. The tree flowers abundantly in mid-June, the flat white heads standing in lines above the bright green foliage in quite a spectacular fashion. It is as good again when bearing the blue-black fruit in September. One at Westonbirt in Gloucestershire is 17 m × 52 cm but few others exceed 12 m × 40 cm.

Bentham's cornel (*Cornus capitata*) is the only evergreen dogwood and it is sub-evergreen in some less mild places. It comes from the Himalayas and China and is really only a tree of Cornish and Irish gardens as it is fairly tender. It has been grown at Kew and at Edinburgh but it needs milder areas in order to flower properly. Its leaves are covered on both sides with soft, fine, pale grey hairs.

The **Prickly castor-oil tree** (*Kalopanax pictus*) from Japan, China, Korea and Manchuria has the large, handsome, rich green foliage of a hothouse plant yet it is very hardy indeed. The typical tree has shallowly-lobed leaves and the variety has them very deeply lobed, but there are trees with leaves intermediate in the depth of lobing and it is hard to decide which to call them. Both forms have stout, very

sharp prickles on the bole, those on the oldest stems having become little upcurved spines on swollen bases although still sharp. The bark is dull grey with thick purple-grey intertwined ridges, becoming pale grey ridges between black, broad fissures.

The leaves emerge red in mid-May. Late in summer the flower-heads expand from the tips of shoots, with about 30 white radiating stalks, each tipped by a little umbel of white flowers ripening to five mm black berries which stay on the tree after the leaves have fallen, until the New Year.

The variety **Maximowiczii** has even larger leaves, to 20 cm × 20 cm, thick and hard. It is slightly more commonly seen than is the type and, oddly, the biggest are the furthest north.

The **Snowbell tree** (*Styrax japonica*) was first sent from Japan in 1862, but most of the trees in gardens are probably from the Chinese seed sent after 1900. Although said to be hardy, it is in practice planted almost entirely in southern England and probably needs hot summers for it to bear the great profusion of flowers for which it is grown. It is at best only a small tree of up to 12 m × 30 cm and slow to grow, but its shapely, broad crown has good fresh green foliage before the flowers open and in summer and autumn it is attractive also because of the dense lines of hanging fruit, and the leaves which turn yellow. The bark is at first smooth grey-brown striated in buff-pink and goes on to be dull grey and thickly ridged between orange fissures.

The **Bigleaf storax** (*Styrax obassia*) from Japan is most at home in the south and west where it even seeds itself in many gardens, but is scarce further north into Cumbria. It has smooth grey bark and a broad open crown. Leaves on young plants may have three pairs of large teeth towards the tip or may be cut across and have no tip: they can be 15 cm × 15 cm. The side-buds are enclosed by the bases of the leafstalks.

Hemsley's storax (*Styrax hemsleyana*) is the Chinese form of the Bigleaf storax and is less frequent, but more showy in flower. The side-buds, when exposed by the leaf falling, are bright orange. A tree in Chapel Walk at Bodnant, Gwynedd, is 11 m × 27 cm.

The **Snowdrop tree** (*Halesia monticola*) can be 32 m tall in its native woods in the Great Smoky Mountains in Tennessee, but it was not introduced to Britain until 1897. Although it is quite vigorous as a young plant, it does not grow fast into a big tree so no British specimens are yet above 15 m. It is a coarsely leafed, open tree tending to have several stems but is good when in flower in late May. The four-winged fruit are unusual.

flowers; one spoke

Prickly castor-oil tree

Maximowiczii's variety

Snowbell tree

Bigleaf storax

Snowbell tree

Hemsley's storax

Snowdrop tree

Pacific dogwood

Table dogwood

Table dogwood

Bentham's cornel

Pacific dogwood

Snowdrop tree

Strawberry Tree

The **Strawberry tree** (*Arbutus unedo*) is native to the British Isles but not to Great Britain, being wild only in the counties of Cork and Kerry in the south of the Irish Republic and in Sligo further north. It forms dense low scrub on some exposed cliff-tops, which makes it a little surprising that it needs shelter in England to make much of a tree: it is even then very liable to be blown down. It is frequently no more than a tall bush with branches arising from a bole that is bent parallel to the ground. Few in fact ever exceed 11 m in height and, being unusually slow in growth and evidently not very long-lived, few have a bole of any worthwhile size. One tree at Lower Beeding Church in Sussex has two boles above average size with the larger just over 50 cm in diameter.

The frequent presence of this tree in old parish churchyards is said to be of similar origin to the Scots pines which were a secret sign of Jacobite sympathies in the incumbent, and to signify support for some heresy or other. Gardens in villages are another frequent site for this species, which is not very common in England or Wales and scarcely known in Scotland. A reputation, surely only held by those who rarely see the tree, for a splendid deep red bark has presumably been transferred from one of the other species, for despite small, dark red branches, the bark becomes dull grey and fissured like an oak.

This tree is at its very fine best in October and November when the flowers are out and last year's fruit turn from green to scarlet via yellow. The wood is exceedingly dense and fine-grained and is pale pink and dark brown. It would be better for turning if it did not split and twist so badly when drying. The pink-flowered form '**Rosea**' is not often seen. The Latin adjective *unedo* is one of Linnaeus's many little jests and puns. He made the word from *edo unum*, 'I eat one', because that was enough, so unpleasant is the flavour.

The **Cyprus strawberry tree** (*Arbutus andrachne*) is unfortunately a little tender, slow and difficult to establish, so it is rare and occurs mostly in the south of England. Its bark is of remarkable beauty when it is about halfway through its shedding routine and the old, rich red strips are separated by the smooth new lemon yellow areas. It flowers in April and is distinguished from its hybrid with *unedo* by the untoothed adult leaves.

The **Hybrid strawberry tree** (*Arbutus* x *andrachnoides*) is a cross between the Common and the Cyprus species, found wild in the woods in which both species grow in Greece. It was introduced in about 1810 and grows faster and much bigger than either of its parents. Two were planted on the terrace at Bodnant in Gwynydd in 1905 and are often illustrated. They each have several stems and are 11 m and 12 m tall. Another near the viewpoint in the garden is 16 m × 47 cm. Three big ones at Kew Gardens are more like the Terrace trees, with two and three trunks. Having one parent that flowers in spring and the other in autumn, the hybrid is unsure which to do and may do either, or flower during the summer.

The **Madrona** (*Arbutus menziesii*) called Madrone in Oregon, has its natural range by the coast from southern British Columbia to southern California. It was introduced by David Douglas in 1827 on his first journey to the West Coast. Young trees grow rapidly after a difficult start.

This species flowers in March in California and in early May in England and the fruit are coloured by or before August. The untoothed leaves are like those of the Cyprus species but bigger and are silvery grey or blue-white beneath. As a fine evergreen, flowering and fruiting decoratively, hardy at least to Inverness and with its splendid bark, this tree would surely be more planted were it better known and more available. It is easily raised from seed but can be tender in its first few years.

The **Date-plum** (*Diospyros lotus*) was introduced from India or China in 1597, presumably indirectly through Asia Minor but has not been planted much outside botanic gardens. There are a dozen in Kew Gardens dating from and after 1882. They are all about 13 m × 35 cm but one prominent in Westonbirt on Mitchell Drive has grown more rapidly. Dating from 1926 it is 19 m × 42 cm. A strange heavy scent is noticeable around these trees, particularly when the leaves are beginning to decay on the ground. There are three specimens at Singleton Abbey in West Glamorgan, up to 13 m × 37 cm.

The **Persimmon** (*Diospyros virginiana*) is seen only in a few collections. In Oxford Botanic Garden it is 13 m × 58 cm and is rivalled only by that in the Chelsea Physic Garden, nine m × 43 cm. Female trees bear the fruit, which is popular in America, but in Europe it is the Chinese persimmon which is found in the shops.

The **Sorrel tree** (*Oxydendrum arboreum*) is, like the Strawberry trees, in the great Rhododendron-Heath Family, but unlike those it shares the family failing of disliking lime in the soil. It grows best in the woodland gardens of the acid sands or clays in Sussex, where the biggest are 18 m × 37 cm at both Leonardslee and Sheffield Park. However there are two nearly as big in Holker Park, Cumbria and a six m tree in Branklyn Garden, Tayside, shows that they can grow in the north. Young trees flower well almost from planting and it is difficult to tell when the flowering which starts in July has become fruiting, for the fruit are the same colour and shape as the flowers.

Cyprus strawberry tree	Hybrid strawberry tree	Madrone	Strawberry tree

Strawberry tree
'Rubra'

Sorrel tree

Date-plum

Madrone

Cyprus strawberry tree

female
flower

Hybrid strawberry tree

Strawberry tree

Hybrid strawberry tree

Date-plum

Common Ash

Ash trees belong to the same Family as such splendidly scented and decorative plants as the privets, lilacs, *Osmanthus* and the jasmines, as well as that depressing, scrawny, semi-tree the olive. The **Common ash** (*Fraxinus excelsior*) is one of the ash-trees that has flowers without petals or fragrance. It seems to have become obligatory for poets and other writers in flowery style to find in the ash remarkable elegance and beauty but it is in fact a coarse tree lacking in grace, with a short season in leaf, very little autumn colour and gaunt in winter. The leaves usually fall green and are then relished by sheep. It is native to the British Isles extending to the furthest north. The famous tree of Kirkwall in the Orkneys is an ash.

The late leafing out, open, light crown, and preference for limestone soils where ivy flourishes best, all lead to the branches and boles of old ash bearing a heavy load of that climber. This has no known direct effect on the life-span of the tree, which is short. Growth is rapid and well maintained, yet trees of more than 1.3 m diameter are scarce. These will be around 180 years old and few survive to be 1.5 m through, so anything over 200 years is unusual.

Ash have been known to attain a height of 45 m, but only when sheltered in deep combes and even these are liable to breakage or death before long; none so tall is now known. The tallest is one in a ravine in St Leonards, Sussex, known as Old Roar Ghyll. This is a young tree, 41 m × 48 cm. One in the grounds of Petworth House, Sussex, among other tall trees, is 39 m × 90 cm.

Ash flowers are sometimes sorted according to sex so that one tree may be all male and another all female. More often, a few branches only bear quantities of fruit when the other branches have none. These may, however, have been showing male flowers at first and the filigree styles of the females could have emerged later from the same clusters of flowers, only on those branches. The fruit form an important part of the diet of the bullfinch before egg-laying, and a good season for ash fruit may lessen the damage to fruit-trees and Forsythias.

The **Weeping ash** ('Pendula') must have been a fine sight when grafted 27 m high in a Common ash at Elvaston Park in Derbyshire and its shoots reached the ground. That one has now unfortunately gone and the usual two m graft is a wretched little thing. Its shoots have been broken at their tips by brushing the lawn since its second year in place and it is often asymmetrical and tucked into a shady corner. A few have been grafted at sufficient height to have a chance to make a good crown, like two at Glasnevin Botanic Garden, Dublin, worked at four–five m which have grown up to 16 m, but even they are thinly crowned and not the bowers that they should be.

Single-leaf ash ('Diversifolia') is a splendid, very vigorous tree, handsome in leaf. For an ash, it is also shapely in crown with sturdy, well-spaced branches. The foliage would not suggest an ash at all were it not for the black buds and opposite pairs of leaves. It is not a common tree although most London parks grow several.

Golden ash ('Jaspidea') is most easily located in the winter when the young shoots are highly coloured, and again in autumn when its leaves are a solid yellow, never achieved by the ordinary tree. A few specimens are known over 20 m × 80 cm but younger, smaller trees are more frequent.

The **Manna ash** (*Fraxinus ornus*) is one of the select group of Ash that have petals on their flowers and a strong scent. All but one come from Asia, but the Manna ash spreads into southern Europe. Despite its southern origin, the tree grows well in the north of Scotland, although it is less frequent there than in England. It is also good in towns and has been planted along some arterial roads in London. It grows at a moderate rate and is not long-lived. The biggest was in Regent's Park, London, but died when it was 98 cm in diameter and 160 years old. The tallest is in Kensington Gardens, London, 26 m × 73 cm.

Although very fresh seed will yield plants, it is presumably easier to raise them to saleable size by grafting on to Common ash, for nearly all the specimens seen are grafts. Many show an exceedingly ugly union with the stock where they were grafted at two m, as does an entire group in Hyde Park, London, and those worked at the more sensible heights of below 30 cm are prone to strong basal sprouts of rootstock. In the winter this ash can be recognized by the change at grafting level from criss-cross ridged bark to smooth dull grey, and by the broadly domed crown and the brown buds. The flowers are bright shiny green in bud and open in mid June. The scent is sweetish, reminiscent of dusty upholstery and not to everyone's liking. Grown on Common ash roots, this is a hungry plant and not a good neighbour to other plants on thin soils.

Maries's ash (*Fraxinus mariesii*) is one of the several Chinese species of flowering ash and the most decorative of the few likely to be found. It is a tree of collectors and botanic gardens and is rare and probably short-lived. It has purple where the leaflets join the common stalk and the flowers have pink anthers. The fruit are stained purple during the summer.

Manna ash

Common ash

'Pendula'

flowers

Manna ash

Chinese flowering ash

Single-leaf ash

two forms of leaf

Common ash

'Jaspidea'

Narrowleaf and American Ashes

The **Narrowleaf ash** (*Fraxinus angustifolia*) is a species from the African and European shores of the western parts of the Mediterranean. It should therefore be accustomed to hot, dry summers and wet winters and be adapted best to East Anglia and London. Introduced in 1800, this tree is common only in London: no big ones survive in East Anglia, and there are very few north of the River Thames. One at Powis Castle Garden is the most northerly recorded specimen. It is quite a good size (19 m × 61 cm) but half a dozen trees in both Battersea and Victoria Parks in London are bigger. In 1903 the biggest recorded was at Chiswick House and today at 29 m × 100 cm it is still the champion, although a slender tree at Melbury Park in Dorset is taller, being 30.5 m.

Nearly all the big trees were grafted on to Common ash, and it is very obvious whether this was done at ground level or at two m. About one m is the most commonly seen grafting point, but in Battersea Park there are grafts at 0, 0.5, one, 1.5, two and 2.5 m. The union is often grossly swollen with the Narrowleaf making more growth than the rootstock and the bark changing just below the swelling from relatively smooth, pale ridged Common ash to very rough, knobbly, almost black. At Knepp Castle, Sussex, a tree changes in diameter from 64 cm below the graft to 86 cm above it and one in Kew Gardens at the head of the lake has a much bigger bulge. The bright smooth foliage is light and attractive against the blackish bark and particularly in a variety *lentiscifolia* in which the leaves hang and have more widely-spaced leaflets. About a third of the trees are of this variety.

Veltheim's ash (*Fraxinus* 'Veltheimii') has been regarded as the Singleleaf form of the Narrowleaf ash but in one form it lacks the rough bark and so there is some doubt as to its origins. In the usual form it has a dark, knobbly bark and differs also from the Single-leaf form of the Common ash in its brown buds and dense unswept shoot systems, as well as the complete lack of hairs on the underside of the leaf. This is very much a tree of London parks. Primrose Hill has at least eight and Kensington Gardens five big ones. The only noteworthy specimens seen elsewhere so far are two at Westonbirt. In Kensington Gardens the trees are usefully grouped near the Single-leaf Common ash towards the north-west corner, and the difference between the two forms is instantly seen in summer or in winter.

Caucasian ash (*Fraxinus angustifolia* var. *oxycarpa*) is the form of Narrowleaf ash from the eastern Mediterranean and Asia Minor, and a singularly beautiful tree it is with a dense globular crown of bright green, elegant leaves on smooth, shiny, pale grey branches. These shine out as fine features in Regent's Park, London, but there are not many elsewhere.

Most of the recent plantings in parks have been of the **Claret ash** 'Raywood', a form which was received from Australia in 1925. It is much faster growing and more slender in crown, while the leaves are mostly in whorls of three. It is at least as pretty as the other form in summer but it is grown more for its purple autumn colours and this is not only an uncertain feature in many specimens but in some that do turn purple it soon becomes a heavy, dark brownish colour as bad as the worst 'copper' beeches.

The **White ash** (*Fraxinus americana*) ranges from Nova Scotia to Texas and was first sent to Britain in 1724, so it is a pity that there has been no interest in finding sources of seed to give trees best suited to that climate. It was noted 80 years ago that it grew better on a wider range of soils and gave as good timber as the native British ash. However, apart from eight big trees of varied forms at Kew Gardens, two in the Royal Botanic Garden, Edinburgh, and a few in London parks, there is only the occasional specimen in some big gardens and a none too thriving plot in Bedgebury National Pinetum in Kent. The best is the one on Bell Lawn at Kew, which is 28 m × 88 cm. The white or slightly silvered underside of the leaf is variable as is the presence or amount of toothing on the leaflets, but their one–1.5 cm stalks are a good feature, as is their abruptly tapered tip. In America the leaves turn a fine mixture of pale orange and dark purple but colour in Britain is unusual.

The **Oregon ash** (*Fraxinus latifolia*) grows from the Canadian border along the western slopes of the Rocky Mountains to southern California and was sent to Britain in 1870. It has soft dense down on its shoots and leaves and almost stalkless leaflets. A fine specimen near Hanover Gate, Outer Circle, Regent's Park, London is 18 m × 73 cm. There are also two in the woods at Aldenham Park, Hertfordshire, but it is nevertheless a rare tree.

Green ash (*Fraxinus pennsylvanica*) has an unusually extensive range in America, from Nova Scotia to Alberta and south to the Gulf Coast. Two forms are about equally uncommon in Britain: the typical form with downy shoots once known as Red ash, and the one with stout, smooth bright green shoots and bigger, thicker leaves, var. *lanceolata*. One of the Red ash form in Oxford Botanic Garden is 26 m × 86 cm and one on Bell Lawn in Kew Gardens is 28 m × 71 cm. Trees of this species are either wholly male or female. The variety gives a brief but brilliant display of golden colour early in the autumn at the beginning of October.

Oregon ash

bark

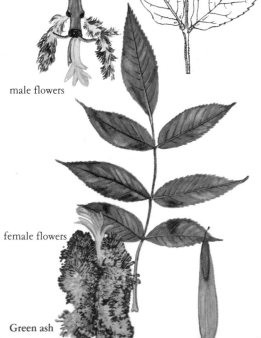

male flowers

female flowers

Green ash

Red ash

Narrowleaf ash

Veltheim's ash

Veltheim's ash

'Raywood'

Caucasian ash

female flowers

female flowers

White ash

male flowers

Narrowleaf ash

White ash

Catalpa and Paulownia

The **Catalpa** (*Catalpa bignonioides*) should be given this name in preference to the common 'Indian bean-tree', as that is doubly misleading, the Indians concerned being Red Indians and the fruit neither being pods nor holding beans. It would be even better to call it, as the Americans do, Southern catalpa, to distinguish it from the next species, the Northern catalpa. It is native to a narrow belt from Florida to Louisiana, but is now grown all over the United States and was brought to England in 1726 by John Catesby. It had thus been known and planted for 154 years before the Northern catalpa, which is in most ways the better tree in England.

The Southern catalpa needs hot summers to grow and to flower well, and is a good flowering tree valuable for its late season – in August – more or less within the region south and east of a line from Bath to Cambridge, and particularly in London. But beyond that area, it is more of a foliage tree and has such a short season in leaf that it is hardly worthwhile.

Golden catalpa ('Aurea') is more tender than the type tree and can also scorch in direct sunlight, so is not an easy tree to grow well and is seen only as far north as the two in the Jephson Gardens in Leamington Spa. The classic specimen is a hugely spreading one in the Botanic Garden in Bath, 11 m × 70 cm at one m.

The **Northern catalpa** (*Catalpa speciosa*) now planted widely across the USA, is native to a small region of the Mississippi Valley around the confluence of that river and the Ohio. It is therefore accustomed to quite long cold winters and hot summers and should be better suited to Britain than the Southern catalpa. It is not very apparent that it is, but there has not been enough planting to give it a fair test. It has grown in Edinburgh but there are very few north of the English Midlands. However, one of the tallest is 20 m tall in a sheltered part of the garden behind the house at Bodnant in Gwynedd. There are very few in London parks but easily the biggest of all with regard to bole measurement is in the tiny Radnor Gardens beside the Thames at Twickenham. This is 20 m × 110 cm, and like one prominent beside the A30 at Hartley Witney in Hampshire it shows very plainly that it was grafted at 1.5 m on to Southern catalpa.

The bark changes from the brown scaling and blistering of the rootstock to a willow-like, dark grey, deeply-ridged bark. This bark is the best way of identifying this species when it is not in leaf. The leaf is variable in the shape at the base, either deeply cordate or broadly wedgeshaped, but it is distinguishable from the Southern species by the down at first on the stalk and by the long drawn out 'drip-tip' and the tendency to hang from the shoot. In autumn it turns bright

yellow unlike the other tree. The flowers open earlier, in late June and are bigger but with fewer in each head. The fruit may be 45 cm long.

The **Hybrid catalpa** (*Catalpa* x *erubescens*) arose in an Indiana nursery, a cross between the Southern catalpa and the Yellow catalpa from China in 1874. It was introduced to Britain in 1891. It is curiously local in occurrence, probably reflecting the first nurseries to stock it, big trees being grouped largely around Bath in Avon and Farnham in Surrey. It has a dark grey, willow-like, ridged bark, huge leaves, to 38 cm × 33 cm on sprouts and they unfold paling from rich purple. The flowers open late, in August or even September and give a powerful, far-carrying scent like the Japanese lily, *Lilium speciosum*. The open panicle of flowers can be over 30 cm long.

The **Yellow catalpa** from China has darker leaves than any other and smaller flowers which are only tinged dull yellow. It is somewhat scarce but a specimen 13 m × 65 cm is the centrepiece of the town of Leatherhead in Surrey.

Farges's catalpa (*Catalpa fargesii*) was introduced from China in 1900 and is very rare. It makes up for its small foliage by a great display of flowers and absurdly slender long fruit to 50 cm long but only three–four mm wide.

Paulownia (*Paulownia tomentosa*) is also called Royal Paulownia, Princess-tree and Empress-tree in America, all due to its being named after Anna Paulowna, daughter of Czar Paul I of Russia and also a princess of the Netherlands. A native of China, but first sent in 1838 from Japan, it is a tree mainly of southern gardens, extending to Ness Botanic Garden, Cheshire, and Rowallane, County Down. It grows remarkably fast, making a stout shoot 2.3 m long in its second year or when cut to the ground a few years later, but soon adds much less to its height.

A tree below Chilham Castle in Kent is 18 m × 74 cm and all those bigger ones known once have died as it is very short-lived. The flower-buds grow out at the shoot-tips in late summer and remain, covered in brown hairs, until they open in May. The fruit are glossy and very sticky until they become woody. Leaves on adult trees can be 35 cm long but on two-year seedlings or new sprouts they may be 45 cm × 45 cm with a few acute teeth each side near the base.

Phillyrea (*Phillyrea latifolia*) is a dark little Mediterranean tree found in churchyards and a few parks and gardens in the counties along the south coast of England, and more seldom north-east to Norfolk. It is in the same Family as the ash and has scented flowers in June and a very dark grey bark. It has grown to eight m × 50 cm, but very slowly.

Paulownia

Indian bean

Northern catalpa

Hybrid catalpa

Yellow catalpa

Farges's catalpa

Indian bean

Golden catalpa   Indian bean   Phillyrea

Conifers
Maidenhair Tree

The **Maidenhair tree** (*Ginkgo biloba*) is the last survivor of an entire Order of plants that dominated the forests of the Jurassic and Cretaceous periods from about 200 million years ago for 60 million years. Ginkgos are not in fact conifers, nor of course, despite the shape of their leaves and the fact that they are deciduous, are they 'broadleaf' trees. They are non-resinous and much more primitive, with fertilization as in the ferns by motile sperms swimming through water instead of a pollen-tube. They are usually grouped with the conifers for convenience, there being only one species and because we have no mental pigeon-hole for ginkgos in the way we accept conifers, 'flowering plants', ferns and mosses.

At least one species was growing in Europe until the start of the Ice Ages, and ginkgo leaves are found as fossils in the London Clay of the Eocene period, showing that they were growing around the shallow seas of the Hampshire and London Basins some 50 million years ago. The present species survived only in Central China in large wooded tracts that were spared cutting because they belonged to monasteries, and are reported still to do so.

A thousand years ago or more the ginkgo was taken to Japan where it was seen by the German traveller Kaempfer in 1690. The first tree in Europe was planted in Utrecht in about 1730 and is still there. The first in Britain was raised in the Mile End nurseries in 1758 and sold to the Duke of Argyll, who was planting at Whitton Park, Hounslow. The Duke died in 1760 and his trees were moved to nearby Kew Gardens which was being established in that year as a botanic garden: several of them remain today. The ginkgo was planted against a boiler-house wall which was demolished in 1860, and the tree flourishes yet although its first 100 years may have left their mark in its low-branched, forked stem.

In China, Japan and Korea, where one is known about 70 m × 400 cm, Ginkgos live to an immense age. In Europe they should also do so and the reason is a strange one. It is that no relative of any sort has lived in either region for a million years or so, and therefore no insect or above-ground fungal pest is adapted to it as a host, nor can they move across from other similar plants since there are none. Only a few general soil-fungi like honey-fungus can attack it and this has been the only cause of the occasional death in Britain.

Ginkgo is very hardy but needs summer warmth, so growth and numbers fall away towards the north. There are only a handful of specimens north of Edinburgh, including one small one as far north as Easter Ross.

There is an inexplicable phenomenon here, for in Philadelphia, Pennsylvania and the surrounding area, where Ginkgo is the street tree exclusively in some city quarters, they cannot grow the female or it would block the traffic. The only females are in gardens and they bear low, sinuous spreading branches. Street trees are males and neatly erect even when not the Sentry Ginkgo, 'Fastigiata'. This is nearly the reverse of the situation in Britain. But, odder still, northwards of Pennsylvania in New York State, the huge Ginkgos in Hudson Valley gardens are the same giant goblet, upswept shape whether male or female, and so they are to the south in the Carolinas and to the west in Missouri and other states.

In Britain there are some trees more flagpole-like than the two mentioned above, very straight to the tip which may be 18 m high, and with only four or five short and level branches, often in pairs like the stays on a mast. These are also the usual form in the drier Middle West states and in Southern California, but the form cannot be due to a hot, dry climate, for in New York State a mast-tree can be seen in a row with other ginkgos of radiating branches, looking like an explosion, as well as dense upright trees, and any mix is possible.

Autumn golds are a wonderful sight in the eastern States and occasionally in England and Wales where they depend on a long, sunny, hot autumn. The fruit are offensively rancid when they rot, and this is another reason for the preference for male trees in streets. **Sentry ginkgo** ('Fastigiata') is scarce in Britain. It is tightly and densely upright. There are two in a shrubbery near Hyde Park Corner in London 18 m tall and a similar one in the Pagoda Vista in Kew Gardens.

Plum fruited yew (*Podocarpus andinus*) from southern Chile is more frequent in western than in eastern gardens and often bushy or with several tall stems, but can be a single-boled tree to 20 m. Male trees are pretty when the spikes of bright yellow flowers on blue-grey stems are at the tips of shoots of blue-green foliage. The bark is smooth and black, sometimes with areas of copper.

Willow podocarp (*Podocarpus salignus*) also from Chile, can be 20 m × 60 cm in Ireland and the far west of Britain and seeds itself in some Cornish gardens. The orange-brown bark is shaggy, peeling away in purplish strips. The leaves can be 12 cm long.

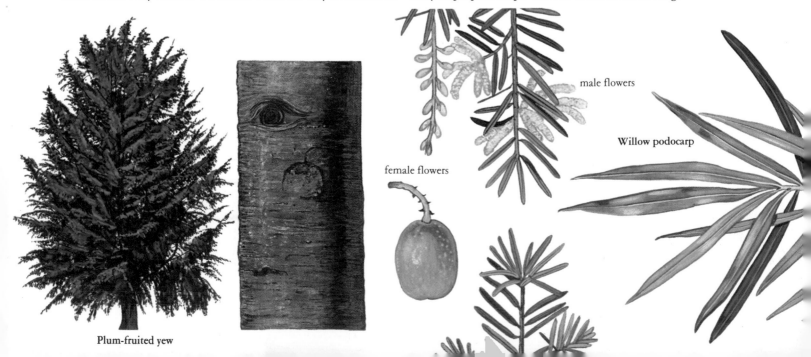

male flowers

Willow podocarp

female flowers

Plum-fruited yew

male catkins emerging

female flowers

leaf from old, weak shoot

Maidenhair tree

'Sentry' ginkgo

Yew

The Yews are a group among the conifers that are much more primitive than those which bear cones. Their berry-like fruit each has a single large seed, partially enclosed in a succulent red aril which grows up around it. The seed itself is, like the foliage, very poisonous to people and to many animals, but deer and rabbits eat the leaves without harm. In conifers of such early origin the sexes are separated on male trees and female trees. Although classed as a conifer and therefore a 'softwood', the yew has extremely strong and durable wood, superior in both qualities to all but a few 'hardwoods'. This factor enables very old trees to hold together and support long branches even when a relatively thin ring of live wood around a hugely hollow bole is all that is left.

With resistance to almost every pest and disease of importance and to stress from exposure, drought and cold, the **Common yew** (*Taxus baccata*) is nearly immortal. It is by a long way the longest-living tree we have. Indeed, whereas among oaks and other venerable old trees the myths and reputed histories exaggerate grossly the real ages, in churchyard yews they greatly underestimate them. It is often said that the yew is as old as the church, even when that is Norman. It is now apparent that the big yews were old trees when the Normans built or rebuilt a Saxon church, that the yew dates back beyond Christianity, and that the site was doubtless a holy one.

There is no record at all of the planting of any churchyard yew before 1640 and many nineteenth-century measurements known for some of the biggest are hopelessly erratic and of no use in calculating ages. Gilbert White, however, gave the yew at Selborne a diameter of 2.23 m at one metre in 1789, where, 195 years later, it was 2.51 m. On reasonable estimates of earlier growth these measurements give an age of around 1400 years for this tree. But a careful re-survey of many others after a twenty years' interval shows that some have made much slower growth and two, smooth-boled and easy to measure accurately, have made no measurable growth at all. Since these are only 1.9 m in diameter, they could take almost any time to achieve 2.5 m. The fine tree at Stoke Gabriel in Devon, only 1.65 m and clean to measure, added 1.6 cm in 23 years and must therefore be around 1000 years old. The Tisbury yew in Wiltshire is, including a little concrete, 3.04 m in diameter and with sprouts as well, cannot be shown to have grown measurably this century. Its age must be measured in thousands of years.

A yew in the northernmost known wild population, on a rocky cliff near Strontian, Argyll, was blown down recently. A section of 14 cm radius shows 310 rings (= 310 years to less than 0.3 m diameter) but in a shaded site at the extreme of the range on the poorest soil this cannot be compared with a warm, open southern churchyard.

If the yews predate the churches and were sacred trees, possibly symbols of immortality and certainly the toughest evergreens available for shelter, the question of why they are in churchyards is seen to be the wrong way round. The church is there because it was a holy site, already equipped with a yew. Had the yews been grown for longbow wood it would be hard to explain why one or two were not used in nearly every churchyard. If the branches only were used (and they are generally far more suitable than the boles) there would be no primary branches found today, nor would it be likely that multiple boles and low forks would be so frequent. In Ireland, male branches of yew are used as 'palm' when in England the sallow takes its place. Probably the Irish usage is the earlier, but there is no suggestion that male trees have been preferred in churchyard planting. The one explanation that is so often in accord with the position on the ground is that, as the toughest evergreen, thriving on any soil found near churches (nearly always locally raised ground; few are ever flooded, and yews can tolerate anything else) yews were placed to give shelter from snow and cold winds to those places where parishioners and pallbearers may need to wait – the lych-gate, the porch and the path between. This view is very often right but it may be that the church was more often placed to take advantage of the yews.

'Adpressa' arose in 1838 in Chester and is a female tree, often bushy but usually with a central stem. It is rarely of notable size but one in Alexandra Park, St Leonards, Sussex 11 m × 62 cm. Its neat little foliage is attractive but sometimes rather sparse.

Irish yew 'Fastigiata'. In about 1770, a farmer named Willis found two little upright yews growing among the rocks on a mountain in County Fermanagh. He took one to his own garden and gave one to the estate, Florence Court, on which he lived. They must have been part of the same plant, for none has ever been found since and two together, both females, is an impossibly unlikely chance. Willis's tree grew better and was the source of trees on the market after 1820. That tree no longer exists, whereas the tree at Florence Court is in reasonable health. Avenues of Irish yew are frequent, especially in western gardens, but are incredibly gloomy and ugly. Many trees are bent irrevocably out of shape by wet snow but when clipped carefully, as by the jousting ground at Dartington, Devon, they can be a fine feature, especially when, as there, they are subtly varied in shape.

West Felton yew 'Dovastoniana'. In 1777 Mr Dovaston decided to plant a yew at the well-head of his house. He probably knew that its roots would make a smooth encasement for the well for a thousand years or more. A pedlar sold him one, at the then exorbitant price of five shillings, and it grew in a remarkable way. It has a good central bole (now 1.17 m in diameter) with strong level branches from which the foliage hangs in curtains. In parks where it has room, as in the Jephson Gardens, Leamington Spa, it spreads widely.

conelet

male flowers

Prince Albert's yew

Golden Irish yew

West Felton yew

Female flowers

Golden form

Chinese yew

male flowers

Yellow-berried yew

male flowers

'Adpressa Variegata'

Japanese yew

'Adpressa'

Common yew

male flowers

Common yew

Irish yew

Monkey-Puzzle

The **Chile pine** (*Araucaria araucana*) was given the nickname 'Monkey-puzzler' by the Victorians after a visitor to Pencarrow in Cornwall, when shown one of the first trees as a novelty, recoiled in near dis-belief with the phrase, 'Well, it would puzzle a monkey to climb that.' The terminal 'r' was lost somewhere and the tree has been known as the Monkey-puzzle ever since. It grows in a restricted area each side of the Chile-Argentina border around the Andean peak of Volcan Llaima. Its introduction to Europe came about when George Vancouver took his squadron to Valparaiso and was invited to a ban-quet by the Governor of Chile. His expedition botanist and general scientist was Archibald Menzies, who had spent the previous two years, from 1792, collecting foliage from many of the finest conifers in the world along the coasts of British Columbia and what are now Washington, Oregon and California. Having no opportunities to collect seed, no cold-store, nor any way to keep plants on a three-year voyage, he could not introduce any of these but brought the foliage from which the original descriptions of many trees like the Douglas fir and Sitka spruce were made. When Menzies saw big nuts in the dessert and his hosts were cagey about their origin, he slipped some into his pocket, raised them on board on the return journey, and brought five seedling trees to Kew in 1795. The irony is that he saw so many fine new species and could not introduce any of them, yet he did introduce this tree which he had never been within sight of.

Two of Menzies' monkey-puzzles were known and had died by 1900 but one, reputedly of this origin, is alive and thriving after having been blown over and re-erected, at Holker Park in Cumbria.

In 1844 large quantities of seeds arrived from William Lobb in Chile and the large majority of the biggest trees are derived from those. The largest planting was the Avenue to Bicton House at East Budleigh in Devon, originally 40 trees. These began bearing good seed and made Britain self-sufficient. One of these, a male on the eastern side, has had the stoutest bole in the country for the whole of this century, and in 1983 was 28 m × 126 cm. A female on the other side at 29 m × 116 cm is one of the tallest.

On the Isle of Skye a fine male is 22 m × 94 cm. The mean height and diameter of all the males and the females in the Bicton Avenue is precisely the same for each sex and no consistent sex difference in the breadth of crown is shown generally. A tree at Nymans in Sussex was noted early this century as bearing both male and female flowers but it has been male for at least 50 years now.

Not all birds are put off by this tree. One in a Surrey town held a nesting colony of house-sparrows and another tree supported a kestrel's nest. The long, curved, woody shoots found under the tree when shorn of their leaves make ideal tapers, burning steadily and slowly with a good flame and little ash. The cone holds over a hundred seeds, and if a male tree is within 20–30 m, they should be over 95% fertile. When sprouting, the cotyledons stay in the seed and only a spiny-leafed slender shoot emerges from the ground. Growth is liable to be eccentric in that each well-marked whorl may represent a season's growth, as one would expect, but it may equally represent two years, or two whorls may show three years and only by watching how it spends the winter can the problem be resolved. Old trees often throw up sprouts from around the base or, where surface roots have been damaged, a good distance away. This is usually the true origin of many taken to be self-sown seedlings.

Norfolk Island pine (*Araucaria heterophylla*) from the island to the north of New Zealand is common in warmer climates. In Britain, it will only survive out of doors on the Isles of Scilly, where one is 30 m tall. In juvenile foliage with out-turned scale-tips, it is a frequent front-room window plant. Adult scales curve over the shoots and hide their tips.

Californian nutmeg (*Torreya californica*) is mostly seen in the west, where it can be over 20 m × 100 cm, but there are some smaller ones in eastern parts. The stiff, spine-tipped leaves give a sour, oily, sage-like scent when crushed. The bark has a shallow network of pale grey ridges. The crown is broad, with level branches from which the shoots hang in lines. The **Japanese nutmeg** (*Torreya nucifera*) is a gaunt, slender, small-leafed version of the Californian. It is rare, and one in the Dell in Victoria Park, Bath, is much the biggest at 14 m tall.

Japanese cowtail pine (*Cephalotaxus harringtonia* var. *drupacea*) makes a broad bush of a very fresh bright green. It is unusual in hold-ing all its leaves up at the same angle, showing the broad, pale, silvery-green banded undersides. Male plants have a pair of knob-like flowers at the base of each leaf; females two pairs at the base of the shoot, on curved stalks. The leaves are acutely pointed but leathery rather than spined.

Chinese cowtail pine (*Cephalotaxus fortuni*) will grow anywhere except in the north-east. It has handsome and luxuriant foliage but only a straggly, leaning, many-stemmed crown. It appears to make long healthy growths but hardly increases in size and a nine m open bush is its limit. The red-brown bark has coarse purplish scales and shreds lifting away.

Californian nutmeg

Chinese cowtail pine

Japanese nutmeg

male flowers

female flower

Monkey-puzzle

Japanese nutmeg

Japanese cowtail pine

Californian nutmeg

male flowers

Monkey-puzzle

var. *drupacea*

Norfolk Island pine

juvenile foliage

Chinese cowtail pine

Norfolk Island pine

var. *drupacea*

Japanese cowtail pine

Young Monkey-puzzle

Monterey Cypress

The entire British population of **Monterey cypress** (*Cupressus macrocarpa*) comprises about as many trees as can be found in a few villages along the coast of Devon, where they grow much faster to three times the size. On the headland of low conglomerate cliffs at Point Lobos south of Carmel in California, old trees have wide crowns flattened at seven–eight m on rugged grey-barked branches. Young trees are quite bizarre, with a central pole densely and closely foliaged and two or three branches like thick ropes, level and snaky. In western Ireland and to a smaller extent in Devon and Cornwall, young trees have numerous branches spreading straight at a low angle. In eastern England, however, they are closely and densely erect making a narrow, columnar crown to an acute long tip. They usually broaden only a little with age but in Beauport Park near Battle in Sussex there are at least a dozen enormous trees over 30 m × 220 cm (measured low) with the great, branchy, broad crowns of Cornish and Irish trees except that they have, or had, an acute apex.

The first seeds in Europe were taken from cones found in 1838 on a desk in Lambert's office at Kew. He gave them to the Horticultural Society and, their origin being unknown, it was called '*Cupressus lambertiana*'. Before this, however, the wild groves had been found by Hartweg, who sent quantities of seed in 1846 and published the name *Cupressus macrocarpa*, the big-fruited cypress.

Gales and wet snow tear branches from big trees, especially those heavy with cones, but the tree is not often blown down. Crushed foliage gives a scent of lemon-verbena, a useful feature in distinguishing among the several similarly foliaged cypresses. **'Lutea'** has a strong tendency to be bushy and needs good pruning to have a proper bole. It arose in 1892 in Chester and an original tree at Castlewellan, County Down, is now 33 m × 152 cm at one m but it does not always grow as fast as the green form and no others are of this size.

The **Arizona blue cypress** (*Cupressus arizonica* var. *glabra*) is of moderate rate of growth, has a neat crown of smoky blue-grey, decorated through much of the year with bright yellow male flowers. It is unmoved by drought or heat, by limey or very acid soils and is extremely hardy. It is remarkable that such a paragon of a tree is not planted more widely. It is frequent in small, roadside gardens only in the south of England and is very scarce north of the Midlands. **'Pyramidalis'** is even bluer, with thicker shoots more densely spotted white, and its hardiness is shown by one at Drum Castle west of Aberdeen 13 m × 61 cm. It is also very largely a tree of the south. Crushed foliage of both kinds is redolent of grapefruit. The **Arizona cypress**

(*Cupressus arizonica*) in some collections, has stringy, ridged grey bark.

The **Italian cypress** (*Cupressus sempervirens*) is hardy at least as far north and east as Perth but is passably frequent in only Somerset, Wales and the English Midlands. The very narrowly conic form is the one usual in formal lines and may be 22 m tall, but a broadly columnar, more bushy form is also often seen. The crushed foliage has only a faint, resinous scent.

Mexican cypress (*Cupressus lusitanica*) is tender enough to have suffered the loss of most of the big trees beyond the western and southern coastal areas in the 1963 frosts, but five survived at Wisley Gardens in Surrey where one is now 24 m tall. Young trees have much more open crowns than the Monterey cypress and grow a sinuous pink leading shoot one m long in a year, bearing blue-grey foliage turning dark green. Each scale has a fine tip which projects from the shoot.

The **Bhutan cypress** (*Cupressus torulosa*) is very hardy and several big trees are in Scotland and in cold gardens in the Midlands, but by far the biggest at 30 m × 144 cm is at Nettlecombe Court in Somerset. The long, slender foliage has a scent of grass-mowings. The **Gowen cypress** (*Cupressus goveniana*) occurs in a tiny clearing in a forest near Carmel, California, and holds its dark, petrol-scented foliage in short, right-angled sprays from the orange shoot. It is very much a tree of the south and the west although there are two at Thorp Perrow in Yorkshire.

Patagonian cypress (*Fitzroya cupressoides*) named in honour of the Captain Fitzroy of the *Beagle*, with whom Darwin sailed, is a small tree mostly found in the west of Britain. It has upswept branches from which the foliage of bluntly round-ended little leaves in whorls of three is pendulous.

The **Incense cedar** (*Calocedrus decurrens*) comes from Oregon and California where it is a conical, level-branched, open-crowned tree. Introduced in 1854 and planted in large gardens everywhere, it is nowhere in the British Isles anything like the shape that it is in the natural stands. From the start, numerous shoots rise vertically pressed close to the stem and in central and eastern England it remains pencil-slim when 30 m tall. In the west, the far north and in Ireland, big branches diverge at a small angle to make a broad column widest near the top. The foliage readily emits a scent of polish. Male flowers and cones are sporadically abundant in time within and among the trees. Seedlings sometimes arise and seed collected in years of plenty is very fertile.

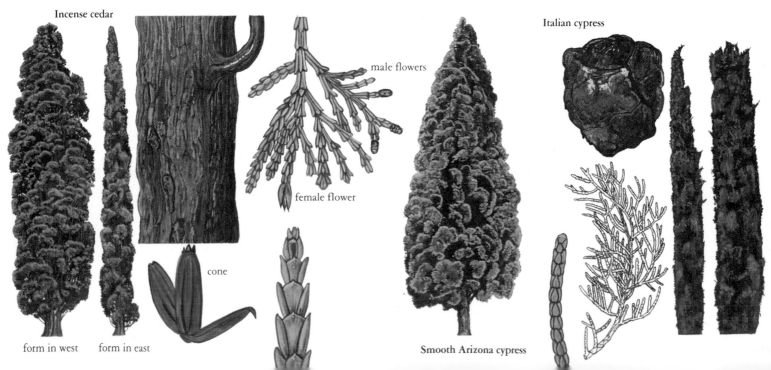

Incense cedar

male flowers

female flower

cone

form in west   form in east

Italian cypress

Smooth Arizona cypress

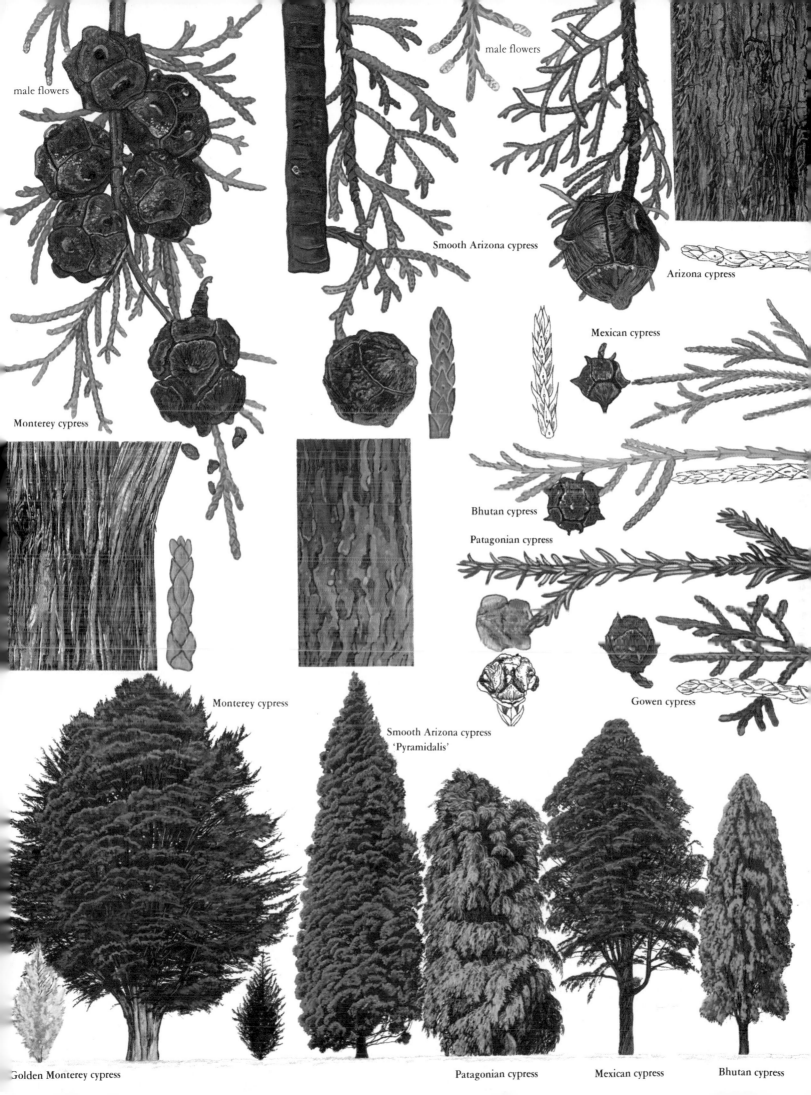

male flowers

Monterey cypress

Smooth Arizona cypress

male flowers

Arizona cypress

Mexican cypress

Bhutan cypress

Patagonian cypress

Gowen cypress

Monterey cypress

Smooth Arizona cypress
'Pyramidalis'

Golden Monterey cypress

Patagonian cypress

Mexican cypress

Bhutan cypress

Leyland and Japanese Cypresses

The **Leyland cypress** (*Cupressocyparis leylandii*) arose at Leighton Hall near Welshpool, Powys, when seeds were raised from a Nootka cypress in 1888. The plants were sent in 1892 to Mr Leyland's property, Haggerston Castle, near Berwick, where all six stand today among the caravan holiday-homes. It arose again in 1911 at Leighton Hall when seed was picked from a Monterey cypress and two odd plants were put out on the hill above the Hall in 1912. One of these survives and is today 30 m × 110 cm, the original 'Leighton Green' with foliage differing from five of the Haggerston trees but very much like the sixth.

This hybrid vigour also shows in its robust indifference to soil, polluted air and, to some extent, exposure and sea-winds. This has led to such intensive planting in town and suburban gardens that unless wholesale topping and clipping starts very soon, all these areas will in 40 years be under dense high forest 30 m tall. Young trees all grow one m a year and in the Savill Garden, Windsor Great Park, the one planted in 1947 was 27 m tall when 34 years old. One of two dating from 1916 at Bicton Gardens in Devon is 37 m × 93 cm. These are both 'Haggerston Grey' the commonest form, which has slender, well-separated, fine shoots often showing some grey and arranged in angular systems, bunched in places.

'Leighton Green' is less common generally but is the clone that was first sold by Hilliers and is thus the one likely to be the biggest tree in older gardens. It is also the commonest in Ireland. It grows a sturdy bole more rapidly, and its long, ferny, very green sprays are flattened, while the finest shoots are broad and closely set. It also flowers freely, while 'Haggerston Grey' very rarely flowers at all.

'Castlewellan Gold' will diversify the impending urban forests as it grows about as fast and is now being planted with abandon. It came from a cone on a branch broken by 1963 snows from a Golden Monterey cypress beside a golden Nootka cypress at Castlewellan in County Down. Its foliage is in angular sprays whereas that of 'Robinson's Gold' is in thick, flattened sprays like 'Leighton Green'.

The **Hinoki cypress** (*Chamaecyparis obtusa*) sent from Japan in 1861 is a cheerful green, broadly conical tree, growing best in soils that never dry out and preferring cool, wet summers. The 'obtuse' part is the tip of the shiny scale-leaf. The rather dull golden 'Aurea' that came with it from Japan is 19 m × 67 cm at Bicton Gardens but this form has been eclipsed by 'Crippsii', Cripps' Golden cypress, which was a seedling in a Tunbridge Wells nursery in Kent in 1900. This is as bright a gold, when in full light, as any conifer and is better

adapted to the drier east than are other forms.

Club-moss cypress ('Lycopodioides') came from Japan in 1861 and in Europe is regarded as a dwarf, but at Leonardslee in Sussex it is 20 m × 45 cm and in the Highlands a remarkable tree is 16 m × 83 cm at Stonefield Castle. Unless thriving, it is a poor thing. **Fern cypress** ('Filicoides') looks even more sad unless it is growing well in a damp, sheltered site, for the long fern-like sprays hang in lines and need to be solidly leafy for the little tree not to appear to be dying. This was another Japanese import in 1861, while 'Tetragona aurea' came in 1873. The green form came earlier but has been completely lost. The golden plant is a very bright colour and very slow to grow, but is far from being a dwarf.

Sawara cypress (*Chamaecyparis pisifera*) from Japan has pale orange-brown bark in regular, flat ridges and hard, fine foliage. It is common in the larger gardens but tends to be dismissed as an impoverished form of Lawson cypress. The forms 'Plumosa' and 'Plumosa aurea' however, prominent in town parks and churchyards as dense, broad columns, are little known to the general public largely because they lack common names. An 1863 cutting from the first import, at Golden Grove, Carmarthen, is 19 m × 93 cm and other old ones have made 26 m in height. 'Squarrosa' has a rich chestnut red stripping bark and soft, fluffy foliage, blue from a short distance, and is common. 'Filifera' is a dull, very open tree usually surrounded by a ring of upswept, often rooted branches. 'Filifera aurea' is very bright and may be either bushy or a thinly branched slender tree.

White cedar (*Chamaecyparis thyoides*) from the east coast of the USA is a short-lived tree mainly seen in southern England in the major gardens. Its fine shoots give a warm gingery scent when crushed.

Nootka cypress (*Chamaecyparis nootkatensis*) inhabits the slopes just beneath glaciers and snow from Alaska to Oregon so it is very hardy but it is apt to blow down in severe exposure. It was much planted after 1855 but is not fast growing and the tallest are all close to 30 m although few are above it.

Yellow male flowers show from midsummer through to April, contrasting with dark blue cones with a beak on each scale, which take two years to ripen. 'Pendula' differs in its flat plates of foliage hanging in lines from strongly upcurved branches.

Formosan cypress (*Chamaecyparis formosensis*) has a broad U-shaped crown, and dark yellowish-green foliage, lacking white marks beneath. It has a scent of old seaweed when crushed and is rare outside some southern collections.

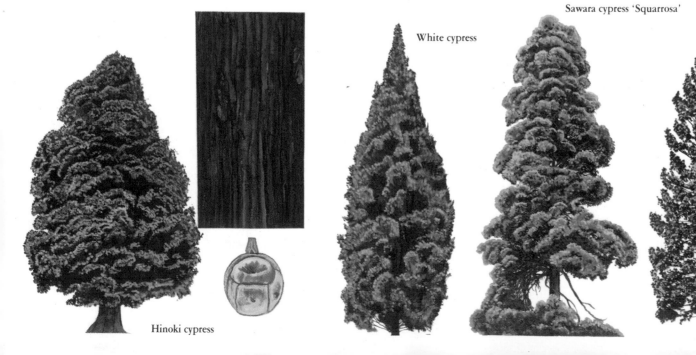

Hinoki cypress

White cypress

Sawara cypress 'Squarrosa'

Sawara cypress

Hinoki cypress

cone (enlarged)

Fern cypress

'Tetragona Aurea'

Club-moss cypress

'Filifera Aurea'

'Crippsii'

Formosan cypress

'Squarrosa'

Nootka cypress

'Plumosa'

Sawara cypress

cones

White cypress

'Haggerston Grey'

cone

'Leighton Green'

Nootka cypress   bark

Leyland cypress

'Castlewellan Gold'

Leyland Cypress

'Robinson's Gold'

bark

'Naylor's Blue'

Leyland cypress
'Haggerston Grey'

Nootka cypress

Weeping Nootka
cypress

Lawson Cypress

The **Lawson cypress** (*Chamaecyparis lawsoniana*) is, in its highly various forms, the dominant tree of British gardens, parks and suburbs. Without it the country would look very different and its urban bird-life would be very much the poorer. In garden design it is the first tree to plant in order to give shape, shelter, background, and diversity of colour and form, and is the prime source of winter colour. But it was unknown until 1854. Its native stands are of very limited extent each side of the border between Oregon and California from near Port Orford to beyond Crescent City and in the mountains behind them. An isolated area further inland in the Upper Sacramento River Valley was found first, and seeds were sent by the discoverer, Andrew Murray, to his employer, Lawson's Nurseries of Bangholm, Edinburgh.

In the wild, the tree is remarkably uniform, dark sea-green and narrowly conical to 60 m tall. No variants seem to have been noted, but among miles of seedlings springing up beside the recently-widened highway there is at least one that is as bright blue-grey as some named forms. It is, however, inexplicable that a species so uniform as a forest tree should, almost from the start in cultivation in Europe, become the most prolific source of variants in colour, form and foliage of all the world's conifers, and do so almost entirely in British and Dutch nurseries. The tree yields quantities of seed in its early years and screens planted commonly from local seeds always show numerous subtle variants from deep green to blue-green. Few trees are known which came from the earliest seeds because big trees are liable to be blown down, but the biggest boles are nearly all in Scotland and Ireland in damp areas with cool summers.

It is singularly fortunate that a tree so universal in and around towns is so beneficial to birds, as is the Leyland cypress also. The Lawson cypress is in constant use as high cover, songpost, nesting-place and roost, particularly by greenfinches, chaffinches, goldfinches, song-thrushes, blackbirds and robins. Since about 1970 the collared doves extended into it and now siskins have started eating the seeds. It is remarkably adaptable to any soil that is not water-logged, or where even brief flooding can cause it to be killed by collar-rot from *Phytophthora* fungi. The species and all its variants usefully have a distinct scent of parsley when the foliage is crushed.

'**Erecta Viridis**' was the first variant to arise and did so from the first import of seed, at Knaphill in Surrey in 1855. A coarse tree seldom with a single stem or proper bole and with branches easily bent out by wet snow and staying bent, it is in nearly every churchyard in the land. One in the ravine at Bodnant, Gwynedd, has grown in 105 years to 31 m × 130 cm but this is exceptional. A much improved form, '**Green Spire**' was raised at Woking, Surrey before 1947, and is neat and narrow with the vertical shoots springing strongly back into place and very rarely bent by snow. It is a pleasing pale green with shiny smooth bark.

'**Pottenii**' was raised at Cranbrook in Kent in 1900. As a young tree its flame shape and pale, feathery, nodding shoot-tips recommend it for formal plantings in a line, or better, a group; but when above about ten m tall it is liable to suffer from displaced branches or even colonies of nesting jackdaws. '**Intertexta**' was a Lawson addition to the early variants in 1869. Its hard, distant foliage is pendulous from a narrow crown, often forked above ten m. Slow to root and for the first few years, this then grows quite fast to 25 m. '**Wisselii**' is a very odd variant, arising in the Netherlands in 1888. The congested foliage suggests a dwarf form but this is far from the case and it grows with great vigour in height and diameter.

'**Allumii**' is the commonest conifer seen in small gardens around towns, fronting on to roads or backing on to railways. The neatly formal shape of young trees deteriorates as a bushy base develops. One at Glamis Castle, Tayside, is 30 m × 78 cm. '**Fraseri**' is much less common, less blue, more grey-green and stays neat at the base. '**Columnaris**' arose in the Netherlands in 1941 and has been widely planted in Britain since 1950.

'**Triumph of Boskoop**' is a good but softer blue and of quite different shape. It grows rapidly into a medium-broad, rather open conic shape. Arising in the Netherlands in 1895, it has outgrown other varieties and the type tree when planted with them, and has made a very big tree, particularly in the north of Scotland and in Northern Ireland. Many trees now exceed 25 m × 80 cm. '**Pembury Blue**' is a smaller, more bushily inclined tree, but of the brightest yet softest blue-grey of any Lawson cypress. '**Fletcheri**' arose in Chertsey, Surrey in 1912, and its fluffy, dark blue-grey multiple-column crown is familiar in gardens everywhere. '**Ellwoodii**' is a seedling from 'Fletcheri', with more adult, greyer foliage, more tightly erect and slower growth, although it has achieved 11 m.

'**Lutea**' was the earliest good golden form and arose at Tooting, London in 1870. It is still as bright as any and hangs its shoots from a slender crown occasionally 25 m tall. '**Stewartii**' from Ferndown, Hampshire in about 1920 is becoming as common as 'Lutea' but is very different in aspect. Broadly conical, it has rising shoots bearing fern-like sprays arched down from each side, their bright gold contrasting with bright green interior foliage which is slightly revealed.

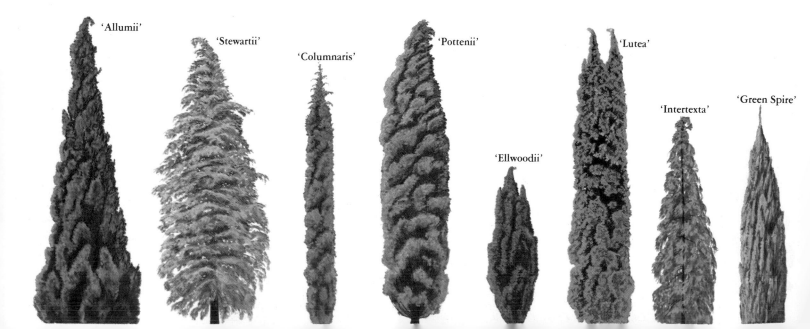

'Allumii' 'Stewartii' 'Columnaris' 'Pottenii' 'Ellwoodii' 'Lutea' 'Intertexta' 'Green Spire'

'Intertexta'

'Lutea'

'Ellwoodii'

Lawson cypress

male flowers

male flower enlarged

'Fletcheri'

'Allumii'

'Filifera'

'Pottenii'

'Wisselii'

female flower enlarged

Lawson cypress

'Triumph of Boskoop'

'Erecta Viridis'

'Fraseri'

'Wisselii'

'Fletcheri'

'Pembury Blue'

Juniper

The **Common juniper** has the most extensive range of worldwide of any tree. It is the only one growing in the wild on both sides of the Atlantic Ocean, one of the very few to cross America to the Pacific Ocean and to span Europe and Siberia to reach that ocean on its opposite side. In Britain it is slightly eccentric in its distribution. On chalk and limestone in England it grows in fully open, sunny places, but on wet acid peats in the north of Scotland where the sunshine is much less strong it grows in shady woods of old Scots pines. It grows very slowly in the wild and few trees exceed five m. The only plant of known date, a cutting in a garden in Northern Ireland, was, however, four m when 26 years old. That, and one other are the only two plants seen in a garden. So although a widespread, if local native species, it is about the rarest tree of any in gardens.

The **Irish juniper** ('Hibernica') is quite common. It is often planted to give a vertical contrast to low hummock plants in rock-gardens or among heaths and grows to seven–nine m tall. It is not known to have originated in Ireland. The **Swedish juniper** ('Suecica') is less tall and frequent. It is distinguished by the nodding tips to its shoots. **Dwarf juniper** (var. *nana*) grows at high altitudes in northern Great Britain but on lowland bogs also in Ireland, and has softer, less prickly foliage.

The **Chinese juniper** (*Juniperus chinensis*) is by far the commonest tree-juniper in gardens and parks, although distinctly uncommon in Scotland. The bole is deeply fluted and is sometimes more like two stems roughly fused together. The juvenile foliage is spiny and hard so it is better to crush the adult smooth shoots to find the slightly sour resinous scent.

Golden Chinese juniper ('Aurea') arose as a seedling in Young's Nursery at Milford, Surrey in 1855. It is common in towns in southern England but less widely seen in the north. It is a male tree, so the gold of the new foliage is freely speckled with yellow flowers from mid-summer until pollen-shedding in early April. Many of the shoots are clad in entirely juvenile foliage.

'Keteleerii' came to Britain from Belgium by 1910 and is a choice, though rare form with a regularly conical crown and almost entirely of adult, shining grey-green foliage. It is female and bears blue-green, bloomed fruit.

Temple juniper (*Juniperus rigida*) from Korea and Japan has been in Britain since 1861 but is only found in large gardens and collections. Despite the specific name there is nothing rigid about it. The leaves are almost soft if handled sensibly and they are on weak, hanging shoots.

The **Pencil cedar** (*Juniperus virginiana*) is an abundant tree of open countryside in the eastern half of North America and was introduced to Britain more than 320 years ago. With one or two remarkable exceptions, however, it is a short-lived tree and so undistinguished that there is no reason to plant it at all and it is quite uncommon. Unlike the Chinese juniper, the juvenile foliage is fairly soft and much of it at the tips of the shoots. Also, the foliage is well scented with the smell of fresh paint and the fruit is half the size. '**Glauca**' is an upright tree with smooth adult foliage in erect tufts and is female. It is a good little tree, to 12 m and moderately frequent.

Drooping juniper (*Juniperus recurva*) from the Himalayas and China is more often seen in the west of Scotland and in Ireland than elsewhere. Its branches turn upwards, the low ones on old trees in the west at two–three m from the bole. The bark is deeply ridged and peeling dull grey-brown. An occasional specimen is silvery blue instead of the usual light grey-green.

Cox's juniper (var. *coxii*) was sent from Upper Burma where it is the largest and most beautiful of all junipers, in 1920. It is now planted rather more in British gardens than the Drooping juniper and is more widespread. There are four in Sheffield Park, Sussex. The bark is more orange and stringy, hanging in loose strips and the leaves, instead of overlapping closely and hiding the shoot, are spaced well apart and spread to reveal it.

Syrian juniper (*Juniperus drupacea*) was introduced to Britain in 1854 but there are few trees of any great age to be seen. Only three of 17 recorded before 1931 have been found. It seems prone to be blown down unless well sheltered. One old one is the finest specimen yet seen. By the 18th hole on Brickendon Golf Course in Hertfordshire it is an absurdly slim, dense column 19 m × 40 cm. This juniper has the most handsome foliage, with the longest, brightest green leaves of any and it also has the biggest fruit. No female tree is known in Britain, but if there were, the fruit should be over two cm across, pale brown and soon woody like the cone of a Monterey cypress.

Meyer's blue juniper (*Juniperus squamata* 'Meyeri') is a garden selection of a widespread and variable juniper on the Himalayas and in China. It was found in a Chinese garden by F. N. Meyer in 1910 and is now among the most commonly planted junipers in small-scale features. That is perhaps an unwise place for it, since it grows at what by juniper standards, is a great rate, and soon spreads widely in an irregular high table-top manner with many acute peaks. It begins life as such a neat little conical, dense, electric blue cutting that this development is often not foreseen.

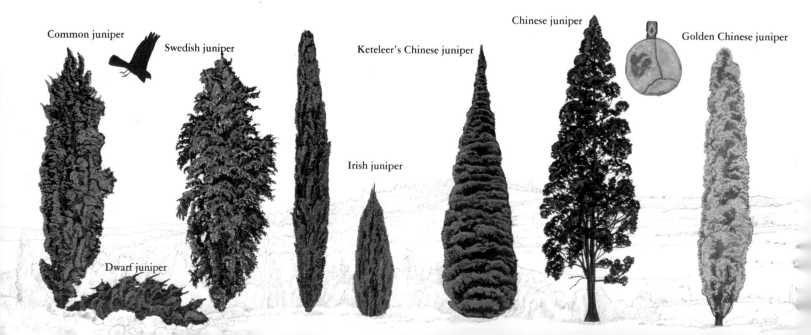

Common juniper
Swedish juniper
Keteleer's Chinese juniper
Chinese juniper
Golden Chinese juniper
Irish juniper
Dwarf juniper

Swedish juniper

Irish juniper

Chinese juniper

underside

Syrian juniper

Golden Chinese juniper

male flower

Drooping juniper

Common juniper

Cox's juniper

Meyer's blue juniper

...s juniper bark

fruit

fruit

male flowers

Pencil cedar

'Glauca'

Syrian juniper

Temple juniper

Meyer's blue juniper

Drooping juniper

Temple juniper

Western Red Cedar

The **Western red cedar** (*Thuja plicata*) is one of the many cypress and juniper relatives given the name of 'cedar' by settlers in North America. At that time, if a coniferous timber had a scent it would sell better as a cedar than under some new name, but this practice has led to some confusion, particularly since the Pencil cedar – a juniper – is known as 'Red cedar' in the eastern States. A grove of magnificent

This thuja was introduced to Britain by William Lobb in 1854 and a few of his trees can still be seen today. It was planted in almost every large garden as soon as it was available and throve exceedingly in the cool damp north and west and on moist clay sites in the east. It was planted as a crop on a local scale and it yields a quick return of strong but light timber useful for ladder-poles and rugby goalposts. It is used for shingle cladding of houses but in the British climate it does not season to become decay-resistant without the aid of preservative. The heavy, fruity scent carries far from a group of trees in mild humid weather and when the foliage is crushed it gives a sweeter scent suggestive of pineapple.

The male flowers are minute and shed their pollen early in March. Cone crops are often heavy and seedlings arise in large numbers around groups of trees on damp soils. Growth is good on heavy clay and on chalky soils and since the early years benefit from shade, this tree is valued for underplanting old oak, larch or beech where very few other conifers would succeed. It also grows well as a mixture with larch or beech and is useful in shelterbelts to give them more solidity.

Golden barred thuja ('Zebrina') seems not to have arisen until about 1900 since none is known to date from before 1902. It varies in the amount and brightness of the gold. It grows at much the same speed as the green one and if it goes on to become as big it will be the biggest golden conifer until the Leyland cypress variants catch it up and surpass it. A splendid specimen at Stourhead is 22 m × 90 cm. Others are taller; at Gregynog, Powis, 24 m × 77 cm, and at Orchardleigh in Somerset, 24 m × 63 cm.

Northern white cedar (*Thuja occidentalis*) was probably the first American tree grown in Europe, whether it came in 1536 or in 1596, but it has little to show for its long innings beyond an array of cultivars. It grows slowly, rarely looks happy and gives up early. Not one of 15 specimens listed by 1931 was still there in 1970. It has at times been used as a hedge, no doubt in error for the western species, and can grow in land that is too swampy for any but a very few trees, it is then, however, liable to be blown down. At Logie House, Grampian, a tree 13 m × 64 cm must be about 100 years old, and has much the biggest bole. The foliage is slightly roughened above by a raised gland

on each scale-leaf and is uniformly matt pale green beneath. It is held on young trees in upright, curved plates and on old trees it hangs as if dying.

'Lutea' is, however, a robust, bright and healthy-looking tree with solid, handsome foliage, uncommon, sometimes 15 m × 50 cm and known to reach 20 m. **'Spiralis'** sometimes shows some winter-bronzing, a feature of other forms of the species, on its deep green foliage, but often does not. The 'spiral' part is the arrangement of the minor, leafy shoots on the erect branchlets of the outer crown. It is a splendid little tree for small gardens but is not often encountered.

Japanese thuja (*Thuja standishii*) has the most deliciously scented foliage of any conifer, sweet, lemony and spicy, and with a good hint of eucalyptus. The sprays are thick and heavy, often dusty blue-grey when new, and nod at the branch tips. The bark has some shiny patches of rich deep red among stringy-edged, lifting plates. It is found in important gardens everywhere, sometimes 20 m tall.

The **Korean thuja** (*Thuja koraiensis*) has flat, thin foliage brilliantly white beneath almost all over and scented more strongly than the Japanese but less sweetly. It has an appetizing scent of almonds, like a rich fruit-cake or a scented tobacco. The trees grow slowly, and having been in Britain only since 1918 none can yet be big. The tallest was planted in 1925 in Park Wood at Hergest Croft in Hereford and is 13 m × 22 cm. It is seen only in collections and the trees are either bright, fresh green or slightly silvered dark blue-green.

Chinese thuja (*Thuja orientalis*) was introduced to Britain in 1752 and seems to be a tree of Midland village gardens and churchyards rather than one of big gardens, where there are few. It is seldom seen in Scotland. Normally a gaunt tree with an open, upswept crown, it holds its foliage, the same green on both sides, in erect plates and rarely exceeds 15 m in height. **'Elegantissima'** is a semi-dwarf much planted in patios, tubs and rock-gardens and around houses and cottages, where it has slowly grown to ten m. It is brightest in summer and fades to dark green faintly tinged yellow in winter.

Hiba (*Thujopsis dolabrata*) from Japan is a glossy-foliaged, many-stemmed tree common in large gardens, or else a single-boled conical tree in a few western gardens, to 23 m tall. Many specimens dating from soon after 1860 have died in drought years when 20 m tall. This tree really needs high rainfall areas or moist soils. It has flat, broad, hard foliage and bears two cm woody cones sporadically. The bark of the many-stemmed trees comes away in fine strings as if scratched by cats, as it may well be, but on the stout stems of single-boled trees it is mostly shiny rich purple-brown.

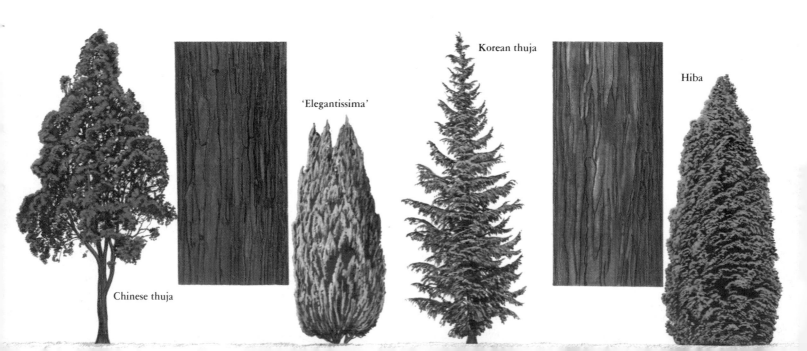

Chinese thuja

'Elegantissima'

Korean thuja

Hiba

'Zebrina'

Hiba

underside

cone

Chinese thuja

cone

cone

Western red cedar

underside

Northern white cedar

cone

Japanese thuja   bark

bark

cone

cone

underside

Korean thuja

underside

cone

Japanese thuja

'Zebrina' 23m

'Lutea' 18m

'Spiralis' 10m

Northern white cedar
15m

Western red cedar

Redwoods

The two Sequoias grow only in California, if you ignore a mile or two in Oregon. It is therefore not helpful to refer to either of them as 'Californian redwood', while the often heard 'Canadian redwood' is an unforgiveable error. The Americans dealing with trees distinguish the two by their very distinct distributions as 'Sierra' and 'Coast' redwood. In Britain, the Sierra redwood is known commonly as the 'Wellingtonia', a parochialism not acceptable elsewhere and the name Giant sequoia is preferred.

The **Giant sequoia** (*Sequoiadendron giganteum*) is well known to be the biggest tree in the world – not in height, nor in diameter, but in the two combined and therefore in the volume of timber. The holder of this record is 'General Sherman' in Sequoia National Park. Quoted as 83 m × 9.7 m or its equivalent (272 ft × 101 ft) the diameter (girth) refers to ground-level and a fair measurement has to be made at 1.5 m. To the dead stump of the apex the tree is now 90 m × 7.75 m. 'General Grant', a finer tree in a nearby grove but in King's Canyon National Park is 77 m, also by 7.75 m but measured at two m. 'Grizzly Giant' in Mariposa Grove near Yosemite, a rugged veteran estimated to exceed 3000 years in age, is 60 m × 7.05 m at 2.3 m.

This species was first observed in 1833 by a traveller named Leonard, whose notes were not published until long afterwards and it was not known to botanists until 1852. It was introduced in August 1853 to Errol near Perth and in December 1853 by William Lobb to Veitch's Nurseries, both lots from Calaveros Grove, the tree's most northerly outpost in the Sierra Nevada. It was a much celebrated tree and was at once planted on every estate of any standing throughout the British Isles. Within 80 years or so it was the biggest tree in every county, the lightning-conductor of England and, with its spongy, thick, fibrous bark, the roosting place for all treecreepers as well as the tree that every schoolboy could punch with impunity.

Of the great number of original trees, those in Scotland, untroubled as they are by lightning, are growing steadily with long tapered tops. Two of the finest are at Castle Leod, Easter Ross, 50 m × 280 cm and Taymouth Castle, by Loch Tay, 50 m × 244 cm. The biggest boles in Wales are at Powis Castle, 38 m × 293 cm and Dolmelynllyn Hotel near Dolgellau, 40 m × 281 cm. Two fine trees in England are, Hutton-in-the-Forest, Cumbria, 33 m × 280 cm and off Rhinefield Terrace, New Forest, 47 m × 250 cm. In Northern Ireland one at Castlewellan, County Down, is 37 m × 252 cm and in the Irish Republic one of 1861 planting at Powerscourt in County Wicklow is 35 m × 262 cm. In the Wellingtonia Avenue, near Crowthorne, Berkshire, 108 trees were planted in 1869 at 18 m spacing. One died of honey-fungus in 1981 and in 1984 the three biggest, all with very sharply-tapered boles, are over 262 cm diameter: the best specimens are 46 m × 163 cm and 40 m × 237 cm. In the avenue at Benmore, Highlands, of about 1870 planting, the best trees are 50 m × 183 cm and 47 m × 208 cm.

This tree has never blown down and many of those in Scotland and England may begin to rival those in California for diameter of bole and height. Pollen is shed in February but once the flowers start to open they are vulnerable to frost and are often caught so that seeds in those years may not be good. **'Pendulum'** can be a straight flue-brush to over 30 m like those in the Bodnant ravine and by the Aray Bridge in Inveraray Castle gardens but more often it arches over into a hoop with a few erect spires.

Coast redwood (*Sequoia sempervirens*) grows a little inland from the coast from just inside Oregon to a few miles south of Big Sur in California. The official tallest tree in the world is seven miles from Orick by Redwood Creek, a Coast redwood 112 m tall. A far finer tree with a bigger bole is two miles north of Orick, 'Big Tree, in Prairie Creek Grove 98 m × 5.72 m and, unlike 'Tallest Tree' which has a dead, forked top, it is green to the tip. So are many trees 110 m tall in Giant Tree Grove and others around Weott along Bull Creek Flats.

The first seed came to Britain from Leningrad in 1843, originating in the Russian colony at Fort Ross, north of San Francisco. Several trees of this history are known today but the great majority of the huge specimens came from seed sent by Hartweg in 1846 and by Lobb in 1851. They are all in the west and north for this tree needs humid summers for it to grow rapidly for long and is scorched, although not seriously injured, by freezing dry east winds. It grows in eastern counties but is slow and becomes thin in the crown, as it does in towns. To continue to grow in height and not to flatten out at the top, it needs at all times to be deep in shelter.

Growth in youth is more rapid in height than in the Giant sequoia but less rapid in diameter. A planting each side of Rhinefield Drive in the New Forest in 1955 is on a warm, damp, very sheltered site. One tree was just over 28 m tall when 28 years old: another was 70 cm in diameter. At Speech House Arboretum in Gloucestershire a tree only 26 years old is 77 cm in diameter and 20 m tall.

'Adpressa' with new, cream foliage turning silvery blue has a thinner and more slender crown and hence grows more slowly. A few are over 20 m and one at Nymans, Sussex is 28 m × 67 cm. This tree is almost entirely confined to similar large gardens.

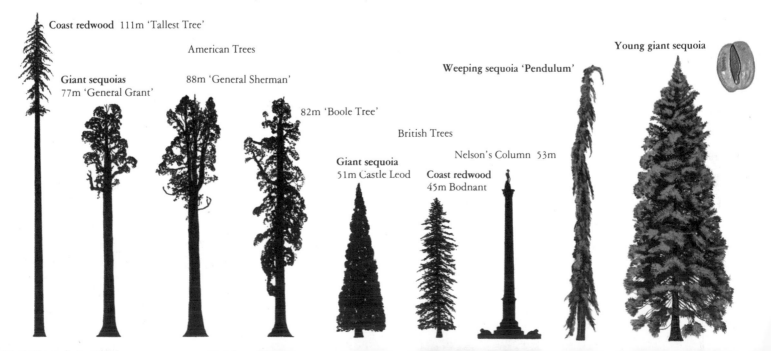

Coast redwood 111m 'Tallest Tree'

American Trees

Giant sequoias
77m 'General Grant'

88m 'General Sherman'

82m 'Boole Tree'

British Trees

Giant sequoia
51m Castle Leod

Weeping sequoia 'Pendulum'

Nelson's Column 53m

Coast redwood
45m Bodnant

Young giant sequoia

Male flowers
Young cones

Underside of leaves

Male flowers

Giant sequoia

Mature cone

Coast redwood

'Adpressa'

Mature cone having shed seed

Seedling

Japanese Red Cedar

The **Japanese red cedar** (*Cryptomeria japonica*) was first sent in 1842 from the south of China, where it is also a native tree. This form, (var. *sinensis*) is separable from both of the Japanese forms, which came many years later, by its loose, open foliage of longer, less branched shoots. All the oldest trees and some of the biggest are of this form. The common Japanese one was sent in 1879 and has been very widely planted. It grows most luxuriantly in Devon and Cornwall, North Wales, the north of Scotland and all Ireland. It likes cool, rainy summers. It is little less frequent in drier eastern parts where it is less vigorous and has a narrower crown. In the west many big trees have huge, upcurved, low branches and some grow pap-like protuberances on the bole.

Male flowers crowd the shoot-tips from about the fifth year from seed and shed pollen in February. Female flowers are numerous at the same age. They consist of spiny green rosettes that ripen into woody cones which stay on the tree for several years.

'Lobbii' is a Japanese form brought from Java in 1853. It is much more dense and bunched in the foliage than the common form. It makes up a fair proportion of the trees seen, as at Westonbirt Arboretum, where all the big ones are 'Lobbii' and it grows to the same size.

'Elegans' is a fixed juvenile form of ancient origin in Japan that was brought to Britain in 1861. It has brighter red, more finely stringy bark and seldom makes a respectable tree although it grows big. All too often it branches low, or forks, and both or all the crowns arch over, sometimes right to the ground, blocking paths and getting in the way generally. The fluffy-looking but quite hard foliage, so blue in summer, takes on a dull purple-red stain in late autumn and is nearly all this colour in the winter. Luckily it recovers completely in the spring. A rare, shapely one at Leonardslee, Sussex is 23 m × 71 cm. Bigger, sprawling ones at Stonefield, Highlands, and Johnstown Castle, Wexford, have boles 97 cm in diameter. 'Cristata' is rare. There are three at Bedgebury in Kent 15 m tall: they are narrow, upswept, quite bright little trees.

The **Chinese fir** (*Cunninghamia lanceolata*) is a redwood although it looks like a bright green monkey-puzzle with adhering dead orange shoots. Its bark is pure redwood and has parallel flat ridges, while the cones are small. It is named after James Cunningham who discovered it in 1701, on Chusan Island in the East China Sea. It was introduced in 1804 and the tree at Claremont, Esher in Surrey is thought to have come from that seed, being planted in 1819 after a slow start, perhaps potbound. It certainly has taken things quietly since and is now only 19 m × 67 cm. This tree is not reliably hardy in the east, so the two groups of eight in Bedgebury National Pinetum in Kent, planted in 1925, have done well to have been undamaged by frosts (one tree is now 18 m × 54 cm). The big trees are all in the west. At Bicton, Devon, one has been 31 m tall for at least 25 years, and the brownish tuft at the top shows no promise of further progress.

The **Japanese umbrella pine** (*Sciadopitys verticillata*) is another, even more aberrant redwood, long without any surviving relative even faintly like it. The slight knobs on the otherwise smooth shoot are the tips of long scale-leaves pressed to the shoot, but these are not working, green leaves. Near the shoot-tip they crowd and swell to buttress the whorl of glossy 12 cm working leaves, which, being grooved deeply on both surfaces, may each derive from a pair of leaves, loosely fused, or may be a form of shoot.

The **Tasmanian cedars** are an isolated group of three closely related members of the redwood Family linked to the Sequoia. They are restricted to the mountains of central and western Tasmania and were all introduced in 1857.

The **King William pine** (*Athrotaxis selaginoides*) has fully free, spreading, rigid, sharp, shining green leaves and the biggest cones (three cm across). It is not hardy north of the River Thames and east of Hereford. It grows best, seldom affected by the worst frosts, in Sussex, Cornwall and Ireland. Even then it takes about 50 years to grow to 12 m. The biggest are in County Wicklow, at Mount Usher, 17 m × 53 cm and at Kilmacurragh, 16 m × 59 cm. At Killerton in Devon, it is 15 m × 20 cm. The cones are in pairs, each cone on a three cm stalk. During the summer when changing from rich, glossy green through yellow and orange to brown, with some of all of these colours present, they are highly attractive.

Summit cedar (*Athrotaxis laxifolia*) is midway between the other two in that only the tips of its scale-leaves are free. It has the peculiarity of growing pale yellow new shoots and is, by a small margin, the most vigorous of the three.

Smooth Tasmanian cedar (*Athrotaxis cupressoides*) has its scale-leaves tightly pressed to the shoot with the tips turned in. It is the least frequently grown of the three and the one most likely to die. But it has grown for many years in and near Edinburgh, and there are three big trees at Kilmacurragh, one of them 16 m × 47 cm.

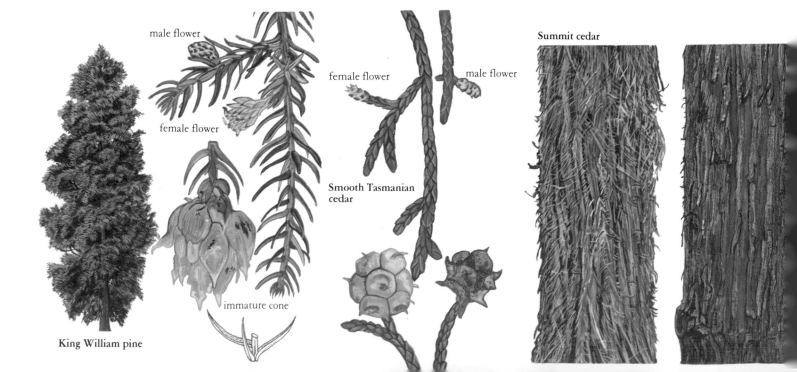

male flower

female flower

immature cone

King William pine

female flower

male flower

Smooth Tasmanian cedar

Summit cedar

female flower

male flowers

'Elegans'

summer

winter

'Cristata'

Chinese fir

cone

Japanese umbrella pine

cone

Japanese red cedar

Chinese fir bark

conelet

seed

cone

Summit cedar

ripe cone

male flower

Japanese red cedar   'Lobbii'   Chinese fir   Japanese umbrella pine

Deciduous Redwoods

The **Swamp cypress** (*Taxodium distichum*) was the first of the scattered and highly various remnant species of the Redwood Family to become known to botanists. It was classed as a cypress, '*cupressus disticha*', since its spherical, woody cones were similar and it differed in having its leaves in two ranks. Why this factor prevailed over its deciduous habit in the decision of Linnaeus so to name it is not clear. It was brought to England by John Tradescant in about 1638 but the first planting in numbers was probably that of Lancelot 'Capability' Brown at Syon Park, Middlesex in about 1750, where there are still a dozen or more. Since the largest of these is less than 1.6 m in diameter, it is tempting to suggest that two trees known more than 1.8 m – one at Dean's Court, Wimborne, Dorset and the other hidden by a little pool in Burwood Park near Walton, Surrey – are Tradescant trees, since growth is slow in trees over 220 years old.

This tree is thought to live for 1000 years or more in its native swamps and a dying or dead one in Britain is extraordinarily rarely seen. It is native along the tidal, brackish creeks from Chesapeake Bay in Delaware south to Florida, extending inland along river bottoms, but not down the Florida Peninsula where, to English eyes, although not apparently to American, it is replaced by the Pond cypress. It spreads along the Gulf Coast to Texas and along the Mississippi bottom-lands nearly 1000 miles up to the Ohio River and into Indiana. All this wide range enjoys long, hot summers and this characteristic shows in its distribution and growth in the British Isles.

The big trees are in and around London and southern England. North of Derbyshire, where both Melbourne House and Elvaston Park have trees around 25 m × 120 cm, size and numbers fall away sharply. In Scotland, Castle Kennedy in Dumfries has one of 18 m × 62 cm, and the furthest outpost is a surprisingly good tree, 17 m × 73 cm in 1970 at Kinfauns just north of Perth. Dulwich in south-east London has an unusual number of good specimens.

The 'knees' arise like wooden anthills or termite hills only where the ground near the tree floods annually, and very rarely in a non-flooding damp hollow. It takes about 45 years for a tree to grow them and they presumably help to take air to the roots since they are constructed internally of very open tissue. The timber of the tree is extremely durable when repeatedly wetted and dried so it used to be imported for holding the glazing in quality glasshouses.

Because this tree is used to hot, early summers it is the last into leaf in Britain and is often only hazed with green in mid-June and not fully leafed out until nearly July. It colours late in the autumn and

some trees may still be holding dull brown foliage into December. The lateral shoots fall with the leaves. Male catkins are prominent through the winter on some or all branches of many trees while others seem to flower rarely. The female flowers are on the same tree.

Pond cypress (*Taxodium ascendens*) has a very different appearance, being a small, narrow-crowned tree with level branches and foliage in cords of closely appressed leaves. Many trees in the wild, and a few in Britain, are however neither one thing nor the other, and the Americans tend to ignore the variation and call them all 'baldcypress'. This is the tree of the Florida Everglades, and is scattered among ordinary Swamp cypress in the south-eastern states. It is less hardy and is grown only in the south of England. Most of the trees are the form 'Nutans' in which the branch tips curve over and the leafy shoots, at right-angles, radiate stiffly at first and then hang from the ends late in the season. The biggest is at Knaphill Nursery in Surrey, 21 m × 75 cm; one by the drive to the House at Beauport Park in Sussex is 20 m × 51 cm, and one as far north as Woburn Abbey in Bedfordshire is the same size.

The **Dawn redwood** (*Metasequoia glyptostroboides*) had long been a well-known fossil from rocks 80–100 million years old almost worldwide, north to Spitzbergen. It was one among numerous fossil species allied to the Sequoias and Swamp cypresses and there was no reason to suppose that any had been alive for millions of years. Then, in 1941 it was decided that a small group of these fossils which had opposite leaves and shoots should be separated from the rest which were spirally arranged and they were named '*Metasequoia*'. In the same year a party surveying the resources left to the Chinese government found a few odd trees around a paddyfield in Hupeh Province. In 1944 specimens were acquired by botanists and in 1947 seed was collected by the Arnold Arboretum, Boston, and sent in January 1948 to gardens all over the world.

A feature that would be botanically unique were it not occasional in the Coast redwood is that in Dawn redwood lateral buds are not axillary, that is between the main shoot and side shoots but on the outside just below the side-shoot. Growth is best beside water or by a spring-line or damp hollow. In frost hollows, however, the first shoots, unfolding in late March, can be killed by a late frost, although without lasting harm. The lateral shoots, as in Swamp cypress, are shed with the leaves. Cones are numerous after a hot summer but no summer in Britain has been hot enough to ripen male flowers so the seeds are infertile.

Dawn redwood

cone

male catkin

Dawn redwood

female flower

Pond cypress

cone

Swamp cypress

'Nutans' form

male flower

Pond cypress

Swamp cypress

Swamp cypress 'knees'

Silver Fir

Silver firs (*Abies alba*) are smooth and leathery whereas spruces are rough, scaly and spiky, and they hold their cones vertically until they break up on the tree. The common European silver fir is the largest in stature outside the Rocky Mountains. It was first grown in Britain in 1603 and planted extensively after 1700. From probably 1850 until 1930 it was the tallest tree in Britain. At that date it was equalled by a Douglas fir and since then it has been surpassed by many scores of that species and by the western American silver firs, the Grand and Noble firs. Once these American trees were available in numbers, after 1851, few European silvers were planted and the old ones have now, to a large extent, gone. Some remain only in the areas where they grow best, from central Perthshire to Argyll, where several are 44–46 m tall, and that remarkable monster at Strone House which is 9 m round its brief bole. Others grow in southern Ireland, but all that remain in England are younger, smaller trees, mostly already with dead tops.

There are some magnificent natural stands of this tree on the northern slopes of the Pyrenees Mountains where they grow pure, and in eastern France where they grow among beech. In natural woods the seedlings arise in dense masses and for twenty years or so grow very slowly in the fairly deep shade. They grow more sideways than upwards and compete strongly. Grown in seed-beds they still tend to have long, level side-branches until put in transplant lines after 3–4 years, when the leaders begin to dominate.

When growing in the open or well spaced, old trees tend to have many large branches which turn sharply upward near the bole and vie with the central stem. The several very big trees at Armadale Castle, Isle of Skye, include one rather extreme example. Cones, as in most silver firs, are borne only on the shoots near the top of the tree. Every few years these carry dense rows of the slender, pale green fruit. They are seen closely only when squirrels or high winds deposit some of the shoots on the ground, or when an old tree is blown down.

Grecian fir (*Abies cephalonica*) is one of the few silver firs rather more spiky than leathery, as its sharply-pointed leaves radiate stiffly all round the shoot. It grows better than most in dry areas and soils and above limestone and chalk, but its new growth comes out early and progress is retarded in a frosty place for many years. Although there are big trees in eastern England, over 30 m tall and 1.3 m in diameter, the biggest are in the cool, damp northern regions where other silver firs thrive best. One at Bodnant in North Wales is 42 m tall, and several in Scotland exceed 1.4 m in diameter.

The Grecian fir was first sent here in 1826, and one of these first trees survives in Surrey, although it is not as big as many younger trees elsewhere. The Bodnant tree is 50 years younger. When young the trees are broadly conical and sturdy and most of them continue to become hugely branched with wide spreading tops, but a few make narrower, lightly branched crowns on impressive boles. Coning is frequently profuse and can lead to the weight breaking out high branches. New shoots are bright green but by the end of the year, and especially during the second year, they are deep orange and, with the radiating, slender leaves, help to identify the tree. The pale orange or pinkish cast to the bark is also a useful sign.

Algerian fir (*Abies numidica*) is a relict of an earlier age when silver firs were more numerous than today around the Mediterranean Sea. Some species remain from Asia Minor through Sicily to Spain, and one survives as a tiny population on Mount Babor in Algeria. (The one on Sicily is reduced to 21 trees on Monte Scalone.) The Algerian fir was discovered, among Atlas cedars, in 1861. It is by no means common yet and specimens are frequent only in important collections of trees. It grows unusually well for a silver fir in dry areas and on limestone soils but also tolerates cool damp summers, so it is found as quite a large tree from East Anglia and the south to Argyll and Easter Ross. It is rarely other than very shapely, with a regular conic crown and small, level branches. A strong shoot from some vigorous specimens is unlike any other fir in the density of the leaves, and those in the interior rows are hard, short and broader than they are long. The two prominent white stripes on the upper surface are also unusual and contrast with the orange shoot.

The **Spanish fir** (*Abies pinsapo*) is another southern relict species. It is found only in a few small groups around Ronda in the Sierra Nevada. The botanical name 'pinsapo' is derived from *Pinus saponis* (the 'Soap pine') because the shoots crushed in water give a useful detergent. This fir will grow for many years on dry and chalky soils but, as can be seen in a number of south-eastern churchyards, it becomes twiggy and full of dead wood and the top fails. However, the locations of the two finest specimens indicates their adaptability – one is in mid-Sussex (24 m × 116 cm) and the other near Inverness (23 m × 115 cm).

Although as young trees Spanish firs are usually shapely, rounded-conic, there is a distressing tendency for huge low branches to develop, turn upwards and become competing boles. This sort of tree has a short bole, maybe 1.2 m through, where it can be measured at one metre or below, and seldom exceeds 25 m in height. There is some variation in the blueness of the foliage, from deep blue-green through the commoner pale grey to quite bright blue-grey, which last can be called variety *glauca*.

An unusually slender Spanish fir beside the Ornamental Drive at Rhinefield, New Forest, is the tallest known at 33 m × 67 cm.

Grecian fir

Algerian fir

Spanish fir

Cone

Spike left by cone

Silver fir

Seed

Female flower

Male flowers

Spanish fir

Algerian fir

Female flowers

Male flowers

Silver fir

Cone

Female flowers

Cone

Silver fir

Male flowers

Cone

Grecian fir

Grand Fir

The **Grand fir** (*Abies grandis*) grows from southern British Columbia to northern California and inland to Montana. In the valleys near the coast it has been known over 80 m tall, scattered among other conifers, while east of the Cascade crest it is often found in pure stands but with smaller trees. In Britain it has been found that seed from the western American lowlands yields trees of faster growth than the more easily procured seed from the interior stands.

David Douglas introduced the tree in 1832 and more seed from the west coast came from William Lobb in 1851. Growth in the British Isles is very rapid everywhere at first, and it continues to be rapid in the cool, moist western and northern areas in sheltered valleys. Trees from seed received 30 years after Lobb's commonly exceed 50 m in height.

The tallest Grand fir is one of the four equal tallest trees in Great Britain, a magnificent tree at Strone House, Cairndow, Highland Region, planted in 1875 and now 60 m × 178 cm.

Growing upwards beyond its shelter, as the Grand fir soon inevitably does unless in a deep valley, it is liable to have its top blown out. In high rainfall and cool summer areas this damage is soon repaired, and the tree sets off again with four or five leading shoots. However, where summer winds are dry, new growth is short, becomes bunched and starts to die back.

The foliage of Grand fir is smooth and leathery, strongly fragrant of oranges when crushed. Male flowers, very small and purple in bud, are in a close row beneath one-year shoots. A few old trees have strong growth near the ground, even in one case bearing them on rooted branches, but normally the flowers are some 30 m from the ground, and are seen closely only on the shoots broken from the crown by high winds or squirrels. Similarly, few trees cone before they are about 50 years old. Thus the cones, which are only borne on strong shoots around the apex, are some 40 m from the ground and are sparsely borne and so little seen. Grand fir is sensitive to impure air and will barely grow near towns. It is common as a big specimen in the policy woods of Scottish castles and in small plantations in forests. The very rapid growth on a variety of non-peaty soils is attractive to the forester, but planting is limited to small areas as the wood is of little use except for pulp and its cellulose content is not high.

The **Santa Lucia fir** (*Abies bracteata*) grows in a few small groves in the Santa Lucia Mountains near the Californian coast south of San Francisco. These are hot, dry hills with no rainfall in summer but in Britain the tree grows well only in cool, moist places. This is because the native groves are in ravines and beside creeks just above Coast red-woods, and are to a small extent subject to summer sea-fogs. Introduced in 1854, this tree was quite widely planted in southern collections after 1900, but hardly one of these now survives.

The **Red fir** (*Abies magnifica*) from the Cascades of Oregon and the Sierra Nevada of California, where it is sometimes 70 m tall, was introduced in 1851. In damp, well-sheltered sites it grows fast after a few years, but it is short-lived in England except in Northumberland, where one in Cragside is 41 m × 94 cm, and only there and in Tayside does it thrive and persist. The stout boles, prominently ringed by branch-scars, often appear to be barrel-shaped and sometimes really are. The branches are upswept, with very regular whorls. The leaves are keeled beneath and ribbed above and so, unlike those of the similar Noble fir, can be rolled between finger and thumb.

The **Korean fir** (*Abies koreana*) is semi-dwarf if it comes from Quelpaert Island, but mainland and Manchurian seed yields trees which can grow 60 cm a year. These trees also flower when very young but less densely. Female flowers may be pink, purple or pale yellow. Brown bracts hide much of the fine blue-purple of the cone, which disintegrates in winter leaving the central spike. The bark is dark brown or black and often smooth and leathery.

The **Cilician fir** (*Abies cilicica*) from Asia Minor has foliage like a sparsely leafed Nordmann fir, but its trunk is smooth grey, ringed by branch-scars of concentric circular folds. It is seen only in collections and may be a slender tree like the one beside the Rhinefield Ornamental Drive in the New Forest, 31 m × 77 cm, or broadly conical with more luxuriant foliage like the one planted in 1916 in the Speech House Arboretum near Coleford in Gloucestershire, which is now 25 m × 94 cm.

The **Subalpine fir** (*Abies lasiocarpa*) grows beside almost every pass in the Rocky Mountains that is above 3000 m in altitude. It has an extraordinarily slim crown, a mere spike of level shoots a few cm long. It does not take at all kindly to the less rigorous conditions in Britain and has probably never survived in England for as long as 40 years. In Scotland a plot at Kilmun in Argyll grows good, slender trees 41 years old and 14 m tall. Further north-east, three 20 m trees are known.

The **Arizona cork fir** (var. *arizonica*) lives longer and grows a little better in England as well as Scotland, either as a slender tree or candelabra-branched. The foliage is bright blue and the bark becomes corky and pale very early in life.

Manchurian fir (*Abies holophylla*) makes a neat, sturdy tree with bright green leaves standing up from smooth pink-brown shoots. It can be seen in many of the big gardens everywhere.

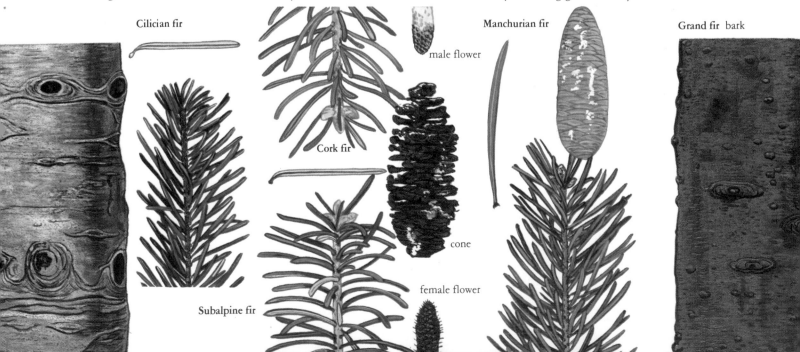

Cilician fir

Cork fir

Subalpine fir

male flower

Manchurian fir

cone

female flower

Grand fir bark

Red fir

female flower

Grand fir

male flowers

Santa Lucia fir

female flower

male flowers

cone

female flowers

male flowers

Korean fir

cone

Grand fir 55m

Subalpine fir 20m

Santa Lucia fir 36m

Korean fir 10m

Red fir 37m

Caucasian Fir

The **Caucasian fir** (*Abies nordmanniana*) is one of the commonest of the silver firs in gardens, locally outnumbered by Grand and Noble firs, but more widespread. It will grow on more alkaline soil than they will and tolerate dry eastern winds a little better, although in less than good, damp sheltered surroundings it does not become a big or impressive tree. Like most conifers and virtually all the silver firs it needs to be in the cool glens of Scotland, Ireland or North Wales to grow at its best and to live longest. In England the oldest trees, which date from the raising of tens of thousands of plants in 1850, have ceased upward growth at about 35 m and some are dead at the top. In Scotland and Ireland this is far from the case, however. A pair of superb trees by Loch Tay is still growing steadily and the larger, by a very small margin, is 41 m × 141 cm.

The Caucasian fir does not grow well near towns, and in many old gardens or estates encroached by building or industry there are specimens that are now in poor condition. The foliage varies remarkably, not entirely as a result of the site, from relatively thin with twisted, short leaves lying almost flat to splendidly luxuriant with bright, shiny, long leaves standing crowded above the shoot. Young trees benefit greatly from the high, light shade of birch or other trees for their first 15 years or so until they are growing strongly. This minimizes damage to the newly-flushed shoots from late frosts, but must be removed as soon as the trees are about five m tall and thinned before that if there are signs of a big infestation of aphids, which weakens the tree and builds up under shade. Cones are borne only on trees about 30 m tall, not every year and only around the tip. Self-sown seedlings have been found but this is a very rare occurrence.

The **Pacific silver fir** (*Abies amabilis*) or Lovely fir has its natural range from southern Alaska to northern California and in Washington it is a remarkably silver-barked, black-foliaged narrow tree to over 60 m. David Douglas sent seed in 1830 but none of the trees lived long and it was some 1881 seed which produced the few oldest trees now alive. In England almost the only trees are those in a few thriving plots barely 20 years old, but there are a few splendid trees further north and west.

The long leaves, which broaden towards the tip, are pressed flat, fanning out over the shoot, and are often blue-grey in their first year. When crushed they emit a scent of tangerines. The bole is usually very stout for the height of the tree except in the tallest specimens, and is rather the reverse in the wild. In dry eastern areas the trees are often afflicted by gouty swellings on the shoots caused by an aphid. Even when young trees are not making leading shoots more than 50 cm long, they usually bear side-shoots in their first year, which is a rare feature in a silver fir.

Maries's fir (*Abies mariesii*) from Japan is very similar to the Pacific silver fir but has shorter leaves with a ginger scent, dark brown hairs instead of pale on the shoot, and the bark marked by rings round the branch-scars.

The **Szechuan fir** (*Abies fargesii*) has hitherto usually been known as *Abies sutchuenensis* and a similar species but with much longer leaves and very rare was called *Abies fargesii*. Recent study has however shown that this latter is *Abies chengi* and its previous name belongs to this species. They both have shining mahogany brown and purple shoots. The Szechuan fir is grown in many collections in each country and makes a slender tree with light, level branches, and very glossy, deep green leaves.

Bornmuller's fir (*Abies bornmuellerana*) comes from a small area in north-western Asia Minor. This is geographically between the ranges of the Common and the Caucasian silver firs and Bornmuller's fir may be a hybrid between these. In some features it is more like the Cilician fir, notably the form of that species growing in the Speech House Arboretum mentioned on page 146. Although scarce and normally found only in collections like Bicton in Devon, where one planted in about 1916 is 30 m × 82 cm, there are trees in smaller gardens and even outside them. One is on a triangle of land at Welford in Berkshire, and another in a little churchyard, Bolton's Bench at Lyndhurst in Hampshire. The biggest, 30 m × 118 cm, is in a surprisingly good group of conifers on the chalklands near Andover at Red Rice, Farleigh School. The species is notable for the luxuriance of its foliage, the big leaves tipped with white and standing up from shining red-brown, stout shoots.

Veitch's silver fir (*Abies veitchii*) sent from Japan in 1879 is very short-lived in England and the few survivors of numerous plantings before 1910 are thin and waiting to die. Even in northern Scotland there has been an occasional death, although the biggest trees are still in full vigour. One in a large private garden near Inverness is 23 m × 95 cm, a size of bole far beyond any seen elsewhere. A sturdy tree by the fence at Dunkeld Cathedral, Tayside is 23 m × 75 cm, and can be seen as a three m sapling in a photograph in Blair Castle taken in about 1908. At Dawyck, the biggest of many is 26m × 72 cm. The species has a distinctive bole, with deep rounded fluting and hollows under the branches. In the seed-bed and transplant lines, this tree grows faster than most silver firs and is soon an attractive little tree, so it is frequently planted.

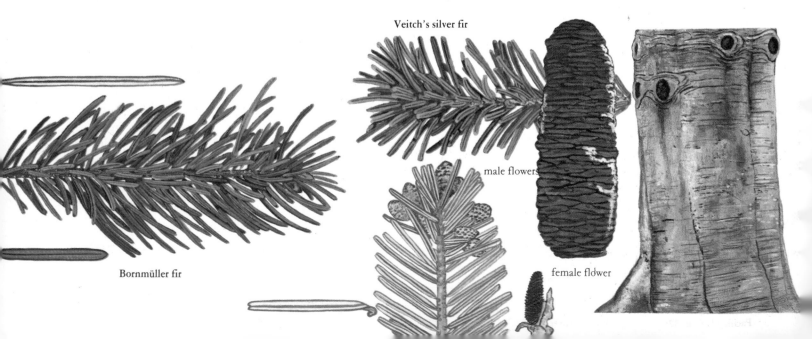

Veitch's silver fir

male flowers

female flower

Bornmüller fir

Caucasian fir

female flower

Maries's fir

Pacific silver fir

cone

cone

cone

female flower

male flowers

Szichuan fir

Pacific silver fir 32m

Veitch's silver fir 25m

bole

Caucasian fir 40m

Noble Fir

The **Noble fir** (*Abies procera*) comes from Washington and Oregon and was sent to Britain by David Douglas in 1830. A second, larger import in 1851 and another around 1870 were the origin of the great majority of the big trees in Scotland. It is most at home in the eastern Highlands from Aberdeen northwards, and seedlings spring up in great numbers there, in lines along rotting logs where there are any. It is common as one of the biggest specimens in castle policies, where unless very sheltered, the tops tend to be broken and be deformed into thick twisting branches. This tree is particularly susceptible to a mis-shapen top because its cones are borne there and they are big, 25 cm tall, heavy and often numerous. They bend the shoots down until the seed are shed and the cones disintegrate in November, but there can be gales before then. Even some young trees less than nine m tall will have many cones, although this is mostly in drier districts where the tree is less thriving.

In May the male flowers, crowded along the underside of the shoot and often within five m of the ground, swell and turn bright crimson-red before shedding great quantities of yellow pollen. Fertile seed is gathered but a seedfly drastically lowers the numbers germinating in some cases. Three old and big specimens can be seen to have been grafted on to Common silver fir rootstock just above ground level. The most prominent of these is the now rather senile but majestic tree beside the east path at Stourhead, Wiltshire, 43 m × 146 cm.

Some of the big trees, including that mentioned at Stourhead, are the variety *glauca* with very blue-white young foliage. This type of foliage occurs among the trees in the wild, but some specimens in gardens may be grafts from a particularly well-coloured tree.

Forrest's fir (*Abies forrestii*) is the most frequently seen of a complex of similar species in China, named after the collector, George Forrest, who discovered and introduced it in 1910. Very handsome, it does not grow well in England where it is slender and short-lived, but thrives exceedingly in Scotland and Ireland. Typically, the stout shoot is bright orange but where seedlings have been raised from garden trees the shoots may be dark brown. The leaf undersides are brilliantly white-banded. In Tayside a tree is 26 m × 91 cm and with two others it added 40 cm to its diameter in 19 years. An original tree in the Royal Botanic Garden in Edinburgh is 19 m × 50 cm. Var. **Georgei**, also named after George Forrest, is the high-altitude form and has hairy shoots and shorter, bluer leaves.

King Boris's fir (*Abies borisii-regis*) is a rugged, vigorous tree from Greece and Bulgaria, closely related to the Common silver fir and differing mainly in its densely hairy shoot and tapered leaf. There are single specimens in a number of the larger gardens. One by the drive at Penrhyn Castle, Gwynedd, is 36 m × 110 cm.

The **Himalayan fir** (*Abies spectabilis*) has foliage on a grand scale and is brilliantly silvered beneath even in the south and east of England, where it does not live long. It has dark grey bark with large loose scales and very level branches. The fine dark blue cones remain in one piece through the winter.

The Himalayan fir is the high-altitude form of its close relative, the **Pindrow fir** (*Abies pindrow*) and although they are so very different, there are intermediate forms in the wild. Pindrow fir foliage is on the same bold scale but is pale green under the leaf and the shoot is shiny pink-grey. Its branches are level but shorter, with a narrowly conical crown, the long leaves making brushes at the tips. Opening its buds early for a silver fir and suffering for it in late frosts, this species has also been failing almost everywhere east of Devon and Herefordshire, while thriving from Cumbria northwards.

The **Nikko fir** (*Abies homolepis*) from Japan is one of the best silver firs for growing near towns and in dry eastern areas, although it too grows best in the cool, wet northern and western climate. Also, unlike many Japanese conifers it has not, at least so far, begun to fail in early middle age. A sturdy tree with strong branches, straight and raised at a uniform angle, it is recognizable by the orange-pink tinge on parts of the finely-flaking bark and by the smooth creamy, plated, stout shoots. The male flowers are large globules ripening bright orange-yellow and may be within three–four m of the ground on trees 50 years old, while cones on somewhat older trees are sometimes within less than two m, which is most unusual in a silver fir.

The **Momi fir** (*Abies firma*) from Japan resembles the Nikko fir but has thicker leaves that are green beneath, not bright white: they are very broad but narrowed to a distinct stalk.

The **White fir** (*Abies concolor*) is native to the southeastern ranges of the Rocky Mountains from Idaho to Arizona and was introduced in 1872. The 5 cm leaves, the same blue-grey on either side, hence the botanical name, stand largely vertically from the stout pale shoot and the bark is smooth, dark grey. It has not been planted very widely and big trees are scarce and largely confined to Northumberland and Scotland.

Low's white fir (var. *lowiana*) is the form of White fir that was introduced first, in 1851, and grows so much better that it is the one most commonly seen. Often towering out of groups of conifers which are failing at height in exposure, it is frequent as a conic young tree with a leading shoot 1 m long. It ranges from Oregon through the length of California and connect the White fir to the Grand fir. It makes a superbly shapely stem and crown. There is one over 46 m tall at Bodnant, Gwynedd and Cragside, Northumberland and 50 m tall at Durris, Kincardineshire. One 120 years old at Kilravock Castle, Nairn, is almost 2 m in diameter – as big as any twice this age in California.

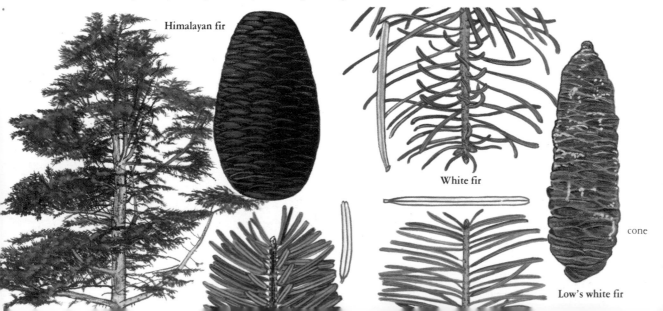

Himalayan fir

White fir

Low's white fir

Noble fir   bark of young tree

cone

female flower

male flowers

female flower

female flower

male flower

cone

spike of disintegrated cone

Bract of cone

Pindrow fir

George's fir

Forrest's fir

Momi fir

seed

King Boris's fir

Noble fir   cone

cone

Nikko fir

Noble fir

Low's white fir

White fir

King Boris's fir

Douglas Fir

The **Douglas fir** (*Pseudotsuga menziesii*) is one of the great trees of the world and may have been the tallest ever to grow. One was felled in 1895 on Vancouver Island that was 128 m tall. Today a stand at Lake Quinault Park, Washington, has trees 85–90 m × 240 cm with clear cylindrical boles nearly 60 m to the first branch. The English and botanical names commemorate the two men who discovered and introduced it (in reverse order). Archibald Menzies found it and brought foliage to Kew for description when travelling with George Vancouver in 1793, and David Douglas sent seed in 1827. Douglas sent a large quantity and the members of the Horticultural Society were all able to have a share. Original trees from that packet are quite numerous, particularly in Scotland. Douglas came from Scone near Perth and naturally the local lairds were keen to have his first trees. It so happens that the tree grows particularly well around Perth and by another peculiar chance, the small area of Washington State from which Douglas sent the seed has been found since, from numerous trials, to yield the best trees for growth in Britain of all the vast area of wild stands, which occur throughout the Rocky Mountain system in the United States and southern British Columbia.

Two of the original trees at Dawyck in the Borders Region are 49 m × 135 cm and 34 m × 163 cm, while one at Bowood in Wiltshire is 41 m × 153 cm. No more seed is thought to have been sent until 1846, and some trees planted in or a little before that date were probably sown late and grown in pots for some years. The biggest single bole, on a tree near Dunkeld Cathedral in Tayside, and now 32 m × 213 cm was one such tree. It was planted in 1846. Many of the finest trees, often in groves, are of much later date. The stand at Bolderwood in the New Forest was planted in 1859, and has many trees of 46–47 m in height. Sutherland's Grove by the coast road south of Oban, Highlands, is of about the same date. Its best tree is 53 m × 144 cm. The avenue at Glenlee Park, New Galloway, planted in about 1864, has slender spires on many trees to over 50 m, the biggest being 53 m × 163 cm. The grove at Broadwood Farm, a Forest Walk near Dunster, Somerset, was planted in 1874 and has many near rivals to the tallest, 53 m × 144 cm.

Since the timber is strong and hard, such growth makes the tree of interest to foresters but its popularity waxes and wanes. It does need a deep, well-drained mineral soil and some shelter. It also suffers an apparent decline when about 20 years old after good growth, together with infestation by aphids. After thinning it normally regains health and vigour, except on some particular soils and areas, like the Coal Measures in South Wales, and it is no longer planted there.

The Douglas fir grows well when young under a moderate degree of summer shade and so it was planted under old oak and other deciduous woods where these were to be brought into quick yielding productive forest. It soon requires full overhead light so the overcrop has to be thinned and then felled within some ten years for the underplanting to remain vigorous. Old deciduous woods are now too much prized for wildlife and amenity value, and for some years now, in State Forests, they are preserved as broadleaf woods.

As young plantation Douglas fir closes its crown, it becomes, until the first thinning, as dark inside as any wood and shades out all the vegetation beneath. In this stage, which is prolonged if thinning is neglected, these woods gave commercial forestry a bad name for impoverishing the countryside, but they breed numbers of goldcrests and, as more light is let in, the ground plants return. In tall, older stands, some trees usually suffer broken tops and bush out at height. These trees are used for nesting by sparrowhawks and buzzards. Commercially there is no point in leaving Douglas fir to grow bigger than about 40 m tall as the logs become too big for ordinary equipment, but in many forests a ride-side line or belt, where the biggest trees in the stand usually are, is left to grow on for its scenic value. The soft foliage has a sweet, fruity scent when crushed.

Blue Douglas fir (var. *glauca*) extends over the Rocky Mountain system inland of the western slopes which are the home of the Green or Coastal form. It grows much more slowly and is seen here and there in gardens. Some foliage is very blue, but mainly it is dark blue-green and known best by the long, spreading or down-curved bracts on the coppery brown cones. There is a semi-avenue to 23 m × 43 cm outside the fenced garden at Nonsuch Park near Epsom, Surrey, and there are more specimens within it.

Golden Douglas fir ('Stairii') arose at Castle Kennedy, Dumfries, but there it only made a six m bush, almost white with the wool of infesting aphids, *Adelges*. It always has these but is sometimes seen to 20 m high, mostly in Scotland.

Bigcone Douglas fir (*Pseudotsuga macrocarpa*) grows on the mountains just north of Los Angeles, California, and was introduced in 1910. It is very rare and the two grafted plants at Bedgebury National Pinetum, Kent, dating from 1925 and now 22 m × 60 cm are the biggest and probably the only ones to have borne a cone or two.

Japanese Douglas fir (*Pseudotsuga japonica*) has a very poor growth and survival record in Britain, and the few ten m trees, at Bedgebury, Wakehurst Place, Sussex and Armadale Castle, Isle of Skye, give no sign of improving it.

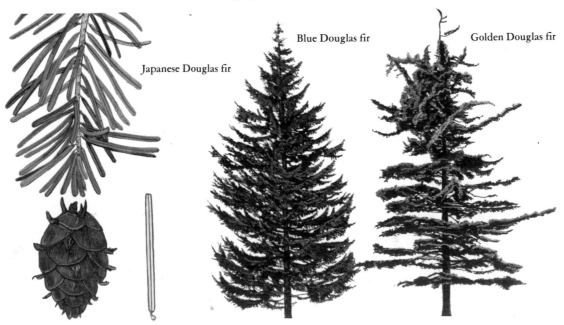

Japanese Douglas fir

Blue Douglas fir

Golden Douglas fir

Big-cone Douglas fir bark

male flowers

buds

leaf

Big-cone Douglas fir

Douglas fir

seed

female flowers

Blue Douglas fir

Douglas fir   cone variations

male flower

cone

Douglas fir

Big-cone Douglas fir

The Cedars

The true cedars are four species from the Mediterranean and western Himalayan regions and have no near relationship with the many New World trees called 'cedars' which are junipers and cypress relatives and even, in the case of 'cigar-box cedars', broadleaf trees.

The **Cedar of Lebanon** (*Cedrus libani*) occurs on mountains in southern Turkey as well as in the famous grove on Mount Lebanon. Although known and written about from early times, this tree was not brought into cultivation as early as is often assumed and the legends about it being brought back by the Crusaders and associations of some trees with Queen Elizabeth I cannot be sustained. The earliest definite references go back no further than 1679 when John Evelyn raised many trees, but there is considerable evidence that seed was brought by Dr Edward Pocock to Wilton House in about 1637. The story goes that one tree was kept for him until he took the living at Childrey Rectory, Wiltshire, where he planted it in 1643. It is now 252 cm in diameter.

Lancelot 'Capability' Brown used the Cedar of Lebanon in many of his schemes. Working in around 1750, he had probably not seen one more than ten years old, when they are narrowly conic, and of course he had none of the western American conifers now so widely used. He may therefore have intended a design of different aspect from that which the cedars gave when they matured. Many of the biggest specimens have huge low branches or their main stem divides low down and here only one can be spared a mention, at Pains Hill Park, Cobham, Surrey, 37 m × 313 cm at 0.5 m.

Clean, single boles are immensely impressive when they are big, and none is finer than one of the 1000 cedars planted at Goodwood Park in Sussex in 1761. This survivor, near the cricket pitch, is 34 m × 282 cm with three m clear. At Rousham Park, Oxon, a tree with six m clear is 42 m × 179 cm and at Claremont, Esher, in Surrey a tree with 15 m of cylindrical bole is 32 m × 206 cm. At Stowe Park in Buckinghamshire, a magnificent tree is 31 m × 259 cm, with a six m clear bole. At Blenheim Park, Oxon, a fine tree near the Cascade is 29 m × 269 cm. Some trees are deep green and many are quite bright blue. In some cases, they are scarcely distinguishable from an Atlas cedar but usually the Lebanon species have a more pinkish brown bark. **Golden cedar of Lebanon** ('Aurea') is occasionally seen as a small, slender young tree or a tree of moderate height with a broadly-spreading crown.

The **Cyprus cedar** (*Cedrus brevifolia*) found only on the Troodos Mountains, has much the shortest needles of the four species and a dark grey bark of nearly square plates. A tree normally seen only in big collections, there is one front garden roadside tree 17 m tall where a one-time nursery has been built over at Pitt Corner on the western outskirts of Winchester. A scattered group of six trees in Botany Bay near Totem Pole Ride in Windsor Great Park includes one 22 m × 48 cm.

The **Atlas cedar** (*Cedrus atlantica*) from the Atlas Mountains of Algeria and Morocco, has been grown in Britain only since about 1844, and so is not equal in size to the older Cedars of Lebanon, although several are now more than 32 m × 140 cm. It is common in churchyards and in garden surrounds but is much outnumbered, and virtually replaced in recent plantings by the **Blue Atlas cedar** (var. *glauca*) which grows among the dark green-leafed trees in the wild stands. The first seeds were brought in 1845 by Lord Somers who planted one of the trees by his garden gate at Eastnor Castle in Herefordshire, where it now is 31 m × 139 cm.

All the cedars flower in the autumn, the Atlas before the others in mid-September. The male flowers have been standing there all the summer, bright grey-green, making people think they are cones, and expand to four cm long, curving over at the tip as they shed masses of pollen before they fall off and carpet the ground beneath. **'Fastigiata'** arose as a seedling in France and, for a neat, shapely tree tolerating drought and liking lime in the soil, it has been peculiarly neglected as a valuable garden tree where space is limited. **'Pendula'** can be a hoop that does not increase in size noticeably for 20 years or, more rarely, a splendid cascade from seven–nine m high. One on the rock garden at Glasnevin Botanic Garden is pictured in Dublin papers on the rare occasions of heavy snowfalls there.

The **Deodar** (*Cedrus deodara*) was first sent from the Punjab in 1831 and is very common in gardens of Victorian houses around towns as well as in parks and larger gardens everywhere. The leading shoot arches over and the branch tips droop, a feature that is most prominent in young trees, a number of which have blue-grey foliage for many years. The male flowers and the cones are taller than in the other cedars and tend to be on separate branches. The female flowers, in the centre of the whorls of leaves, six mm tall and pale green tinged with pink, open when the males shed pollen in early November. The cones expand to half-size during the following summer and to their full 12–14 cm during the second summer, to break up on the tree in the winter. A few of the original trees survive around 34 m × 140 cm: and a few others are bigger, to 180 cm diameter, but there are many losses among old trees, as well as some younger ones, from honey-fungus or windblow.

Fastigiate Atlas cedar 20m

Atlas cedar bark

Weeping Atlas cedar 10m

Blue Atlas cedar 32m

male flower

Deodar

Cedar of Lebanon

Blue Atlas cedar

male flower

male flower

Cyprus cedar

bark

cone

bract from cone

Golden Cedar of Lebanon   Cedar of Lebanon 40m

Deodar 35m

The Larches

The **European larch** (*Larix decidua*) grows wild in the Alps from France to near Vienna and on the Tatra and Carpathian mountains, with a few woods of a distinct form on the plains of Poland. It was first grown in Britain in about 1625 and became common – and an important timber tree – only after the Dukes of Atholl made extensive plantations in the Tay Valley, beginning in about 1770. Some of the plants used were raised from five trees at Dunkeld and twelve at Blair Castle which had been planted in 1737 and had grown with remarkable vigour. One remains by Dunkeld Cathedral and is 32 m × 1.68 m. Six are left at Blair where the best, by Old Blair Bridge, is 43 m × 1.4 m.

Several other estates in Scotland have larches from the same 1737 parcel. All the big old Scottish larches tend to be claimed to be among them but few can be. In 1750 eleven trees were planted on Kennel Bank near Dunkeld Cathedral, probably the first plants raised from the old trees. They are now preserved and include one with a superb, clean bole 27.5 m long before the first branch. In 1789, twelve trees from Blair Castle seed were planted six each side of the road by Loch Earn at Ardvorlich. The best are 39 m × 1.51 m and 42 m.

An earlier Scottish planting had less impact on forestry but trees of 1725 planting still grow at Kailzie and Dawyck in the Borders Region. A curious trick of twisting a larch on its roots in increasingly big pots seems to be the cause of a few 'pedestal' or 'pot' larches of about 1740 planting. At Dunkeld and near Auchterarder in Tayside and at The Whittern in Herefordshire, a base two metres high and over two metres across supports a very big bole.

Larch comes into leaf early, and into flower just before that, but the leading shoot starts to expand much later, in May. By June, a strong young tree will be adding 10 cm a week. It then slows a little but regains speed and is fastest in early September before stopping in early October, by which time it is sometimes 1.3 m long.

In general, larches from the western Alps have stout, pink shoots and big cones, while eastwards the shoots become progressively more slender, yellow turning to white, and the cones smaller, until the Polish larch is at the extreme for all these features. Eastern seed yields trees growing here later, longer and faster than western, but less straight. Seed from the Sudeten Mountains gives a good compromise, fast and straight in stem.

Japanese larch (*Larix kaempferi, L. leptolepis*) grows in central Honshu and on Mt Fuji. It was introduced in 1861. The Japanese larch was very rare indeed until the Atholl and Dunkeld plantings of 1886, after which it began to be used in forestry. By 1940, wide expanses of hillsides, particularly in central Wales, were under plantations on thin bracken soils where this tree grows faster than European larch. Main shoots bear many side-shoots, so the crown is more dense, the bole expands more rapidly and more shade is cast. Given space, many Japanese larch grow strong, long, level branches making a broad crown, as have the eleven by the drive at Dunkeld, but the twelfth, separated from them and the biggest (33 m × 1.01 m) is less broad.

Flowering starts within about four years of planting and is profuse in most trees. The female flowers are often open in February and the males shed pollen a week or two later.

Hybrid larch (*Larix* x *eurolepis*) was first recognised in 1904 at Dunkeld when some seedlings from the Japanese larches there were noted in the nursery as larger and paler than the others. They were planted in several places on the Atholl Estates and one of the two near Blair Castle has now the biggest bole of any – one metre in diameter. After that, the seedlings from the Avenue trees were selected to make plantations of hybrids. The hybrid is intermediate between the parent species in all features except that it has taller cones and more flowers than either and can grow faster than either on many difficult sites – for example, on thin peats, in polluted air and on spoil-heaps. Young trees on good soil can add 1.5 m in height in a year, with 15 cm in a week, and can be 20 m tall in as many years. The leaves on the most rapidly-grown part of the leading shoot can be eight cm long. Hybrid seed is now obtained from seed-orchards where grafts from the most healthy, shapely and vigorous trees of each parent species are grown together and pollinate each other.

Siberian larch (*Larix sibirica*) grows from north-eastern Russia to mid-Siberia along the Yenisei River, beyond which is the **Dahurian larch** across to the Pacific Ocean. Siberian larch is like the European but has softly hairy shoots and cones. It can hardly grow in Britain, where it leafs out in January, but very shapely specimens grow in Finland, Iceland and eastern Canada.

The Dahurian larch is more like the Japanese, having dark red shoots and often a broad, branchy crown. It leafs out densely with grassy slender leaves in late January. A few at high altitudes are over 23 m tall but in lowland collections they are mostly branchy and bent at the top.

Tamarack (*Larix laricina*) grows from Labrador to Alaska and southwards around the Great Lakes. The few in Britain have good straight boles and slender crowns of curved, whippy shoots. Tamarack will grow where the soil is too wet for other larches and starts away rapidly but seldom achieves 20 m, nor does it live long.

Golden larch (*Pseudolarix amabilis*) differs from all others in having male flowers in clusters of 20, replacing the leaves on some spurs, cones with thick leathery scales on separate branches from the males, and spurs which grow longer every year. Sent from China in 1853, it remains rare, a broad tree, mainly in southern England, notable for its bright gold and orange autumn colouring.

Golden larch

Golden larch

Male flowers

Female flowers

European larch

Seed

Female flowers

Male flowers

Japanese larch

Seed

Cone

Hybrid larch

Siberian larch

Cone

Hybrid larch

European larch

Tamarack

Japanese larch

Norway Spruce

The **Norway spruce** (*Picea abies*) ranges widely in the mountains of Europe from the Balkans to Scandinavia, but is absent from the North European Plain. It is known to have been growing in Britain by 1548, but it may have been sent earlier. It is now most familiar as the Christmas tree, having replaced the Scots pine, which was used at first but upon which it is not nearly so easy to slip the rings from which most decorations are now hung. The Norway spruce was extensively planted as a forest tree in the eighteenth century and as much again, perhaps as cover for pheasants, during the century following. Since 1920 its place in forestry has been mainly limited to sites which are too frosty or exposed to dry winds for the best growth of the Sitka spruce. It was often planted in shelterbelts and as a screen around big gardens on the outskirts of towns where it is now thin in the crown, not being at all suited to urban air.

Growth is best on north-facing slopes or in deep northern glens and young trees will add one m a year for 15 years or so. Old trees grow very slowly in diameter and although the life-span is capable of exceeding 200 years, very many die when considerably less than this and few achieve diameters of 130 cm. Of the 72 trees noted as specimens before 1931, 63 have now gone, a very high proportion in comparison with other conifers.

The lower shoots of trees that look a little thin often have spindle-shaped swellings or pineapple galls showing the chambers where the larvae of the insect responsible have lived. These are made by an aphid which migrates to the larch to feed, and returns to the spruce to lay its eggs. Most Norway spruce that one encounters have a 'brush' crown in which the shoots spread in all directions from the branches, but here and there in any planting there are a few 'comb' spruce in which the shoots hang in lines from well-spaced branches. This crown-form, perhaps evolving to shed heavy snow, is frequent in the wild stands in the Carpathian Mountains and in Sweden where it is favoured as being superior in growth.

'Aurea' is seen in a few collections but seems not to have appealed to gardeners in general. It is attractive when the new shoots are expanding but from midsummer to the following May it can be recognized only by the not very pleasing yellowish tinge left on some leaves and by a generally pallid look. One in Specimen Avenue at Westonbirt Arboretum has grown fast and is now 33 m × 58 cm when about 80 years old. An older tree at Castlewellan, County Down, near Cypress Pond is 28 m × 74 cm.

Siberian spruce (*Picea obovata*) is the eastern extension of the Norway spruce across Siberia and to some extent grades into it in European Russia, but the eastern form grown in Britain is very different. A scarce tree found in some collections, it has a conical crown with upcurved branch-ends; slender and often bright green needles with a pair projecting widely wherever there is a bud on the shoot; and small, five–eight cm cones with down-curved scale-tips. Introduced in 1908 and of rather slow growth, few are 15 m tall.

The **Serbian spruce** (*Picea omorika*) is a relict of a pre-Ice Ages flora in which spruces with flattened leaves spread widely. Today flat-leafed spruces are confined to each side of the northern Pacific Ocean and through China to the eastern Himalayas only, with the exception of this Serbian species discovered in 1875 in the Upper Drava Valley, Yugoslavia. Introduced in 1889 it has shown a remarkable ability – for a spruce – to thrive on chalky or acid, peaty soil and in towns. Unfortunately it is also unusually susceptible to honey-fungus and most of those planted before 1910 have now died. Many have not waited so long and it is all too often that a specimen noted in an arboretum on the first visit as a good tree is thin and sickly on the second visit and has gone by the third. There are, however, some notable early trees at present in robust health. None more so than the three planted in 1897 on Jubilee Terrace at Murthly Castle by the River Tay, all similar in size and slender crown, the tallest being 33 m × 65 cm. Another in good condition is the extraordinarily dense, columnar one planted in 1910 in Conifer Walk, Sheffield Park, Sussex and now 29 m × 56 cm. The first tree planted to start the Savill Garden in Windsor Great Park in 1933 is now a fine specimen 26 m × 48 cm. Serbian spruces flower at the same time as other spruces, in early May but open their vegetative buds later, three weeks after the Sitka spruce. They are therefore rarely damaged by frost.

Sargent spruce (*Picea brachytyla*) was sent from China in 1901 and is a beautiful tree grown in most collections. The flattened leaves are as thickly white-covered beneath as any tree, and are pressed down slightly each side of the smooth white shoot.

The **White spruce** (*Picea glauca*) spreads across Canada from Labrador to Alaska but has a very poor survival record in Britain, where it has been grown since 1700. The square-sectioned leaves usually stand stiffly above the smooth white or pinkish-tinged shoot and when crushed have a scent somewhere between mice and grapefruit.

Schrenk's spruce (*Picea schrenkiana*) from East Siberia and China seldom looks happy here. One prominent in Wisley Gardens, Surrey, is 17 m × 30 cm and few are bigger, but despite the stout shoots bearing leaves all round them, the foliage is thin.

female flowers   male flowers   White spruce   Siberian spruce   female flower   male flowers

Norway spruce

male flowers

female flower

Schrenk's spruce

Serbian spruce

male flowers

female flowers

underleaf

bark

Sargent spruce

cone-scale

'comb' type

Norway spruce   Northern Swedish type   'Aurea'   Sargent spruce   Serbian spruce

Sitka Spruce

The **Sitka spruce** (*Picea sitchensis*) extends for 4000 km on a chain of islands and in a belt by the mainland coast from Kodiak Island off Alaska to mid-California. This is one of the most intricately fretted coastlines in the world and even where the belt is at its broadest the tree is near tidal water. Low and bushy in western Alaska, Sitka is the world's biggest spruce: many in Washington are 80 m × 350 cm. In the last stand southward, at Caspar in California, mixed with the southernmost Grand firs, the trees are 40 m tall.

David Douglas sent the first seed in 1831 and three trees from this seed survive in Ireland, but the majority of the immense trees in Scotland, now 45–55 m × 200–220 cm, were raised from seed sent in 1851 by John Jeffrey and William Lobb. Even in 1920, the way that the Sitkas towered from the castle policy woods everywhere, however high the rainfall or northerly the site, was so marked that the first Forestry Commissioners adopted it as the main species for planting on the large areas of peat in the western Highlands that they had acquired for afforestation.

Sixty years later, after extensive trials of every other tree at all likely to succeed on these sites, none has been found to rival Sitka spruce and it is the mainstay of productive forestry in all the western hills. It is less successful where rainfall is below 1000 mm a year or on sites liable to late frosts. In the drier areas, particularly after a mild winter, the trees suffer infestation by the Green spruce aphid: all needles except the last year's turn brown and are shed, making the trees look thin and sick, although they usually recover.

Although anathema to many naturalists and countryside bodies, Sitka is not only highly attractive in late spring with bright green brushes of new foliage on blue-green and silvered crowns, but new plantings are among the richest of all habitats for nesting warblers and finches in variety, tree-pipits and many other birds. After early thinnings, plantations have high populations again of many birds, and provide cover and roosts. Since these trees are often covering what had previously been man-made semi-desert in a high rainfall area, a gross misuse of land, with barely a meadow-pipit per hundred hectares, they increase the diversity of wildlife spectacularly.

Brewer spruce (*Picea brewerana*) grows in small groves at around 2000 m in the Siskiyou Mountains straddling the border between California and Oregon. The first import was of a single tree sent to Kew Gardens in 1897 and planted near the pagoda. It is now a thinly foliaged 14 m × 22 cm. Many seedlots were received between 1907 and 1911 and it is from these that the finest trees have derived.

Whenever a Brewer spruce is reported to be 30 m tall it is an erroneous identification and the tree is, and must be for the next 30 years or so, a **Morinda spruce** (*Picea smithiana*) from the Western Himalayas, which is quite often of that height and occasionally 38 m tall. Unlike the Brewer spruce, which is in the group with flattened needles banded white beneath, the Morinda has nearly round dark green needles, slender and four cm long. The original tree, received in 1818, grows at Hopetoun House near the Forth Bridge, together with a graft made from it on to Norway spruce in 1826.

Colorado blue spruce (*Picea pungens* var. *glauca*) occurs among the wild stands in the eastern Rocky Mountains of the United States. Anthony Waterer brought cuttings back to his Knaphill Nursery in 1877 from a selected blue seedling growing at Harvard, Massachusetts.

A remarkably silver-blue, rather slow form 'Hoopsii' has been imported from America more recently. **Blue Engelmann spruce** (*Picea engelmannii* var. *glauca*) is also bluer than the usual Blue Colorado spruces and differs in its soft, menthol-scented foliage and orange bark with small papery flakes. It is found in the wild stands in the Rocky Mountains and is grown only in collections, more in Scotland than elsewhere.

The **Hondo spruce** (*Picea jezoensis* var. *hondoensis*) is the hardy form from Honshu, Japan, of a spruce widespread in north-eastern Asia. It is common in collections everywhere but uncommon in gardens. The leaves, very blue-white banded beneath, stand stiffly above the stout white or cream shoot. It makes a sturdy tree, to 28 m × 108 cm at Benmore, Highlands, and sometimes to over 30 m.

The **Likiang spruce** (*Picea likiangensis*) from Tibet and western China was introduced in 1910 and is common in some collections. There are 20 trees in Wakehurst Place, to 22 m × 57 cm, and seven at Bedgebury to 19 m × 69 cm. This tree is, however, scarce in gardens, one of the few being a splendid one 21 m × 69 cm at Beaufront Castle, Northumberland. The very blue foliage is held on widely spreading upcurved branches with pale grey bark. The great feature of this species is the abundance of the rich red flowers opening in early May and often almost covering the crown. It is well represented at Bedgebury in most years by the trees grouped along a stream.

The **Purple spruce** (*Picea purpurea*) is a form of the Likiang spruce which has more hairy shoots, rough, scaly, dark bark and dark green foliage on its densely upswept crown. **Koyama's spruce** (*Picea koyamai*) comes from Korea and a single grove of about 100 trees in Japan.

female flowers

female flowers

Likiang spruce

male flowers

Hondo spruce

Koyama's spruce

female flower

male flower

Sitka spruce

Morinda spruce

Colorado blue spruce

male flowers

Brewer spruce

female flower

Englemann spruce 'Glauca'

Sitka spruce   Englemann spruce   Colorado blue spruce   Morinda spruce   Brewer spruce

Other Spruces

The **Dragon spruce** (*Picea asperata*) is native to the mountains of western China and was introduced to cultivation by Ernest Wilson in 1910. It is a rather variable tree and in a blue-foliaged form it makes a respectable specimen. As generally seen, however, it is dull, twiggy and untidy with loose papery bark. It has seldom been planted in gardens although it is frequent in collections. Gardeners may also have been discouraged by the rigid spined needles, but Borde Hill in Sussex and Westonbirt in Gloucestershire have at least 18 trees each and Bedgebury Pinetum has 23. The best specimens, however, are at Powerscourt in County Wicklow, one by the Pepperpot, 19 m × 48 cm and the other beside a path below, 23 m × 45 cm. In flower the Dragon spruce is not much inferior to the Likiang but is less prolific. Its stout leading shoot is usually about 30 cm long and held at a slight angle from true vertical.

Alcock's spruce (*Picea bicolor*) is one of the only two spruces to have blue-white bands on the underside of needles that are not flat in cross-section but nearly square (this is denoted by the adjective 'bicolor'). It has a distinctive crown with strong low branches gently curving upwards, densely clothed in foliage. Sent from Japan in 1861, it shares the tendency of some other spruces from that country to have a short life and to prefer cool, moist sites.

Tigertail spruce (*Picea polita*) was also first sent from Japan in 1861, and is very often short-lived, to a greater extent than Alcock's or other spruces. The group of half a dozen planted at Bedgebury in 1925 was reduced to one by 1980. Despite this, a few old trees live on and look very healthy although they are growing slowly. The best of these are: one to the south of the lake at Stourhead in Wiltshire, 27 m × 77 cm; one by the drive at Pencarrow in Cornwall, 22 m × 100 cm; and one at Petworth House in Sussex, 26 m × 70 cm. The needles are rigid and very sharply spined such that they will draw blood if grasped with any appreciable grip. The Latin word *polita* means 'polished' and may refer to the shining chestnut brown buds or the general shininess of the yellow-green leaves which may be dark or a fresh grassy green. The tree can be identified from afar by this colour, by its short, level branches and by the amount of dead twiggery carried in the crown even of a healthy tree.

The **Black spruce** (*Picea mariana*) grows across Canada from Labrador to Alaska, and is the tree with extraordinarily slender spires that stands in small groups by the Icefield Parkway to Jasper, Alberta. It extends round the Great Lakes into the United States and in about 1700 was sent to Bishop Compton at Fulham Palace. Like the Japanese spruces, it has a short life but unlike them it grows very slowly while it is alive. It is quite a pleasing tree with its dense crown of pale bluish foliage but upward growth is so slow that instead of the very slender crown of the wild tree it tends to acquire a rounded, bushy top once it is over ten or 12 m in height. A pair of unusually good trees is at Nymans, Sussex (both 22 m × 55 cm) and Wisley Gardens in Surrey grows a reasonable tree, 18 m × 46 cm.

The **Red spruce** (*Picea rubens*) is closely related to the Black spruce and hybridizes with it where its limited range overlaps to the east of the Great Lakes. The species as grown in Britain, however, are quite distinct and whereas the Black spruce has blue, soft leaves all round the shoot, the Red has hard, grassy green leaves standing up from it. It is a tree seen in collections only and of no great size.

The **Sikkim spruce** (*Picea spinulosa*) is a flat-needled spruce with the forward-pointing needles all round the hanging shoots, slender and sharply tipped. The crown is very open, there being almost no interior foliage and the branch whorls far apart, often one m or so because young trees make an annual shoot of that length. One planted in 1911 in Warren Wood, Borde Hill, Sussex is 30 m × 80 cm and in the Woodland Valley at Wakehurst Place not far away, there is one, 31 m × 66 cm, that is probably not as old. It has been planted only in collections but is found in those everywhere except in western Scotland.

Wilson's spruce (*Picea wilsonii*) is the Chinese form of the Siberian spruce. It has very slender needles on slender, pallid white shoots and can either be bushy and broad or quite slender. In some collections it is 17 m tall, a dark and not very robust-looking tree.

The **Oriental spruce** (*Picea orientalis*) from the Caucasus and north-eastern Turkey was introduced in 1839 and was one of the standard set of conifers used in the great surge of pinetum planting from 1850 to 1880. It is frequent also in large gardens generally. It has the shortest needle of any spruce, shining dark green with a broad, bevelled tip, held closely all round the main shoots and remaining green for up to ten years. Young trees have singularly regular, whorled branches and make Christmas trees far superior in shape, ease of dressing and retention of needles to the Norway spruce but can rarely be obtained for the purpose. After rapid early growth, it tends to slow markedly from about the fiftieth year. In England, but not in Scotland, some of the oldest trees, over 30 m tall, are dying back at the tips. An original tree, however, planted in 1840 at Stanage Park, Powys, was green to the tip when 34 m × 105 cm in 1978.

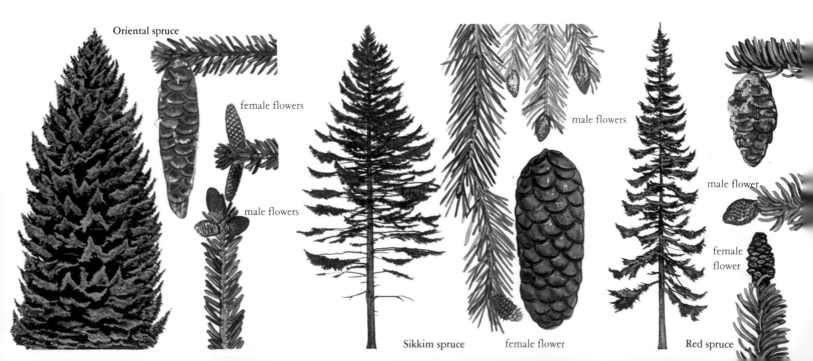

Oriental spruce

female flowers

male flowers

male flowers

male flower

female flower

Sikkim spruce

female flower

Red spruce

female flower

male flowers

Dragon spruce

Alcock's spruce

male flower

female flower

Tigertail spruce

leaf underside

cone scale

Black spruce

male flowers

female flowers

bark

end view of shoot

cone scale

Wilson's chinese spruce

Alcock's spruce

Dragon spruce

Tigertail spruce

Black spruce

Hemlock

The hemlocks are a small group of conifers related to the spruces, and are now native to the eastern and western sides of North America, the Himalayas, China and Japan. They acquired the name of the famous poisonous herb merely because the scent of crushed leaves of the first one known to western botanists, the Eastern hemlock, was thought to be similar to that of the herb.

The **Western hemlock** (*Tsuga heterophylla*) is the giant of the genus and in Washington State, near the middle of its long range from Alaska to Northern California, some roadside trees below Mount Rainier are 70 m tall. The tree was introduced in 1851 by John Jeffrey but he did not send much seed and only one tree, at Hafodunas in Clwyd, now 37 m × 138 cm, and one at Boturich Castle, Loch Lomond, are known from his seed. The numerous very big specimens elsewhere were planted in and after 1860 from later seed. In Tayside and the Highlands of Scotland, the long, slender spires are in many places over 45 m tall and growing fast.

Young trees grow one m a year or more in some shelter on a variety of soils from light sands to heavy clays and deep peats, and will do so for many years under considerable shade. This recommends the tree to a forester wishing to underplant old oak, larch or pine, although the timber is not of high quality and is used mostly for pulping. In dry eastern regions, growth falls away once the tops are out of shelter and it is in the cool, wet west and north that the fine big trees grow. This species is also intolerant of any but the best air and is hopelessly thin and unsightly as an ornamental tree near big towns.

The Western hemlock shares a feature of growth with the Deodar and Lawson cypress alone among the world's trees. It dangles its leading shoot as a 'dropper' in a wide arc, an adaptation to growing up beneath other trees and threading its way through them, eventually to dominate them. The fragile new growth is always pointing downwards and out of harm's way when the woody top of the arc is blown against an adjacent branch. In the middle of the growing season much of the old drooped leader straightens up, going past the offending branch and bringing the now hardened new shoot up to become the new dropper, the terminal bud still hanging safely below.

Eastern hemlock (*Tsuga canadensis*) is as shapely as the Western and a pale green in its natural woods from Nova Scotia down to Georgia, but in Britain it is a dark, dull tree nearly always with big low branches making a broad crown. The leaves taper from near the base and on most shoots: those along the centre are twisted to show their white-banded undersides, which gives the foliage a distinctive pattern. Being usually bushy when young, it is occasionally planted as a hedge, but the Western hemlock makes a superior one. There are trees in many old gardens in the countryside, with nearly black, coarsely-fissured bark. Few of them are good trees.

The **Carolina hemlock** (*Tsuga caroliniana*) is a rare tree, found in a few deep valleys in the Allegheny Mountains, and rare in Britain too. It is ten–14 m tall in some collections and has handsome dark shining green foliage in a dense crown, although each individual leaf is slender and stands out well from the shiny brown shoot.

The **Chinese hemlock** (*Tsuga chinensis*) is a broad tree with a dark grey flaking bark, yellowish-green leaves banded pale green beneath, but otherwise like the Western hemlock, and nodding branch-tips.

The **Southern Japanese hemlock** (*Tsuga sieboldii*) is a broad, often branchy tree in a number of gardens and collections, but usually it has a central stem, sometimes two, to make an acute top to the crown. The smooth shoot is shiny and may be white or brown and the leaves vary from broad, stubby and well silvered beneath, similar to the Northern species (below) to rather slender and dull white beneath, although always with a blunt, notched tip.

The **Northern Japanese hemlock** (*Tsuga diversifolia*) is as frequently seen as the Southern, but tends to be more bushy. Positively distinguished from it only by the hairy grooves in the shoot shown under a lens, it is often fairly safely separable by its orange-brown shoot and very stubby leaves brightly silvered beneath.

The **Himalayan hemlock** (*Tsuga dumosa*) is somewhat tender and makes a good tree only in Ireland and from Cornwall to the Highlands. Its drooping foliage of long leaves heavily silvered beneath is very handsome and its bark is pink-brown and finely flaky.

The **Mountain hemlock** (*Tsuga mertensiana*) was sent from the western ranges of the Rocky Mountains by Jeffrey in 1854 and is widespread although not abundant in large (and occasionally small) gardens everywhere. For a snowline, glacier-foot tree it grows quite well on sandy soils in eastern England, where its slow start gives it a bushy base and later growth of moderate speed surmounts that with a slender spire of drooping, variably dark blackish green and blue-white foliage. Fine, level branches grow from a bole with dark orange and black scaling bark.

Jeffrey's hybrid hemlock (*Tsuga x jeffreyi*) is not often seen but is of interest for its strange origin. The first plant was the only seed to germinate in a packet of Mountain hemlock sent by Jeffrey in 1851. The next arose from a packet of rhododendron seeds and it was only in 1969 that wild trees, hybrids between the Mountain and Western hemlocks, were found in Washington.

Southern Japanese hemlock

Northern Japanese hemlock

Mountain hemlock

Eastern hemlock

Western hemlock

Southern Japanese hemlock

Northern Japanese hemlock

Jeffrey's hybrid hemlock

Carolina hemlock

Himalayan hemlock

Chinese hemlock

Eastern hemlock

Carolina hemlock

Mountain hemlock

Western hemlock

Scots Pine

The **Scots pine** (*Pinus sylvestris*) has the widest natural range of any pine, growing from the mountains of Spain and Scotland eastward through the Crimea to Eastern Siberia. In Scotland the old native stands remain from the Black Wood of Rannoch to Glen Finnan and around Loch Maree in Wester Ross, with some of the best in the Spey Valley and Upper Dee. It has been planted as the chief forest tree on most Scottish estates until replaced on many after 1850 by the western American conifers of more rapid growth, available since that time. It remains the favoured tree on high ground on many estates in the Grampian and Highland Regions, and also over large areas of Northumberland. It was the usual species for forests on lowland English heaths like the Breckland in Norfolk, but except in a few special cases like Windsor Forest it is being replaced by the Corsican pine, which grows much faster.

The seed used for the Breckland plantings mostly came from unsuitable sources, mainly the Harz Mountains, and although very easy to grow and starting well, the trees make little progress above 12 m tall. The New Forest Scots pine first came from Grampian in 1777, and this has grown well, but the Corsican is better still.

The first Scots pine planted in England are thought to date from 1660 when a few were planted at Eversleigh and Bramshill in north Hampshire and survive today. From these and other plantings, Scots pine ran wild over the Berkshire and Surrey heaths. To preserve parts of these for the rare and threatened Dartford warbler, smooth snake and natterjack toad, conservationists have to cut the thousands of young trees which spring up. Planted on light, well-drained soil, this is a reliable, easy tree to establish and many soon make annual shoots up to one metre long, but this growth is not sustained. The top becomes diffuse and domed, usually below 25 m, and not many trees exceed 30 m with the tallest being only 37 m.

The boles of open grown trees at their most rapid will add one cm diameter for a few years but this slows down markedly and older trees increase very slowly. Boles bigger than one metre in diameter are found only on the occasional tree, whether in deep wooded combes in Sussex or in castle gardens in the Highlands. An exceptional tree by the drive at Ballogie, Aboyne is 34 × 1.4 m and one in the picnic site at Speymouth Forest, Fochabers is 30.5 m × 1.38 m. The most remarkable is at a house in Somerset and has a bole clear for seven m and 1.55 m in diameter.

Female flowers, soft pink, are borne by trees only five or six years old. They are at the tips of the most vigorous shoots, usually the leading shoot and those from the whorl below. As the tree grows, the vigorous shoots and hence the female flowers are increasingly high in the crown. As maturity approaches and vigour falls away, these flowers begin to grow at the tips of weaker shoots. Old trees bear them, and thus cones, all over the crown. Male flowers arise only on weak, dangling shoots. Young trees take some years before there are such shoots, until which time they bear no males. Old trees are all weak shoots and have male flowers, with the females, all over the crown. The females open a week or two before the males on the same tree, so avoiding inbreeding by fertilization from their own pollen. The pollen enters the female flower in June and the flower closes into a conelet but remains the same size. The actual fertilization occurs the next spring and the cone then swells, becomes shiny bright green during the summer and woody and ripe by late autumn.

'Fastigiata' is a rare tree but is becoming better known and more widely planted. One of the very few older trees is at the RHS Garden at Wisley in Surrey and has begun to open out somewhat.

Austrian pine (*Pinus nigra* var. *nigra*) is the Black pine of Central Europe and was not grown in Britain until 1840. It is, however, very common, especially in shelterbelts, including those around large old gardens in suburbs; on railway embankments; in town parks, and near the sea – in fact on those sites which few other conifers can tolerate. It is exceptionally tough, on chalk, clay or sand and is easy to raise from seed, making sturdy young plants. It has the blackest, scaliest and most rugged bark of all four Black pine forms and the shortest, most curved and stiffest needles. These help to identify those less usual specimens which have respectable crowns on single straight boles.

Crimean pine (*Pinus nigra* var. *caramanica*) comes also from Asia Minor and the Caucasus region and is the most vigorous and largest growing of the Black pines. Many are around 40 m tall and 1.5 m in diameter. They all have a curious feature which distinguishes them from a distance. The bole divides some 6 m up into several closely-held, vertical branches or secondary boles. The foliage is halfway between the short, stiff, markedly whorled Austrian and the lax, long, unwhorled Corsican. This is not a common tree and is seldom seen growing around fields but is in many big gardens and collections and is generally the biggest pine there.

Pyrenean pine (*Pinus nigra* var. *cebennensis*) grows also in the Massif Centrale in France. It is infrequent in Britain and is known from afar by its domed crown densely hung with lax, slender pale needles, yet it is obviously a Black pine.

Mountain pine (*Pinus uncinata*) grows on the Pyrenees and the Alps and is often merely a big bush, but the tree form, more often seen in the Pyrenees, makes a sturdy plant up to 18 m tall. The two best are in the churchyard at Patterdale, Cumbria, but more are seen struggling to make trees along the top of some of the highest plantations.

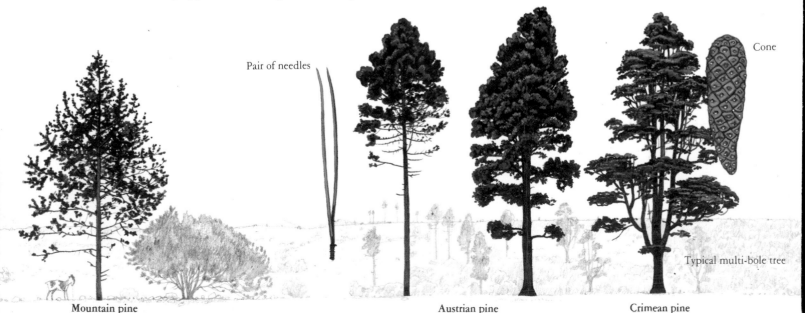

Pair of needles

Cone

Mountain pine

Typical multi-bole tree

Austrian pine

Crimean pine

conelets

Female flowers

Pine-looper moth

Scots pine

Pair of needles

Seed

Ripe cone

Shoot with young cones

Cone

Mountain pine

Seed

Scots pine

'Fastigiata'

Scots pine

Corsican pine

Stone Pine

The **Stone pine** (*Pinus pinea*) was probably the first exotic conifer to be grown in Britain, around 500 years ago, and although it comes from Mediterranean parts with long dry summers it has been grown successfully everywhere in England north to Cumbria and in the Border Region of Scotland. Unexpectedly, it shows no preference for the hotter and drier eastern side, rather the reverse, with many of the biggest trees in South Wales, especially, and in Devon and Cornwall. It is fun to grow. The big seeds, which are made into a flour in Italy, and eaten raw or cooked in many countries in vegetarian foods, sprout unusually big seedlings with a dozen five cm pale green cotyledons on a stout three cm stem.

As in all pines, the first leaves are the flat, long-pointed 'primordial leaves', but in this species (and a few others) these are the only foliage for many years; long, toothed and silvery blue. In four to five years, the plant is an upright-branched narrow bush over one m tall before the green paired needles emerge between these soft primordial leaves. By the time it is about ten years old it is starting to grow the broad umbrella crown typical of the old tree, and beginning to bear flowers and cones. Even old trees will sprout primordial leaves again if they are browsed or otherwise cut back on low branches.

The **Maritime pine** (*Pinus pinaster*) from the western Mediterranean was also introduced at an unknown, very early date, and has similar seedlings to the Stone pine, juvenile and silver-blue until one m high. It differs, though, in growing further north, to the Highlands, and in the biggest specimens being in the Midlands and southeast of England. Most of them are hidden deep in large estates in Sussex. It also grows much faster with young trees adding well over one m a year even on very poor sandy soils, and can be 34 m tall. There are a few plantations, generally near the sea and on sand-dunes and they have an unmistakable aspect with swept bases to the boles and very open canopies. The cones adhere in clusters on the tree for many years and when picked newly ripe they are ornamental, shining rich redbrown and up to 12 cm long.

The **Red pine** (*Pinus resinosa*) from the Great Lakes and St Lawrence Basin is a handsome but rare tree seen only in collections and mostly in the south of England. It has the feature that the long, paired needles snap cleanly and readily when bent into a curve. The upper bole and branches develop a dark red bark very like the Scots pine.

The **Japanese red pine** (*Pinus densiflora*) is, in effect, a Scots pine with slender, dark green needles in tufts on green shoots and numerous clusters of pointed cones. It makes an attractive young tree in many collections but tends to decline into a twiggy, low-domed,

thinly-foliaged tree. At Wisley in Surrey it is 14 m × 36 cm and past its best, but in Warren Wood, Borde Hill, Sussex, one is 22 m tall and in fine shape.

Japanese black pine (*Pinus thunbergii*) is one of the few conifers in the world to grow on the shore where seawater washes its roots, but it has not been tried in that position in Britain. It is also notorious for its lack of restraint in flowering. Always prolific, it often goes about it with such enthusiasm that all the needles on a year's growth of some shoots are replaced by female flowers. There can be 200 of them in a long whorl, densely packed so that the cones cannot develop. Young trees are attractive, narrow, upright and very dark with the silky white buds prominent. Old trees become picturesque in a Japanese style, a few long branches snaking out with thin foliage in whorls, and often leaning.

The **Bishop pine** (*Pinus muricata*) is scattered in small groves along the coast of California and was first described from a little patch on low hills near San Luis Obispo in 1846 when seed was sent. The few old trees with hugely domed crowns are of this or similar origin. One is at Ebernoe House in Sussex, 29 m × 134 cm; one is by the moat at Eastnor Castle, Herefordshire, 26 m × 105 cm; and a third is in Claremont, Surrey, 25 m × 100 cm. However, northern groves in Mendocino County are very different, with tall, slender-conic trees of blue-black foliage, and young plots grown from this northern seed have shown extraordinary vigour. At Wakehurst Place in Sussex several trees planted in 1917 and now to 29 m × 105 cm are also of a northern, 'blue' origin. The spined cones adhere tightly for 60–70 years and if a crown-fire were to sweep through, the seed would be released and germinate.

The **Macedonian pine** (*Pinus peuce*) is a five-needle pine not only resistant to the blister-rust but seemingly to everything else. It grows, steadily, if not precipitately, wherever it is, from mountainsides at 600 m to chalklands or coastal heaths. It is always shapely, rather upswept, neat and dense, and full of health. Except for the very different Chinese white pine, it is the only five-needle species with a smooth, bright green shoot.

The **Jack pine** (*Pinus banksiana*) grows across most of Canada as a scrubby plant of the muskeg bogs and is little better in the many collections that grow it in Britain. It resembles a thin, scrawny Lodgepole pine, but with its cones smooth and pointing forwards, not backwards. Some of them remain on the tree until, grey with lichen and algae, they are partially embedded in the branch. Old trees have pendulous shoots and are sometimes over 22 m tall.

Japanese black pine

Japanese red pine

Shore pine

Ponderosa pine
female flowers

male flowers

male flowers

Lodgepole pine

Aleppo pine

female flowers

male flowers

Western white pine

Calabrian pine

Limber pine

Lodgepole pine

male flowers

Japanese white pine

Western white pine

female flowers

Ponderosa pine

Japanese white pine

Corsican Pine

The **Corsican pine** (*Pine nigra* var. *maritima*) is the form of Black pine found in Corsica and southern Italy. It was the first of the four forms to be introduced, in 1729, and is the only one important in forestry. Today it is replacing Scots pine on southern heaths and in the Norfolk Brecklands because it yields timber in much greater volume. It is of generally lower quality but for many uses this matters little. It is very common in old gardens around country towns, like the coarser, darker Austrian form, but of superior shape and with more open, lax foliage. Young plantations show the foliage and branches in regular layers, from whorls separated by 60–90 cm of the clean stem of each year's growth. At the size used for planting out, about 80 cm, the needles are very long, much twisted and are in bundles of three–five near the tip of the shoot instead of the normal pairs. Great spotted woodpeckers will pick cones and take them to an old stump to extract the seed, building up piles of discards. In places seedlings sow themselves but they usually grow into spindly plants and come to little.

The tree is an unusually useful conifer for shelter as well as forestry since it can grow well on chalk, clay and poor sands and is highly resistant to pollution. Although there are good 36 m specimens as far north as Skibo Castle in Sutherland and bigger around Inverness, Corsican pine is not generally successful as a plantation tree in Scotland away from coastal plains. At any significant altitude a fungus, *Brunchorstia*, can be devastating and make it look as if fire has swept through the trees. It is the cool summers that make the tree susceptible.

Montezuma pine (*Pinus montezumae*) is a complex of pines in Mexico which can be regarded as a varying number of separate species or as varieties of the one. It is said to have been introduced under 50 different names in many forms, with the first being sent in 1839. The form usual in Britain with great sweeps' brushes of stiff grey-blue needles, is, however, not seen today in Mexico. All the various forms seen over a thousand miles of wooded mountains have grey or yellowish-green drooping needles. The typical British specimen has needles in fives, 30–45 cm long, on very stout shining orange-brown shoots and strong level branches holding a big broadly-domed crown.

Hartweg's pine (var. *hartwegii*) is the form which grows at 4000 m on the shoulders of Popocatepetl and was also introduced in 1839. It has its needles arranged as much in threes as in fives and slender, grey-blue shoots.

Bigcone pine (*Pinus coulteri*) sent from the mountains between Los Angeles and Monterey, California in 1832, is very vigorous indeed as a young tree but of the 26 specimens recorded by 1931 only one, which was then only six years old, could be found by 1956. The oldest known today is probably about 70 years old. It is at Stanway, Gloucestershire and 21 m × 92 cm. In 19 years a tree at the Hillier Arboretum, Hampshire, is 13 m × 52 cm and one at Wisley Gardens, Surrey, 26 years old is 13 m × 51 cm. The first cone may be borne within 12–15 years of planting but then there is often a gap of 15 years or so before regular bearing starts. Several old trees now dead were bearing barrowloads of cones each year right to the end.

The **Weymouth pine** (*Pinus strobus*) once covered vast areas from Newfoundland to west of the Great Lakes and after 1705 it was planted in almost every garden and estate in Britain. At Longleat, the heir to the Earldom of Bath planted it so widely that it was named from his courtesy title, Lord Weymouth. It grew rapidly and the timber is remarkably even in its structure and so of value in specialist uses, such as the making of musical instruments. However, by 1900 the blister-rust fungus had struck, and today there are very few plantations, and old trees are dying.

The **Chinese white pine** (*Pinus armandii*) is a five-needle pine with pale green leaves, a green shoot marked with resin and barrel-shaped cones. It is usually thinly foliaged and looks in poor health but at Fota Island in County Cork it was 19 m × 77 cm in 1966.

The **Lacebark pine** (*Pinus bungeana*) from China has the most decorative bark of any conifer. It can be mainly blue-grey or rich green and in both cases it sheds large flakes to leave patches which start white or yellow and turn through browns to dark red. It has its smooth, hard needles in threes, cones freely and may be low-branched and bushy like two of the original trees from 1846 seed near the Palm House at Kew.

The **Bhutan pine** (*Pinus wallichiana*) is the only five-needle pine which is frequent in or near towns, growing in many of the older, now semi-suburban gardens and parks. It grows and ages rapidly, dying at the top but healthy below and bearing quantities of the long, very resinous cones. It has stout shoots with a blue-grey bloom and fissured bark coloured pinky-brown or orange.

The **Arolla pine** (*Pinus cembra*) is preserved in the High Alps and planted even higher to hold the snow on slopes liable to avalanches. Its cones, deep blue in summer, are borne only rather high on old trees and fall complete with the seeds. Rodents eat the seeds out and leave the cores with glistening white hollows. A five-needle pine with densely-held foliage, it grows a level-branched columnar crown rather slowly and is reasonably common in small numbers in all parts of the British Isles.

female flowers

male flowers

Bhutan pine

Arolla pine

male flowers

female flower

male flowers

female flowers

Bigcone pine

Weymouth pine

Lacebark pine

Montezuma pine

Chinese white pine

male flowers

Corsican pine

female flower

female flowers

male flowers

male flowers

Montezuma pine

Hartweg's pine

Chinese white pine

Weymouth pine

Corsican pine

Monterey Pine

The **Monterey pine** (*Pinus radiata*) is in several ways a remarkable tree, as the name by which it is known to many of the older gardeners and more widely in Cornwall, 'Insignis pine' denotes. In the few kilometers of the largest part of its few native groves, on Carmel peninsular in California, it is of no account, infested by a sinister brown and lethal mistletoe and barely 23 m tall and 50 cm diameter when it dies about 100 years old. Yet only 90 km to the north, on an irrigated lawn in San Francisco it can grow 16 m tall in five years; in Devon, Cornwall, and Ireland in 40 years it can be 30 m tall and in 80 years two m in diameter, while in New Zealand it has become 60 m tall in 41 years. In the semi-tropics it grows continuously without setting a bud and is the mainstay of many timber industries. In Cornwall it has sometimes grown 15 cm by the end of January.

It is a fire-climax tree, holding on to its cones until a fire comes through the crown. In the general absence of such fires in Britain, the cones remain unopened for 20 years or more, their weight being often the chief cause of a branch being blown out of the crown. In a few southern places, seeds are eventually shed and seedlings grow up, usually under too much shade for vigorous growth. Cones wrested from a branch can be put for an hour or two in a hot oven and the seeds will be expelled and grow well. They transplant poorly, however, unless they are put out around midsummer and never allowed to become at all pot-bound. They grow very fast on almost any soil, even just above chalk, but in that case they begin to turn yellow once about 30 years old and 20 m tall and soon deteriorate.

The male flowers turn bright yellow as the new shoot expands, often before April. In eastern parts, height growth, starting in late March, often ceases with a set bud by July and may or may not start again through August to early October.

Mexican pine (*Pinus patula*) is a three-needle pine at once recognizable by its scaly, bright orange bark and hanging lines of unusually pale green, sometimes grass-green, slender needles on white shoots. In the wild, the orange bark persists solely on the higher branches when the trees are 40 m tall. In Britain it has been replaced by the purple-grey mature bark, at the base of the bole, only in one or two Cornish gardens. It is a rare tree there, and severe winters take a toll so it is mainly seen in southern and Irish collections.

Northern pitch pine (*Pinus rigida*) ranges from New England along the Appalachian Mountains to Georgia and is grown in a few collections, mostly in England. There is one, however, 14 m × 65 cm at Cairnsmore, Dumfries, and one in Inveraray Castle garden 17 m × 86 cm. It is a three-needle pine and resembles a rough Monterey pine with small cones and with a habit found among pines only in two others from the southern parts of its range, which are not seen in Britain. This is to grow sprouts on the bole and larger branches – short tufts of needles on slender, often hanging shoots, sometimes making a grassy mat on the bole.

The **Jeffrey pine** (*Pinus jeffreyi*) is a beautiful tree whether it is 55 m tall in the granite mountains above Yosemite or 25 m tall and even more shapely in a British garden. It replaces the closely allied Ponderosa pine above 2000 m throughout California and differs from it in having blue-grey bloomed shoots; greyer and stiffer 23 cm needles; bigger, broader cones and, in Britain, a dark, nearly black bark. It is rather less frequent but equally widespread, and young trees are even more handsome, very vigorous and easily raised, although it has been shorter-lived in some gardens. It almost invariably maintains a regular, narrow, conical crown with a single stem to the tip until it is 30 m tall, after which it may make a dome at the top. One 120 years old at Scone Palace in Perth is 41 m × 128 cm.

Knobcone pine (*Pinus attenuata*) grows on the foothills of southern Oregon and northern California beneath 60 m Sugar pines and is bright grassy green and encrusted with cones, the main stem just below the leading shoot being covered by them for two to three m.

Sugar pine (*Pinus lambertiana*) is, in southern Oregon and in California, the biggest pine in the world, often reaching a height of 60 m across miles of hillside and sometimes even 70 m as for example around Giant Forest Village in Sequoia National Park. It also bears the longest cones which can be 60 cm long and hang at the ends of level branches. Introduced by Douglas in 1827 and again by Lobb in 1851 it grew rapidly and there were many big trees bearing cones freely by 1900. It is however, like other five-needle pines from America, susceptible to the blister-rust fungus and by 1930 only a few remained.

The **Mexican white pine** (*Pinus ayacahuite*) is the hardiest of the trees from Mexico grown in Britain and although a five-needle pine, it resists blister-rust quite well. The slender needles droop in arcs all round the leading shoot. Cones are up to 30 cm long and taper to a long narrow tip. There is variation depending on the original source of the seed in how far from the base of the cone the tips of the scales are curved out and in one origin every scale is strongly decurved.

Jeffrey pine   Northern pitch pine   Mexican pine

female flower

male flowers

Jeffrey pine

female flowers

male flowers

Monterey pine

old cones retained

Northern pitch pine

male flowers   female flowers

Mexican pine

cone

male flowers

Mexican white pine

bark

male flowers

female flowers

Knobcone pine

female flowers

Mexican white pine

Monterey pine

Sugar pine

Palms

The **Cabbage tree** (*Cordyline australis*) is not a true palm but an agave, related to the Yuccas. It is native to New Zealand and was first sent to Britain in 1823. It thrives in the western region near the coast, even to the extreme north of Scotland at Tongue, Highland Region and is much grown in Ullapool. The Isle of Man, and the Isle of Wight are equally crowded with Cabbage trees and in Ireland they grow even better especially from Dublin to Cork. A few grow inland in the south, in Surrey, but these are slow and rarely flower so they remain as unbranched poles with a single crown at the top. This plant can branch only where it bears a flowerhead. Seedlings spring up like grass in some Irish gardens. Sisal is a close relative, and Cabbage tree leaves are very strong. The bark becomes quite thick and corky.

True Palms can have leaves like fans or pinnate leaves like feathers. The only palm hardy outside Torquay and the Isles of Scilly is the **Chusan palm** (*Trachycarpus fortunei*) from south China. Robert Fortune, who brought the tea plant out of China, brought this palm in 1839 and these plants were grown under glass. In 1843 he brought the first to be grown out-of-doors. It is quite a hardy tree and can be grown in the Midlands north to Lancashire and by the west coast far up into Scotland. It flowers freely almost everywhere, with several huge heads each summer, but no palm can ever grow a branch. Seedlings spring up in a few Sussex gardens and they always arise deep in the shade of big shrubs. Growth is very slow indeed. A tree from the 1843 lot at Kew is only 10 m tall and none is yet over 13 m. The mode of growth of palms gives only minimal increase in diameter except in a few species, so the stem remains slender. It looks much stouter than it is while the big leaf-bases adhere to the trunk with a thick cover of fibres.

The **Canary palm** (*Phoenix canariensis*) is a pinnate-leafed palm and the noblest of the tribe, with a crown of a hundred or more leaves up to 6 m long. In Britain it grows only at Tresco Abbey, Isles of Scilly but it is commonly grown in warmer countries, and can be 24 m tall in South California.

The **Dwarf fan-palm** (*Chamaerops humilis*) is the only palm wild in Europe where it covers hillsides in Sicily, Spain and the south of France but is no more than a hard, spiny, ground-cover plant.

fruit

Cabbage-tree

Chusan palm

Canary palm

Dwarf fanpalm

Practical Reference Section

A concise guide to the practicalities of the
selection and cultivation of trees.

Contents

Suitable Trees for the Garden

This table contains a wide range of trees and is not confined to those that are only appropriate for small gardens. Some will grow very large indeed, and these are indicated by (L) in the 20-year height column. Those trees that will never make large spreading specimens are marked (S).

The list is, however, limited to the more desirable trees, with an emphasis on year-round features, bark and shape, and foliage. The use of the common English names creates a few infelicities like the incense cedar among the true cedars, and the southern beeches scattered under 'Beech', 'Dombey's', 'Rauli' and 'Roble'. The fancy Japanese cherries are so numerous that they have been combined under 'Sato' cherry, and their details generalized.

Height after ten years is bedevilled by the deplorable range in the size of plants sold, but evens itself out somewhat since trees planted when two or three metres tall will not grow, while 60 cm plants grow fast. Standard trees unavoidably start at over two metres and so grow slowly.

'Spread' is a loose concept and varies according to individual characteristics as well as the space available. The figures given are for 20-year-old, average shaped trees growing in the open.

Key
B Broadleaf
C Conifer
L Trees that grow to a large size
S Trees that remain relatively small

Common Name	Height after 10 years (metres)	Height after 20 years (metres)	Spread (metres)	Good Features	Failings
Alder, Italian (B)	8–12	15–20 (L)	6	Vigour, catkins, shape, foliage	No autumn colours
Apple (B)					
Hupeh crab	6–9	12	6–8	Vigour, flower, fruit	
Japanese crab	3–4	4–7 (S)	5–8	Unfailingly floriferous	Low, densely twiggy crown
Magdeburg	5	6–8 (S)	6–8	Beautiful flower	Dull out of flower
Pillar	7–9	10–15	3	Shape, new foliage, autumn colour	
Ash (B)					
Caucasian/Claret	6–10	10–17	6–8	Bark, bright elegant foliage	
Manna	5–8	7–12	5	Flowers, scent	
Beech (B)					
Dawyck	6–9	14–17	2–3	Shape, spring and autumn colour	
Dombey's (Southern)	7–12	10–17 (L)	4–6	Evergreen, pretty foliage, vigour	Can scorch in east
Golden	6–8	9–14 (L)	5	Spring, early summer foliage	
Birch (B)					
Chinese redbark	5–9	9–12	3–4	Bark, foliage	
Erman's	8–10	12–15	3–4	Bark, foliage, shape	
Fastiagiate	6–8	10–15	1–2	Bark, shape	Can become untidy
Himalayan/Kashmir	8–11	12–17	3–5	Bark, foliage	
Swedish	8–11	14–18	2–4	Bark, crown, foliage	
Transcaucasian	3–4	5–6 (S)	5–6	Crown, foliage, autumn colour	Low and rather slow
Buckeye, Yellow (B)	5–6	7–10 (L)	3–4	Foliage, flower, autumn colour	
Catalpa (B)					
Hybrid	7–9	10–12	5–7	Foliage, flower	Short season, gaunt
Northern	6–8	10–12	4–5	Foliage, flower	Short season
Cedar (C)					
Blue Atlas	6–8	12–15 (L)	8–10	Vigour, colour	Spreads with age
Incense	6–8	12–14 (L)	2	Crown, colour	
Cherry (B)					
Bird	3	5–6 (S)	3–5	Flower, autumn colour	
Japanese 'Sato'	2–6	4–10 (S)	1–5	Flower, autumn colour (some)	Coarse foliage, poor crown
'Kursar'	4–6	6–9 (S)	3	Flower, autumn colour	
'Pandora'	6–8	9–10 (S)	2–3	Flower, autumn colour	
Sargent	6–8	9–12	3–6	Flower, autumn colour	

Common Name	Height after 10 years (metres)	Height after 20 years (metres)	Spread (metres)	Good Features	Failings
Tibetan	6–8	8–10	2–4	Bark	
Wild	7–10	15–18 (L)	3–5	Vigour, flower, autumn colour	Suckering roots
Winter	4–6	5–8 (S)	3–7	Six months of flower	Twiggy, sprawling crown
Yoshino	3–4	4–8 (S)	4–6	Flower	Coarse foliage, poor crown
Chestnut (B)					
Indian horse-	6–8	12–14 (S)	4–6	Opening leaf, flower, foliage	Shape needs watching
Japanese horse-	7–9	9–13	4–5	Huge foliage, flowers, autumn colour	
Sunrise horse-	3–4	5 8 (S)	4–6	Opening leaves	
Cypress (C)					
Smooth Arizona	6–7	10–14	3–4	Any soil; shape, colour, tough	
Cripp's Golden	3–5	5–8	5–6	Shape, colour	
Leyland	9	17–20 (L)	5–6	Vigour, shape, tough	Green forms dull
Swamp	3–6	6–12	2–3	Wetland, shape	Long season leafless, twiggy
Dove-tree (B)	4–6	6–12	4–6	Flower, foliage, interest	Rather gaunt when leafless
Fir (C)					
Grand	8–11	15–20 (L)	4–5	Vigour, shape, height	Not in dry or much exposure
Korean	1–3	3–6 (S)	2	Flowers, cones, shape	Usually bushy, slow
Santa Lucia	3–8	10–15 (L)	3–6	Shape, foliage	Not in dry or much exposure
Ginkgo (C)	3–6	5–8	2 3	Interest, shape, foliage	Unreliable shape and growth
Gum (B)					
Broadleaf	8–15	15–25	6–9	Vigour, bark, foliage	Non-rural
Cider	8–12	15–20	5–9	Vigour, bark, foliage, flowers	Liable to blow when young
Snow	7–10	12–18	3–5	Bark, new leaves, foliage, flowers	Variable bark and growth
Hazel, Turkish (B)	6–8	10–15	5–9	Vigour, tough, flowers, shape	
Hemlock (C)					
Mountain	3–5	6–10	2 3	Shape, colour, tough	Best in wet west, and north
Western	8–14	10–18 (L)	3–4	Shape, vigour, clay or sand	Poor in east, dry, towns
Honeylocust (B)	3–7	8–12	4–6	Foliage, autumn colour, dry	Needs heat, short season
Sunburst	3–6	6–10	5–9	Foliage, shape	Short season, twiggy when bare
Judas tree (B)	4–6	6–8 (S)	3–5	Foliage, flowers, autumn colour	Slow, reclines with age, fragile
Katsura tree (B)	6–10	9–14	4–7	Vigour, shape, foliage, autumn colour	Resents late frost and drought
Keaki (B)	5–8	7–10	5–8	Shape, foliage, autumn, bark	May spread when young
Laburnum, Voss's (B)	6–8	9–10 (S)	2–4	Flower	Poor thing for 50 weeks
Larch, European (C)	8–11	12–17 (L)	3–5	Vigour, early and late colour	
Lime (B)					
Cutleaf	5–7	8–10	3–4	Shape, foliage, flower	

Common Name	Height after 10 years (metres)	Height after 20 years (metres)	Spread (metres)	Good Features	Failings
Mongolian	6–8	10–12	3–4	Foliage, flower	
Silver	6–8	12–15 (L)	4–6	Vigour, shape, flower, towns	
Silver Pendent	8–10	12–17 (L)	3–5	Vigour, shape, foliage, flower	
Small-leaf	7–8	9–12 (L)	3–5	Foliage, flower	With age sprouty and burrs
Madrone (B)	6–8	9–13 (S)	3–5	Foliage, bark, flowers	May be short lived
Magnolia (B)					
Veitch's	6–8	9–12	4–7	Flowers early in life	Coarse foliage
Willow	5–7	8–9 (S)	4–5	Shape, foliage, flower	
Maple (B)					
Amur	3–6	6–8 (S)	4–6	Foliage, autumn colour	Bushy, sheds leaf early
Ashleaf	7–9	11–12	5–6	Cultivars – foliage	Revert to green, short life
Hornbeam	3–5	5–8 (S)	5–8	Foliage, flower, autumn colour	Broad bush, slow
Japanese (Downy)	2–5	4–8 (S)	1–3	Foliage, flower, autumn colour	
(Smooth)	2–4	3–6 (S)	3–5	Foliage, shape, autumn colour	Variable growth
Lobel	8–11	12–17	2–3	Shape, foliage	No autumn colour, gaunt winter
Norway	6–10	12–15 (L)	4–5	Flower, autumn colour	
Oregon	8–10	12–15 (L)	3–5	Foliage, flower, shape	
Paperbark	2–4	5–8 (S)	4–5	Bark, autumn colour, flower	Slow, needs pruning to bole
Silver	8–14	12–20 (L)	6–10	Vigour, foliage, size	Brittle high branches
Snakebarks	6–9	8–12 (S)	6–9	Bark, foliage, autumn colour	Spreading upper crown
Monkey-puzzle (C)	2–5	5–12	3–5	Character, foliage, contrast	Slow to start, harsh litter
Moosewood (B)	6–9	7–11 (S)	9–11	Bark, foliage summer and autumn	Can be short-lived
Mulberry (B)					
Black (Seedling)	1	2–4	2–3	Shape, foliage, fruit	Slow to start, fruit mess paths
(Truncheon)	2	3–5	3–5		
Oak (B)					
Common	4–6	9–12 (L)	3–6	Wildlife, character, autumn colour	Galled, often sprouty
Cypress	6–8	10–14	2–3	Shape, foliage, autumn colour	
Hungarian	8–10	12–16 (L)	5–8	Vigour, size, foliage	Soon enormous
Mirbeck	6–8	11–15 (L)	3–5	Vigour, shape, foliage	Some leaves fall in spring
Pin	8–11	12–15	4–6	Vigour, crown, foliage, autumn colour	Best with hot summers
Red	7–10	12–15 (L)	6–8	Vigour, new foliage, autumn colour	Variable autumn colours
Scarlet	7–9	12–15	4–6	Foliage, autumn colour	May be gaunt in winter
Sessile	6–8	11–14 (L)	5–7	Vigour, shape, foliage	
Paulownia (B)	9–14	12–15	5–7	Flowers, foliage	Short life and season
Privet, Chinese Glossy (B)	4–6	6–10	3–5	Foliage, flower	Some are bushy
Rauli (B)	8–14	13–18 (L)	5–6	Vigour, shape, foliage, autumn colour	Seedling can be tender
Redwood (C)					
Coast	6–14	12–18 (L)	3–6	Vigour, interest	Browns in cold dry winds

Common Name	Height after 10 years (metres)	Height after 20 years (metres)	Spread (metres)	Good Features	Failings
Dawn	8–11	10–17	3–5	Interest, foliage, shape, autumn colour	Needs moist site
Roble (B)	9–13	13–20 (L)	3–6	Vigour, shape, autumn colour	High branches brittle
Rowan (B)					
Hupeh	7–9	10–12 (S)	3–5	Foliage, fruit	Grafts sprout at base
Joseph Rock	4–6	7–9 (S)	2–4	Foliage, fruit, autumn colour	Grafted, may sprout
Scarlet	8–10	9–11 (S)	4–7	Foliage, fruit, autumn colour	
Vilmorin	2–4	5–7	5–8	Foliage, fruit, autumn colour	Low, spreading, slow
Sequoia, Giant (C)	6–8	12–17 (L)	4–5	Size, shape	Often struck by lightning
Snowbell tree (B)	3–5	6–8	4–6	Flower, shape	
Spruce (C)					
Blue Colorado	3–6	6–10	2–3	Colour, shape	Spruce aphid, red spider
Brewer	2–3	5–6	2–3	Shape	Seedlings best, but slow start
Serbian	5–8	10–13	3	Shape, tolerance soil, town	Susceptible to honey fungus
Sweetgum (B)	5–7	9–12	3–4	Foliage, autumn colour	Variable colour, needs good soil
Thorn (B)					
Carrière's	3–5	7–8 (S)	4–6	Flowers, fruit, tolerance	Possibly fireblight
Plumleaf	3–3	5–8 (S)	4–6	Foliage, autumn colour	Bushy unless legged
Tulip tree (B)	5–9	9–15 (L)	3–6	Foliage, autumn colour, flowers	Best with warm summers
Chinese	6–10	12–15 (L)	3–5	Foliage, autumn colour, flowers	
Tupelo (B)	2–5	5–10	2–4	Autumn colour	Slow, needs warm rich site
Walnut (B)					
Black	3–6	8–13 (L)	3–5	Vigour, shape foliage, autumn colour	Needs deep rich soil, warmth
Common	3–6	9–12	4–6	New and summer foliage, fruit	Needs deep rich soil, sun
Whitebeam (B)	5–6	10–12 (S)	3–4	Foliage, flowers, fruit	Birds eat fruit
John Mitchell	8–10	10–13 (S)	3–5	Foliage, vigour, shape	
Willow (B)					
Bay	6–8	7–10 (S)	2–5	Foliage, flower	Needs cool, damp site
Coralbark	8–12	12–15	5–7	Bark	
Corkscrew	8–12	10–15	5–6	Interest, early and late foliage	Prone to anthracnose disease
Violet	8–9	9–12	3–4	Bark, early vigour	May be short lived
Weeping	6–9	10–15	8–12	Shape, early foliage	Prone to disease, thirsty roots
Yew (C)					
Common	2–4	4–6	2–4	Dark background, immortal	Slow
Irish	2–4	3–5 (S)	1–2	Shape	Slow, dull in numbers
West Felton	3–5	6–8	6–10	Shape	Spreads low
Wingnut (B)					
Hybrid	9–12	15–18 (L)	6–9	Vigour, foliage, autumn colour	Suckers luxuriantly
Zelkova, Caucasian (B)	6–8	10–12 (L)	4–7	Foliage, autumn colour	May turn out ordinary shape

Planting a Tree

Preparing the Hole

Nearly all trees make more reliable, sturdy growth in their first few years if they are transplanted than when seed is sown and the plants left undisturbed. Nonetheless, it is a wholly unnatural break in its growth pattern for a tree to be planted – one to which it cannot have evolved a response – and the operation should be planned to cause the least possible disruption to growth. The crucial point is to make the move as early in the tree's life as possible, to allow it the formative first five or six years in its final position. The bigger and older a tree is when planted, the more its growth is retarded, the longer it takes to make the big root-system it needs for growth and stability. A tree three metres tall is easily crippled for life by being moved, and no tree so big should even be considered for purchase unless it has a big root-system prepared over several years in the nursery.

The best size for planting is 30–50 cm, from open ground or a large container, where the roots have never been cramped. Such a plant, with all its roots, planted firmly, is stable from the start, must not be staked and will grow away rapidly to build a stout bole and shapely crown. A tall plant has already made its lower crown in response to conditions in the nursery lines, and so it will be drawn up with a slender, weak stem and often made worse by being tied to a stake. For a healthy plant, this vital part must be grown in the place where the tree is to spend its life, and in response to its surroundings there. The foliage of a tree feeds the roots and the roots feed the foliage. A tree planted out is usually in less shelter than it was in the nursery and its foliage is under more stress from drying wind. So it needs a vigorous root-system. With the usual tiny cramped, incomplete one of a tall plant, it can scarcely leaf out at all, much less make new shoots. So there is little leaf to feed the roots during their vital time for expansion into new soil. Thus, little growth can be made on roots, and little again on the shoots and the tree is locked in this stage of minimum growth and dire struggle to survive, for many years.

A small plant with almost natural rooting evades this trap. Roots must be spread to reach the new soil, not left in a ball. Pot-bound roots must be at least partially unravelled even if some break and need to be cut back. The size of hole needed can then be seen – big enough to take the spread roots with a small margin extra. The bottom of the hole is dug out to allow 15 cm of good soil or leaf-mould beneath the tree, and the base well broken up if it is a heavy soil. A mixture of the surrounding soil, compost and sand is put round the spread roots, and gently firmed.

In poor, sandy soils, a little superphosphate fertilizer spread over the bottom before placing the tree in the hole aids rapid root-growth; while some slow-release nitrogenous fertilizers like bonemeal added to the backfill improve early shoot-growth.

The level of the surface on the stem before planting can be seen, and filling brings the new soil to the same place; then after heavy firming it is made good to that level again. In light soils the new tree and one metre radius around is left ten cm below the surrounding level to help keep the frequent waterings needed from flowing out of reach.

Preparing the Hole

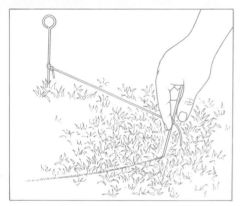

1. *A circular area of cleared ground is most suitable, and easily marked for the new tree. Swing a marker one metre from a pin.*

2. *Remove a thin top layer and put it aside. Most of the good topsoil stays to be dug out and mixed to make the backfill.*

3. *Break up the bottom of the hole well, if it is compacted, to give good drainage. If it is good loam, it can be dug over.*

4. *Break up the turf taken from the top and put it at the bottom of the hole, where it will break down into good rooting-soil.*

5. *Spread a layer of well-rotted manure, leaf-mould or compost over the turves to conserve moisture and allow easy rooting.*

6. *Firm in the bottom layers before the tree roots are put in place, to ensure there are no pockets of air in the lower layers.*

Planting a Tree

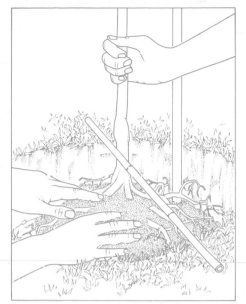

1. *Hold the tree roughly in position and shake it up and down a little as the soil is spread around and among the roots.*

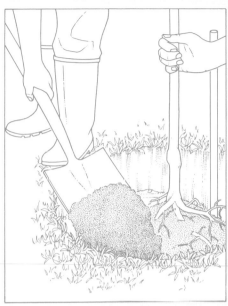

2. *Using a cane to mark the soil level, hold the tree for final filling to the old level and firming.*

3. *Tread the top firm: then lightly fork the surface to break it up slightly and to allow in water and air.*

Staking and Tying

Standard and other large trees need a stake, not to hold the stem up but just to hold it still until the new roots have grown out. After that it is bad for the tree, which needs to sway to grow its proper, stout stem. A short stake, strong and firmly set 30 cm away holds a tie on the bole 30 cm from the ground and is removed after the second growing season and winter gales.

A large tree from a container is best held by a triangle of three short stakes, because driving one into the root-ball would very likely damage important roots. (One stake each side is adequate for trees of moderate size.)

Stakes should not be longer than is needed to hold the ties at 30 cm. Projecting into the crown they can damage branches, and serve no purpose unless sometimes, in public places, lessening vandal damage. The heaviest standards with big tops may need their support at one third of the height of their stem, and 30 cm is better for normal trees.

Stakes should be long enough to allow 40–60 cm in the ground, and be knot-free and straight-grained for strength. They must be free from disease, preferably tanalized or otherwise treated with preservative unless they are Western red cedar.

Ties must have some elasticity to allow unhindered expansion of the stem even in the two seasons at most that they are needed. They must have spacers to prevent the stake rubbing the tree and be fixed on the stake to prevent slipping down in rough weather.

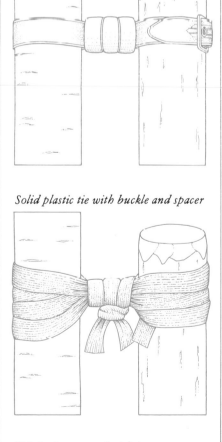

Ties

Solid plastic tie with buckle and spacer

Fabric tie arranged with knot as spacer.

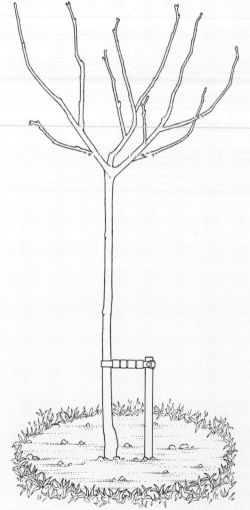

Pruning and Shaping

Trees normally assume their best shape in their own way. Only those grown for their fruit need annual pruning to increase the size, number or accessibility of the fruit. In the case of all other trees, the term 'pruning' has a very different meaning, covering two separate operations.

The first of these is to aid the natural process of shedding the first, lowest branches in order to give a clean, smooth bole. In woodland these are soon shaded out and shed, but on single trees the strongest branches extend into the light and keep growing at their tips while their inner shoots and smaller branches become bare. Left alone, these make a tangle of dead wood hiding the bole and soon full of nettles and rubbish, while big low branches disfigure the tree. Even where a lawn-tree is intended to be feathered to the ground, the early removal of the branch-tangle on the bottom 1.5 m allows the next layer to droop around a clean bole. Other trees can have two m of clean stem by the time they are six m.

The second operation – shaping – is required only to rectify a fault in growth. A forking leading shoot can be singled as soon as it is seen. A forked, two-stem tree is ugly and vulnerable to storms. Misplaced or over-vigorously protruding branches should be removed when necessary.

Where to Cut

Cleaning a stem of side-branches early in its life removes dead and living wood only a few cm in diameter. It can be done at any time of year and the small scars will close within one or two years, leaving a smooth stem. Cleaning older stems and taking branches from the crown leave big scars. Branches usually swell out at their origin to a conic protrusion. This causes conflict between the two desired aims – a minimum size of scar and a cut flush with the major branch or stem to leave it smooth. Controversy raged for 400 years and decay followed pruning whether the cut was flush, left a marked stub, or if a rough unreasoned compromise were made.

Recent study by Dr A. Shigo of New Hampshire has shown exactly where the cuts should be and why.

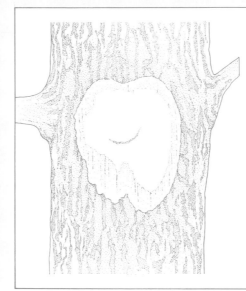

The Wrong Way

Cutting flush with the stem does leave a smooth surface, but usually a branch has a conical base so the nearer the stem, the bigger the scar. Worse, however, such a cut removes the collar of tissues whose function is to grow new tissue to heal the scar. Healing will thus be slow and have a greater area to cover. Wound-dressings are not the answer. Few of them inhibit decay at all and many make a skin which soon cracks and allows water to lodge against the scar. Unless re-painted regularly, dressings thus encourage decay. The correct cut leaves the collar intact to grow protective barriers and to close the scar. Left open to sun and air the wound heals most rapidly.

The Shigo Method

In beech alone there was an old method of pruning small branches leaving a five cm stub. Coral-spot fungus was sure to infect this but by the time it reached the main stem, the tree had sealed off the scar and the stub would fall off with the fungus to leave a healed scar. Were the cut flush with the bole the fungus could have entered the stem and decayed a large, deep scar.

Dr Shigo has shown that *all* trees isolate areas of decay with barriers of resistant cells; that the junctions of branches have the tissues for growing the barriers already disposed in a pattern to prepare for natural shedding, and he has described how these show on the tree. A 'branch bark ridge' on the upper side and a 'branch collar' on the underside mark the outer rim of tissues that will grow the barrier, which is conical, pointing inwards.

The natural death of a branch causes the collar to enlarge. When the branch is decayed and breaks off it will tend to take with it the conical insertion. However, if this remains and rots, it is isolated from the main stem, and the exterior is sealed in by active growth from the enlarged collar. The cut must be close to but clear of the collar.

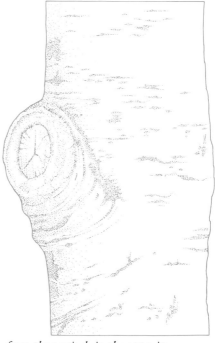

The correct cut is from just clear of the 'branch bark ridge' above to just clear of the collar beneath. The collar may not show and then the angle of the cut is shown by the angle that the branch bark ridge makes away from the branch. The cut is at the same angle from the vertical, in the opposite direction. With a branch arising almost vertically this makes a cut very close to the stem, but it is not flush, for it leaves the vital collar. Heavy branches must be cut off first to 15 cm stubs before the final cut.

Singling a Fork

 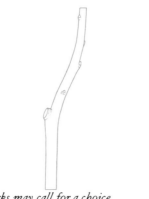

A symmetrical fork in new growth on a very young tree may be left until new growth begins next season but no longer.

Unequal forks may call for a choice between a weak shoot and a strong one that is more offset.

Cutting

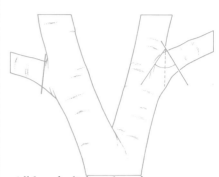

All but the lightest branches are cut to a stub before pruning, to prevent tearing. First a shallow undercut, then the full cut a few cm outside it.

Singling Sprouts

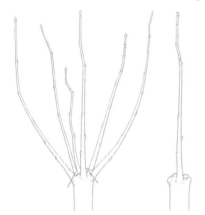 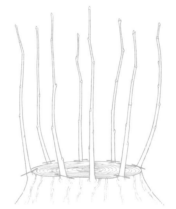

A eucalypt or similarly strong growing tree may regrow after a hard frost as many shoots from ground level. Choose one strong, straight shoot and cut the others.

A sprouting stump can be re-grown as a tree cutting out all but the single strongest and most shapely new shoot. Having a big root-system it will grow fast.

Cleaning the Bole

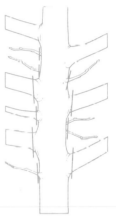

A neglected tree may have its bole spoiled by low branches which should have been removed with secateurs when still small. Now it will need a saw.

Crown Thinning

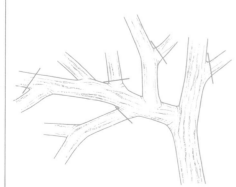 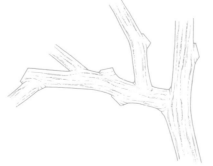

Some broadleaf trees have crowns which can become congested. They may take too much light and be untidy. Savage cutting makes them worse, and ugly.

Thinning the crown by intelligent removal of excess leafage on complete branch systems, always cutting back to a main branch, cures the trouble.

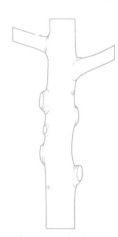

A bole can be rescued when branches are 10–15 cm across. Beyond that it would leave too much scar. A clean bole for 1.5 m is a minimum aim.

Improving Growth of Young Trees

Trees are sociable plants and in nature they normally arise and grow in groups of varying densities, either of their own species only or amongst others. Even the pioneer species – the first to colonize bare ground – usually spring up in numbers together.

The new, bare sites are very largely those cleared by fire (due to lightning before the arrival of man and often afterwards also) but greatly increased by deliberate burning to clear the land for grazing and crops. In Britain today, the fire-sites available for regrowth of trees are mostly on heaths and commons and are all the result either of pure mischief or the carelessness of smokers and campers. The extent of past fires can often be seen from the areas of dense, pure silver birch.

In western North America most of the coniferous forests have large areas of uniform age which can be dated back to a fire and most of the trees have a life-cycle adapted to the average period between fires, which itself is fixed by the time needed for enough combustible material to accumulate. Other new sites arise on a smaller scale from landslides, rivers changing course and swamps drying out.

Pioneer species have light seeds, often with fluff or wings and are carried by the wind much further than heavier fruits which rely on birds or mammals, which mostly frequent developed woodland. The trees bearing the heavier fruits therefore come in only after the pioneers have created a form of woodland. Hence the successor species also are adapted to growing up among trees – at first those of a different species from themselves.

The aspen, sallows, bay willow and related shrubbier forms have fluff on their seeds and, among native British trees are the long-distance pioneers. The silver and downy birches with minute winged seeds can travel a fair distance, and Scots pine, with its heavy winged seeds, is a short-distance pioneer unless a crossbill should carry a cone and drop some seed further away.

The first trees on new land grow in conditions very different from those found in woodlands. There will be an open sky and either newly formed soil or newly burned surfaces. If new, the soil will usually be short of the nutrients needed for growth, particularly in nitrogen, and lacking entirely in humus. If burned it will also lack nitrogen but be high in potash, and the top at least will lack humus. So pioneer species need to adapt to poor, often open, sandy soils and have low demand for nutrients. But the overwhelming factor on new sites is the wind. Such sites are always more exposed than those in wooded areas and usually to a very high degree. This causes the soil, at best open and poor in humus, to dry out rapidly and often, so pioneer trees must be able to withstand drought. They can do so by deep and wide rooting early in life and by having small or thick-skinned leaves.

The most profound effect is however, from the wind on the foliage. Here again, small, tough leaves or dense hairs on shoots and leaves lessen the damaging drying effect. Big, thin leaves can be grown only by trees whose entire life is spent in the shelter of old woods. The pioneer trees, in full light, have no need of dense foliage to catch enough of it for their needs. Their leaves work only in nearly full light, and are shed when they become shaded by others and the crowns remain light and open. This allows the wind to filter through

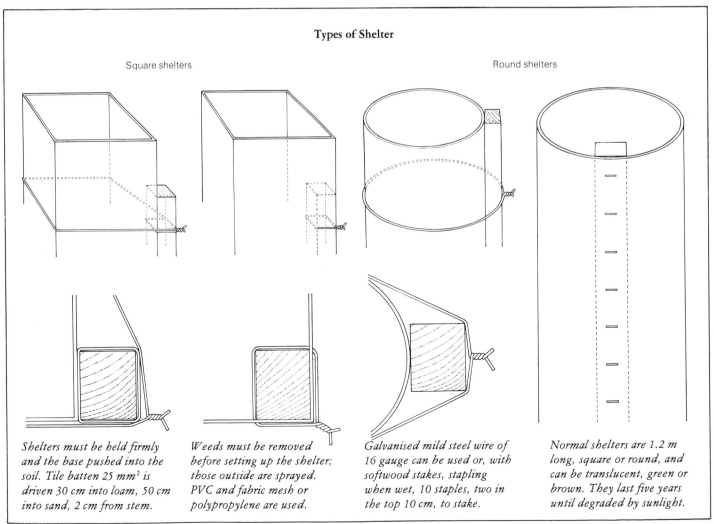

Types of Shelter

Square shelters

Round shelters

Shelters must be held firmly and the base pushed into the soil. Tile batten 25 mm^2 is driven 30 cm into loam, 50 cm into sand, 2 cm from stem.

Weeds must be removed before setting up the shelter; those outside are sprayed. PVC and fabric mesh or polypropylene are used.

Galvanised mild steel wire of 16 gauge can be used or, with softwood stakes, stapling when wet, 10 staples, two in the top 10 cm, to stake.

Normal shelters are 1.2 m long, square or round, and can be translucent, green or brown. They last five years until degraded by sunlight.

where a dense crown would be damaged by strong gusts. It also allows strong growth of the early arrivals among the ground herbs, and, later, the growth of the more shade-bearing trees that will take over when the pioneers have created shelter and their leaf-fall has built up a much improved soil.

The pioneers make rapid early growth, flower and fruit within a few years of germinating from seed and tend to be short-lived. These qualities are further adaptations to their life-style. They do need, however, to modify the severity of their surroundings in order to grow well, or, in the more extreme sites, to grow at all. This can be done only by growing in large numbers together from the start, which is the normal result of seeding on to bare ground. Each tree then benefits from the shelter of the others and this common shelter increases as the trees grow and improves greatly the microclimate within the stand. Even the trees on the periphery benefit, since the trees behind retard the wind that sweeps through them. Height growth increases with distance from the edge, giving a wedge-shaped profile.

The pioneer stands are usually fairly open, but there are exceptions such as the birch tracts following heath fires in Britain and the lodgepole pine stands in the interior Rocky Mountains, which arise and largely remain in very dense groups, despite a high rate of suppression and death.

Successor species are adapted to starting life in the sheltered, relatively humid conditions of woodlands, in a developed, humus-rich, reasonably fertile soil. Many need open sky above them after varying periods and achieve this end either by outgrowing the species around them or by biding their time until the canopies above them fail and fall with age. The conclusion to be drawn from all these factors is that a tree of any kind, either planted singly, or widely spaced on an open site as in most amenity plantings in parks or around buildings, faces conditions from which its natural manner of growth largely shields it. To make matters far worse, it is usually planted out when it is far too big, and has spent too many years in the very different conditions of the nursery. The worst aspect for the tree is the sudden subjection to exposure.

Tuley Tubes

Graham Tuley of the Forestry Commission experimented with translucent plastic 'tree-shelters' of different materials, widths and heights. A narrow shelter gives a 'greenhouse effect', retaining within the heat it receives from radiated light – an effect that is very apparent if you put your hand into one on a cool day. In the calm, damp warmth, the side shoots grow big leaves which promote good growth in the stem and leading shoot. They are short and congested but are due for removal when the stem is cleaned-up. The shelter at the same time protects the tree from damage by animals. Growth in many broad-leaf trees is given a rapid early start, most spectacularly in Sessile oak but all that have been tried have shown the benefits. Among conifers, only Japanese larch responds strongly. Some trees, notably the oaks, cannot hold up the big crown. They must be secured to the stake that held the shelter when the plastic has degraded away after the expected five years.

Materials and methods are still being developed but over 500,000 Tuley tubes were used during 1983.

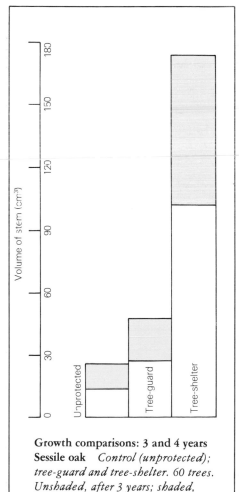

Volume of stem (cm³)

Growth comparisons: 3 and 4 years
Sessile oak *Control (unprotected); tree-guard and tree-shelter. 60 trees. Unshaded, after 3 years; shaded, fourth year. Tree-guard is plastic net.*

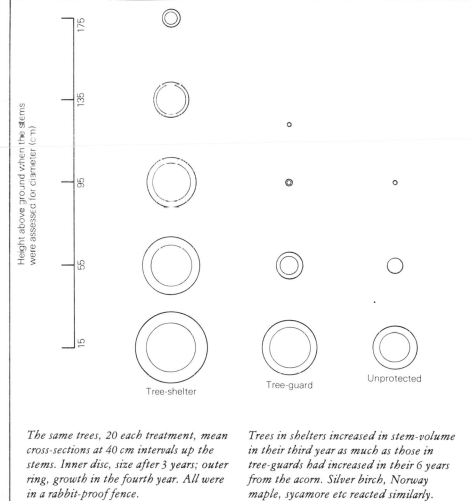

Height above ground when the stems were assessed for diameter (cm)

Tree-shelter   Tree-guard   Unprotected

The same trees, 20 each treatment, mean cross-sections at 40 cm intervals up the stems. Inner disc, size after 3 years; outer ring, growth in the fourth year. All were in a rabbit-proof fence.

Trees in shelters increased in stem-volume in their third year as much as those in tree-guards had increased in their 6 years from the acorn. Silver birch, Norway maple, sycamore etc reacted similarly.

Measuring Height

The height of a tree less than about six m tall can be measured accurately with a rod. A tall tree can be measured easily and reasonably closely by several homemade methods, and more accurately and reliably by an instrument. Exact measurement of its height is, however, normally impracticable. Even climbing the tree can rarely solve the problem. The path for the tape down the bole cannot be quite direct, the precise tip often cannot be seen by the climber or judged closely to be level with his rod, and the tree may lean.

Height is reckoned from the highest point of the crown and this may, in an old, many-headed conifer, and in a broad, domed broad-leaf tree, be many metres from the central axis. Its position has to be decided from a distance and the point directly beneath it estimated from under the crown. The bottom of a tree is the highest point to which the soil reaches up the bole. This prevents the extended bole and roots on the downhill side of a steep slope from counting in the height.

Having observed the points between which the measurement is to be made, the next thing to decide is the point from which to make it. Accuracy is best at a distance from the tree which is equal to its height and from the same level as its base. In fact even quite a marked slope makes little difference because measurement is made down to the base as well as up to the top, but an uphill shot from much below the tree is best avoided. So a rough estimate of the height of the tree – 20, 30 or 40 m – is made and a position found at about the equivalent distance (with an instrument an exact distance is required) as nearly level with the base as possible, from which the top and the bottom can be seen. A tree with an obvious lean is sighted at a right-angle to the direction of lean if possible. If it cannot be, then, as is worth doing for all very tall trees, two shots from opposite directions give a mean which is the height.

Interestingly, unpractised estimates by eye usually much underestimate trees of six to twelve metres, and grossly overestimate trees of 25–30 m in height.

Method 1

The top of a tree, its base and your eye form a triangle with a right-angle between the stem of the tree and the ground. Hence, when the whole tree makes an angle of 45° from your eye, the two sides formed by the tree and your distance from it are equal. You are the same distance from the base as the tip is, and were the tree to fall, its tip would land at your feet. This distance can be measured precisely along the ground. To find the point at which the angle is 45°, a miniature of the real triangle is made. Break a stick so that its length is exactly equal to the length of your fully stretched arm. Hold it vertically at arm's length. Move to where the top and bottom of the stick align with those of the tree. You are then at the desired point.

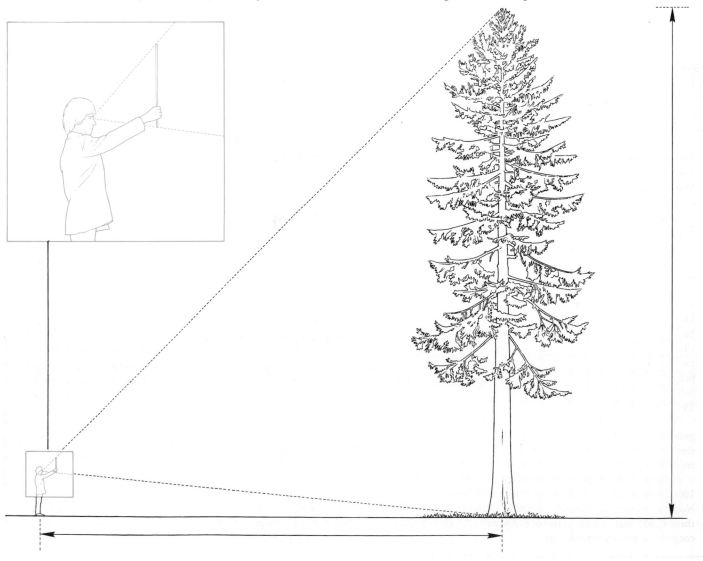

Method 2

Unlike Method 1, this requires two people. A small nick is cut into a ruler, or a rod similarly marked, at the one-inch mark or at five cm on a 50 cm rod. Hold the ruler at full stretch (which is a constant and the easiest distance) and move to where the tree top and base line up with those of the ruler. Now ask your assistant to move a white marker (a notebook page folded into a broad triangle will do) to bring it exactly into the notch. The height at which this occurs is one twelfth or one tenth, depending on the measure used, of the full height of the tree.

Method 3

The sun is not always out and tree shadows are not very often thrown on to open ground, but for lawn specimens the shadow method can be useful. The height of the sun at any hour and day can be determined by reference to a Nautical Almanack but this process can be short-circuited by a simple device. The length of the tree-shadow is compared with that of the shadow of a two m rod taken at the same time and the height arrived at by simple proportion.

Using a Hypsometer

A hypsometer is an instrument for measuring height. A free-hanging needle reads directly on several scales or else a bob rotates a cylinder with scales against a marker. Most have scales for distances from the tree, marked 15, 20, 30 and 40 and these can be feet, yards or metres, whichever is used for the baseline. Hypsometers are expensive. Workable ones can be devised.

Estimating Age

The height and spread of a tree increase with age until senility begins and then they decrease again. Both fail as indicators of age beyond the early years. Diameter and bole circumference must increase every year of life, a ring of new wood being added annually. The circumference, measured at 1.5 m is a guide to the age.

For big-growing trees (not those like apples and holly) the broad rule 'one inch a year' (roughly 2.5 cm) increase in circumference applies regardless of species, region or altitude of site, over a wide span of ages. The reason is that most trees add well over one inch a year in youth and gradually decline first to one inch and then to less. Once they are past one inch a year their mean annual increase becomes nearer to that rate every year and in an old tree it is on or close to it over a very long period. Wood added depends on the amount of foilage, so a tree crowded in a wood or having lost branches adds less each year and may fit 'one inch in two years'. A fully crowned oak 20 feet (about six m) round will usually be about 250 years old.

There are, however, both hares and tortoises among trees. Fast growth, that is three to four inches (7–10 cm), is made each year by the best eucalypts, willows, giant sequoias, coast redwoods, dawn redwoods, some grand firs and poplars.

A few trees grow more than one inch (2.5 cm) a year for less than 100 years and then become very slow. Examples are Scots pine, Norway spruce, sycamore and common lime. Approximate age for these is 100 years plus 2 years for every inch (2.5 cm) of circumference above 100 inches (40 cm).

Gilbert White recorded the Selborne Yew to be 23 ft round at three ft up in 1789. In 1984 it was 25 ft 7 in (7.8 m) at the same point. A uniform decline from ½ in/yr in youth gives the age as about 1200 years in White's day, 1400 years today.

Notable Tree Collections

Abbreviations

BC — Borough Council
CC — County Council
D of E — Department of the Environment
For Comm — Forestry Commission
Min of Ag — Ministry of Agriculture
NT — National Trust
NTS — National Trust of Scotland

Some National Trust properties have seasonal opening times. Many open only in the afternoon.

Other properties are open either seasonally or on certain days, and details need to be ascertained from appropriate annual publications.

Ownership and opening policies are always liable to change, and the current position should be checked before a visit.

England

South-east

BERKSHIRE

1. **Windsor Great Park** *(H.M. the Queen.)* Extensive plantings, conifer and broadleaf, Obelisk Pond, Totempole Ride, Botany Bay. Notable Cyprus cedars, Limber and ponderosa pines, old coast redwoods, rare birches, maples and rowans.
Savill Garden Notable Metasequoia, southern beeches, bigleaf magnolia, Serbian spruce.
Valley Gardens Magnolias, maples.

2. **Whiteknights Park** *(University of Reading.)* Notable old Turner, Lucombe and cypress oaks – shagbark hickory. Recent varied planting.

HAMPSHIRE AND ISLE OF WIGHT

3. **Blackwater Arboretum** off Rhinefield Drive. *(For Comm.)* 1960 planting of great variety of conifers, a few hardwoods.

4. **Bolderwood Arboretum** nr Lyndhurst. *(For Comm.)* Huge 1859 conifers; notable noble fir, Hartweg pine, Crimean pine, Thuja, stand of Douglas fir (46 m top height).

5. **Broadlands**, Romsey. *(Lord and Lady Romsey.)* Outstanding swamp cypress, good northern catalpa, horse chestnut, cedars, ginkgo.

6. **Exbury Gardens**, Beaulieu. *(Mr E. I. de Rothschild.)* Notable prickly castor-oil tree, Farrer's spruce, Chinese tulip-tree, snakebark maples, oakleaf beech.

7. **Hackwood Park**, Basingstoke. *(Lord Camrose.)* Notable sugar maple, giant sequoias, Norway spruce. Adjacent to:
Herriard Park, Basingstoke. *(Mr Jervoise.)* Short avenue of 1851 conifers, big limes, sugar maples, Daimyo oaks, dove-trees.

8. **The Hillier Arboretum**, Ampfield. *(Hampshire CC.)* Founded 1954 to grow every species that climate and availability allow. Notable crabs and cherries in flower but remarkable assemblage of extreme rarities of all kinds.

9. **Jenkyn Place**, Bentley. *(Mr and Mrs G. E. Coke.)* Notable 1823 Lebanon cedar, paper-bark maple, Cyprus strawberry-tree, Judas-tree.

10. **Leigh Park**, Havant. *(Public park.)* Huge tulip-tree, good fernleaf beech, giant sequoia, Kentucky coffee-tree, yellow buckeye.

11. **Longstock Gardens**, Stockbridge. *(The John Lewis Partnership.)* Wide range of species and ages. Good cherries.

12. **Osborne House**, Isle of Wight. *(Royal Parks.)* Open April–October, weekdays. Fine old conifers and some hardwoods. Lucombe oak avenue.

13. **Rhinefield Ornamental Drive**, nr Lyndhurst. *(For Comm. Public road.)* 1859 background Douglas firs with mixed conifers. Outstanding Lawson cypress, Spanish fir, white spruce, giant sequoia, white pines. 1955 avenue of coast redwoods.

14. **Stratfield Saye**, nr Swallowfield. *(Trustees of the Duke of Wellington.)* Open daily spring to autumn. Outstanding Bosnian pines, sweetgum, Hungarian oaks, fine Metasequoias, Lebanon cedars, giant sequoias, Chinese sweetgum, in arboreta each side of the House.

15. **Ventnor Botanic Garden**, Isle of Wight. Recent planting of a wide variety of tender trees among old pines and cypresses.

KENT

16. **Dunorlan Park**, Tunbridge Wells. *(Public park.)* Fine deodars, ponderosa pine.

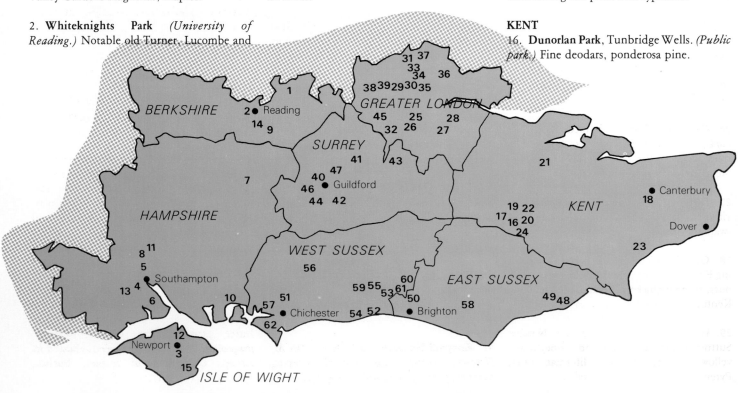

17. **Emmetts**, Ide Hill. *(NT.)* Good variety; outstanding prickly castor-oil trees, Dawyck beech, maples, good sessile oak.

18. **Howletts Park Zoo**, nr Canterbury. *(Mr John Aspinall.)* Vast sweet chestnut, tallest Huntingdon elms, female Ginkgo.

19. **Knole Park**, Sevenoaks. *(NT.)* Parkland hardwoods, fine sessile oaks, beech. Garden with some conifers etc.

20. **Ladham House**, Goudhurst. *(Lady Betty Jessel.)* Outstanding Metasequoia, good magnolias, mixed conifers, flowering trees.

21. **Mote Park**, Maidstone. *(Public park.)* Huge beech, black walnut (in field), cucumber-trees, good honeylocust, Chinese elm.

22. **National Pinetum**, Bedgebury, Goudhurst. *(For. Comm.)* Always open. World's most comprehensive collection of conifers. Main plantings 1925–6, constant additions. Species and cultivars. Forest plots conifer and broadleaf. Some rare maples, oaks.

23. **Sandling Park**, Hythe. *(Mr A. Hardy.)* Outstanding common alder, some fine old conifers, many younger trees, fine Dombey's beech, Monterey pine, weeping and fernleaf beeches.

24. **Scotney Castle**, Lamberhurst. *(NT/Mrs Hussey.)* Big limes, Corsican pines, fernleaf beech, Lucombe oak.

LONDON

25. **Battersea Park** *(Public park.)* Huge collection of rare hardwoods. Notable hybrid horse chestnuts, Italian alders, Kentucky coffee-trees, Lobel maples, outstanding black walnut.

26. **Cannizaro Park**, Wimbledon. *(Public park.)* Outstanding sassafrases, fine nettle-trees, maple collection, unusual oaks, good Metasequoias, tupelo, poplars.

27. **Dulwich Park** *(Public park.)* and environs. Many fine and unusual hardwoods, swamp cypresses.

28. **Greenwich Park** *(Public park.)* Outstanding Euodia, fine paper birch, old sweet chestnuts, shagbark hickory, ginkgo, Metasequoia, Kentucky coffee-tree, prickly castor-oil trees.

29. **Holland Park** *(Public park.)* Notable Suttner plane, bur oak and honeylocust, yellow buckeye, pin oak, Californian laurel, Pyrenean oak, manna ash, catalpas.

30. **Hyde Park/Kensington Gardens** *(Royal Parks.)* Extensive plantings of unusual hardwoods. Outstanding manna ash, pin oak, chinkapin oak, true service tree, group of single-leaf and Veltheim ashes, fine Zelkovas, wingnut etc.

31. **Kenwood**, Hampstead. *(Public park.)* Fine swamp cypress, sessile oak, beeches, big old Zelkova, fine poplars, red oak, London plane.

32. **Marble Hill Park**, Twickenham. *(Public park.)* Outstanding Lombardy poplar, black walnut, Italian alder, big London planes, bat willows.

33. **Osterley Park** *(NT. Public park.)* Outstanding Daimyo, Hungarian and blackjack oaks, fine sweetgums, maples, poplars, Crimean lime, shagbark hickories, scarlet and pin oaks, small pinetum.

34. **Primrose Hill** *(Royal Parks.)* Fine single-leaf ash in numbers, big thorns, Crimean limes.

35. **Regent's Park** *(Royal Parks.)* Wide collection of mostly young, unusual hardwoods; Indian horse chestnut, Caucasian ash, fine large Oregon ash, big whitebeams, Zelkova.

36. **St James's Park** *(Royal Parks.)* Big catalpas, an 'Augustine Henry' London plane, euodias, cherries, thorns, swamp cypresses, Italian maples, Crimean limes.

37. **Syon Park Gardens**, Brentford. *(The Duke of Northumberland.)* Open daily. Outstanding Chinese catalpa, Zelkovas, Hungarian and swamp white oaks, swamp cypresses, Turkish hazels. Many fine rare oaks, maples.

38. **Victoria Park**, Hackney. *(Public park.)* Many unusual hardwoods. Washington thorn, yellow buckeyes, narrowleaf ash, Oregon maple, Zelkova.

39. **Waterlow Park**, Highgate. *(Public park.)* Fine black walnuts, Paulownia, catalpas, wingnut.

SURREY

40. **Albury Park**, Guildford. *(Mutual Household Association.)* Open May–September, Wednesdays and Thursdays pm. Fine London planes, Corsican pine, Bhutan pines, Monterey pine, outstanding Zelkova.

41. **Knaphill Nurseries**, nr Woking. *(Mr M. Slocock.)* Outstanding original weeping beeches, pond cypress, willow oak, quercitron oak, fine swamp cypress, cypress oak, Jeffrey pine.

42. **Mosses Wood**, Leith Hill. *(NT.)* Public road. Fine big conifers, Nootka and Sawara cypresses, sequoias, Norway spruce, Hinoki cypress.

43. **Nonsuch Park**, Epsom. *(Public park.)* Garden within usually open. Fine ginkgo, black pines, southern magnolias in garden. Several big hardwoods outside, horse chestnuts.

44. **Ramster**, Chiddingfold. *(Mr and Mrs P. Gunn.)* Open May weekends and Wednesdays pm. Some fine hardwoods and conifers, big Colorado blue spruces, blue Atlas cedars, incense cedars, dove-tree.

45. **Royal Botanic Garden**, Kew. *(Trustees of Royal Botanic Garden.)* Unrivalled collections of oaks, ash, beech, hickories etc. Outstanding chestnut-leafed oak, Maryland poplar, original ginkgo, large pinetum, golden larch.

46. **Winkworth Arboretum**, Godalming. *(NT.)* Big collections of whitebeams and rowans, maples, oaks, limes; fine southern beeches, line of tupelos and blue Atlas cedars, magnolias, eucryphias, madrone, hybrid wingnut etc.

47. **Wisley Garden**, Ripley. *(Royal Horticultural Society.)* Open daily except Sundays am. Notable Metasequoias, cherries, apples, moosewood and other maples. Extensive pinetum.

SUSSEX

48. **Alexandra Park**, Hastings. *(Public park.)* Long valley including Bohemia Park and Thorpe Wood. Fine rare oaks (1880 planting), maples, varieties of beech, fine wingnuts, poplars, cherries, alders, eucalypts, cypresses.

49. **Beauport Park**, Battle. *(Public park and golf course.)* Miles of hills and valleys of beech and oak studded with collections of rare oaks, maples etc. Scatter of huge giant sequoias, coast redwoods, Monterey cypresses and monkey-puzzles. Outstanding silver pendent lime, Crimean pine, giant sequoia (Ring Wood).

50. **Borde Hill**, Haywards Heath. *(Mr R. Clarke.)* Garden and Warren Wood. Great variety of rare trees. Outstanding Californian laurel, Japanese lime, Chinese stuartia, magnolias. Park and many woods abound in rarities. Collections of maples, birches, spruces etc. (By permission.)

51. **Goodwood Park**, Chichester. *(Goodwood Estates Co Ltd.)* Open mostly May–early October. Outstanding Lebanon cedars, fine oaks, Paulownia, cork oak, limes.

52. **Highdown**, Goring-by-Sea. *(Worthing BC.)* Famous chalk garden. Fine maples, cherries, hybrid strawberry tree, outstanding Chinese hornbeams.

53. **Leonardslee**, Lower Beeding. *(Mr and Mrs R. Loder.)* Open daily spring and autumn. Rare and large trees along seven km of paths. Drive, rock-garden, long bank, the Dell, Coronation Wood, Mossy Ghyll, Azalea Garden, Pinetum. Outstanding Metasequoias, tuliptree, golden larch, Nootka cypress, Fraser and Campbell magnolias, fine coast redwoods, Brewer spruce, sessile oak, Syrian juniper, Serbian spruce, Japanese thujas.

54. **Munton House Crematorium** *(Worthing BC.)* Huge reclining Judas-tree, fine coast redwoods, cypresses, deodars, Morinda spruce.

55. **Nymans**, Handcross. *(NT/The Countess of Rosse.)* Open daily spring to autumn. Outstanding Southern beeches, Eucryphias, rare and tender species in garden. Two pineta, wall-garden, magnolia garden and wilderness. Big Metasequoias, Torreya, guttapercha tree, monkey-puzzle.

56. **Petworth House** *(NT/Lord Leconfield.)* Pleasure Grounds to north. Very tall old hardwoods; oaks, limes, sycamores, sweet chestnuts. Outstanding Lebanon cedar, hybrid catalpa, tiger-tail spruce, good Likiang spruce, Hinoki cypress.

57. **St Roche's Arboretum**, Singleton. *(Mr E. F. W. James.)* Open late spring; last Sunday in October. Large area of remarkably large conifers on a chalk slope, and some hardwoods. Huge Douglas firs, thujas, coast redwoods, fine Sitka spruce, pines, grand fir, southern beeches, Lucombe oak.

58. **Sheffield Park**, Uckfield. *(NT.)* Spring to autumn. Extensive plantings round three lakes and East Park. Grove of giant sequoias. Conifer Walk, 1910. Outstanding Brewer spruces, Serbian spruce, 150 tupelos (1908 planting), Palm Walk, fine Japanese umbrella pine, cider-gums, Metasequoias, Nikko maples, Montezuma pine, common oaks, pond cypress.

59. **The High Beeches**, Handcross. *(Hon. E. Boscawen.)* Large glades of rare trees, Stuartias, oaks, Brewer spruce, magnolias.

60. **Tilgate Park**, Crawley. *(Crawley BC. Public park.)* Mixed old trees; 1906 pinetum. Fine swamp cypress, bur oak, cucumber tree, keaki, Hondo spruce, dove-tree, Virginia magnolia.

61. **Wakehurst Place**, Ardingly. *(NT.)* Huge area, six pineta, Bethlehem Garden, Heather Garden, Japanese Garden, Himalayan Valley, Bloomer's Valley, Mansion Lawn, the Oaks. Outstanding Sikkim spruce, Dawyck beech, dove-tree, Campbell magnolia, fine rare pines, southern beeches, crested beech, cider-gums, rare maples, Gowen cypresses, Leyland cypresses, Hondo spruce, western hemlock, southern catalpa, Chinese wingnut, blackjack oak.

62. **West Dean House**, Singleton. *(The James Trust.)* Outstanding horse chestnut, female ginkgo, fine cedars, oak species.

South-west

AVON
1. **Bath Botanic Garden** Outstanding Chinese necklace poplar, yellow buckeye, papermulberry, golden catalpa, fine Metasequoia, ginkgos, silver pendent lime, hornbeam, Balearic box.

2. **Henrietta Park**, Bath. *(Public park.)* Outstanding line of seven double horse chestnuts, Lombardy poplar. Good smooth Arizona cypress, ginkgos, Tree of Heaven, purple sycamore.

3. **Sydney Park**, Bath. *(Public park.)* Notable hybrid catalpa, golden Cappadocian maple, golden poplar, London planes and several beeches.

4. **Victoria Park** *(Public roads.)* Huge honeylocust, fine Zelkova, Kentucky coffee-tree.
   The Dell Fine conifers; notable Arizona cypress, ginkgo, coast redwoods, Cedar of Goa.

5. **Blaize Castle**, nr Bristol. *(Public park.)* Big old Ginkgo and another; Lucombe oak, Lebanon cedar, Himalayan birch.

CORNWALL
6. **Antony House**, Torpoint. *(NT.)* Open April–end October. Outstanding cork oak, Japanese hemlock. Fine ginkgo, Metasequoia, black walnut, Siebold hemlock, lacebark pine.

7. **Caerhays Castle**, nr Truro. *(Mr J. Williams.)* Open occasionally. Collection of rare Asiatic oaks unrivalled in variety and size; innumerable other trees of great rarity.

8. **Glendurgan**, Mawnan Smith. *(NT.)* Open March–end October, Mondays, Wednesdays, Fridays. Fine willow oak, Rauli, Cunninghamias, Bentham's cornels, western red cedars, Monterey pines, swamp cypress.

9. **Lanhydrock**, Bodmin. *(NT.)* Open daily. Good conifers in old avenue, fine magnolias, Japanese black pine, Douglas fir.

10. **Mount Edgcumbe Country Park**, Torpoint. Open daily. Outstanding cork oak, fine stone pine, Lebanon cedars, ginkgo.

11. **Pencarrow**, Bodmin. *(Sir J. Molesworth-St Aubyn.)* Open daily Easter–October. Avenue of 1840–1860 conifers, outstanding oriental spruce, Japanese red cedar, Cunninghamia in American Garden, pinetum, fine monkey-puzzles, southern beeches, tiger-tail spruce, drooping juniper.

12. **Trebartha**, Launceston. *(Mr C. Latham.)* Open daily. Outstanding 50 m Sitka spruce, 46 m Norway spruce, fine Oregon maple, noble fir, European larch, western hemlock, hiba.

13. **Trelissick**, nr Truro. *(NT.)* Open March–end October, not Sundays. Notable Japanese red cedar, Cornish elms, fine maritime pine, sawara cypress varieties.

14. **Trengwainton**, Penzance. *(NT.)* Open March–October, not Sundays, Mondays or Tuesdays. Many rare and tender trees. Notable magnolias, podocarps, eucryphias, myrtles, Dove-tree.

15. **Trewithen**, Probus. *(Mr and Mrs A. M. Galway.)* Outstanding rare maples, birches, southern beeches, dove-tree, Michelia.

DEVON
16. **Bicton Gardens** *(Lord Clinton.)* Open daily. Very big collection of outsize old conifers and hardwoods; additional 1916 pinetum; many trees added around 1960. Oak collection. Hickories.

17. **Castlehill**, Filleigh. *(Lady M. Fortescue.)* (Must phone estate office, Filleigh 336.) Outsize Sitka spruce, Douglas firs, Thuja, golden-barred thuja, Lucombe oak, fine Japanese red cedars, grey poplars, western hemlocks, deodar.

18. **Cockington Court**, Torquay. *(Torbay BC. Public park.)* Large collection hardwoods, conifers (some tender). Notable Cashmir

cypress, Metasequoia, Mexican pine, Taiwania, paper birch, roble beech.

19. **Coleton Fishacre**, Kingswear. *(NT.)* Open Wednesdays, Fridays and Sundays throughout year. 1925–40 planting of wide variety of unusual trees. Formosan cypress, Forrest fir.

20. **Exeter University Campus** *(Public roads and gardens of Reed Hall, Streatham Hall.)* Outstanding Torreyas, Santa Lucia firs, fine bishop pine, fernleaf oak.

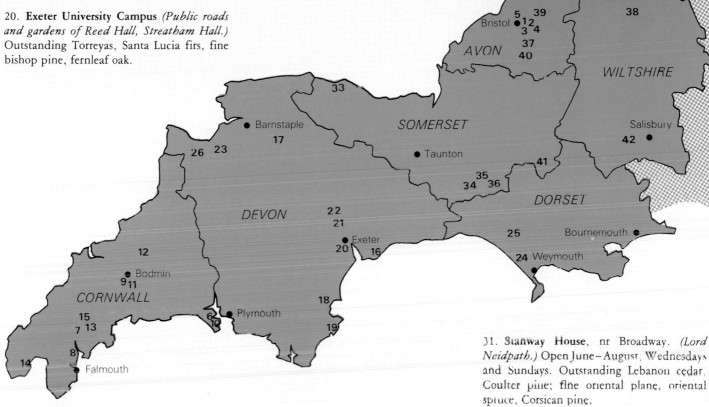

21. **Killerton**, Silverton. *(NT.)* Open daily. Outsize Chinese sweetgum, Monarch birch, quercitron oak, Pacific dogwood, Stuartia. Fine magnolias, incense cedar, thuja, Metasequoia.

22. **Knightshayes Court**, Tiverton. *(NT.)* Open daily April–October. Outstanding Turkey oak, fine Lucombe oak, rare maples, Dombey's beech, giant sequoia, western hemlock, grove of Douglas firs.

23. **Rosemoor**, Great Torrington. *(Lady Anne Palmer.)* Great variety of post-1970 rare trees.

DORSET

24. **Abbotsbury** *(Strangways Estates.)* Outstanding wingnuts, Idesia, Madeira laurel. Many fine tender trees. Magnolias, orangebark myrtle.

25. **Forde Abbey**, Chard. *(Trustees of Mr G. D. Roper.)* Open spring to autumn. Pagodatree, fernleaf beech, wingnut, coast redwood, cedars.

26. **Melbury House**, nr Yeovil. *(Lady Teresa Agnew.)* Open National Gardens days. Outstanding Caucasian wingnut, coast redwood, cypress oak, Grecian fir, Caucasian oak, Monterey cypresses.

GLOUCESTERSHIRE

27. **Batsford Arboretum**, Moreton-in-the-Marsh. *(Lord Dulverton.)* Open April–October. Extensive collection since 1880. New oak collection. Notable oaks, cedars, Metasequoia, Syrian juniper etc.

28. **Hester Park**, Cheltenham. *(Public park.)* Good varied planting 1953; many unusual trees.

29. **Lydney Park** *(Viscount Bledisloe.)* Outstanding London plane, fine limes. Garden planted 1956, sourgum.

30. **Speech House Arboretum**, nr Coleford. *(For Comm.)* Always open. Large array unusual conifers and hardwoods begun in 1916. Outstanding Cilician fir, Himalayan birch, fine pines, spruces.

31. **Stanway House**, nr Broadway. *(Lord Neidpath.)* Open June–August, Wednesdays and Sundays. Outstanding Lebanon cedar, Coulter pine; fine oriental plane, oriental spruce, Corsican pine.

32. **Westonbirt Arboretum**, nr Tetbury. *(For Comm.)* Open daily. Vast collection, almost continuous planting since 1829. New glades and collections in Silk Wood. Outstanding maples, oaks, birches, limes, hollies etc.

SOMERSET

33. **Broadwood**, Dunster. Forest road through grove of 1877 Douglas fir to 53 m tall and larch, with recent additions.

34. **Clapton Court**, Crewkerne. *(Capt S. Loder.)* Open daily, not Sat. Outstanding monster ash, notable Metesequoia, dove-tree.

35. **Cricket House Country Park**, nr Chard. Good deodars, beech lime.

36. **Montacute House**, nr Yeovil. *(NT.)* Outstanding Monterey cypress, line of 'family circle' regrowth of coast redwood, several giant sequoias.

37. **Orchardleigh**, Frome. *(Mr Duckworth.)* Fine tall Silver pendent lime, incense cedars, coast redwoods, Bhutan pine.

WILTSHIRE

38. **Bowood**, Calne. *(The Earl of Shelburne.)* Open spring to autumn. Outstanding Lebanon cedars, ponderosa pine, hybrid poplars, grove of coast redwoods, fine Morinda spruces, black pines, Atlas cedars, Monterey pine, lodgepole pine.

39. **Corsham Court** *(Lord Methuen.)* Not open Mondays. Notable Oriental plane, Lucombe oak, Lebanon cedars, ginkgo, black walnut, Ohio buckeye.

40. **Longleat** *(The Marquess of Bath.)* Open daily. Pleasure grounds, notable ginkgo, Spanish fir, coast redwood, fine Douglas fir, Brewer spruce.

41. **Stourhead** *(NT.)* Open daily. Outstanding tulip-tree, tiger-tail spruce, Macedonian pine. Fine coast redwoods, dove-trees, Japanese white pine, Metasequoias, thuja, noble firs.

42. **Wilton House** *(The Earl of Pembroke.)* Open spring to autumn. Outstanding Lebanon cedars, Golden oak, Lucombe oak, big Bhutan pine, London plane.

Eastern England

BEDFORDSHIRE

1. **Woburn Abbey** *(Trustees of the Bedford Estates.)* Pleasure Grounds open daily in summer, weekends in winter. Evergreens, splendid variety of conifers of about 1920 planting, some 1860 conifers.

2. **Wrest Park**, Silsoe. *(D of E.)* Open weekends, April–September. Notable giant sequoia, Jeffrey pine, Small-leaf limes.

CAMBRIDGESHIRE

3. **Anglesey Abbey**, Lode. *(NT.)* Open daily in summer except Mondays and Tuesdays. Extensive planting since 1930; fine Hungarian oak, honeylocust, catalpa etc.

4. **Cambridge University Botanic Garden** Open daily. Outstanding single-leaf nut-pine, Gerard's pine, pecan, spurleaf, Metasequoia, hybrid catalpa.

5. **Clare College Gardens**, Cambridge. Open daily pm. Big Metasequoia, Ohio buckeye.

6. **The Fen**, Cambridge City. *(Public park.)* Fine line Italian alders, huge Lombardy poplars.

HERTFORDSHIRE

7. **Ashridge Park**, Berkhamsted. *(Management College.)* Open April–October, Saturdays and Sundays. Fine Blue Algerian cedar, ring of incense cedars, Lobel maples, grand fir.

8. **Bayfordbury House** *(Agricultural College.)* Notable 1760 Lebanon cedars; pinetum with outstanding western larch, fine ponderosa and Crimean pines.

9. **Hatfield House** *(The Marquess of Salisbury.)* Open May–September, not Mondays. Some fine old hardwoods; new plantings.

LINCOLNSHIRE

10. **Belton Park**, Belton *(NT.)* Open April–October, not Mondays or Tuesdays. Some fine hardwoods. Silver and sugar maples, sycamores, weeping beech, Trees of Heaven, limes.

11. **Boultham Park**, Lincoln. *(Public park.)* Outsize 40 m railway poplar, Japanese thuja.

12. **Lincoln Arboretum** *(Public park.)* Black walnut, wingnut, silver pendent lime.

NORFOLK

13. **Holkham Hall**, Wells-next-the-Sea. *(The Earl of Leicester.)* Open June–September most days. Garden with notable snakebark maple, old Corsican pines, fine junipers, tupelos.

14. **Lyndford Arboretum**, Mundford. *(For Comm.)* Always open. Large collection 1950 onwards of rare and common conifers and some hardwoods, already fine trees. Notable old Crimean and Corsican pines. Chinese tulip tree, groups of bishop pine, southern beeches.

15. **Sandringham Hall** *(HM The Queen.)* Open April–September, variously. Some fine older trees, much recent planting, blue spruce, incense cedar.

16. **Talbot Manor**, Fincham. *(Mr M. Mason.)* Open occasionally. Huge variety planted since 1950; notable poplars, alders, beech forms, oaks, maples.

NORTHAMPTONSHIRE

17. **Althorp** *(Earl Spencer.)* Open daily, pm. Arboretum with notable Santa Lucia fir, limber pine, coast redwoods, Likiang spruce, limes, giant sequoias, sweetgums, Dawyck beech, cypress oak, Crimean oak (nr stables).

18. **Castle Ashby** *(The Marquis of Northampton.)* Open Sundays April–October. Notable horse chestnut, Bhutan pine, Bhutan cypress.

SUFFOLK

19. **Abbey Garden**, Bury St Edmunds. *(Public park.)* Notable Trees of Heaven, Père David maples, Turkish hazel.

20. **East Bergholt Place** *(Mrs Maxwell Eley.)* Outstanding rauli; large collection of fine, rare, often tender trees.

21. **Hardwick Park**, Bury St Edmunds. *(Public park.)* Fine cypress oaks, junipers, Algerian firs, Lucombe oak, cedars.

22. **Ipswich Arboretum / Christchurch Park** *(Public park.)* Fine cider-gum, alders, willows, big horse chestnut, common oak, white willow.

23. **Somerleyton Hall**, nr Lowestoft. *(Lord and Lady Somerleyton.)* Open summer, not Saturdays. Cider-gum, monkey-puzzles, Monterey pine.

Midlands

BUCKINGHAMSHIRE

1. **Ascott House**, Wing. *(NT.)* Open April–September, Wednesdays and Thursdays. Fine colour-planting, golden Atlas cedar; 1897 Jubilee group, paper birch, paperbark maple.

2. **Cliveden**, Maidenhead. *(NT.)* Open March–December. Outstanding butternut, fine cypress oaks, black locust, blue cedars.

3. **Stowe Park** *(Stowe School.)* Open mid-July–early September, Fridays and weekends. Outstanding Lebanon cedar, good Dawyck beeches, Leyland cypresses, yellow buckeye.

4. **Waddesden**, Aylesbury. *(NT.)* Open April–October, not Mondays or Tuesdays. Fine Arolla pine, noble firs, Grecian fir, small-leaf lime, cedars, ginkgo, oriental spruce, giant sequoias, Chinese privet, silver pendent lime.

CHESHIRE

5. **Granada Arboretum**, Jodrell Bank. *(University of Manchester.)* Recently established wide selection of hardwoods; notably alders, birches, apples, cherries, Leyland cypresses, limes.

6. **Ness / Liverpool University Botanic Garden** Open daily. Mostly fairly young specimens; notable Paulownia, collection of rowans, flowering trees, pin oak.

7. **Tatton Park**, Knutsford. *(NT.)* Open daily. Chilean incense cedar, fine Metasequoias, Colorado blue spruce, Père David's maple.

DERBYSHIRE

8. **Chatsworth**, Bakewell. *(Chatsworth House Trustees.)* Open April–October, daily. Outstanding Weymouth pine, tupelos, sweet chestnut, good pinetum.

9. **Elvaston Country Park** Open daily. Fine junipers, cedars, pines, monkey-puzzles.

HEREFORDSHIRE & WORCESTERSHIRE

10. **Eastnor Castle**, Ledbury. *(Hon Mrs Harvey Bathurst.)* Open Sundays spring and summer; Wednesdays, Thursdays, July–August. Outstanding deodars, Lobel maple, original blue Atlas cedar, fine pines, incense cedars, rare oaks and conifers over wide area. Tall grand, pindrow and Algerian firs; outstanding bishop pine, Nootka cypresses, Morinda spruces, Turner's oak.

11. **Hergest Croft**, Kington. *(R. A. and L. Banks.)* Open daily mid-April to mid-September. Huge collection, many from original seeds from China; fine and rare conifers, maples, birches.

12. **Jephson Garden**, Leamington Spa. *(Public park.)* Fine collection of unusual trees. Notable ginkgo, keaki, catalpas, wingnut, Hungarian and Caucasian oaks, Indian horse chestnut.

13. **Queenswood**, Hope-under-Dinmore. *(Hereford & Worcester CC.)* Open daily. Varied planting since 1953, many rarities.

14. **Spetchley Park**, Worcester. *(Mr and Mrs J. Berkeley.)* April–September, not Satur-

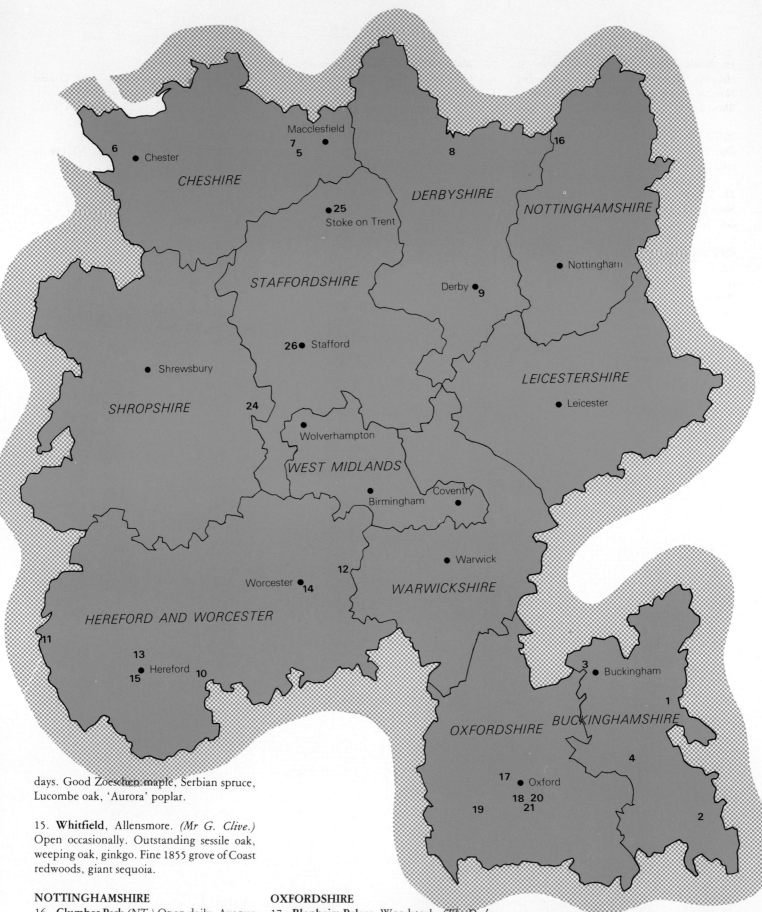

days. Good Zoeschen maple, Serbian spruce, Lucombe oak, 'Aurora' poplar.

15. **Whitfield**, Allensmore. *(Mr G. Clive.)* Open occasionally. Outstanding sessile oak, weeping oak, ginkgo. Fine 1855 grove of Coast redwoods, giant sequoia.

NOTTINGHAMSHIRE

16. **Clumber Park** *(NT.)* Open daily. Avenue of common lime with one notable broadleaf lime. Fine young pines, Jeffrey, ponderosa, jack pines.

OXFORDSHIRE

17. **Blenheim Palace**, Woodstock. *(The Duke of Marlborough.)* Open mid-March to end October. Notable Lebanon cedar, sugar maple, incense cedars.

18. **Nuneham Arboretum** *(University Botanic Garden.)* Open pm. Fine old conifers, oak, incense cedars; new plantings.

19. **Pusey House**, Farringdon. *(Mr M. Hornby.)* Open most days April–October. Notable London plane, swamp cypress, Bhutan pine.

20. **University Botanic Garden**, Oxford. Open daily. Outstanding service trees, green ash, fine ginkgo, black walnut, persimmon.

21. **University Parks**, Oxford. *(Public park.)* Notable poplars, pagoda-tree, Turkish hazel, rare thorns etc.

SHROPSHIRE

22. **Hodnet Hall**, Market Drayton. *(Mr & Mrs A. Heber Percy.)* Open May–Aug. Fine Metasequoia, Grecian firs, catalpas, dove-trees, cherries, magnolias; fine oaks.

23. **Walkcot Park** *(Mr Parish.)* Open occasionally. Original Douglas fir, many fine conifers, Low's fir, hemlocks.

24. **Weston Park**, Shifnal. *(The Earl of Bradford.)* Open summer, daily except Mondays and Fridays. Outstanding oriental plane, giant sequoia, good Corsican pines, cypress oak.

STAFFORDSHIRE

25. **Trentham Park**, Stoke-on-Trent. *(Public park.)* Unusual hardwoods; yellow buckeyes, trident maple; pinetum, fine Lows and Nikko firs, Japanese thuja, Macedonian pines.

26. **Shugborough Park**, Stafford. *(NT.)* Many fine old trees.

Northern England

CUMBRIA

1. **Aira Force**, Ullswater. *(NT.)* Notable Sitka spruce, Himalayan fir, Bhutan cypress, Norway spruce, grand fir.

2. **Fallbarrow Park**, Bowness-on-Windermere. *(Public park.)* Fine conifers, deodar, Morinda spruce, mountain hemlock, Bhutan pine.

3. **Holker Hall**, Cark-in-Cartmel. *(Mr H. Cavendish.)* Open April–October, not Saturdays. Probable original monkey-puzzle, outstanding Hungarian and Mirbeck oaks, fine Hupeh crab, sourgum, ginkgo.

4. **Hutton-in-the-Forest**, Penrith. *(Lord Inglewood.)* Always open. Outstanding giant sequoia, Low's fir, hornbeam, fine Sitka spruce, elms.

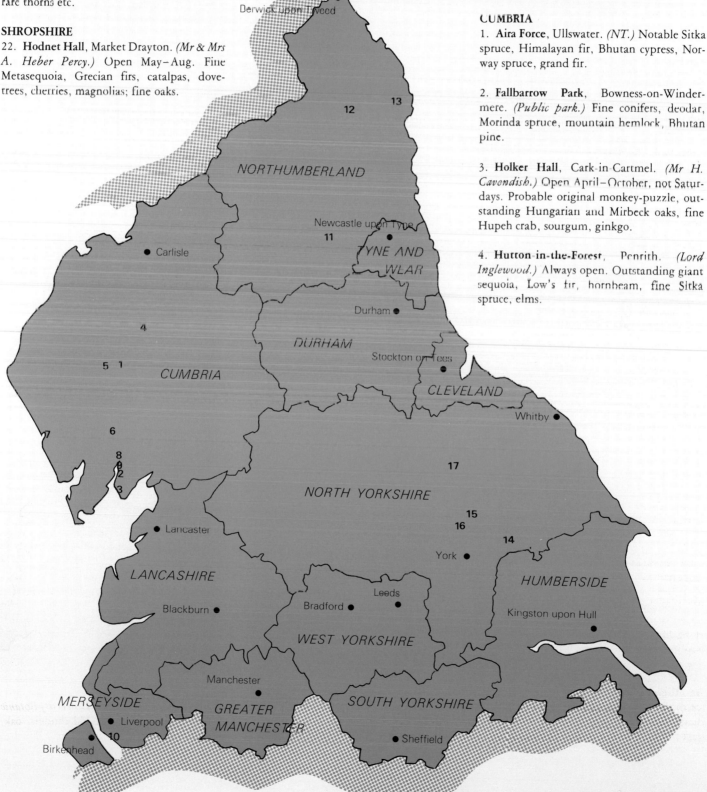

5. **Lingholm**, Derwentwater. *(Viscount Rochdale.)* Open April–October, weekdays. Outstanding Norway spruce, fine Scots pines, giant sequoia, silver firs, cucumber-tree.

6. **Monk Coniston**, Coniston. *(The Holiday Fellowship.)* By permission. Outstanding pindrow fir, Douglas fir, Sitka spruce, Japanese red cedar, fine old larches.

7. **Muncaster Castle** *(Sir W. Pennington Ramsden Bt.)* Daily except Mondays. Outstanding Dombey beeches, rauli, fine coast redwoods, noble firs, Leyland cypress.

8. **Skelgill Wood**, Ambleside. *(NT.)* Beside Stagshaw Garden. A few superb conifers, grand firs, Douglas fir to over 50 m, Hondo spruce.

9. **Wray Castle** *(NT.)* Fine big coast redwood, giant sequoia, Thujopsis, monkey-puzzle, Douglas fir, Atlas cedar, fernleaf beech.

MERSEYSIDE
10. **Calderstones Park**, Mossley Hill, Liverpool. *(Public park.)* Wide selection; notable rowan, apple, cherry glades; avenue of American lime; notable Italian alder.

NORTHUMBERLAND
11. **Beaufront Castle**, Hexham. *(Mr A. Cuthbert.)* Open occasionally. Outstanding beech, cutleaf lime, Likiang spruce. Pinetum with fine foxtail pine and other rarities.

12. **Cragside**, Rothbury. *(NT.)* Open April–September daily; October–March weekends. Many huge conifers; notable 46 m + Low's firs, Douglas firs, western hemlocks, red fir.

13. **Howick Gardens**, Craster. *(The Howick Trustees Ltd.)* Fine maples, birches, katsura-trees, Hungarian oak.

NORTH YORKSHIRE
14. **Castle Howard** *(Lord Howard of Henderskelfe.)* Open daily April–October. Old hardwoods and vast new collection of unusual, rare and very rare trees, as comprehensive as any, with recent cultivars 1975 on. (1978 arboretum not currently open.)

15. **Harlow Carr**, Ripon. *(Northern Horticultural Society.)* Open daily. Fairly recent wide collection.

16. **Studley Royal/Fountains Abbey** *(NT and North Yorkshire CC.)* Outstanding wild cherry, sweet chestnuts, fine oaks, sycamores, a few big conifers.

17. **Thorp Perrow**, Bedale. *(Sir J. and Lady Ropner.)* Open April–October. Enormous collection, 1880 with 1930 colour glades, collections of rare and notable maples, cherries, oaks, beech poplars, spruces, pines, white beams, rowans, crabs, laburnums, thorns etc. Outstanding line of rare limes; many pillar apples.

Wales

CLWYD
1. **Gwysany**, Wrexham. *(Mr P. Davies-Cook.)* Open occasionally. Lines of old conifers being landscaped with young trees.

2. **Vivod Forest Garden**, nr Llangollen. *(For Comm.)* Always open. At 300 m and above, huge array of plots of unusual and rare conifers 1950. Small pinetum, 1953 on.

GWYNEDD
3. **Bodnant Garden**, Tal-y-Cafn. *(NT.)* Mid-March–mid-October. Huge collection with outstanding Grecian, Low's and grand firs, weeping giant sequoia, western hemlocks, Chinese hemlock, Mexican white pines, coast redwood, magnolias, maples, tender species.

4. **Penrhyn Castle**, Bangor. *(NT.)* Spring to autumn, daily except Tuesdays. Outstanding Douglas firs and silver fir species along drive; maritime pine, umbrella pine, Metasequoia, Italian cypresses in garden.

POWYS
5. **Leighton Arboretum** *(Royal Forestry Society.)* Open daily. Grove of 1857 redwoods, original 'Leighton Green' Leyland cypress, big Morinda spruce, Japanese red cedar, medium age and recent pinetum.

6. **Powis Castle** *(Earl Powis/NT.)* Park open daily. Outstanding oaks, ponderosa pine, giant sequoia, Douglas firs. Gardens, open daily pm. Fine coast redwoods, silver firs, maples, ginkgo, dove-tree.

7. **The Gliffaes Hotel**, nr Crickhowell. *(Mr and Mrs Brabner.)* Outstanding Japanese red cedar, fine yellow buckeyes, giant sequoias, coast redwood, Metasequoia, Lucombe oak.

SOUTH GLAMORGAN
8. **Cathays Park**, Cardiff. *(Public park.)* Good ginkgos, Leyland cypress, beech.

9. **Dyffryn Gardens**, St Nicholas. *(Public park.)* Huge variety of fine and rare trees. Outstanding paperbark maples, Brewer spruces, Chinese wingnut, Chinese elm, tupelo, many

oaks, birches, maples, southern beeches.

10. **Roath Park**, Cardiff. *(Public park.)* Pagoda-tree, ginkgo, black walnut, paperback maple.

WEST GLAMORGAN
11. **Clyne Castle**, Swansea. *(Public park.)* Fine winter's bark, bigleaf storax, Cunninghamia.

12. **Margam Abbey** *(Swansea/West Glamorgan CC.)* Open April–October, not Mondays. Fine fernleaf beech, bay laurels, old tulip-trees, oriental plane, Cedar of Goa.

13. **Singleton Abbey**, Swansea. *(Public park.)* Fine Laurelia, a rare wingnut, big Metasequoia, Italian cypresses, Montpelier maple, Idesia.

Northern Ireland

ARMAGH
1. **Gosford Castle**, Markethill. *(Forestry Department.)* Open daily. Outstanding Himalayan fir, noble fir, fine redwoods, cypresses.

DOWN
2. **Bangor Castle** *(Public park.)* Fine blue gums, Santa Lucia and noble firs, bishop and Monterey pines.

3. **Castlewellan**, nr Newcastle. *(Forestry Department.)* Open daily. Extensive and expanding collection with many huge old conifers, rare and tender species. Outstanding Algerian fir, Brewer spruce, California nutmeg, eucalypts; fine Himalayan hemlock, New Zealand red beech, Japanese thuja, junipers. Morinda spruce, Himalayan fir, cypresses.

4. **Mount Stewart**, Portaferry. *(NT.)* Large garden with big blue gums and other eucalypts, redwoods, King Boris fir, Kashmir and Monterey cypresses, outstanding Monterey pines and many rare, tender trees.

5. **Rowallane**, Saintfield. *(NT.)* Open daily, except weekends in winter. Remarkable collection of southern beeches, big monkey-puzzles, fine bishop and Macedonian pines, Likiang and Brewer spruces, dove-tree, Paulownia.

6. **Tullymore Castle** *(Forestry Department.)* Open daily. 'Seven Sisters', very big old silver firs, notable Grecian fir, deodars, Monterey

pine, J
Japane

TYRO
7. **Dr**
Dep
we

LONDONDERRY

DONEGAL

LONDONDERRY

ANTRIM

TYRONE

Omagh

Belfast

2

Enniskillen

Armagh

1

DOWN

5

FERMANAGH

ARMAGH

7

4

Down Patrick

6 3

SLIGO

MONAGHAN

MAYO

LETTRIM

CAUAN

LOUTH

Castlebar

ROSCOMMON

LONGFORD

MEATH

GALWAY

WESTMEATH

Galway

DUBLIN

OFFALY

Dublin

17

KILDARE

12

Dortlouise

21

15

20

LEIX

WICKLOW

Wicklow

22

16 Limerick

CARLOW

LIMERICK

TIPPERARY

KILKENNY

WREXFORD

19

8

KERRY

WATERFORD

18

14

CORK

9 10

13

Cork

11

pine, Japanese white pine, willow podocarp, Japanese thuja, tulip-tree.

TYRONE

7. **Drum Manor**, Cookstown. *(Forestry Department.)* Open daily. Outstanding western hemlock, Himalayan fir, noble fir, fine redwoods, cypresses.

The Irish Republic

CORK

8. **Annes Grove**, Castletownroche. Open Easter to end September, not Saturdays. Notable willow podocarp, Cornish elms.

9. **Ashbourne House Hotel**, nr Fota. Notable Kentucky coffee-tree, ginkgo, dove-tree, katsura-tree, fine deodar, Serbian spruce, blue gum.

10. **Fota**, Carrigtwohill. *(University College of Cork.)* Open April–end September. Outstanding Himalayan cypress, Japanese red cedars, Torreya, Gregg pine, notable grand fir, sorrel tree, Hungarian oak and several great rarities.

11. **Ilnacullin**, Garinish, Glengarriff (by boat). *(Comm of Public Works.)* Open March–October. Renowned collection of plants from southern hemisphere, mainly 1910–1940. Notable Mexican pine, Japanese black pine, Totara.

DUBLIN

12. **Glasnevin Botanic Garden** *(Dept of Agriculture.)* Open daily. Outstanding collection of Euodias, Algerian fir, Chinese elms, several willows, good collection of pines, cypresses, maples, oaks, spruces. Fine Zelkovas, Idesia.

KERRY

13. **Derreen**, Kenmare. *(Hon David Bigham.)* Open April–September, Sundays, Tuesdays and Thursdays. Outstanding Monterey cypress, Monterey pine, Pacific fir, Japanese red cedars, blue gums, Lawson 'Erecta' and 'Gracilis Pendula'.

14. **Dunloe Castle Hotel** Outstanding varigated table-dogwood, Stoll's maple, fine Wissel cypress, paperbark maple, Mexican and bishop pines, Taiwania, crested beech, rare limes, Zoeschen maple.

LEIX

15. **Abbeyleix** *(de Vesci Estates.)* Open

Easter–end September. Original David Douglas Sitka spruce, notable silver firs and spruces in variety, Bhutan pine, Japanese larch, Zoeschen maple, single-leaf ash.

LIMERICK

16. **Currah Chase**, Adare. *(Forestry and Wildlife Service.)* Open daily. Big silver fir, monkey-puzzle, Monterey cypress, Monterey pine, European larch, Bhutan pine, manna ash.

OFFALY

17. **Birr Castle**, Birr. *(The Earl and Countess of Rosse.)* Open daily. Extensive collections of Asiatic conifers, maples and others, mostly from original seed. Outstanding Macnab cypress, drooping juniper, Sichuan fir, hybrid wingnut, grey poplar, Henry's lime etc.

WATERFORD

18. **Curraghmore** *(The Marquis of Waterford.)* Open April–September, Thursdays only. Original David Douglas Sitka spruce and grand fir. Outstanding giant sequoias, Mexican white pine, Caucasian fir, Japanese red cedars, coast redwood.

WEXFORD

19. **John F. Kennedy Arboretum**, New Ross. *(Forestry and Wildlife Service.)* Open daily. Extensive plantings, species collections and plots begun in 1960.

WICKLOW

20. **Avondale Forest Garden**, Rathdrum. *(Forestry and Wildlife Service.)* Open daily. Outstanding Wissel and Arizona cypresses, Veitch's silver fir, three old common silver firs, Macedonian and western white pine. 1904 plots. Many fine eucalypts.

21. **Powerscourt**, Enniskerry. *(Mrs Slazenger.)* Open Easter–end October. Large area of huge trees. Outstanding blue gums, monkey-puzzles, Mexican pine, Coulter pine, Likiang spruce, dragon spruce, Himalayan fir, winter's bark. Mile of drive with lines planted 1866. Notable Nordmann's fir, Himalayan cypress, sequoias.

22. **Mount Usher**, Ashford. *(Mrs Jaye.)* Open mid-March–end September. Outstanding Dombey southern beeches, eucalypts, Canary pine, Chinese firs, Montezuma pines, rare maples and birches, Tasmanian cedars.

Scotland

(The names of former Scottish counties are given in brackets after the regions for ease of reference.)

Borders Region

(PEEBLES-SHIRE)

1. **Dawyck Arboretum**, Peebles. *(Royal Botanic Garden.)* Open daily April–September. Huge collection with many outstanding Asiatic silver firs and spruces, maples; original Dawyck beech, fine Brewer spruces, Douglas firs etc.

2. **Kailzie Gardens**, Peebles. *(Mrs A. M. Richard.)* Open daily March–October. Fine 1725 larches, sugar maple, wych elms.

(ROXBURGHSHIRE)

3. **The Monteviot Pinery**, Jedburgh. *(The Marquis of Lothian.)* Open daily. Notable Macedonian pine, Sitka spruce, varigated oak, Hungarian oak, mountain hemlocks.

(SELKIRKSHIRE)

4. **Dryburgh Abbey**, Selkirk. *(Scottish Dept.)* Open daily. Fine Cedars of Lebanon, deodar, Atlas cedar, big common lime, Low's fir.

5. **Dryburgh Abbey Hotel** *(Adjacent to Abbey.)* Outstanding fastigiate Scots pine, big Chinese juniper.

Central Region

(STIRLINGSHIRE)

6. **Culcleuch Castle**, Fintry. *(Baron Hercules Robinson.)* Open daily. Outstanding Grecian firs, Sitka spruces, single-leaf ash, fine Jeffrey, ponderosa, lodgepole and Crimean pines, Hungarian oak.

7. **Gargunnock** *(Miss V. Stirling.)* Open at times. Line of fine giant sequoias, outstanding common oak in field, fernleaf beech behind house.

8. **Stirling University Campus**, Airthrie Castle. Outstanding giant sequoias, line of fine incense cedars, Arolla pine.

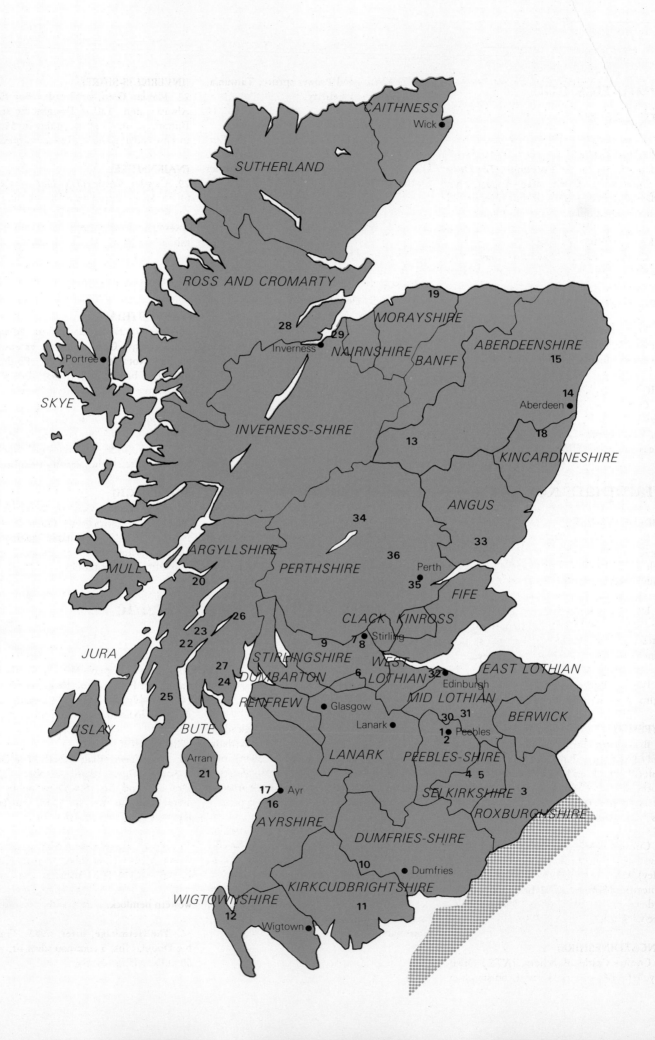

Dumfries and Galloway

(DUMFRIES-SHIRE)

9. **Drumlanrig Castle**, Thornhill. *(The Duke of Buccleuch.)* Open May–August, not Fridays. Original Douglas fir, fine silver fir, old larch, Eugene poplar, biggest sycamore.

(KIRKCUDBRIGHTSHIRE)

10. **Glenlee Park**, New Galloway. *(Mr Agnew.)* Open occasionally. Outstanding Douglas firs, giant sequoia, larch, Norway spruce, all 40–55 m tall.

11. **Threave Garden**, Castle Douglas. *(NTS.)* Open daily. Large and varied recent planting, fine alders, poplars, pines, maples, cherries.

(WIGTOWNSHIRE)

12. **Castle Kennedy**, Stranraer. *(The Earl and Countess of Stair.)* Open daily April–September. Fine avenues of monkey-puzzle, bishop pine, cider-gums, thujas, Monterey pines.

Grampian Region

(ABERDEENSHIRE)

13. **Balmoral Castle** *(HM the Queen.)* Open May–July. Fine Low's and red firs, many good noble firs, Douglas firs, western hemlocks, small younger pinetum.

14. **Drum Castle**, Aberdeen. *(NTS.)* Open May–September. Delavay fir, smooth Arizona cypress, Jeffrey hemlock, Brewer spruce, Chinese necklace poplar, yellow buckeye.

15. **Haddo House**, Methlick. *(NTS.)* Two original giant sequoia, notable beech.

(AYRSHIRE)

16. **Blairquhan**, Straiton. *(Mr John Hunter-Blair.)* To be opened in 1985. Orchard of huge conifers; notable jack pine, shore pine, rare spruces; Maria's Walk and two mile drive of fine silver firs, spruces, hemlocks of mixed ages. Vast beech above house.

17. **Culzean Castle**, Maybole. *(NTS.)* Open daily. Fine Montezuma pine, red fir (Happy Valley), Monterey pines, two big Sitka spruces, Crimean and Scots pines. Hybrid catalpa (Wall Garden), fifty Chusan palms, Katsura trees, three wingnuts.

(KINCARDINESHIRE)

18. **Crathes Castle**, Banchory. *(NTS.)* Open daily. Fine Douglas fir, deodar, outstanding

rare Zelkova, good Brewer spruce, Taiwania, madrone, Tibetan cherry.

(MORAYSHIRE)

19. **Innes House**, Llanbryde. *(Mr Iain Tennant.)* Open some days. Outstanding larch, Lucombe oak, madrone; many unusual species for the region.

Highland Region

(ARGYLLSHIRE)

20. **Ardineisaig Hotel**, Taynuilt. Outstanding noble and Caucasian firs, monkey-puzzle, Sitka spruce, Douglas fir, southern beeches, Chinese beech.

21. **Brodick Castle**, Arran. *(NTS.)* Numerous huge old conifers and many tender evergreen broadleaves.

22. **Crarae Garden**, Furnace. *(Sir Ilay Campbell Bt.)* Open March–October. Notable eucalypts, tender broadleaves and rare conifers, Kawakami fir, Cunninghamia, sugar pine, cypresses.

23. **Inveraray Castle** *(The Duke of Argyll.)* Open April–October variously. Notable grand firs, deodars, larch, weeping sequoia, Leyland cypress (Frews Bridge), cucumber tree.

24. **Kilmun Forest Garden**, nr Dunoon. *(For Comm.)* Always open. Hillside of plots and specimens of rare and unusual conifers and broadleaves, notable eucalypts; post 1950.

25. **Stonefield Castle Hotel**, Tarbert. Remarkable clubmoss cypress, King Boris fir, fine Sawara cypress forms, willow podocarp, Himalayan hemlock.

26. **Strone House Arboretum**, Cairndow, Arrochar. *(Lady Glenkinglas.)* Open daily. Tallest tree in Britain (grand fir 60 m), outstanding thujas, Fitzroya, Sawara cypresses, immense common silver fir, fine larch, oriental spruce, mountain hemlock, Hinoki cypress.

27. **Younger Botanic Garden**, Benmore, Dunoon. *(Royal Botanic Garden, Edinburgh.)* Open April–October. Towering 55 m Douglas firs everywhere; avenue of giant sequoias to 50 m; Sitka spruce and western hemlock to 50 m; outstanding Pacific fir, Forrest fir, rauli, roble beeches, Hondo spruce; Nordmann firs to 48 m.

(INVERNESS-SHIRE)

28. **Moniac Glen**, nr Beauly. *(For Comm.)* Always open. Tallest Douglas fir stand in Britain, 1880, to 60 m; grand fir 55 m; big incense cedar, silver fir, Lawson cypress.

(NAIRNSHIRE)

29. **Cawdor Castle** *(The Earl of Cawdor.)* Open May–September. Outstanding Low's fir, western hemlock, Douglas fir, fine horse chestnut, coast redwoods, noble fir, single-leaf ash.

Lothian

(EAST LOTHIAN)

30. **Smeaton House**, East Linton. *(Mr and Mrs G. G. Gray.)* Open at times. Extensive collection. Notable Italian alder, Pindrow fir, roundleaf beech, original sequoias, a gutta-percha tree.

31. **Tyninghame**, East Linton. *(Earl of Haddington.)* Open June–September. Outstanding Bosnian pine, Crimean pine. Fine Hers's maples, Cornish elm, katsura-tree, beeches.

(EDINBURGH)

32. **Royal Botanic Garden**, Inverleith Road. *(Minister of Agriculture.)* Open daily. Outstanding Van Volxem maple, golden beech, Likiang spruce; big collections oaks, maples, birches, pines and rarities.

Tayside

(ANGUS)

33. **Glamis Castle** *(The Earl of Strathmore and Kinghorne.)* Open May–September, not Saturdays. Policies; notable grand firs, hybrid larch, noble fir, thujas. Pinetum nearby, notable Nikko fir, oriental spruces.

(PERTHSHIRE)

34. **Blair Castle**, Blair Atholl. *(The Duke of Atholl.)* Open April–October. Diana's Grove, grand firs, 50–55 m, noble firs to 46 m, Douglas firs to 55 m, outstanding Japanese larch, red fir, Low's fir.

35. **Scone Palace Pinetum** *(Earl of Mansfield.)* Open May–mid-October. Square of four immense 1851 Sitka spruces, lines of 1866 mixed conifers, outstanding giant sequoia, western hemlock, Jeffrey pine, noble firs.

36. **The Hermitage**, Inver. *(NTS.)* Group of big Douglas firs, a common silver fir, view of 60 m Douglas across the river.

Index

Trees are listed mainly under their popular name, in roman, with their generic name in italics. Names of cultivars appear in inverted commas.